English Pottery
1620–1840

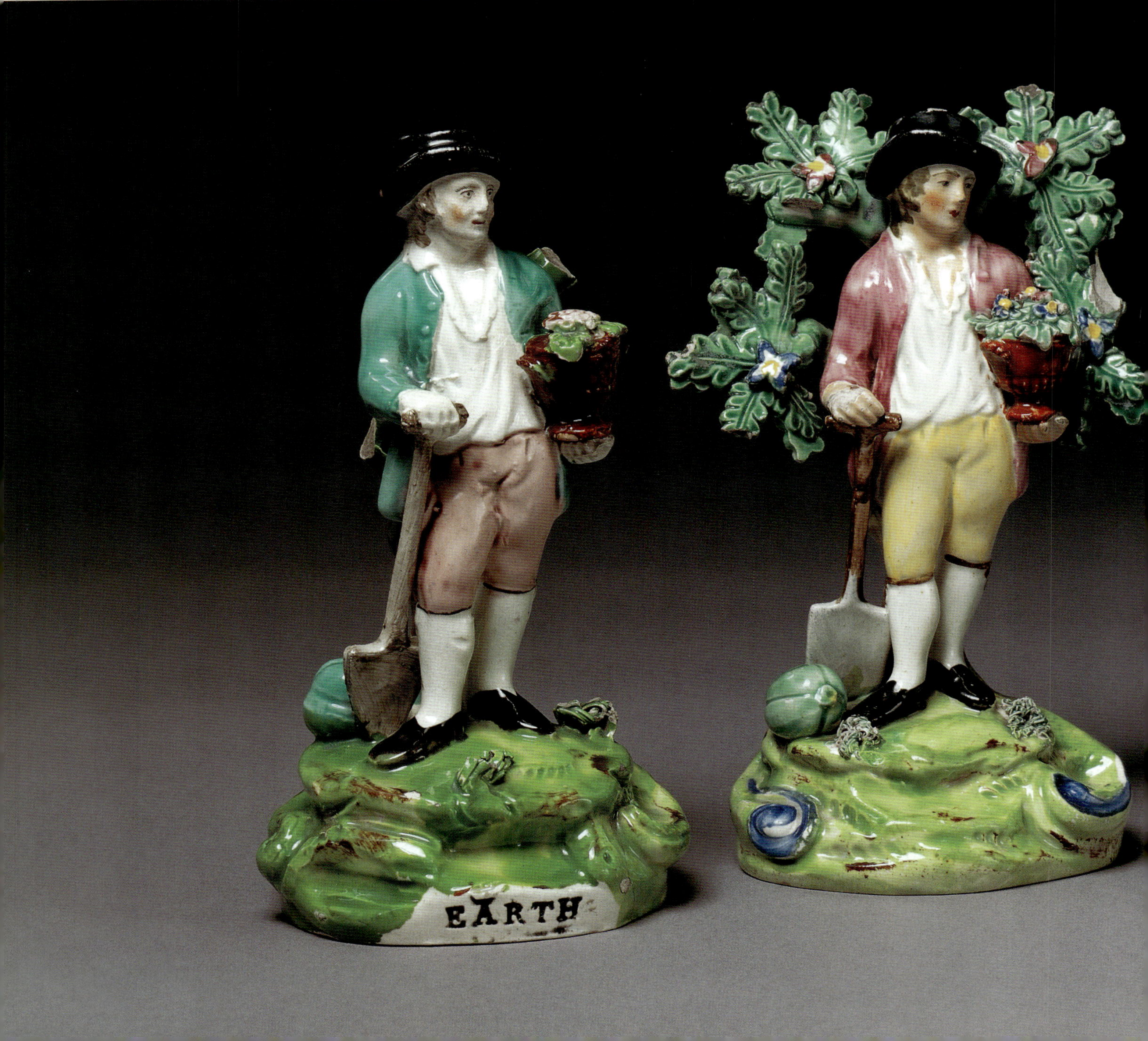
EARTH

English Pottery
1620–1840

Robin Hildyard

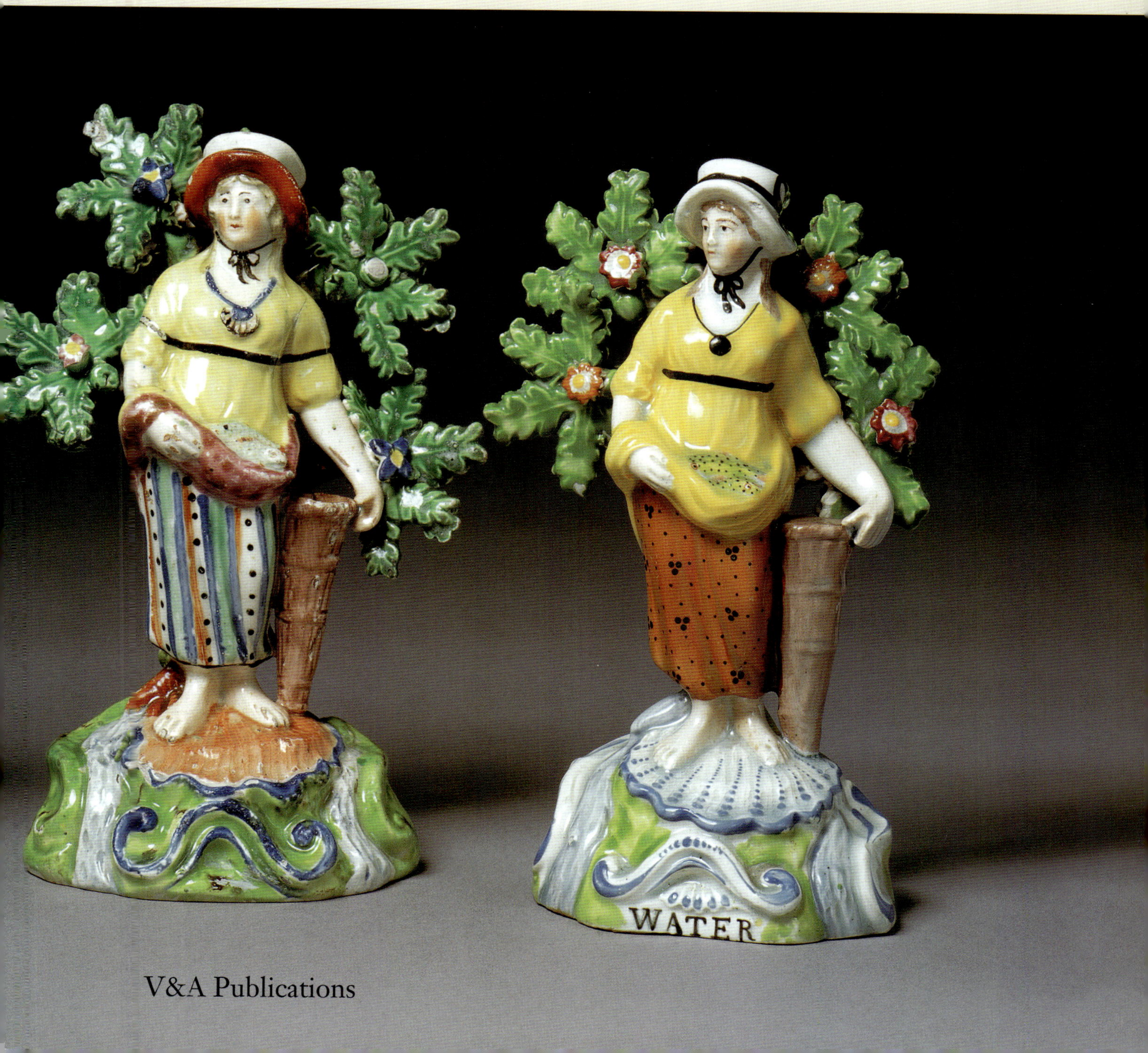

V&A Publications

First published by V&A Publications, 2005
V&A Publications
160 Brompton Road
London SW3 1HW

Distributed in North America by Harry N. Abrams, Inc., New York

ISBN 1 85177 442 4

Library of Congress Number 2005923381

A catalogue record of this book is available from the British Library.

Designed by Andrew Shoolbred
New V&A photography by Richard Davis

Front jacket illustration: figure of deer with underglaze decoration, *c.* 1800 (see plate 86)
Back jacket illustration: late seventeenth-century English delftware (see plate 57)
Frontispiece: bocage figures of the 1820s–1830s (see plate 91)

Printed in Hong Kong

V&A

V&A Publications
160 Brompton Road
London SW3 1HW
www.vam.ac.uk

Contents

The publication of this book has been assisted by a generous grant from the Ceramica-Stiftung, Basel.

Acknowledgements

My thanks go to all members of the V&A Ceramics & Glass Collection, in particular Oliver Watson for his early encouragement, Jennifer Opie, Reino Liefkes, Hilary Young, Judith Crouch, Alun Graves, Fi Gunn, and especially Terry Bloxham for organising the new photography by Richard Davis. For the privilege of spending time in the Research Department, I am indebted to Paul Greenhalgh, Malcolm Baker and Carolyn Sargentson. Dr David Barker and Miranda Goodby of the Potteries Museum have greatly helped towards understanding the intricacies of Staffordshire pottery, while most generous hospitality and assistance were received from Janine Skerry at Colonial Williamsburg, Pat Halfpenny at Winterhur, Henry Weldon in New York, and Walter Ostrom of the Nova Scotia College of Art & Design. For the production of this book, I am most grateful to Mary Butler and Ariane Bankes of V&A Publications, as also to the copy-editor Delia Gaze and designer Andrew Shoolbred. Lastly, I would like to thank my wife Kate for her support and patience with a project that all too easily veered towards obsession.

Introduction

When the literature on British pottery began in the mid-nineteenth century, it was possible to make sweeping and comfortable generalizations without risk of challenge from a keen but largely ignorant public. Today, these early studies with their woolly assumptions have entirely given way to narrowly focused monographs, which, however beneficial to the serious student and collector, must inevitably exclude much of the context of the subject. Moreover, the sheer size of the field now presents a major obstacle in gaining the sort of confident overview enjoyed by pioneer ceramic historians such as Jewitt, Solon, Rackham and Read, echoes of which were shared as late as the 1960s by important writers such as Donald Towner and Arnold Mountford. In a conscious effort to reverse the swing of the pendulum, the present book – originally conceived purely as a catalogue of the collections of Staffordshire pottery at the Victoria and Albert Museum – has finally evolved as a broad celebration of a craft industry that in the eighteenth and nineteenth centuries took European and New World markets by storm, and the vast legacy of which may still be enjoyed by students of style, by collectors on every level, and, of course, by myriad interior decorators. Though making no claims to be a definitive history, in which the length of the chapters would scrupulously reflect their relative importance, the book does attempt to gather up the increasingly disparate threads of the subject, review the often conflicting evidence between surviving pots and documentation or excavation, identify and follow themes on many levels, scrutinize the established history for dubious myths, offer some mildly contentious theories for discussion, and construct a wider context in which the subject may be studied from new angles.

The illustrations, mainly culled from the rich collections of the Victoria and Albert Museum, were carefully chosen to illumine the text. Unlike the recent catalogues of the Henry Weldon and Longridge collections, these do not necessarily possess that star quality demanded by their owners, for many were chosen simply to represent some vanished class of utilitarian object. But all may enjoy Richard Davis's photography on both visual and intellectual levels, while many of the groups provide unique opportunities to 'compare and contrast'. The intended inclusion of some documentary examples from the Glaisher Collection at the Fitzwilliam Museum in Cambridge was regrettably thwarted by major building work and the consequent clearance of their galleries into closed storage.

As for the title, in view of Geoffrey Godden's pioneering *British Pottery* of 1971, the alternative *English Pottery* was eventually selected as embracing the vast amounts of pottery produced in Scotland, Wales and Ireland, which for the most part, from the delftwares of London, Bristol and Liverpool to the industrial finewares of North Staffordshire and Yorkshire, were directly inspired by developments in England. Regrettably, many of these non-English products take a secondary role in the book, not least because of the lack of existing literature and the difficulties of studying and classifying pottery made almost exclusively for export to North America, India and the Far East.

Considerable thought was also applied to the date range of the book. It could be said that before about 1620 the English pottery trade existed in small independent pockets clustered around the clay beds of the Surrey/Hampshire borders, Essex, the Midlands and elsewhere, heavily dependent on basic prototypes imported from France, Germany and the Low Countries. Even the embryonic delftware industry at Norwich and Aldgate aspired to nothing more ambitious than floor tiles and drug jars. In fact, practically nothing before this date has survived above ground, and what has been reconstructed from fragments tends to hover uncomfortably in that grey area between archaeology and art history. But by about 1620 the situation had altered dramatically with the discovery by northern Europe of blue and white Chinese porcelain, which created almost immediately an insatiable demand for decorated pottery, to which, for example, the Pickleherring Quay pottery at Southwark responded with its innovative series of dated dishes and posset pots. Indeed, from this time onwards, the pressure for constant change and development in English pottery produced successive phases that may be charted, and which provide the backbone and narrative for the book.

Of course, such development did not cease in 1840, nor did the accession of Queen Victoria in 1837 suddenly shroud the arts of England in a mantle of eclectic Victorian ornament. Yet in terms of pottery the date does appear to represent a watershed when – almost symbolically – the British jug went pear-shaped; and when the vast and rapid urban expansion, with all its accompanying social unrest, created a demand for cheap crudely moulded pottery hidden beneath pervasive and inappropriate decoration, and when the last elements of a coarsened Neo-classicism were replaced by anaemic versions of medieval Gothic and the arts of the Middle East, the Orient and India. But the 1840s must also be seen as a run-up to the Great Exhibition of 1851, and for this major landmark the many contemporary catalogues and reports still provide the best classification and analysis, placing British mid-nineteenth-century pottery firmly in context with the rest of Europe. To stray beyond 1840, too, would have made it difficult to ignore not only the explosion of the encaustic tile-making industry, but also majolica, that misnamed but brilliant marriage between moulding technique and French translucent enamel colours that first emerged from Mintons and which continued to flourish well into the twentieth century. And if the last gasp of the eighteenth-century tradition may be heard in the years around 1840, then equally the period 1840–1900, which comprised massive technical advances as well as the artistic upheavals of the Aesthetic Movement, the third Rococo, Christopher Dresser and the beginnings of the Modern Movement, Art Pottery and Art Nouveau, does naturally suggest itself as the subject of another volume.

Inevitably, the inclusion of new material must reduce the space available for repeating old well-worn stories, and this in turn must take for granted a certain degree of knowledge on the part of the reader. It is hoped, however, that the new research included in chapters on the history of collecting and the pottery trade, as well as essential explanations of basic pottery techniques and the chronological table for the whole period, will more than make up for trimming some areas already well covered by encyclopaedias. These include tiles, delft tablewares, Staffordshire figures, blue and white printed wares and Wedgwood medallions. As for Josiah Wedgwood himself, while his creative and marketing genius is never disputed, there are attempts to peer at those behind his giant shadow. For while it was these industrious potters who, decades before, had made the name 'Staffordshire' synonymous with consummate potting skill, they left nothing but anonymous products behind to tease ceramic historians of the future; whereas Wedgwood, alone among his contemporaries, displayed not only a sense of destiny but also concern for posterity. And lest we be tempted to imagine that the Age of Sentiment – portrayed with such delicate feeling on enamelled and printed creamwares and sprigged Jasper wares – was reflected in some slight way in the lives of potters, the book should serve to remind of the harsh reality of the industry, a life of toil, drunkenness, immorality, child labour and lead-poisoning, relieved only by the sober Sabbath and the prospect of the annual Wates Week when the fires were allowed to die down, the bottle ovens were repaired, the smoke cleared enough for windows and doors to be painted, and the inhabitants of the Potteries feverishly enjoyed their brief respite from the treadmill. Against such a background, pure commercialism dictated that, when a pottery failed, like the fate of an ailing chicken in a hen-house, its buildings, pattern books, moulds and copper plates were set upon by its neighbours, to be appropriated or destroyed without trace. It is true that some master potters, driven by a puritan work ethic and astute enough to avoid the ever-present threat of bankruptcy, were rewarded with spectacular success, though it is as well to remember that even the wealthy and paternalistic Enoch Wood could not bring himself to include a single undamaged pot among the time-capsules buried beneath the streets of Burslem. As late as the 1930s, the legacy of this unforgiving way of life infuses bitterly the novels of Arnold Bennett.

Despite all, and with whatever pain they were created, these pots continue to speak eloquently for themselves, their bright oxide colours entirely undimmed, and there is much that they can teach us. In particular, it can never be emphasized too strongly that pots truly come to life only when they are handled. Then their attributes, all their minute idiosyncrasies of potting or decoration and their intimate secrets of manufacture are laid bare, and if there are deficiencies, neither their age nor a reputable potter's mark may excuse them. It is hoped that this book, as the long-ripening fruit of an intimate relationship between curator and a remarkably comprehensive collection of English pottery, will encourage this further: for it is always to the hand as well as to the eye that the handmade pot responds.

CHAPTER ONE 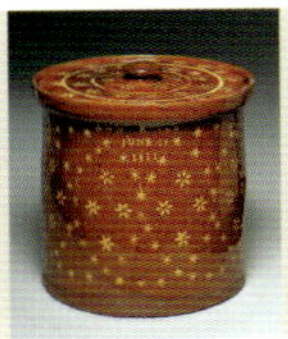

The Story of Slipware

Every potting enterprise, from the making of bricks and tiles to refined tablewares, has owed its existence to the discovery of beds of clay; and when both red-firing and white-firing clays happened to occur in the same locality what we now term 'slipware' came into being. Inevitably, the common iron-rich red was chosen for the body, while the much rarer white pipeclay – suitable for brittle moulded clay pipes but not for throwing on the wheel – was found to be ideal for embellishing the vessel. Given the restrictions of working with two colours only, creative potters rose to the challenge by pushing the repertoire of decorative techniques to the very limit.

But it is important to remember that so universal was this type of coarse pottery that until the early twentieth century, when collectors had begun to classify these interesting *decorated* objects into ever smaller categories, the term 'slipware' was quite unknown, and the technique regarded with only grudging admiration.[1] For example, Hodgkin and Hodgkin in 1891 described it as 'making few pretensions to beauty but wholly picturesque' and suitable to 'gladden the ingle-nook or the homely shelf'. It is also important to recognize that although coarse domestic pottery was essential to the vast majority of the population, it was only among clusters of potteries in areas such as Stoke-on-Trent that slip decoration became the norm, developing at the whim of the potter and quite independently of changing fashion. It is entirely due to the spirited and original 'folk art' decoration redolent of a vanished age of rustic innocence, the obvious handmade qualities, and the very high survival rate of inscribed and dated pieces, that ceramic historians have elevated its status from labourer's cottage to wealthy collector's cabinet. What has been written on the subject, however, has tended to rely on slipware's photogenic qualities, as compensation for the lack of new information about a craft industry that continued to thrive for three centuries, well below the level of fashion and sometimes even of recorded history.[2] Nevertheless, since the objects speak loudly for themselves, here it will suffice simply to put them into a wider context and to single out those many quirky regional idiosyncrasies that distinguish them so clearly from each other.

Like delftware, production of English slipware was inspired by popular imports from the Continent, in this case the slip-trailed bowls and dishes of North Holland. It is also no coincidence that both new products were developed in tandem, each with its own distinct slot in the consumers' hierarchy. Made with cheapness as a primary consideration, this early native slipware made no attempt to copy the sophisticated banding, sgraffito and trailing found on contemporary tablewares imported from potteries along the River Werra in Germany, but

1
Raised outlines produced from a hump-mould greatly simplified manufacture, but deprived the decoration of any spontaneity. Made in Staffordshire by Samuel Malkin about 1720.
Diameter 43.2 cm (17 in.).
V&A: C.135–1930.

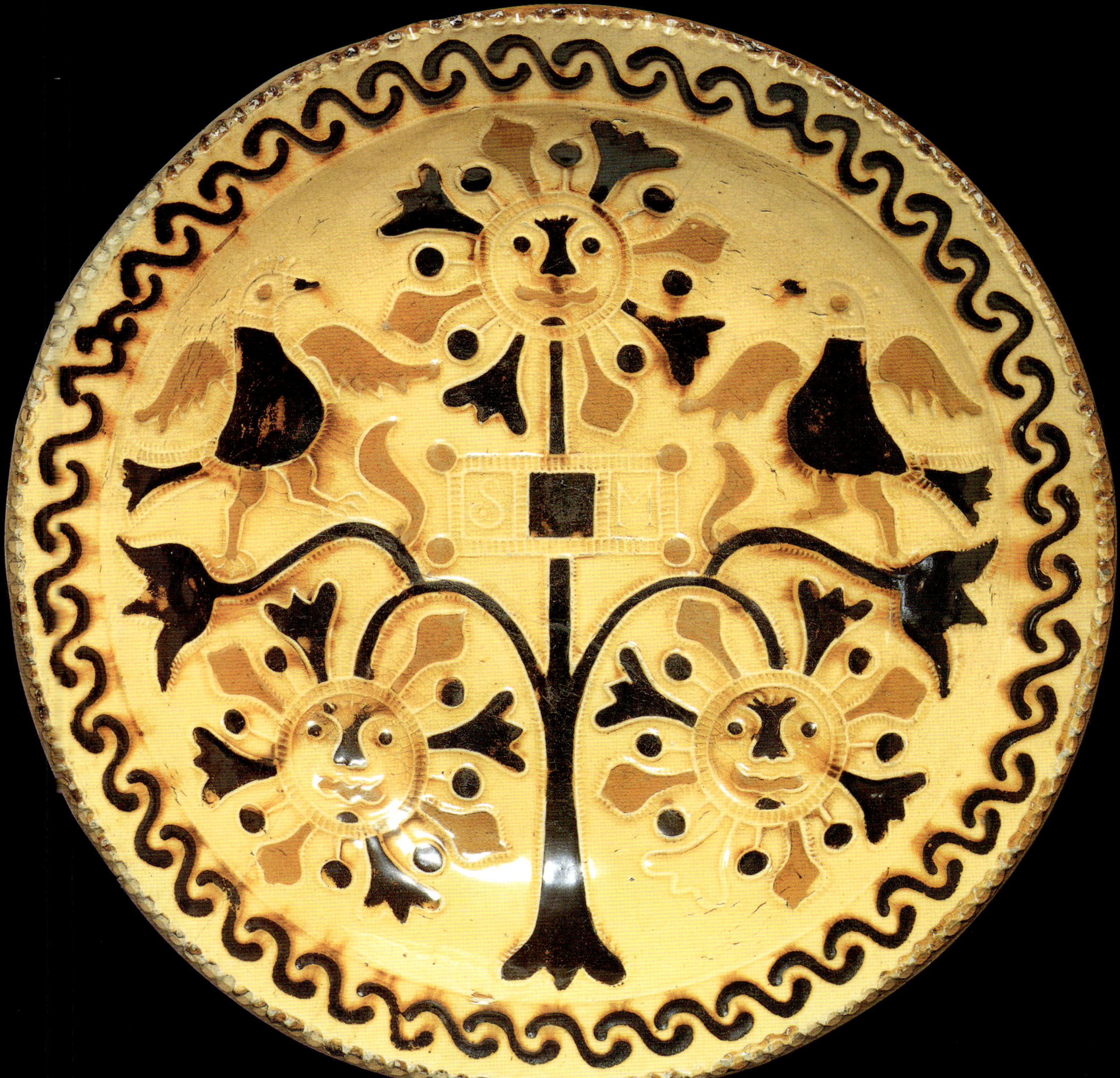
S M

instead relied simply upon a steady hand to lay the trail of slip with cow horn and quill. Although effective brushed-slip decoration had been practised earlier, for example those pots with almost calligraphic designs produced at Cheam in Surrey in the fifteenth century, it is difficult not to consider English potters of the Tudor period as fairly unadventurous, their products always sturdy and proficient but without either aspiration or ability to copy luxury imports from Germany, France and Italy. The green-glazed beer mugs from the potteries of the Surrey-Hampshire borders, for example, had all the necessary qualities – cheapness and practicality – as substitutes for Rhineland stoneware, but without any noticeable individual characteristics.

Thus, it was not until the early years of the seventeenth century that potters at Harlow in Essex began to imitate slip-trailed designs on contemporary

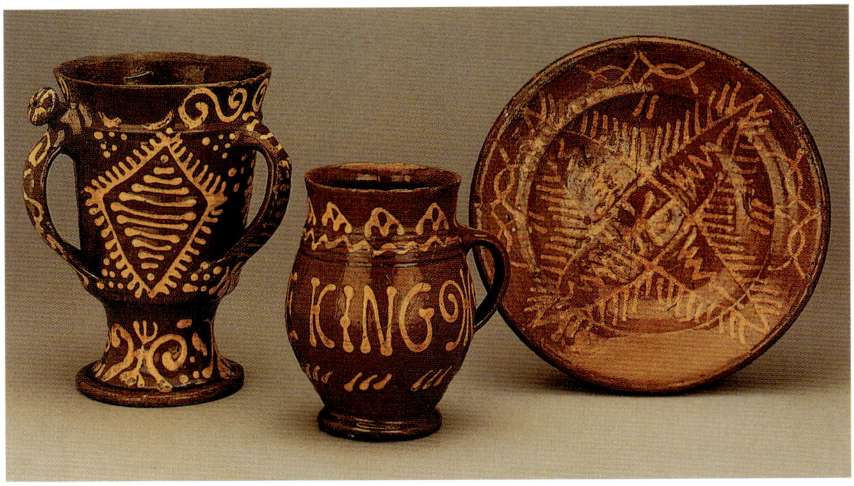

2
'Metropolitan' slipwares for the London market, made at Harlow, Essex, in the mid-17th century. Max. height 14 cm (5½ in.).
Courtesy Trustees of the British Museum.

ear-handled bowls from North Holland. Made principally for the London market, this orangey-red ware, traditionally known as 'Metropolitan Slipware', was mass-produced by several kilns throughout the seventeenth century (plate 2); but being soft and intended for use rather than display, very little of it survived long enough above ground to attract the attention of later collectors. It is evident from excavations, however, that these simple dishes, mugs, candlesticks and chamber pots must have satisfied the needs of most ordinary London households – supplemented by the harder but undecorated white-bodied products from the Surrey-Hampshire borders – for there is little discernible development during their main production period of *c.*1635–70.[3] Following North Holland prototypes, a limited range of elementary geometric, scrolled and leaf-like motifs were used, often accompanied by pious inscriptions reflecting the Puritan austerity of the times, such as 'FAST AND PRAY', 'FEARE GOD' and, after the Restoration of 1660, 'OBEAY THE KING'.[4] Entirely without precedent in England, these trailed-slip inscriptions probably owed their inspiration to the moulded frieze that encircled imported Cologne and Frechen stoneware bottles and mugs of nearly a century before, with such pious exhortations as 'WAN GOT MIT UNS IST' (If God is with us) and 'TRINCK ESST NICHT GOTT VERGESST'

(Eat and Drink, forget not God). Significantly, figure drawing being so much more challenging than mere repeated pattern, the range of designs practised at Harlow never included the fluently drawn birds and animals so commonly found inside North Holland slipware bowls. Towards the end of the seventeenth century, the prolific manufacture of cheap delftware in London, the introduction of salt-glazed stoneware following John Dwight's patent of 1672, and the growing production of refined earthenwares in Staffordshire eventually rendered Metropolitan Slipware obsolete: but the rarity of complete examples today is proof that, as cheap ephemeral tableware unaffected by fashion, it remained in use right up to the point of its destruction.

Rhineland stonewares were imported by the million, and further influence is to be found on the slipwares made for well over 100 years by the farmer-

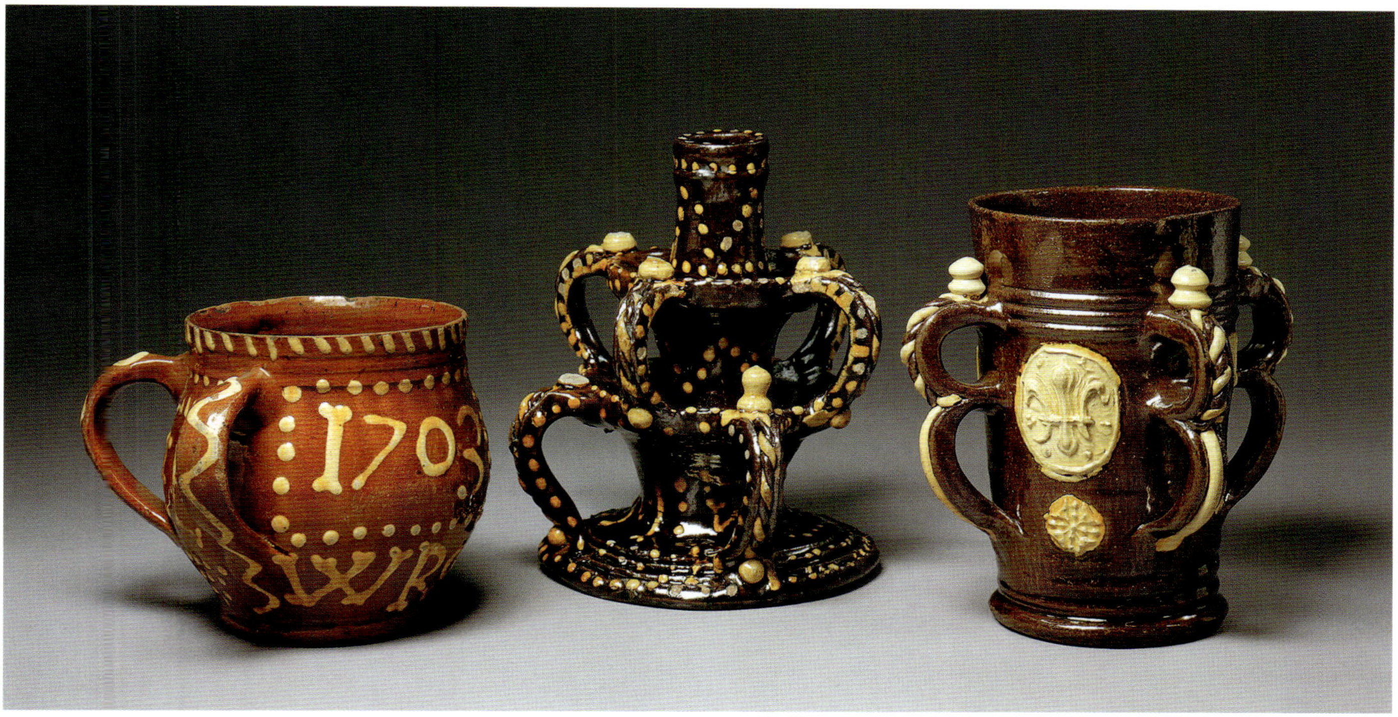

3
The rural slipware potters of Wrotham, Kent, early pioneers whose dated pots span 100 years, had minimal effect on the development of the technique in Britain. Max. height 18.4 cm (7¼ in.).

Mug of 1703, V&A: 3722–1901; candlestick of 1649, V&A: 4736–1901; tyg of 1621: V&A: 4771–1901.

potters at the small Kentish village of Wrotham. Here the potters used applied pads of white pipeclay stamped with moulds taken directly from the Frechen stoneware bottles then in universal use, to ornament their basic beaker-shaped or globular 'tygs' made for the communal drinking (plate 3) that, at least in the form of wassail bowls used for the celebration of Twelfth Night, persisted in rural areas until the very end of the nineteenth century. With the exception of the potter's initials, the repertoire of moulded designs was limited to the more common *Bartmann* medallions, such as lions, flower heads and fleur-de-lis, with an occasional grotesque bearded mask. Excavations at Wrotham have produced fragments of utilitarian wares such as circular chicken feeders with rows of concentric grooves, but significantly not wasters of the decorated wares that would have been fired with extra care. From the almost complete absence of decorated Wrotham slipwares found in London and other likely outlets, it may be deduced that the market for these personalized objects was almost entirely localized; and further, that the hundred or so surviving pots may represent most of the total output of commemorative wares. Because of collectors' and museums' interest in these dated pieces, no doubt stimulated by the publication in 1891 of Hodgkin and Hodgkin's *Examples of Early English Pottery, Named, Dated and Inscribed*, they secured a presence in early collections disproportionate to their importance in the history of English pottery. We do, however, know much more about the makers of these quaint archaic pots than might be expected: for a scholarly resident of Wrotham took up the challenge of identifying the initials that are so often found as part of the decoration.[5] Attributions, based upon his exhaustive study of the hundred or so surviving pots and documentary records of Wrotham inhabitants, consist of four minor potters and what he termed 'The Big Five':

1. 'IL' for John Livermore, with pieces dated 1612–49;
2. 'HI' for Henry Ifield, with pieces dated 1644–69;
3. 'GR' for George Richardson, with pieces dated 1642–77;
4. 'NH' for Nicholas Hubble, with pieces dated 1649–87;
5. 'IE', unidentified, with pieces dated 1687–1721.

Forms other than tygs were attempted, such as large jugs, cisterns, candlesticks, puzzle jugs and dishes, the fabric and glaze varying from almost black with hard brown body to orangey-red with soft red body. The range of techniques employed was not ambitious, and although stylistic links among the village potters were naturally strong, the quality of potting and decoration varied considerably, George Richardson being considered the most proficient. A general partiality for rather messy applied white pads 'stitched' to the pot with dashes of slip has no parallel in the work of other slipware makers in Harlow or Staffordshire. In fact, it seems that these potter-farmers worked almost in isolation, neither absorbing nor imparting influence in terms of the major centres of slipware production that sprung up during their period of operation. And when opportunity offered, they lost no time in abandoning their traditional potting trade and turning to more lucrative agriculture. Any romantic idea that these often appealing pots were made by respected interrelated local craftsmen working harmoniously in an unhurried rural idyll may be quickly dismissed.

At the beginning of the seventeenth century, when the potters of Wrotham began to exploit their local potting clays, the landlocked county of Staffordshire had no direct access to lucrative markets beyond the range of a man on foot and his packhorse. North Devon, however, offered the prospect of extensive sea trade, not only with ports such as Swansea and Bristol, but also with Ireland and America. What is more, there was excellent clay at Fremington, white pipeclay near Torrington and low-grade coal enough to get the local potteries established. Thus it was that here the first large-scale slipware industry sprung up, based upon the familiar sgraffito wares imported from Beauvais and possibly assisted by immigrant potters who were almost certainly responsible for introducing the practice of biscuit-firing.[6] Before London delftware potters migrated westwards and established themselves at Brislington and Bristol in the mid-seventeenth century, the slipwares of Barnstaple and Bideford were a highly popular export to New England, Virginia and Maryland, accounting for as much as 15 per cent of the total output.[7] The range of essential household wares was exactly similar to those of Harlow, consisting of dishes, jugs, chamber pots and candlesticks, and, like the Metropolitan Slipwares, they were used to destruction, leaving behind only the untypical fancy goods such as inscribed posset pots and puzzle jugs. But the sgraffito method of decoration, using various toothed combs and gouges, allowed much greater freedom of expression: these included not only stylized birds, flowers and fruit, but, during the third quarter of the seventeenth century, the highly popular tulip, which showed a familiarity with contemporary delftwares, while unwittingly also following the design of Iznik wares from Turkey of a century before.

At Bideford by 1672 there were 21 men working with 6 master potters, but thereafter the industry slowed down due partly perhaps to competition from delftware, and partly through the imposition of a heavy tax on coal imported from Wales, which allowed the fast-expanding potters of Staffordshire, with their highly accessible coal supplies, to undercut them. So the potteries continued at much the same level throughout the eighteenth and nineteenth centuries, substituting quality for quantity by adding to their range of common pots and clay ovens those intricately carved and incised harvest jugs for which the Barnstaple-Bideford potteries are so well known (plate 4). Several makers, such as the Hollamores, signed their work, all sharing a range of 'folk' motifs such as hearts, heraldic beasts, the royal arms and, of course, the nautical compass. From around 1800 the tradition was taken up vigorously by the Fishley family at Fremington,[8] gradually degenerating to the level of historicist pottery and popular souvenir before eventually handing on their muscular potting style and sturdy pulled handles through Michael Cardew to Bernard Leach.

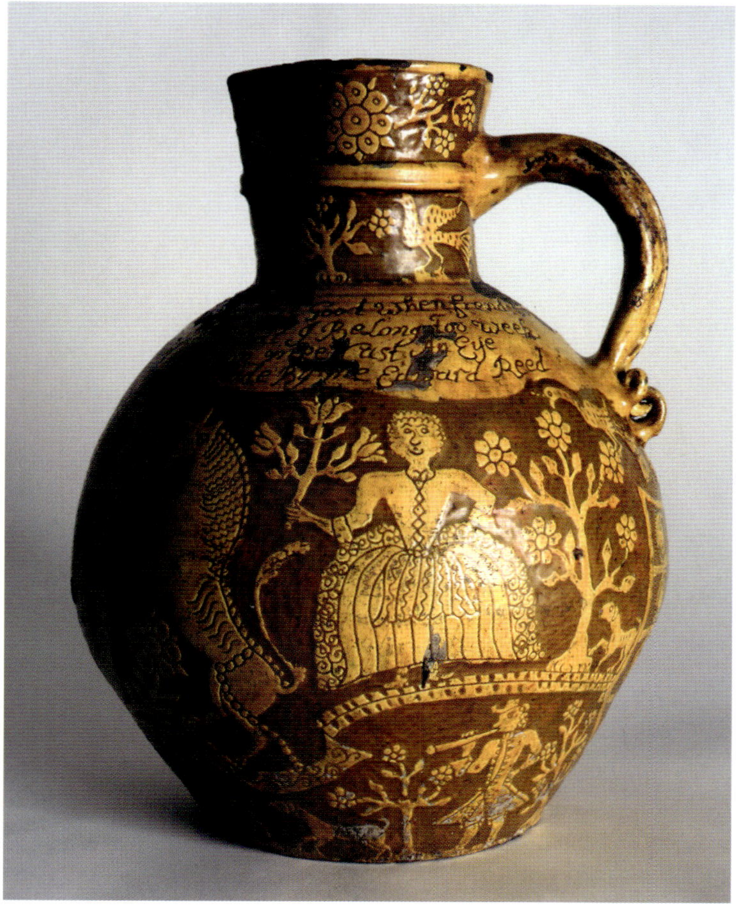

4
Capacious harvest jugs to be filled with cider were a speciality of the potteries in the Barnstaple-Bideford area of Devon. This documentary example signed by Edward Reed and dated 1741.
Courtesy of the Potteries Museum, Stoke-on-Trent.

Other clusters of potteries making use of the excellent West Country clays sprung up at Donyatt in Somerset and at Verwood in Dorset. At Donyatt, from the early seventeenth century, a range of wood-fired pots with simple sgraffito decoration loosely followed those of North Devon, but with splashes of oxide colouring – as found on Spanish pottery and so often the resort of small potteries without a market for more sophisticated decoration.[9] Many rather crude puzzle jugs and miniature barrel flasks have survived, misleading representatives of a local industry that mainly supplied basic pottery to a local community. At Verwood, from the late seventeenth century, the local pink-buff clay required no coating of white slip and proved excellent for basic wood-fired country pots such as large pans and crocks,[10] as well as the archaic squat globular harvest flasks with pinched lugs known as 'Dorset Owls', which, against all probability, continued in production until the 1950s. Often, an apron of impure lead-glaze added a touch of yellow to these attractive pots, sometimes with incised and rouletted decoration; but Verwood products are not strictly slipware.

Part of the West Country tradition, though later in date, were the potteries at Ewenny in the Vale of Glamorgan. Here the local clays, coal and lead ore provided the basis for a successful industry run by potter-farmers to supply local markets. As at Fremington, the inevitable decline at the end of nineteenth century was successfully halted by adapting to historicist and art wares, in which Evan Jones of the Claypit Pottery took a particular interest.[11] The Ewenny potteries were also responsible for the very last multi-handled wassail bowls, ending an English rural custom stretching back two centuries. In complete contrast to the tradition of sgraffito decoration, the Buckley potteries of Clwyd thrived from the late seventeenth century, supplying plain pottery to markets as far away as Ireland via the Dee estuary and the port of Chester. Apart from bricks, Buckley was noted for its robust dark-brown baking dishes, which in the nineteenth century sometimes sported the word 'Beef' in trailed slip.

Ever since slipware was defined as a separate class of earthenware, the name 'Staffordshire' has been firmly attached to it. This is partly a well-deserved association and partly an accident of history; for, as described above, the slipware manufacture in Staffordshire became established only in the 1640s, several decades after its appearance at Harlow and north Devon. Furthermore, although at Burslem dishes press-moulded with geometric designs were being made by the mid-seventeenth century, the complete lack of aesthetic pretension shows that the new process – pressing a sheet of clay over a fired clay mould carved with a pattern – was designed simply to assist mass production by unskilled labour. But Staffordshire, though immune from foreign influence, was not as remote from foreign markets as described by Dr Plot in 1686, recounting the distribution of Burslem pottery by 'poor CRATE-MEN, who carry them at their backs all over the country'. The tall hard earthenware butter-pots for the Irish market were but a small part of the export trade, which also supplied Virginia with butter pots and blackwares from as early as 1610, spreading throughout the century to cover the Eastern seaboard and Caribbean.[12]

The range of good yellow and red clays, however, together with the presence of the rich coalfield upon which Burslem actually stood, not only ensured the economic stability of these small potteries but also established a climate in which ventures into artistic decoration might be made. In the 1660s a local potter, Thomas Toft, appeared as founder and patriarch of a small but active group of makers whose huge display dishes were slip-trailed with bold designs drawn from a wide variety of sources, including traditional moral images (the Pelican in her Piety, Adam and Eve), declarations of loyalty (kings and queens from Charles II to George I, the royal arms, the fugitive Charles II in the oak-tree), heraldic images that fitted the circular frame (lions and unicorns), and many others. These cumbersome dishes were placed upright on their edge in the kiln, and usually display some glaze-runs and bleeding of the iron from the red slip. Even a cursory study shows a wide variance in the technical and artistic ability of the makers, ranging from the schematized and child-like representations of William III and George I by Ralph Simpson to the spirited, almost calligraphic, draughtsmanship of Thomas Toft I (plate 5). It is difficult to avoid the impression of rivalry among these dynastic families of slipware potters (that is, the prolific Tofts, Taylors, Simpsons and Wrights), and even among the handful

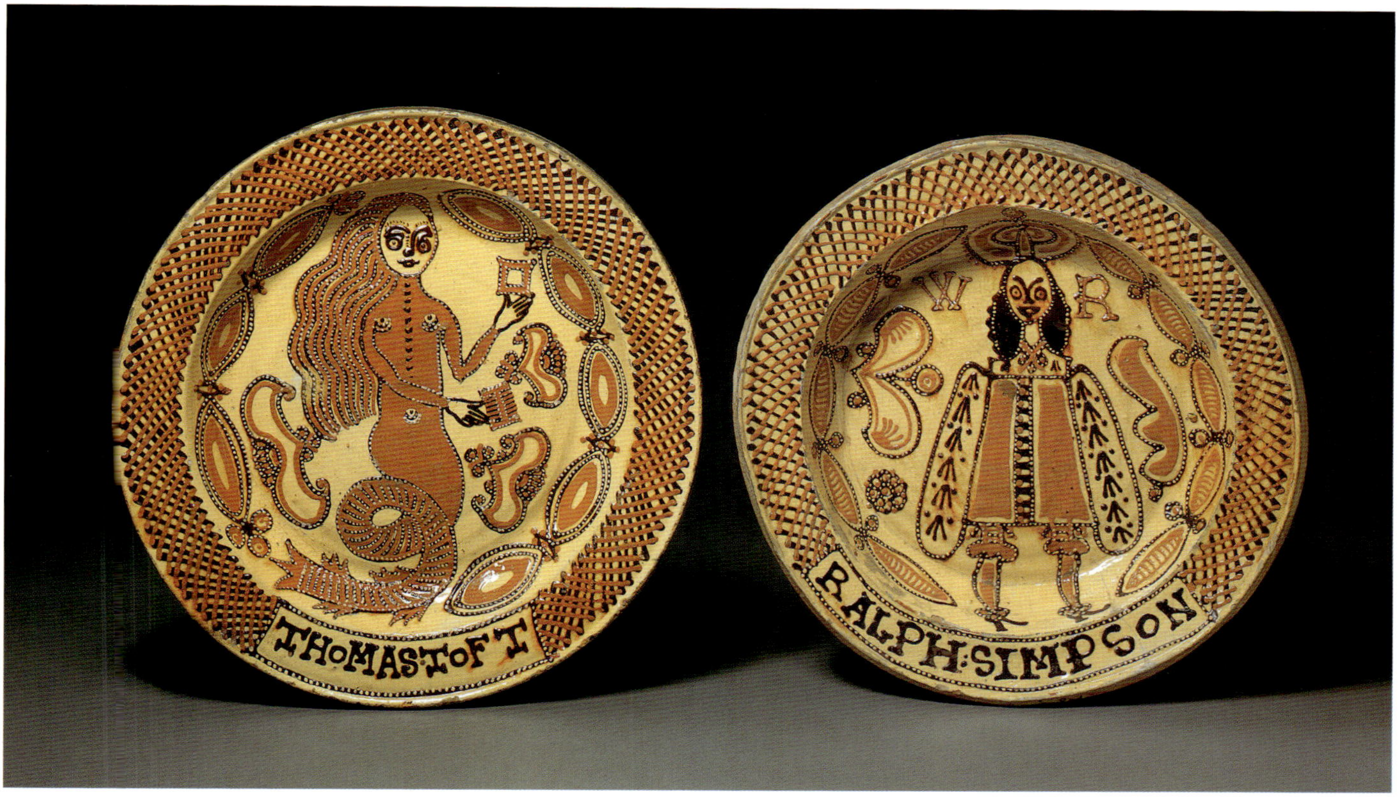

of more obscure followers, since they all applied their very unequal skills in pursuit of the same market.[13] It is, however, equally likely that potting was not their sole occupation and that they may have earned their living, according to the season, as farmers, drovers, carters or even inn-keepers.

Mystery still surrounds the original purpose of these monumental dishes, for almost all are signed by their makers; very few are dedicated or dated as commissions; their popular motifs apparently have no direct connection with taverns of the same name; they show absolutely no signs of wear; no pottery sites have been excavated; and they appear to have strayed little further than the counties around Staffordshire and sometimes into Wales. The discovery of 15 prime

5
The superior slip-trailing skills of Thomas Toft I are well demonstrated by his mermaids, especially when compared with the often schematic designs of his contemporaries. Made in Staffordshire in the late 17th century, the 'WR' dish after Queen Mary's death in 1694. Max. diameter 43.8 cm (17¼ in.).
Mermaid dish, V&A: 299–1869; Simpson dish, V&A: C.116–1938.

examples at Chirk Castle, many of them signed by Thomas, Ralph and James Toft and Ralph Simpson, which were 'exhumed from the precincts of an old Welsh castle wherein they had been left undisturbed for over two centuries', proved something of a red herring, for these dishes were mounted with iron brackets around the dairy and must now be viewed as the antiquarian eccentricity of one of the castle's Victorian owners, one fortunate enough to be able to gather such unappreciated objects long before they were presented to the public as 'Folk Art' by Solon's *The Art of the Old English Potter* in 1883.[14] What may be significant is their availability on the Welsh borders, and herein may lie a clue to their original use: perhaps for the custom of ceremonial breaking of bread on the Welsh family dining table. As for their decoration, there can be little doubt that the inclusion of the potters' names was intended to serve an advertising purpose,

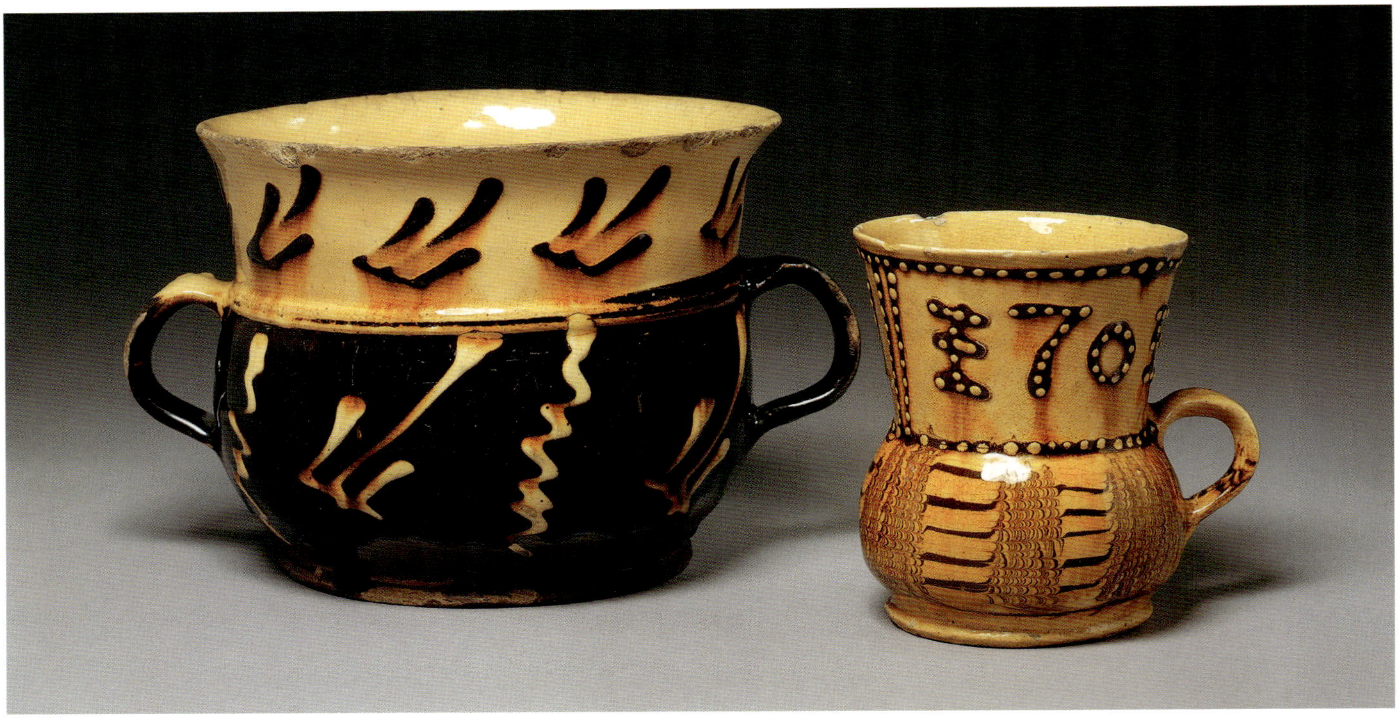

6
After about 1690 Staffordshire slipware makers, forced to compete directly with other refined earthenwares, concentrated on thinly potted drinking vessels, which were widely exported.
Max. height 13.4 cm (5¼ in.).
Made in Staffordshire, the posset pot about 1710, the mug dated 1701.
Posset pot, V&A: C.341–1919; mug, V&A: C.120–1938.

which in turn may point to their display in some public place such as a tavern, or even on their makers' pottery stalls at local fairs. Since their very existence was unknown to the curious Josiah Wedgwood, and remained so until Enoch Wood collected two examples for his factory museum at Burslem in the early nineteenth century, the original inspiration behind this sudden flowering of graphic slip-trailing is likely to continue to tantalize ceramic historians for some time to come.

Although the big dishes have now reached iconic status through the writings of Marc Louis Solon and the art critic Herbert Read, as well as through the links with Japanese folk art forged by the pioneer studio potter Bernard Leach, it was surely the more utilitarian slipware cups and mugs, not to mention the plain lead-glazed earthenwares, upon which the makers depended for a living. These well-potted cups were produced by the thousand and have been excavated all over Britain and in America, for they were cheap, pleasingly decorative and perfectly fitted to the hand of the user, with ring handles of flat section to suit finger or thumb (plate 6). At first, the most basic spots of slip were arranged around these pots, but dated examples show that towards the end of the seventeenth century an important new technique was developed, soon to become the standard decoration on common baking dishes. As early as 1686 Dr Plot described the process, whereby the potters

> *slip* or paint them with their severall sorts of *slip*, according as they design their *work*, when the first *slip* is dry, laying on the *others* at their leisure, the *orange* slip makeing the ground, and the *white* and *red*, the *paint*; which two colours they break with a wire *brush*, much after the manner they doe when they *marble* paper, and then *cloud* them with a *pensil* when they are pretty dry.[15]

This combed or 'feathered' slipware was a highly effective decorative device, simple to produce and adaptable to any shape or size. As an added refinement, the sharp pointed tool or toothed comb could be dragged through with a zigzag motion to create a complex feathered effect. A marbled effect could be achieved by joggling and agitating a mixture of wet coloured slips inside the dish, probably the 'clouding' method mentioned by Dr Plot. Dishes decorated inside in this way were given notched or pie-crust edges so that they could be stacked face-to-face during the firing, protecting the interiors but enabling them to be pulled apart later by cracking off the tiny points of lead-glaze around the edge. Pairs of dishes with unglazed backs could thus conveniently be stacked in the kiln without separators between them, and it is almost certain that the single-glazed surface of these dishes, like the big chargers of Thomas Toft type, was sprinkled with powdered lead ore in the manner described by Simeon Shaw and Dr Plot. Occasionally they bear the maker's initials in relief in the middle, having been cut into the convex mould onto which the clay was pressed. Almost indestructible, a few of these clay moulds survive, such as one in the British Museum made by William Bird as late as 1751.[16]

'Feathering' was also applied to the posset pots made from the 1670s mainly for a local market.[17] The smaller of these were usually cylindrical with two low-set handles, while the larger were multi-handled and of wide thistle shape or tall flaring form. But the predominance of slip-trailed decoration on finely potted examples, consisting of tulips, fleur-de-lis, stylized pomegranates, dark slip ground with white 'jewelling', and often a frieze containing the name of the maker, suggests that trailed decoration was reserved mainly for commissioned pots. Such vigorous hand-drawn decoration on hollow wares and on the big dishes with their increasingly cartoon-like figures of monarchs had apparently ceased by the 1720s, leaving only the debased mass-produced moulded dishes to continue the tradition (see plate 1). The raised outlines on these, produced from a convex clay mould carved with gouges and impressed with bands of rouletting before firing, enclosed areas that could be filled or brushed with contrasting coloured slips in the 'painting-by-numbers' method, perhaps using child labour. Such crude dishes display an almost self-conscious quaintness, some having naïve representations of St George and the Dragon, Charles II in the oak, Adam and Eve, moral exhortations, such as 'Remember Lots Wife / Luke 17: 32 / 1726', or giant sunflowers, and others with archaic motifs such as pomegranates copied from delftwares of 50 years earlier. Just as Thomas Toft has lent his name to an entire class of freehand slip-trailed dishes, so Samuel Malkin has become firmly associated with these later press-moulded examples. Indeed, his name is found proudly displayed on many of them,[18] for example a dish with clock face inscribed 'Samuel Malkin The Maker in Burslem 1722' and a primitive version of the well-known moralizing subject 'Keep with:in Compas:and you:shall be:sure 1726 . . .To avoyd:any troubles:which others:indure', but the identity of other followers who signed their work – or at least their moulds – such as IS, IC and IH remains open to speculation. 'IH' has been attributed, on grounds of probability, to a member of the prolific Heath family of slipware makers.

7
The only signed piece of a group of thinly potted wares with fluent *sgraffito* decoration, with dates from the 1740s–1760s. Made in Staffordshire by John Shaw, dated 1742.
Height 16 cm (6¼ in.).
Courtesy of Sotheby's.

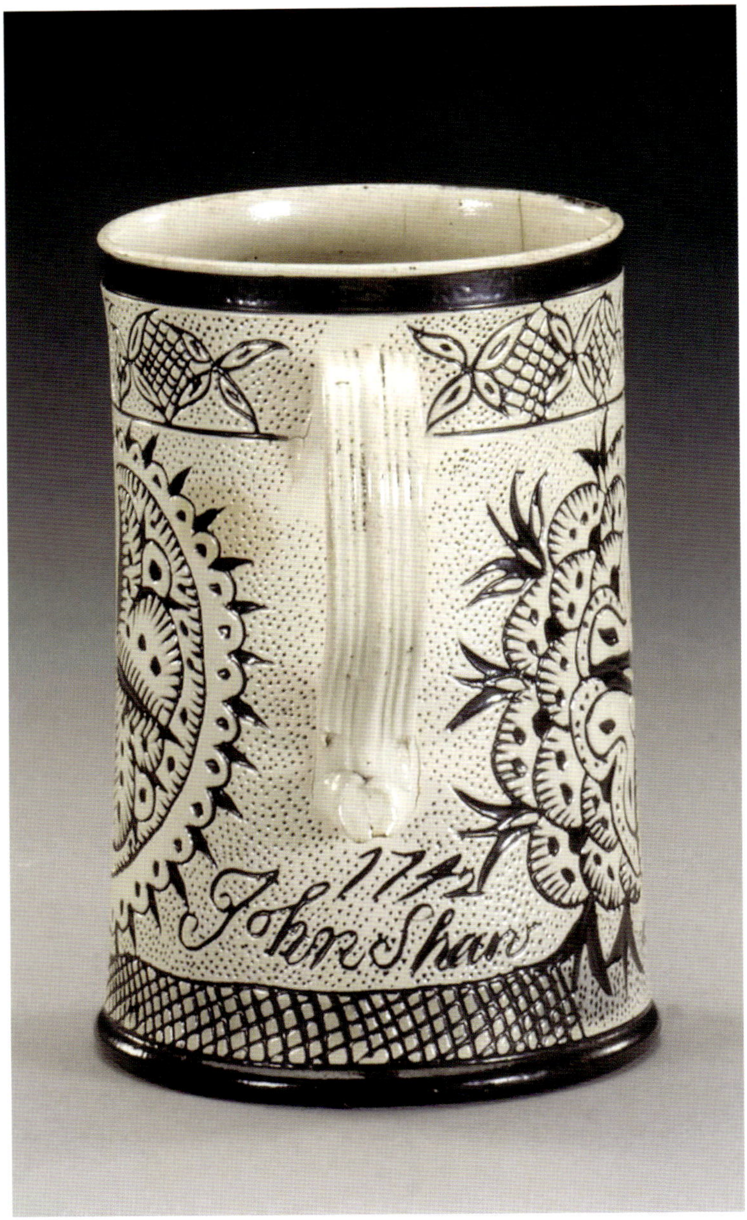

Another, wholly original, class of slipware also appeared in the 1720s, consisting of thinly potted buff-bodied mugs and posset pots coated in dense brown slip and boldly carved with animals and dates.[19] The shapes and fine potting are typical both of Staffordshire and the brown stoneware makers of Derbyshire, but while these remained popular for much of the rest of the century, the fashion for sgraffito decoration seems to have been brief, perhaps an attempt during the 1720s to compete with the fine lathe-turned brown stoneware beer mugs and jugs of Nottingham and Derbyshire. Like the slipware mould-cutters, the decorators of these pots were inclined to use the gouge with a heavy hand, though the best – for example, the mug dated 1727 in the Glaisher Collection – achieved a striking naïve effect, capturing the essence of the beast as in prehistoric cave painting, or indeed in the animals skilfully trailed in *barbotine* by Roman potters. In the 1740s the technique re-emerged on Staffordshire redware, though its extreme rarity in excavations suggests its use mainly for commissioned pieces. The development and decline of this skilful technique during its short lifespan may be traced through dated examples, the earliest of which is an ale mug signed

'John Shaw 1742' (plate 7), followed by a representative series in the Victoria and Albert Museum: namely a brick-red mug with a fox dated 1747, a punch bowl of 1755 with heraldic lions, fish and carved chequering, and a beer jug with coarser decoration dated 1766, all these having animals drawn with great fluency on a background pounced with dots – apparently all by the potter John Shaw, perhaps connected with the salt-glaze potter Ralph Shaw who briefly held a patent in 1733 for chequered white slip decoration on a red/brown body. The vogue for repeated geometric decoration that sprung up after Wedgwood adopted the engine-turning lathe in 1763 offered some scope for these refined slipwares to compete with the products of the big industrialized factories, but in the last quarter of the eighteenth century it was the finer and much more colourful banded creamwares that were to become so popular.

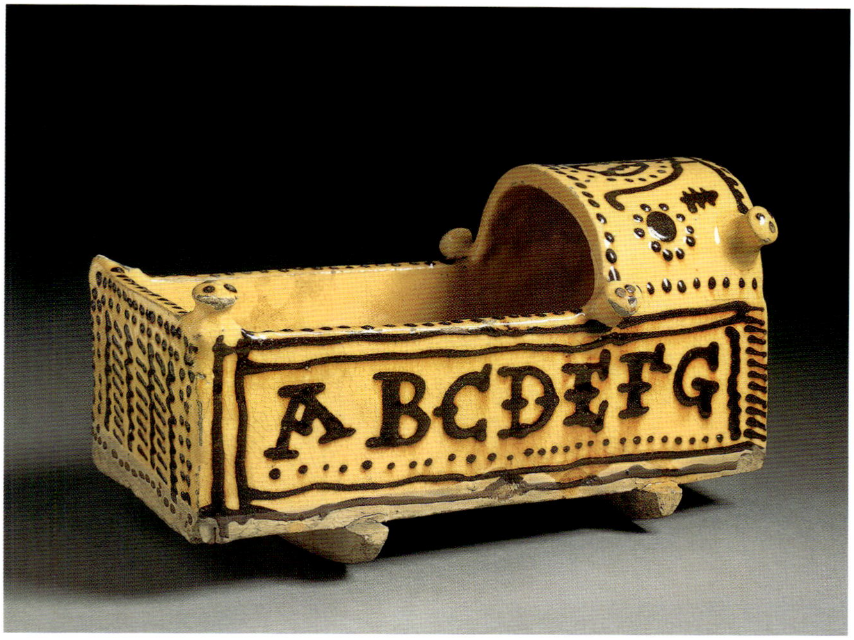

8

Slipware remained popular for commemorating country weddings and christenings until at least the end of the 19th century. Cradles were produced probably not as toys but as symbols of fertility. Probably made in Staffordshire about 1720. Height 27.6 cm (10⅞ in.).

V&A: C.305–1921.

As for the Staffordshire tradition of massive dishes and elaborate posset pots, all the indications are that it declined during the 1720s just as rapidly as the manufacture of fineware expanded; for that watershed decade saw the beginning of white-sprigged red earthenwares as well as the perfection of the new white salt-glazed stoneware. Stimulated as much by the rapidly expanding consumption of tea as by the massive imports of Chinese porcelain teawares, the potters of Staffordshire quickly understood that the future lay in developing a range of cheap fine earthenware teawares, opening up river transport and moving into distant markets far above the level of heavy baking dishes and archaic posset pots.

From this time onwards, the making of slipware and country pottery (plate 8) continued in the neighbouring counties of Shropshire and Derbyshire, but also became established in centres such as Bristol, which offered opportunities for the export trade. Fragments excavated at Bristol show such close reliance on Staffordshire forms that wares from both places are virtually indistinguishable from each other. In Derbyshire, production of slipware baking dishes is thought to have continued throughout the eighteenth century, complementing the major output of lathe-turned brown stonewares. Probably of Derbyshire manufacture are the almost black dishes decorated in white slip with a stylized cockerel and dates in the 1790s, no doubt the work of one individual potter with a particular flair for slip-trailing.

Elsewhere, a number of factors enabled some potteries to thrive, others to decline. In the second half of the seventeenth century the potteries at Potterspury in Northamptonshire fell victim to the two most successful producers of the period, Ticknall in Derbyshire and Burslem in Staffordshire: as John Morton records in his *Natural History of Northamptonshire* (1712), their local clays could not compete with Ticknall wares for resistance to frost, while the higher cost of living in the region allowed the potters of Derbyshire and Staffordshire 'to bring hither their wares upon little horses or asses, usually begging their victuals . . . on that account afford their wares at such under-rates as our potters here cannot live so well upon the trade'.[20] The potters of Ticknall, meanwhile, had long infiltrated markets far afield, with their 'earthen vessels, potts and pancions . . . at Tychnall . . . carried all East England through'.[21] The economic advantages of cheap living in the North, together with the ready availability of the heaviest raw materials of pottery manufacture – refractory clays for kiln bricks and saggars, potting clays and coal – was indeed an unbeatable combination that eventually put out of business many of the potting industries within reach of north Staffordshire and Derbyshire. This rapid expansion of the trade was not controlled directly by the potters themselves, but by a new breed of middleman who bought from a variety of sources and took a percentage from every pot sold through his network of hawkers. The creation of these wider markets resulted, by the third quarter of the eighteenth century, in permanent 'Staffordshire Warehouses' springing up in many small provincial towns, mixing and matching 'sortable' wares from a variety of sources.

After Staffordshire potters had turned to more lucrative finewares during the 1720s, smaller groups of potteries emerged in areas where suitable markets, clay and fuel were to be found, these in turn undermining those old-established country potteries that were ill-placed to serve the shifting and expanding population. In the industrial north, for example, potteries at Potovens near Wakefield declined after 1700, to be replaced by new ones at Halifax, Midhope and Burton in Lonsdale, where idiosyncratic local styles emerged and developed, culminating in the great flowering of decorated slipware towards the middle of the nineteenth century. Slab-built christening cradles, knife-boxes, watch stands, pipe-racks and other fancy forms were embellished with white clay and trailed slip. By contrast, in Wales and the West Country, as described above, traditional sgraffito-decorated wares remained popular until the invasion by cheap printed tablewares from around 1800 forced upon them the role of representing a vanishing world of simple country customs. Almost inevitably, by the end of the nineteenth century this self-consciousness led to essays into kitsch, when the ornament became more important than the form, or indeed the function. Similar tendencies may be seen in the commercial souvenirs made at Swansea and in Devon, where jocular mottos and simplistic decoration seem to echo the faience souvenirs mass-produced at Quimper in Normandy.

In south-east England, London continued to be supplied with basic domestic crocks during the eighteenth and nineteenth centuries by a number of redware potteries along the River Thames, as well as by those using the excellent potting clays on the Surrey-Hampshire borders.[22] It is tempting to suppose that sophisticated London households would have found more elegant Staffordshire substitutes for slipware baking dishes, but surviving accounts of the Isleworth Pottery for the period 1790–1805 show a huge trade in slipware 'moulded' dishes with some of the smart London dealers, with the suggestion that the pottery may have been supplying these from the mid-eighteenth century onwards.[23] Supply was constant, the kiln being fired weekly, with prices of 6d or 7d per piece – probably retailing at about 1d profit, to judge from the three dishes supplied for 2s by the London dealer John Caravella in the early 1770s. Even as late as 1845 John Abbott was making 'Welsh trays' at the former Kishere pottery at Mortlake, marked examples being virtually indistinguishable from unmarked dishes made in the Midlands and elsewhere,[24] and when that venture failed he continued to make slipwares at the Isleworth Pottery from 1849 to 1855. But even before this time, robust dishes with specky olive/brown glaze and simple, assured scrolls trailed in thick white slip were developed by the Sunderland potteries,[25] and, given the existing extensive coal and window-glass trade between London and the North-East, not surprisingly these shared the market in London with more local common household wares from the Hampshire and Deptford areas. By 1873 Doulton of Lambeth was acting as agent for their wares, issuing an illustrated price list that included milk bowls, cream pots, starch pans, parted trays (slip-decorated rectangular dishes with a central division), pipkins (bowls with spike handles), salt-jars, ham and tongue pans. All these heavy domestic pots complemented Doulton's existing range of tougher and more refined stonewares. In the Midlands, however, forms almost identical to Sunderland slipwares were made in salt-glazed stoneware by the potteries of Derbyshire, notably Pearsons of Whittington Moor.

Every region had its local style, and the more isolated the potteries, the more idiosyncratic their products. Sussex had boasted potteries with a distinct local character since the early eighteenth century,[26] but by the end of the eighteenth century these potteries began to develop techniques that were unique to the area: namely, inlaying the russet-brown iron-flecked body with printers' type and metal stamps of tiny stars or other shapes, all filled with white slip and carefully scraped clean (plate 9). A version of this also spread across the Kent border in the early nineteenth century to High Halden in Kent, where red clay storage jars were decorated with fronds of foliage, gouged or impressed and filled with white slip. At Brede in Sussex, a particular style of decoration with bands of interlaced hoops of stars flourished in the 1790s, usually found on cylindrical tobacco jars or tea canisters; but, in terms of output, these decorated and commissioned pieces represented the tip of the iceberg, as a Brede Pottery price list of about

1840 shows,[27] for it was horticultural, architectural and sanitary wares that kept these potteries running throughout the nineteenth century. Inlaid wares were also made at East Grinstead, and from the 1790s at Chailey, where the potters developed the technique into an elaborate art form, displaying familiarity with the Neo-classical forms and motifs of Staffordshire industrial wares. Traditional spirit flasks and small harvest barrels continued to be made at Chailey, including one dated 1839 in the form of a large pocket watch,[28] evidently inspired by the moulded stoneware 'Lady's Watch' and the 'Patent Chronometer' made by the Fulham Pottery at exactly the same time. Not surprisingly, after the mid-nineteenth century competition from big mechanized potteries drove these potters and brickmakers to abandon their time-consuming inlay technique in favour of 'artistic' moulded or hand-modelled decoration, and eventually to making Art Wares, notably at Dicker and Rye.

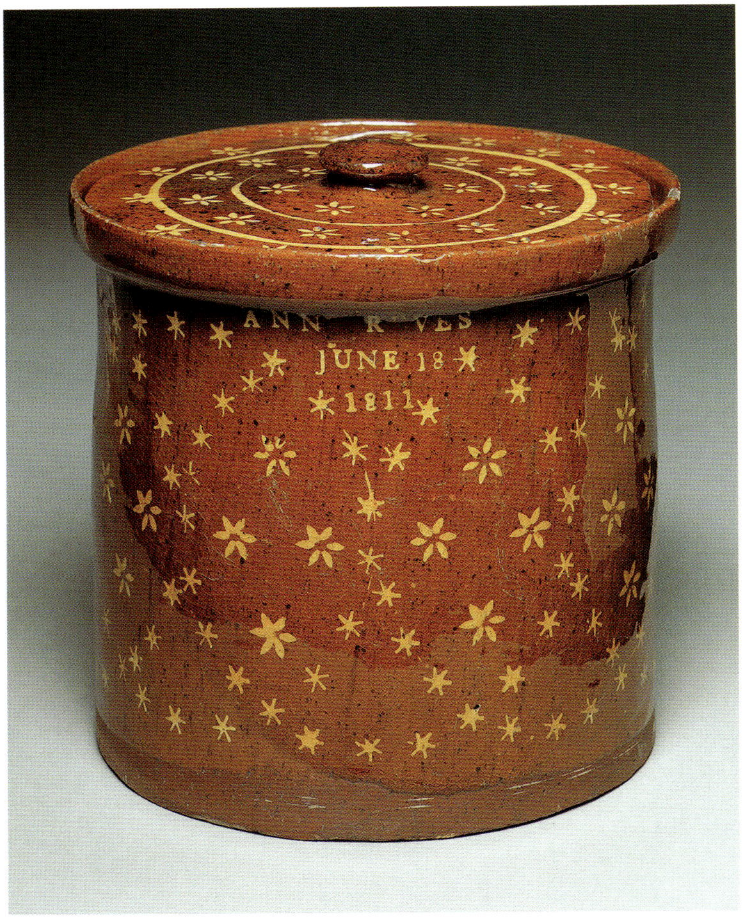

9
Inlaid decoration, using the small metal stamps of bookbinders or type-setters, was a technique exclusively developed by the Sussex potteries. This tobacco jar is inscribed 'Ann Reves 1811', perhaps for the proprietor of an inn. Height 13 cm (9 in.).
V&A: C.71&A–1947.

After slipware had been robbed of its essential domestic function at the end of the nineteenth century, not only by the fireproof stonewares of Derbyshire but also by the introduction of tinned or enamelled pressed steel, and later by aluminium and Pyrex glass, the remaining artistic possibilities of the material rarely proved sufficient to enable small outlying potteries to continue. In the 1920s Bernard Leach borrowed from, rather than breathed new life into, the defunct tradition of Thomas Toft and his followers in order to graft his new studio pottery onto a respected tradition, one that in a period of nationalism had come to symbolize the noble qualities of unsophisticated craftsmanship in a rural Britain fast disappearing beneath the wheels of industry. But the elevation of early slipware potters to the status of artist through the writings of the art critic Herbert Read should not blind us to the fact that, though undoubtedly slipware has a strong claim to be folk art, its place in the development of English ceramics over three centuries is that of a bystander rather than a major player. Unanswered questions remain, for inevitably the whole history of slipware has been written around a tiny corpus of surviving pots, which most probably constitute the least used and the least typical. Fortunately, excavated material from kiln and domestic sites has yielded enough to establish typologies of Staffordshire slipware, but of the makers themselves we know comparatively little. But certain it is that the excellence of their products helped to open new markets and establish Staffordshire as a major force at a crucial time in their development.

1. Dr Robert Plot (1686) fully describes the process of preparing slip and lead-glazing; Josiah Wedgwood's list of potters working in Burslem between 1710 and 1715 includes 'Red Pans' and 'Black and Mottled', which indicate coarsewares and possibly slipware dishes; Simeon Shaw (1829) describes the process of slip-decorating but does not attempt to name it; Jewitt (1878) describes the wares simply as 'coarse brown earthenware'; Solon (1883) and Hodgkin & Hodgkin (1891) classify the material as 'Slip-Decorated'; while the catalogue of the Burlington Fine Arts Club exhibition of 1914 refers to 'Slip Ware'.
2. Rackham (1935), Cooper (1968), Brears (1971 and 1974), Barker (1993), Grigsby, *English Slip-Decorated Earthenware* (1993), Gaimster, 'Regional Decorative Traditions' (1997), Grigsby (2000).
3. Newton & Bibbings (1960).
4. For the range of types, and for Cologne/Frechen bottles with belly inscriptions, see Jennings (1981), and Hurst, Neal & van Beuningen (1986), pp.210–16.
5. Kiddell (1954).
6. Grant (1983) and Outlaw (2002).
7. Grigsby, *English Slip-Decorated Earthenware* (1993), p.29.
8. Strong (1889), Fishley Holland (1958), Exeter, Royal Albert Memorial Museum (1984).
9. Coleman-Smith & Pearson (1988).
10. Algar, Light & Copland-Griffiths (1987).
11. Lewis (1982).
12. In order to make potters accountable for pots of short measure, an Act of 1662 decreed that 'Every person shall sett upon every Pott which he shall sell for packing up of Butter the just weight . . . with the first letter of his or theire Christian name and . . . Sirname'. A rare fragmentary base at the Potteries Museum, Stoke-on-Trent, impressed 'W. DANIEL 4', proves that one potter, at least, decided to follow the new regulations.
13. For lists of these dishes, see Cooper (1968).
14. Solon (1907). These were acquired by Lomax and dispersed at the sale of his collection at Sotheby's on 7 April 1937, many passing to the Burnap Collection.
15. Dr Plot (1686), quoted by Brears (1971), p.119.
16. Illustrated in Gaimster, 'Regional Decorative Traditions' (1997), p.133.
17. Although these are rarely found among groups of excavated Staffordshire slip-wares, it is likely that potters' names were included in the decoration for advertising purposes: for example, a fragmentary posset pot with ' . . . PSON' for 'Ralph Simpson' was found at Norwich (Jennings 1981, note 4 above).
18. Tait (1957).
19. Jug, mug and two posset pots dated 1726, 1727, 1730 and 1732 respectively, Fitzwilliam Museum, Cambridge, Glaisher nos. 314, 315, 318, 319. An undated posset pot at Williamsburg, illustrated in Grigsby, *English Slip-Decorated Earthenware* (1993), pl. 81.
20. Quoted by Brears (1971), p.196.
21. Kinder (*c.*1650), quoted by Brears (1971), p.41.
22. For reminiscences of the potteries at Farnborough and Cove, which supplied London with household pots in the late nineteenth century, see Mackerness (1967). The huge mechanized Doulton factory in Lambeth was seen as a threat, despite the often different roles for earthenware and stoneware. Heavy and bulky objects, such as unglazed sugar moulds and chimney pots, were often made in London itself.
23. Stockspring Antiques (2003).
24. Howarth & Hildyard (2004). Marked Abbott dishes at Williamsburg, at the Fitzwilliam Museum, Cambridge, and at the Victoria and Albert Museum, London.
25. As early as 1828, the London retailer Thomas Goode was supplying Sunderland butter pots, 'trays', pans and foot baths: see Godden (1972).
26. Baines (1980).
27. Illustrated in Baines (1980), p.64.
28. Inscribed 'RICHARD RUSSELL CHAILEY 1839', illustrated in Baines (1980), p.109.

CHAPTER TWO

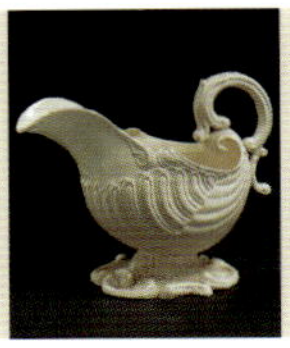

Salt-glaze

'Then I was called to the active kiln to see the first part of the salt-glazing. The fire-holes were successively opened, and, just in the same way that the coal was fed to the flames, the coarse-grained rock-salt was shovelled into what was now really a burning fiery furnace whose glaring white flames sent forth an intense heat: but the salting-off was not yet, for the two burners judged that more time was necessary. So the hours passed. The next operation was the testing of a trial piece which had been placed in a marked position in the kiln and had been glowing white-hot with its multitudinous companions. At the marked position a hole in the wall had been temporarily but effectively stopped. By means of a crowbar this stopping was removed, and standing on a platform I could view, through the hole, the seething fire. Now one of the burners inserted a long iron rod with the end bent, instantly withdrawing it and the trial piece. I wondered at the accuracy and the skill displayed. That hole was closed again by wet clay and bricks. On examination the trial piece, like a small flower pot in shape, gave evidence that the salt-glazing was pursuing its normal satisfactory course and that the time for salting-off was rapidly approaching. Taking up a commanding position from which the dome of the kiln, now in full functional activity, could be viewed, I concluded that there were some sixty apertures, each loosely covered with a brick. From these issued both flames and fumes, which, however, were not very dense at this stage. Each hole glowed like a giant cat's eye in the dim light. Round the dome ran an iron platform having a protecting rail outside, while facing me was a ladder to give easy access to the top of the kiln with two wooden boxes filled with salt. Now the two burners each took a long-handled iron ladle and the two stokers donned their specially thick coarse leather gloves. Working in pairs, one with ladle and one with gloves, they mounted the ladder (*covered their faces, except the eyes, with handkerchiefs*), and the salting off began. Each stoker ran up to the top hole in the dome and with his leather gloves removed its covering brick, while his burner stood ready on the platform with his ladle full of salt, which was soon hissing in the fiery flame below . . . the first hole on each side was covered and the next was opened, salted and covered with

10

Outside Derbyshire, the heartland of 19th-century domestic brown stonewares, potteries making similar wares sprung up where clay was available. The particular sprigged decoration used in Yorkshire at Eccleshill in the 1840s enables its products to be identified. Height 26.4 cm (10⅜ in.).

Private Collection.

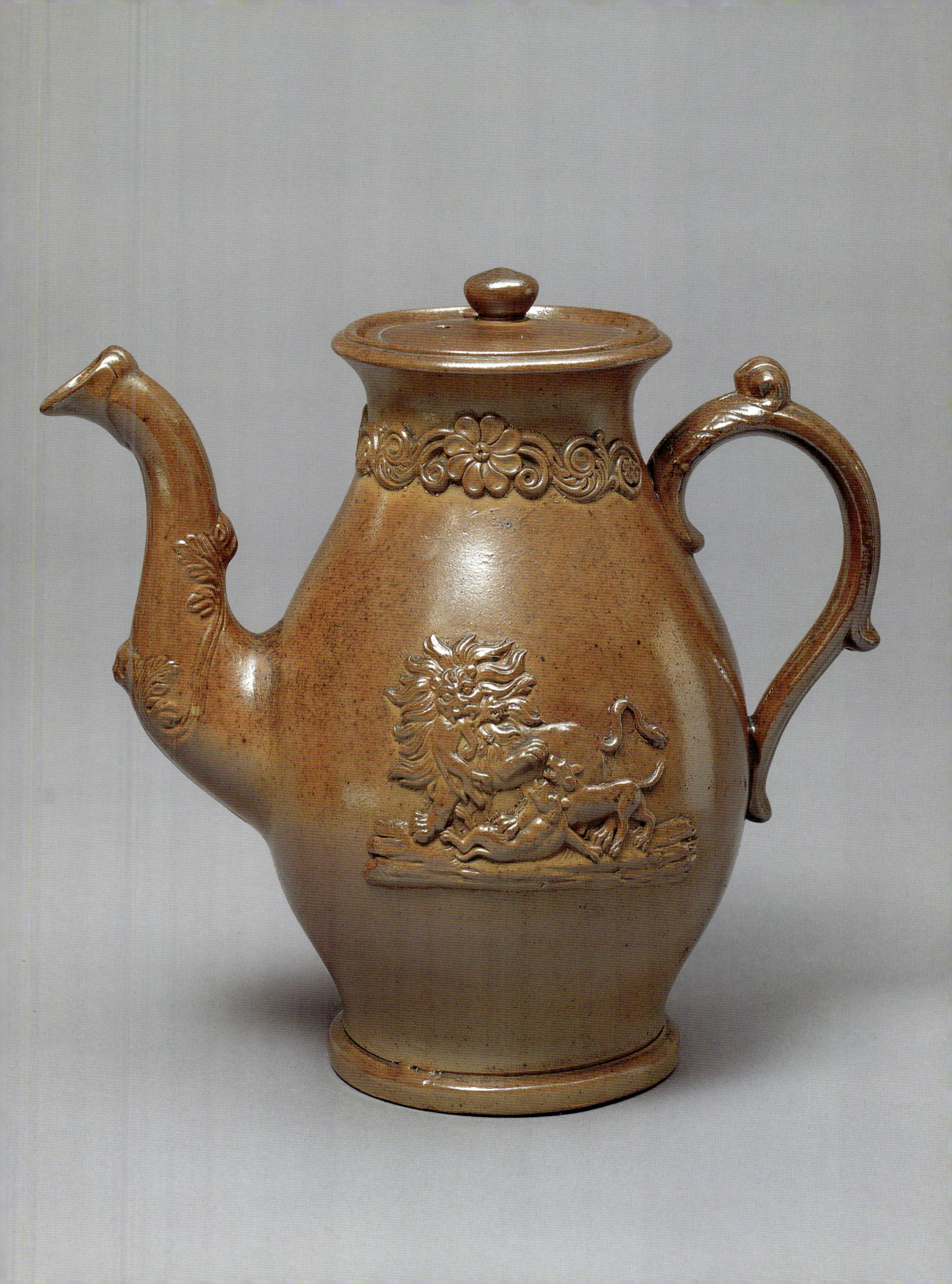

> wonderful celerity. The leaping stokers proceeding to the several holes and the walking burners feeding in the salt with their long ladles were seen through an ever denser screen of fumes.' [1]

This account by J. F. Blacker of a salt-glaze firing on 9 May 1922 at Doulton's Lambeth factory is well worth repeating for the vivid picture it paints of a process that, though almost barbaric in its fiery transmutation of soft clay into flinty vapour-glazed stoneware, nonetheless demanded a high degree of skill and judgement. For upon the success or failure of each firing depended the livelihoods of all the workers in the pottery. Apart from variations in kiln design and slightly differing timings for the salting, the basic process changed little from the time of its chance discovery in Germany sometime around 1400 until the present day: an informed account in *R. R. Angerstein's Illustrated Travel Diary* of 1753–5 described the process thus:

> After the access opening has been bricked up, the firing starts and continues for 38 to 40 hours. The kiln should then have reached its highest temperature and the crockery should be thoroughly heated right through, which is ascertained by taking out small sample cups with an iron bar and breaking them. The glazing then commences and is carried out by throwing common salt into the kiln with a small iron scoop, through little holes in the roof. About half a bushel or 28lb salt is thrown in through all the holes together and the process is repeated each half hour for six hours. The total time for the firing is thus 44 to 46 hours.

His description includes the only known illustration of a salt-glaze kiln with its surrounding scaffold to enable salt to be ladled in from above at the peak of the firing. In recent years, the history of salt-glazing and salt-glazed stoneware in the wider context of English pottery has been thoroughly researched and published.[2]

Paradoxically, it was humble brown salt-glazed stoneware that provided England with its first *fine* ware, and which may thereby claim some responsibility for inspiring the great rise of the Staffordshire Potteries during the eighteenth century. The material was well known in England from at least 1500, after which, until the trade began its sharp decline in the 1660s, an estimated 10 million brown beer mugs and bottles were shipped by Dutch merchants along the Rhine in successive waves from the Rhineland pottery centres of Raeren, Cologne and Frechen. Unlike the lead-glazed earthenwares produced in England, vitrified stoneware – whether glazed or not – had the unique advantage of being impervious to liquids; and, furthermore, it was immensely strong and resistant to the rough handling of tavern or kitchen, while having the capability of being lathe-turned to the thinness of porcelain.

With such unique qualities, and with big profits being made by foreign merchants, it was natural that English entrepreneurs should attempt not only to take over the trade but also to introduce the manufacture of stoneware into their native land. The first recorded application was by William Simpson, who, probably in the 1580s, unsuccessfully petitioned Queen Elizabeth I for an import monopoly – the same 15-year privilege, in fact, that was finally granted to Henry Noel in 1593.[3] In defiance of this monopoly, in 1594/5 Simpson went into partnership with two Dutch merchants, Joos Croppenberch and William Brunynck, to import stonewares direct from the Rhineland potteries. No more was heard of this, though the Noel patent was certainly in force and lucrative enough to pass through various hands until 1601, when it was annulled by Elizabeth I under political pressure.

It is certain that nobody in England at this period had any knowledge of the whereabouts of suitable clays, details of high-temperature kiln design, or the salt-glazing process itself, which, evenly covering every part of a pot without leaving any trace of its method of application, must have seemed almost magical. Since the science of chemistry was still in its infancy, for aspiring stoneware manufacturers the only option was to buy expertise from Germany. Nonetheless, an optimistic consortium of London merchants and tradesmen – Thomas Browne, a tiler and bricklayer, Tobie Steward, a pewterer, and one Nicholas Burghley – obtained a monopoly in 1614 for the manufacture of stoneware jugs and bottles; and although it is not recorded whether or not they attempted to make stoneware, by 1634 Browne was described as 'Potter to King Charles', which implies that he had become a major retailer and importer of pots. In 1626 a similar patent was granted to the merchants Thomas Rous and Abraham Cullen with the proviso that failure to perfect the invention would render the patent void. Having failed the following year to recruit the Frechen potter Hermann Statz to teach them the secrets of making stoneware, their ambitions appear to have receded. However, with the patent for a high-temperature kiln obtained by a courtier, David Ramsay, and his two partners in 1636, one of the major obstacles to manufacture was removed, and it is perhaps surprising that nothing further happened until the middle of the century when unidentified German potters set up a kiln at Woolwich Ferry, bringing not only their own moulds and equipment but even the clay from their homeland.[4] A handful of bottles badly fired from this short-lived kiln – the first stonewares to be made on English soil – have survived.

Meanwhile, the various Dutch Wars that flared up intermittently between 1652 and 1674 caused a hiatus in the trade in Rhineland stonewares and produced a climate in which a native stoneware industry was bound to have a good chance of success.[5] By 1666 the courtier William Killigrew had hired two Germans, Simon Wooltus, father and son, to make bottles for him at Southampton: but although he prepared a patent application in April 1672 for his 'stone bottles and blew canns', a more professional and more ambitious rival, John Dwight, had managed to submit his claim a mere 13 days earlier, securing a 14-year patent for his 'transparent Earthenware commonly known by the names of Porcelane or China and Persian Ware as also . . . the stone ware vulgarly called Cologne ware'.[6] Unlike that other great innovator George Ravenscroft, whose patent in 1674 for 'a perticuler sort of Christaline Glasse resembling Rock Cristall' led directly to the invention of English lead-glass, John Dwight was not a successful merchant using his trade connections to recruit foreign workers, but rather an opportunist whose ten years working as legal advisor to the bishops of Chester had given him the freedom to unravel the secret of salt-glazing through his own experiments at Wigan. In this, he was assisted by having worked in the laboratory of Robert Boyle and Robert Hooke while studying law at Oxford. Having obtained his patent, he sold his legal positions in order to build a pottery at Fulham, where he immediately set about copying a range of brown stonewares from Frechen and the grey, blue and purple mugs from the Westerwald, and hiring the experienced delftware potters Henry Parker and John Stearne in 1675. Notable among these early products were bottles derived from the German *Bartmann* but

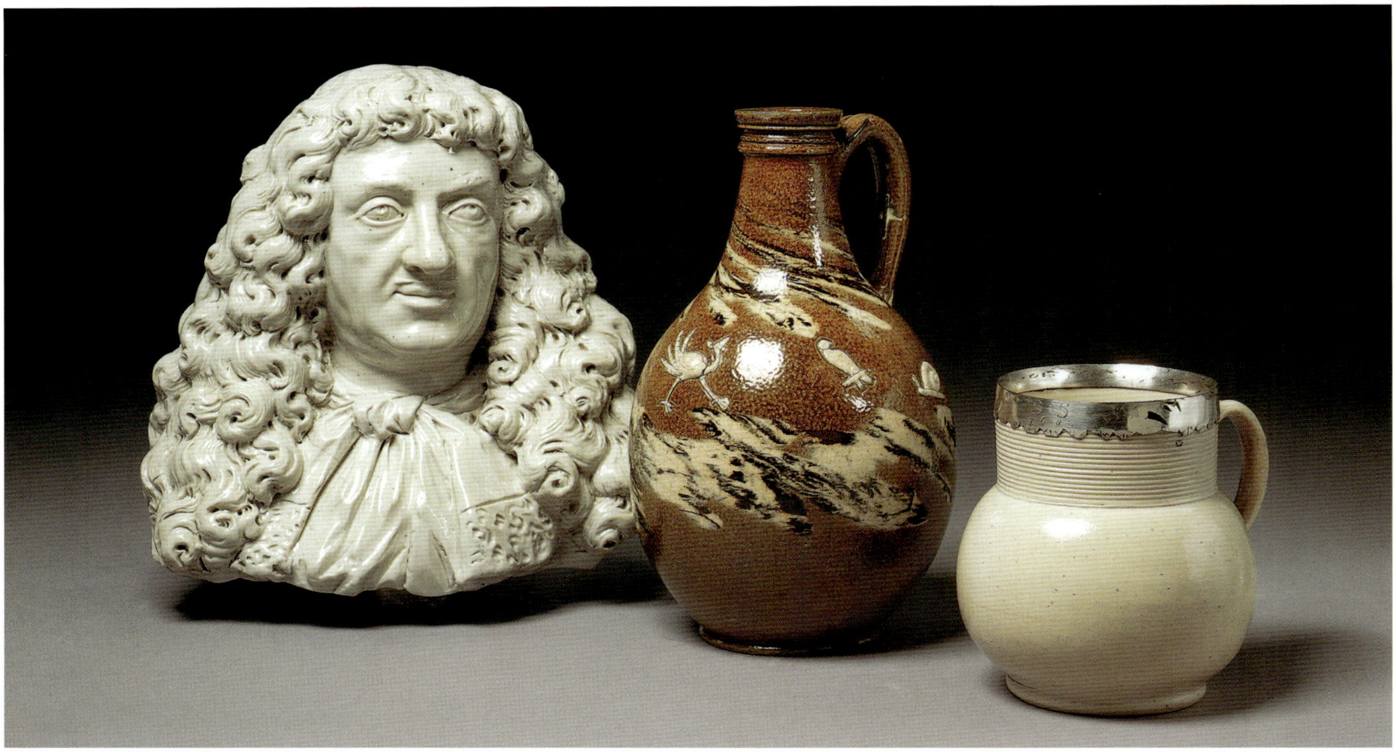

11
John Dwight, father of English salt-glazed stoneware, commissioned an unknown modeller to make busts of his family, including himself. Vessels with marbled inlay and highly refined 'ffine white' mugs (here dated 1682 on the silver rim) were among his most innovative products. Max. height 17.8 cm (7 in.).
V&A: 1053–1871, C.101–1938, Sch.II 58.

bearing personalized medallions in the manner of the newly invented black shaft-and-globe wine bottle. To judge from the large number of different medallions excavated at the pottery, these innovative bottles enjoyed considerable popularity.

In 1676 Dwight and his partner Windsor Sandys made an advantageous agreement with the Glass-Sellers' Company, which controlled not only the retailing of pottery and glass but also its manufacture. The company's guarantee to take the Fulham Pottery's entire output was renewed in 1677 for a further three years, and included 'fine Brown Bottles Juggs and all other sorts of Fine Browne stone wares', as well as 'Fine Flatt Bottom bottles . . . Fine Gorge Potts or Juggs . . . Fine pickling potts and pitchers'. Having got the pottery on a secure footing, in 1684 Dwight applied for a new patent well before his existing patent expired, this now including new applications for stoneware devised from his continuing researches into the mysteries of making porcelain: 'white Gorges marbled Porcelane Vessels Statues and Figures and fine stone Gorges and vessels never before made in England or elsewhere . . . transparent Porcellane and opacous redd and dark coloured Porcellane or China and Persian wares' (plate 11).

Despite the patent, it proved impossible to prevent the highly active Thames-side potteries of Southwark and Lambeth from discovering and exploiting the secret of salt-glazing. Dwight's legal training, however, combined with his commercial ambitions, ensured that no infringement was allowed to escape his zest for litigation. The first action in 1693 was against his former employee John Chandler, whom he accused of revealing his secrets to the brothers John Philip and David Elers, Dutch silversmiths who were making their superb red stonewares in open defiance of Dwight's patent. This action was settled amicably, leaving them free to continue making redware at Bradwell Wood in Staffordshire, as well as a limited amount of brown salt-glaze at Vauxhall (plate 12).[7] A simultaneous action against James Morley in Nottingham was pursued until 1698 without any effect, while yet another against the brothers Aaron, Thomas and Richard Wedgwood in Staffordshire was followed by an injunction. It was eventually answered in 1696 by a Petition to the Privy Council from a consortium of the leading contemporary Staffordshire potters, namely the Wedgwoods, Richard Muchell, Thomas Daniel, Richard Meir and Ralph Shaw. Dwight's London neighbours, however, were less fortunate: in 1694–5 Matthew Garner and his partner Luke Talbot of the Gravel Lane pothouse in Southwark were forced to settle by mortgaging the pottery to the unscrupulous Nathaniel Oade, who later foreclosed and evicted them, while Moses Johnson of the Bear Garden pottery was forced out of business – first to Lambeth, and later to Bristol, where he was probably responsible for introducing the technique of salt-glazing in the early years of the eighteenth century.[8] By 1697, when the Staffordshire potters Moses Middleton, Cornelius Hammersley and Joshua Astbury were added to the list, the action was abandoned due to Dwight's failing health.

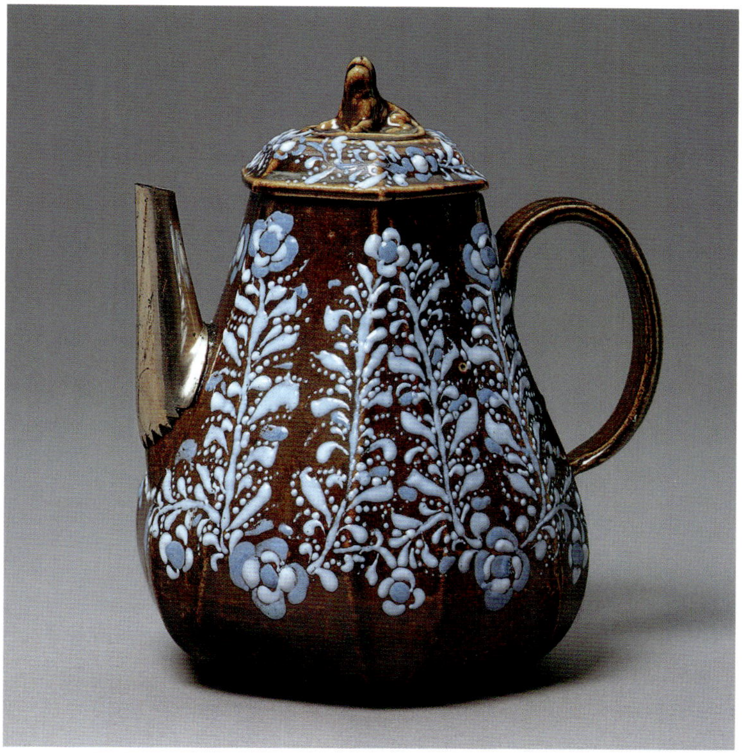

12
One of two known teapots linked to the Vauxhall pothouse of David Elers through its slip-cast technique and the enamelling added by a freelance decorator working in London around 1700. Height 14 cm (5½ in.).
V&A: C.133–1938.

These legal actions provide a fascinating insight into the salt-glaze industry in the mid-1690s (plate 13), at exactly the moment when it was being established in all the future major centres of Lambeth, Nottingham, Bristol and Staffordshire.[9] It is certain that in 1693 James Morley was already making his thin-walled mugs at Nottingham, equally certain that the two Southwark pothouses were producing (probably inferior) copies of Dwight's tavern mugs and bottles, and quite possible that by 1697 the technique had reached Staffordshire. For the vigour with which some of the major potters defended their right to improve their craft without hindrance might well imply guilty knowledge of the secrets of salt-glazing, the technique that was to be the foundation stone of the massive development of the Staffordshire Potteries in the following century.

After Dwight's death in 1703, the quality of Fulham Pottery stonewares remained high for a few more years, along with some of his special products, such as his 'ffine white' wares containing calcined flint, which were now given a dipped brown edge and made into domestic items such as coffee pots.[10] It seems these did not quite overlap with the rather similar early Staffordshire white stonewares

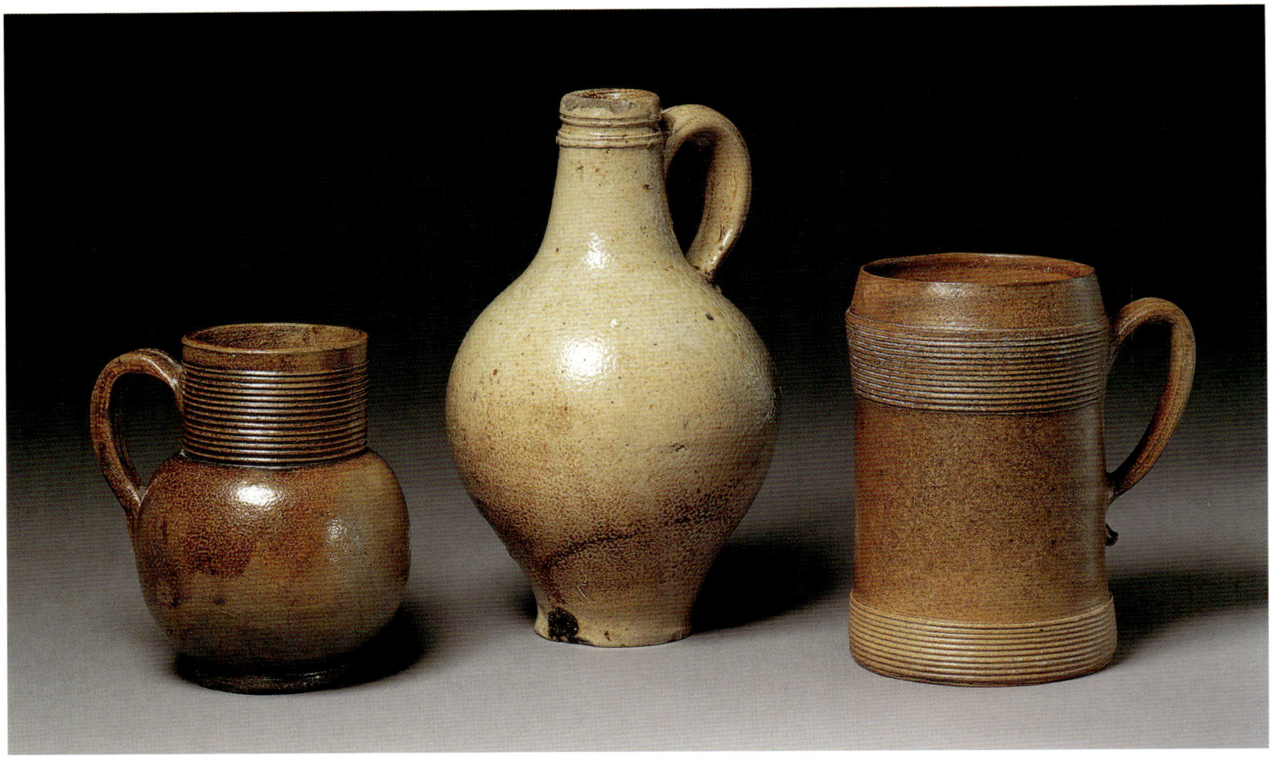

13
At the end of the 17th century basic brown stonewares were the staple products of early London stoneware factories. These tavern wares show that as late as the period 1690–1700 the Fulham Pottery was still unquestionably the most sophisticated. Max. height 21.4 cm (8⅜ in.).
Private Collection.

that made their appearance about 1715–20, nor is there any evidence of a direct link between them: but the likelihood that the last flowering of Dwight's Fulham Pottery must have inspired the Staffordshire potters' first ventures into white stoneware cannot be ignored.

Despite a crippling tax on earthenware in force from 1695 to 1698, which, for example, imposed a tax of 1d on a quart stoneware bottle usually costing about 3d,[11] the end of the seventeenth century was a time of expansion for the potting industries of London and, of course, also of Staffordshire. Once stoneware was added to the existing manufacture of delftware and slipware, hierarchies for different types of English pottery were quickly established: cheap delftware for local and pharmaceutical consumption as well as for export; domestic slipware and the new refined earthenwares emerging from Staffordshire, which were distributed throughout England by packhorse and increasingly intended for export; and salt-glazed stoneware for tavern mugs, general-purpose bottles of all sizes up to three or four gallons (plate 14), pickling pots and storage jars that would not contaminate the contents with lead; and, briefly, a selection of finewares such as coffee pots, teapots and 'capuchines', cups for coffee or chocolate.[12] In homage to their predecessors from the Rhineland, most brown stonewares continued to be dipped in iron-bearing red clay slip in order to replicate the familiar two-tone effect, while the added mantle of dark slip tended to produce that random mottling in the kiln that so pleases the modern eye.

With both delftware and stoneware sharing the same market but having well-defined and complementary roles, only the somewhat isolated Fulham

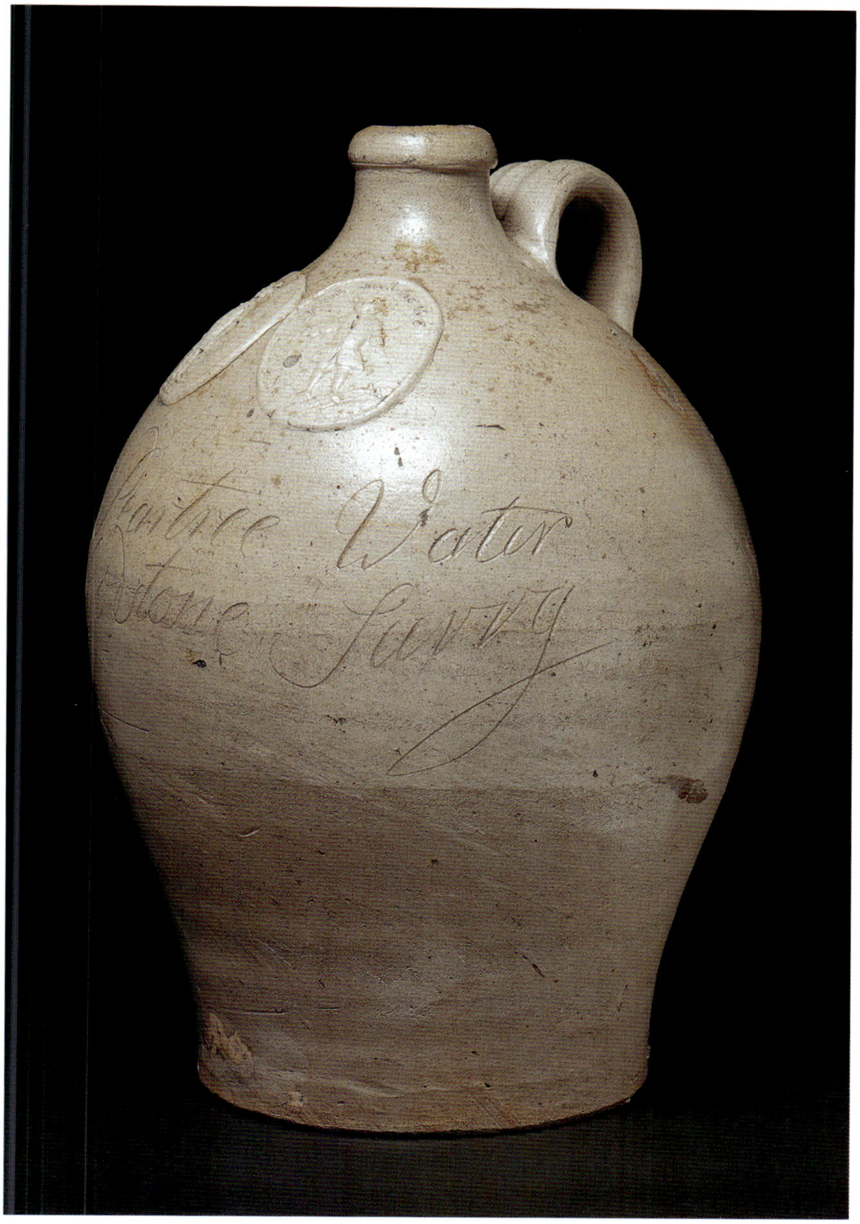

14
Stoneware containers proved ideal for the transport of large quantities of liquid, whether acid, rum, cider, beer or mineral water. In 1752 two-gallon bottles of Iron Peartree Water were carried up from Godstone in Surrey at 2s, plus 2s deposit on the bottle, as a cure for gout in the Metropolis. Height 39 cm (15⅜ in.).
V&A: C.467–1923.

Pottery persisted in making stoneware alone. In Southwark, and later in Lambeth and Vauxhall, the existing delftware factories quickly saw the economic advantages of adding stoneware to their range of products, simply by building a high-firing kiln and arranging supplies of West Country clay and salt from the North-West. The market for stoneware was growing, for by the end of the seventeenth century the import of Rhineland stoneware had dwindled to token numbers of grey-and-blue reduction-fired 'GR' tavern mugs from the Westerwald, while the expansion of Britain and its colonies during the eighteenth century and the high breakage rate in London taverns ensured a ready market for all that the Thames-side potteries could produce (plate 15). Around 1710–15 the Vauxhall Pottery added a range of ambitious stonewares, notably the giant sprigged and dated hunting mugs that, neatly spanning the years of the Jacobite

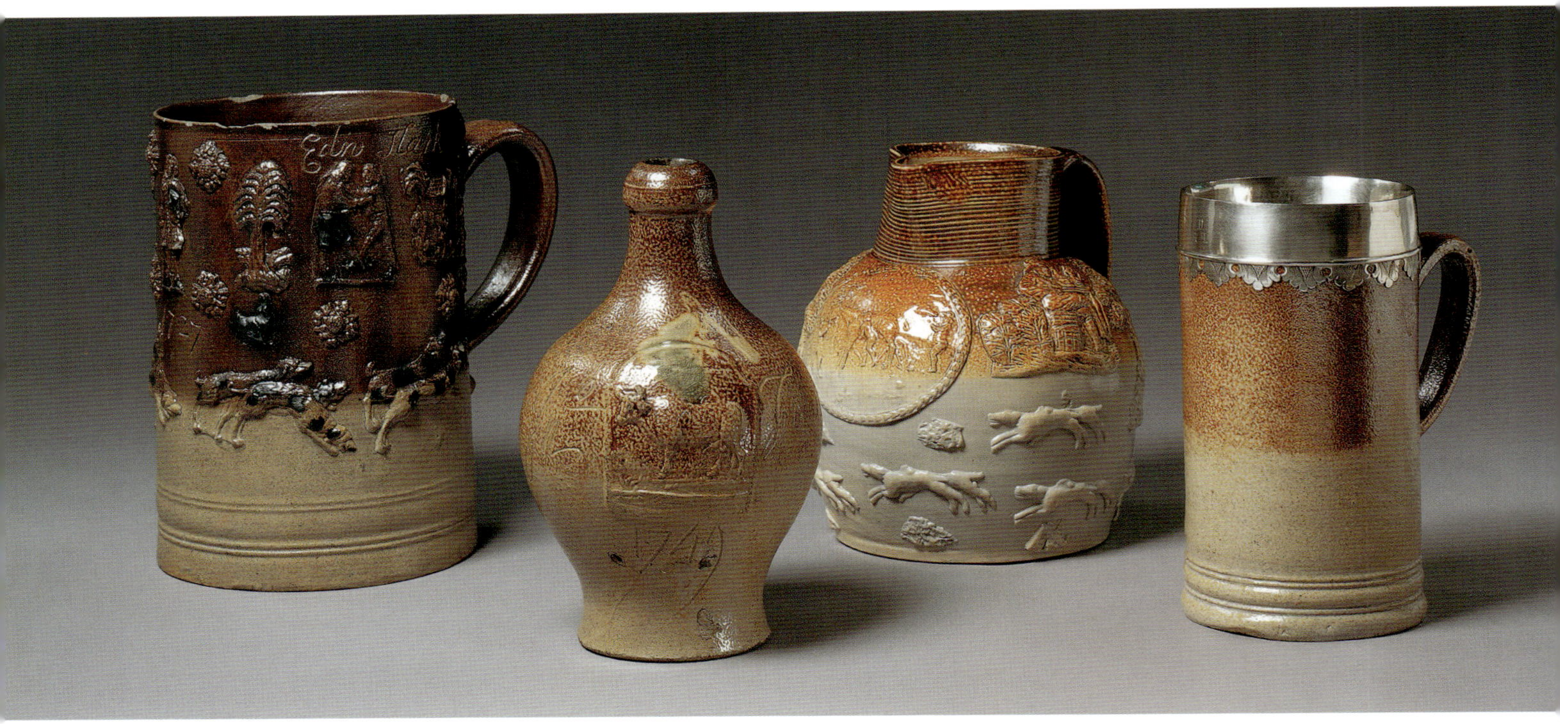

15
During the 18th century both the development of Staffordshire lightweight white stoneware and the continuing manufacture of fine Nottingham ale mugs ensured that London potters supplied the functional and heavy items. The Kishere pottery at Mortlake, however, found a niche market by inventing the 'hunting jug'. Max height 22.8 cm (9 in.).

The mugs, V&A: 3689–1901 dated 1727, and M.199–1939; the bottle of 1749 and Mortlake hunting jug of about 1810. Private Collection.

unrest, 1713–44, and having recurring symbolism among their decoration, were probably made for drinking clubs loyal to the Catholic James II and his descendants James and Charles Edward Stuart. Increasingly the manufacture of stoneware centred itself on Lambeth, but the old Gravel Lane Pottery at Southwark survived until the Oade family offered it for sale in 1748 – the *coup de grâce* being delivered in 1750 by tremors from an earthquake that brought down the roof.

As if to confirm the growing importance of English stoneware at the beginning of the new century, an Act was passed in 1700 that standardized the capacity of beer mugs and obliged the makers to stamp them with a crowned 'WR'. Probably in order to facilitate the production of wheel-thrown mugs of identical capacity, the cylindrical type was now widely adopted in preference to the old German-type globular 'gorge'. Recent excavations at Fulham and Vauxhall have yielded type-series of idiosyncratic ale measure marks used only by those factories, while the incorrect 'AR' and 'GR' marks found in Staffordshire and at Bristol are easily distinguishable. In addition, sufficient dated mugs and bottles have survived to demonstrate the progression of forms.[13] But the popularity of rough salt-glazed tavern mugs waned during the last quarter of the eighteenth century, when first creamware, and then banded 'Mocha' wares, took their place – so much so that by 1800 the Nottingham industry, main supplier in the Midlands of fine lathe-turned lustrous 'Nottingham Ware' ale mugs – had vanished almost without trace.

Despite the loss of the American colonies, by about 1800 the addition of India, Australia, New Zealand and Tasmania to the growing British Empire had brought new demands for containers able to withstand arduous voyages by sea, to which the potters of both London and Derbyshire responded by mass-producing bottles for ginger beer, blue for whitening laundry (the origin, incidentally, of the word 'blue bottle') and liquid boot-blacking on a vast scale, together with food-storage jars with increasingly sophisticated methods of air-tight closure.[14] As early as 1835 Anthony Amatt of Bristol had invented (but never patented) the hygienic non-hazardous liquid 'Bristol Glaze' containing zinc oxide, and although this was more expensive, its use on better-class products inevitably spread to London and eventually to Derbyshire. As for sanitary wares, even as the last delftware pottery closed at Vauxhall around 1840, the recurring great typhoid epidemics demanded vast numbers of new sewers and drainpipes, which were soon to make the fortune of Henry Doulton and to add to the Lambeth waterfront yet more clusters of salt-glaze kilns belching their chlorine gas.

Besides the millions of almost indestructible stoneware containers, the Thames-side potteries developed a range of decorated wares, notably the squat hunting jugs and mugs first made around 1800 by the Kisheres at their Mortlake pottery,[15] where other archaic vessels designed to appeal to the beer-drinking antiquarian, often mounted in Sheffield plate or expensive silver, were also produced. From about 1830 the London potteries successfully adopted the press-moulding technique and began to employ professional mould-makers,[16] exploiting the growing fashion among the working population for wares commemorating popular events typified by the craze for Staffordshire figures. 'Shop Pots' with japanned lids for apothecaries and tobacconists, and round or oval 'Bar Casks', all with sprigged royal arms and labels designed to be elaborately painted and gilded, were staple products. But although the more adventurous potteries attempted heavy brown versions of Staffordshire moulded jugs, their most important innovation was a range of moulded gin-flasks modelled as half-length portraits of the heroes of hugely popular events, such as the Reform Bill of 1832. Such objects, stubbornly surviving against the odds, may now evoke the overcrowded, disease-ridden and gin-soaked Dickensian world of waterfront boatyards, vinegar distilleries, leather-dressers and bone-boilers in the years before the building of the Albert Embankment (1866–70).[17] Competition among the potteries was so fierce that only the most ambitious with the best riverside locations could survive. Even the huge Imperial Pottery of John Cliff simply closed and moved to Runcorn in 1869, while the even larger pottery of James Stiff & Sons was finally absorbed by its rival, Doultons, as late as 1913.

As mentioned above, once the secret of salt-glazing became widely known, such was the need for tough brown stonewares that potteries sprung up wherever fuel and stoneware clays were available, in particular in Bristol, which had access to excellent West Country clay, and in the Midlands, where Nottingham and Derbyshire offered abundant supplies of both. Far from London, the Nottingham stonewares developed their own style and maintained a high standard of fine potting, an all-over appearance of smooth burnished bronze, and a sophisticated range of carved, sprigged, incised and slip-painted decoration (plate 16). Notable decorators who signed their work were William

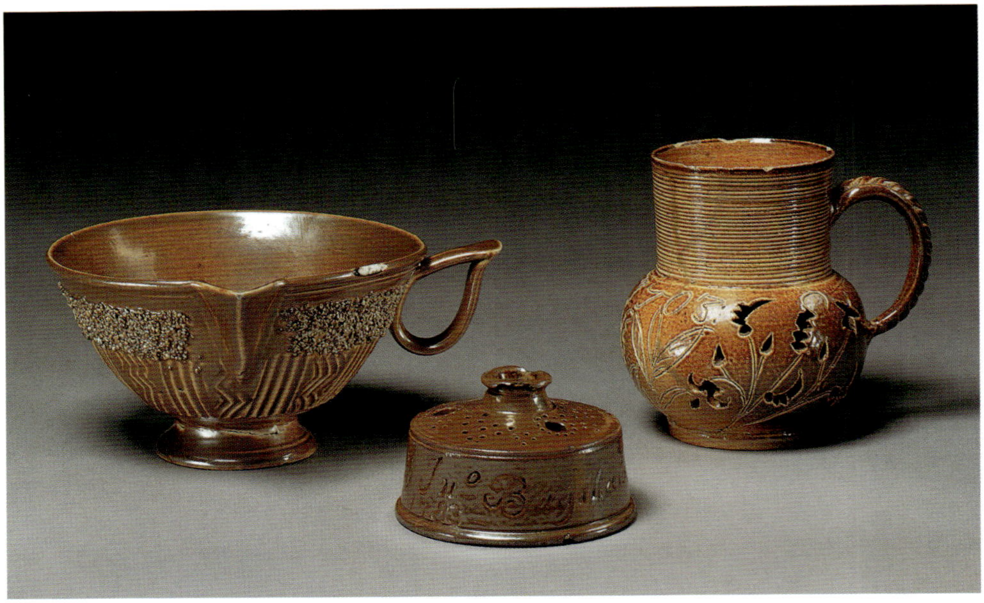

16
As early as 1693 James Morley of Nottingham was sued by Dwight for infringing his stoneware patent, in particular this type of 'Carved Jug', this example dated 1703. The Nottingham potters continued to make their light cylindrical ribbed ale mugs and a limited range of domestic wares, often finely decorated. Max. height 9.9 cm (3⅞ in.).
V&A: C.303–1927, C.26–1967, 803–1872.

Lockett and Thomas Hough; but their scratched signatures are rare glimpses into a thriving industry that has left behind practically no documentation about the location or extent of the individual potteries. The archetypal little double-walled *gorge*, described by James Morley's trade card as a 'Carved Jug',[18] was probably made from about 1690, presumably owing its inspiration either to Chinese porcelains or Westerwald stonewares, which shared the same technique. But soon Nottingham became famous for its tall thin-walled ale mugs, which were imitated elsewhere but seldom equalled. The potteries of Crich in Derbyshire made wares almost indistinguishable from those of Nottingham – in particular the large thistle-shaped loving cups used to commemorate birth, betrothal or marriage – but the advantage of having excellent clay (which the Nottingham potters also used) eventually enabled them to expand and hasten the demise of Nottingham. Surprisingly, these potteries still used square up-draught kilns, although, unlike the Fulham Pottery, which continued to use wood until the 1780s, these would probably have been coal-fired.[19]

Although overshadowed by Staffordshire, Derbyshire has a fine history of ceramic production, including porcelain, creamware and banded wares, and, of course, stoneware. The stoneware clay mined over the coal-measures fired flinty and grey, both body and glaze being vastly superior to that used in London during the eighteenth century. With the growing demand for containers, these potteries flourished, using local raw materials and the cheap labour of women and boys. As with the Doultons in London, the enterprising Joseph Bourne began to take over stoneware potteries in the 1820s, basing his empire on Denby, which is still in production. A vast output of bottles and homely wares ensured their future. After the invention of the iron kitchen range in Derbyshire in the 1820s, there was a constant demand for 'Dutch Pots', or what we know as casseroles, while a large range of domestic wares of excellent design and attractive sprigged decoration flowed from the potteries around Chesterfield, in particular those of the Oldfield and Briddon families of Brampton, and later the Pearsons of Whittington Moor (plate 17). At Brampton a smooth, almost white clay was used to produce the unique toasted honey-colour, with the coarser alternative of dark grey clay coated with iron wash, giving a deep metallic brown.[20]

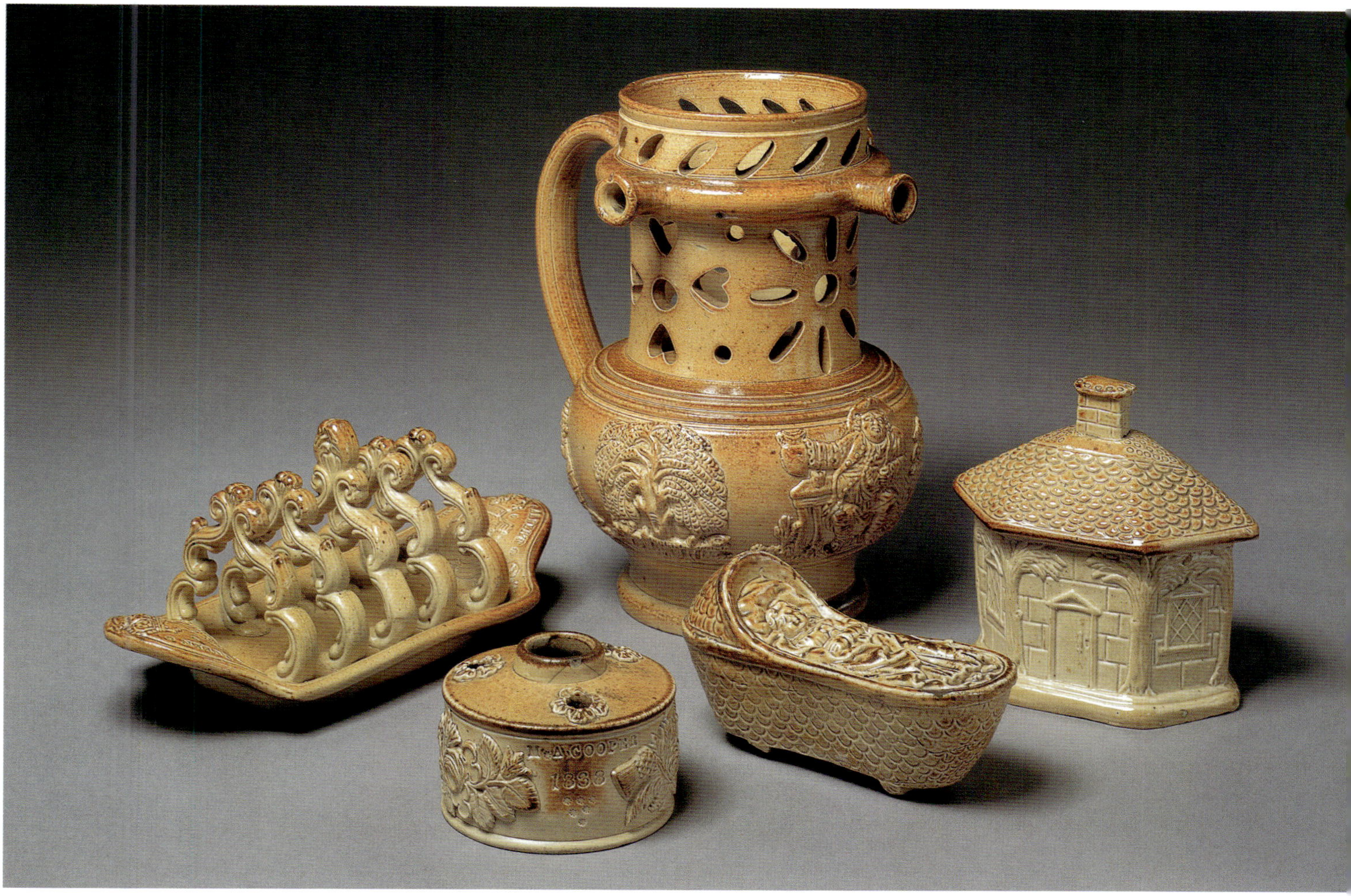

17
Toast racks, tobacco boxes, cradles, puzzle jugs and an inkwell dated 1838 represent a tiny proportion of the honey-coloured novelty wares produced by the potteries of Brampton and Chesterfield in Derbyshire from the 1830s.
Max. height 20.3 cm (8 in.).
V&A: C.3–1935, Circ.1144–1967; puzzle jug and tobacco box, Private Collection.

Bristol, with its existing delftware potteries and great scope for the export trade, was probably making tavern mugs and large spirit bottles from around 1710. Since the potteries mostly now lie unexcavated beneath the city of Bristol, and since the wares themselves were mostly intended either for use on board ship or exported overseas, little is known of the early phase; but by 1738 the talented potter John Harwell had made the first of his splendid 10-pint sprigged tankards and, from this date, if not earlier, large harvest jugs (plate 18)[21] and bottles with the diagnostic ovoid profile were made, culminating in the huge display jugs made by the Powells in the 1830s and now in the Bristol City Museum. Although Bristol is now more famed for its glass, throughout the eighteenth and early nineteenth centuries it was the source of some of the finest stonewares, creamware with the most delicate enamel painting and, of course, millions of glass bottles.

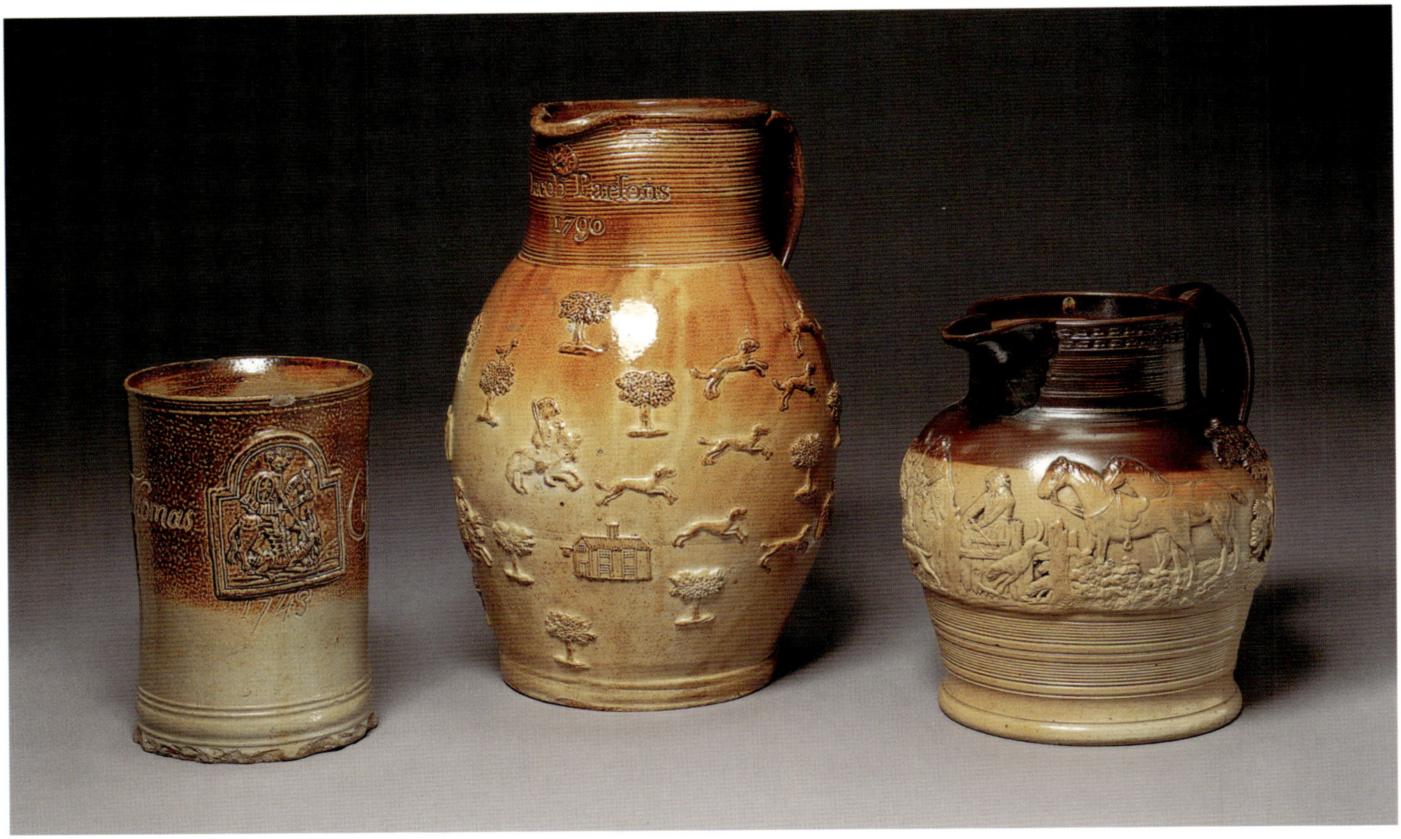

18
The fine stonewares made at Bristol were always distinct from those of London. Typically, ale mugs like this example of 1743 for The George at Nether Stowey bore the incorrect 'GR' ale measure mark; globular shapes were ovoid like this 'Jacob Parsons 1790' jug; and Staffordshire forms like the 'Dutch' jug were copied in the period 1820–40. Max. height 28.5 cm (11¼ in.).
Private Collection.

The invention in 1835 of the 'Bristol Glaze' was to render salt-glazing largely redundant in Britain by the beginning of the twentieth century. Its last exponent, the factory of Messrs Price Powell was still busy making rum casks for the Royal Navy when it was entirely destroyed by enemy action in 1940.

Further north, the manufacture of brown salt-glaze did not come to Liverpool, the West Riding of Yorkshire and the east and west coasts of Scotland until fairly late in the eighteenth century. Like many exporters of utilitarian wares, Liverpool's stoneware has all but disappeared, leaving tantalizing marked early nineteenth-century bottles found on the east coast of America, and doubtless many of the double-handled water-carrier bottles known to have been made for the African market. The Yorkshire stonewares made at Wibsey and Eccleshill tended to follow those of Brampton/Chesterfield in style as either glossy brown or honey-coloured, but in the absence of marked specimens secure attributions are often difficult (see plate 10). The earliest identified Scottish brown stonewares consist of large inscribed and sprigged presentation bottles, moulded hunting jugs and elaborately modelled salt kits (vessels with a hand-sized opening used for storing salt, kept dry by the fireside), made in the early nineteenth century before the industry – notably the Caledonian and Port Dundas potteries in the Glasgow area and the Portobello Pottery near Edinburgh – settled down to making the millions of beer and ginger-beer bottles that are still so plentiful today.

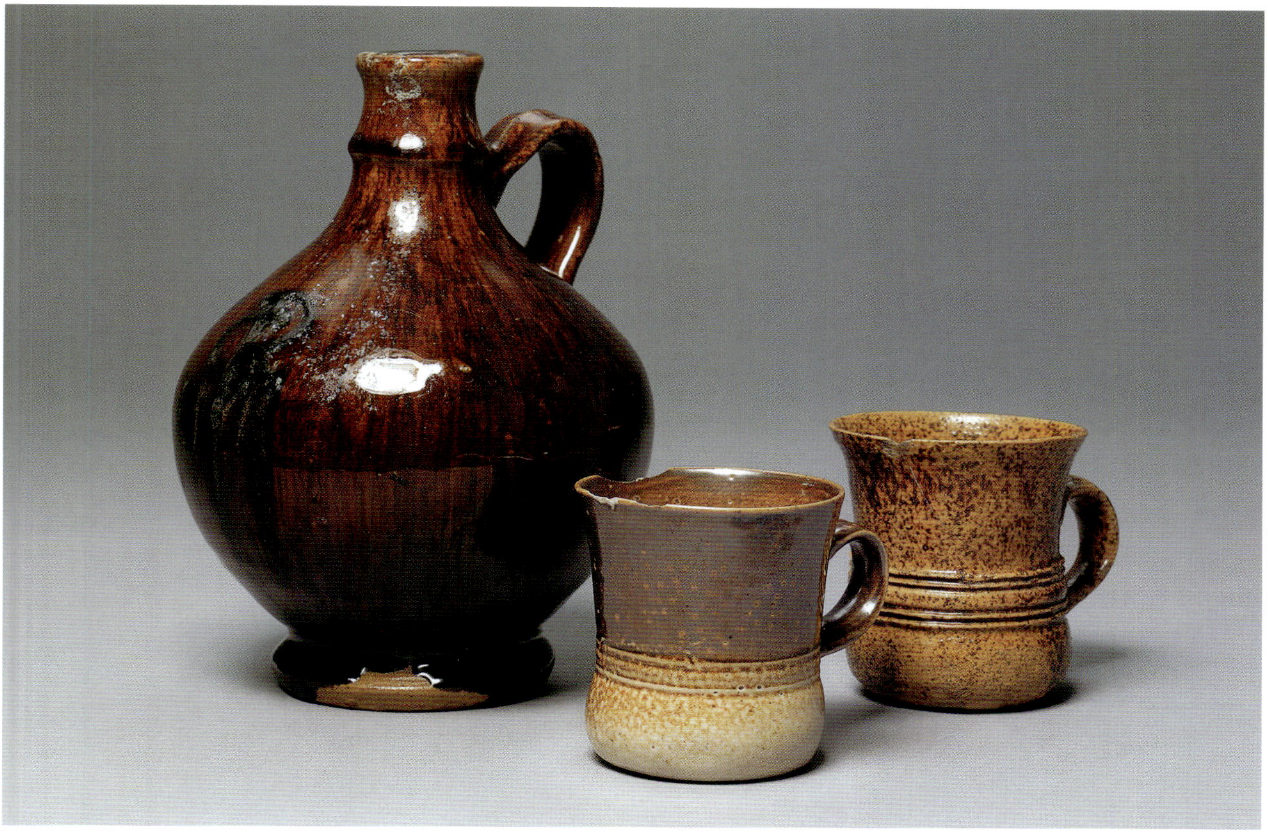

19
Iron-manganese speckled earthenwares, made in Staffordshire from about 1690: bottle and cup, with a similar salt-glazed cup. Max. height 14 cm (5⅛ in.).
V&A: 36–1890, 2092–1901, 2091–1901.

Staffordshire potters may have been late in discovering the secret of salt-glazing, but they were very quick to see the economic advantages offered by a tough once-fired ceramic body, especially after the discovery of rock-salt in neighbouring Cheshire in 1670. In fact, it was as though they had been practising in anticipation of the breakthrough, for by the end of the seventeenth century they were already making a range of finely potted earthenware capuchines and beer mugs, copied from the wares of London and Nottingham but using a speckled brown iron-manganese-lead glaze to simulate brown stoneware (plate 19). When salt-glazing did reach Staffordshire shortly before 1700, the same wares continued to be made, the tavern mugs sometimes rouletted all over and usually stamped with an incorrect 'AR' ale measure mark in supposed accordance with the Act of 1700. Yet with Nottingham already established as the main producer of tavern mugs in the Midlands, these potters needed to find an alternative use for the new material, which, despite its brown colour, had many of the qualities of the Chinese porcelain tablewares that were beginning to flood into the East India Company warehouse in London. There was also a precedent for developing a white body, since, as mentioned above, during the first decade of the eighteenth century the Fulham Pottery had extended John Dwight's original 'ffine white' body to include brown-edged white coffee pots and mugs, creating thereby the first English ceramic alternative to imported Chinese blue and white. Whether or not they knew about these Fulham white stonewares, it is apparent that in the period around 1715 the potters of Staffordshire more or less abandoned their brown tavern mugs and turned their attention to the more lucrative domestic tableware market, at first whitening the naturally grey body with a layer of refined slip containing calcined flint.

It is, however, difficult to pinpoint exactly who was responsible for this important development, which was ultimately to transform north Staffordshire into the most prolific producer of fine pottery in the whole of Europe. It may well be that Dwight's legal action against Moses Middleton, Cornelius Hammersley and Joshua Astbury in 1697 for 'intrudeing themselves unknown into [Dwight's] workhouses to inspect his furnaces and wayes of Manufacturing' might accurately indicate the time, the persons responsible and the method; but given the close working relationship among the potteries in Burslem, and given the fact that several potters must have been working on the problem, the solution may well have been found by several potters simultaneously. The earliest plausible reference to this new product, in the *Victoria History of the County of Stafford*, is contained in the statement that in 1717 Twyford and Astbury set up as partners in a pottery: for Simeon Shaw not only confirms their association but further states that they made 'Red Porcelain, and White Pottery glazed with salt, amidst many small thatched dwellings in Shelton'.[22] Certainly, the perfected ware had reached London by 1719 when the retailer John Akerman at the sign of the Rose & Crown in Cornhill advertised that he 'continues to sell all sorts of Tea . . . China ware . . . Fans, plain and diamond cut Flint-Glasses, white stone ware etc. at the very lowest prices'. Shaw also suggests the early combining of calcined flint with West Country clay. Yet today these very early Staffordshire products defy identification, and apart from the very fine lathe-turned loving cup in the Burnap Collection at Kansas City inscribed 'Mary Sandbach her cup Anno Dom 1720',[23] an equally fine capuchine and a baluster jug excavated at Williamsburg from a pre-1728 context,[24] and a few teapots (plate 20),[25] there is little to show for these early years. An intriguing bankrupt sale notice by the London retailer William Watkinson in 1727 listed 'all Sorts of fine white Stone Ware' without specifying which types. As suggested in chapter Three, 'Red China', however, it is possible that the simultaneous development in the 1720s of a much more popular body, the white-sprigged red earthenware teawares of so-called Astbury type, may have overshadowed and greatly outnumbered these plain white stonewares with their simple mould-applied motifs, bands of rouletting and knife-cut flats around the base.

The Devon clays and calcined flint that, by tradition, had been introduced by either John Astbury or Joshua Heath of Shelton around 1720, were soon added not just to the dip or engobe but also to the body itself, so that two distinct types of white stoneware could be now regularly manufactured in tandem, catering to different markets. For the new refined white body, the technique of throwing and lathe-turning was brought to such a state of perfection that the material was not only as strong as Chinese porcelain but also considerably thinner, lighter, and with better handling qualities. With strictly limited scope for decoration, these potters demonstrated consummate skill in dextrous knife-cut faceting on

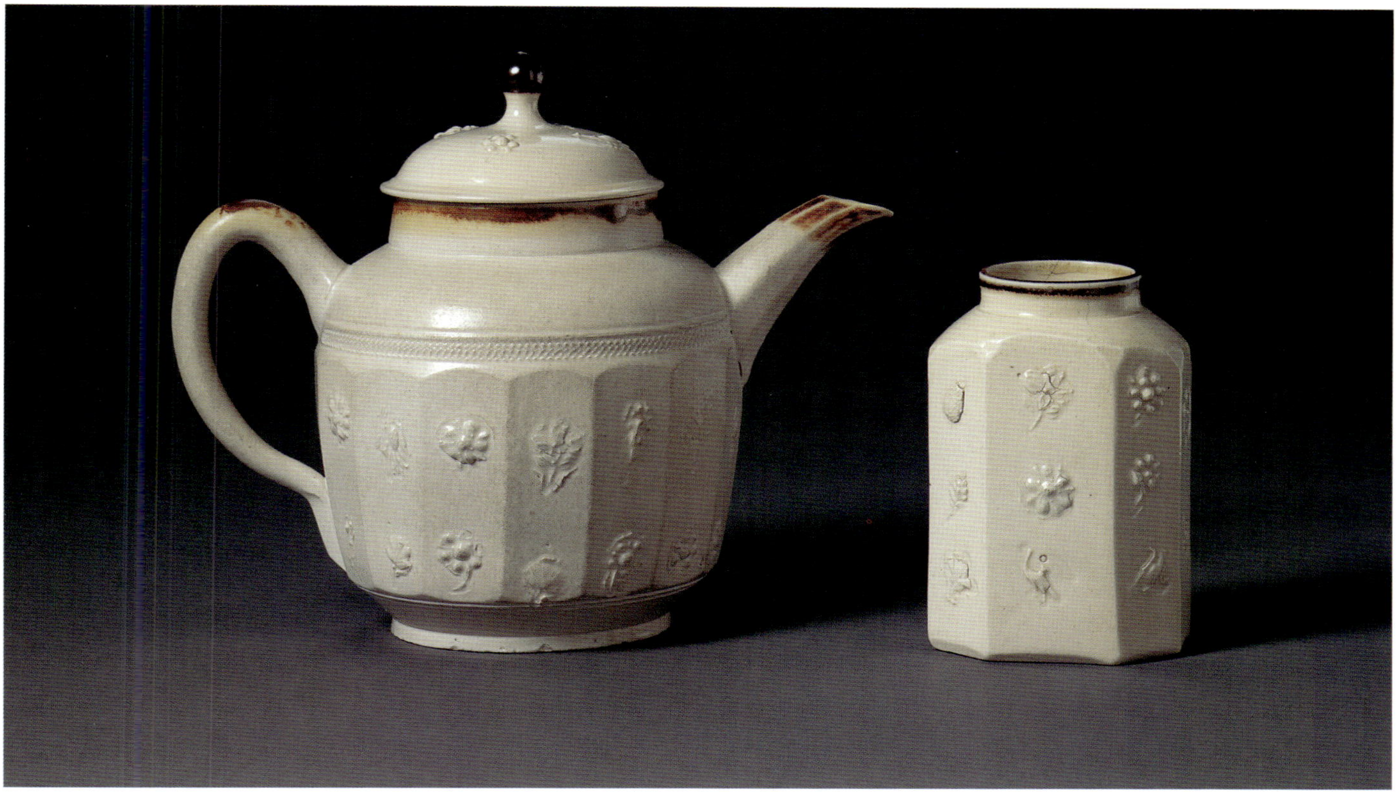

20

The earliest salt-glazed teawares made in Staffordshire in the 1720s owed their shapes to metalwork and their whiteness to an engobe containing flint. Later, flint was incorporated into the clay body. Max. height 15.6 cm (6⅛ in.).

V&A: C.145–1991, C.2–1994.

spouts and bodies, scalloping the edges of cream jugs to imitate contemporary silver, and rolling, cutting, bending and applying delicate tapering handles of exactly the required strength. During the 1720s–1730s many of these handles were pinched in the middle to imitate the wishbone handles of contemporary Meissen porcelain. As for plates, it is just possible that the first examples may have been made during this period, although the absence of any identifiable examples, and the necessity for such thin plates to be press-moulded rather than thrown, make it unlikely. Apart from an ambitious attempt by Ralph Shaw (perhaps the same potter protesting to the Privy Council against Dwight's patent in 1696) to patent in 1733 a type of chequered decoration cut through a contrasting slip, which was annulled by a judge three years later after outraged protests from his fellow potters, the potters' output at this period seems to have been, like the contemporary red earthenware, almost exclusively teawares and cylindrical beer mugs.

It is something of a cliché to say that the whole situation changed around 1740. Yet the closer one looks, the harder it becomes to refute this long-held belief. After the feasibility of porcelain manufacture was proved, with the first patents in Staffordshire closely followed by a migration of potters to the newly established London factories of Chelsea and Bow, suddenly the lid was lifted on a whole new range of techniques as practised on the Continent, notably enamelling, slip-casting in plaster-of-Paris moulds and press-moulding. It is surely significant that Admiral Vernon's naval victory at Portobello in 1739 was

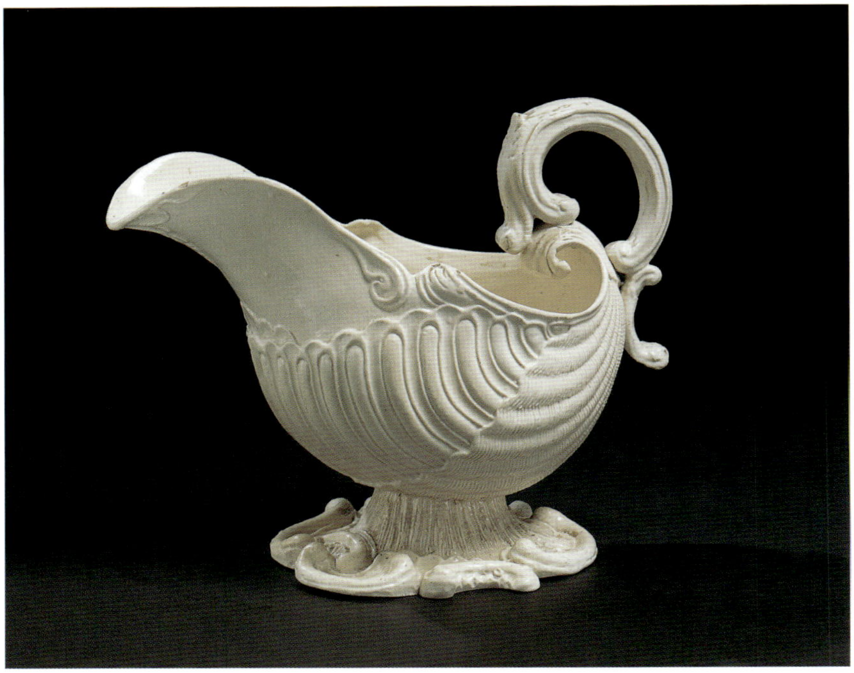

21
Press-moulding and slip-casting from plaster moulds enabled Staffordshire potters to copy elaborate and fashionable silver or porcelain shapes. Here the two techniques are successfully combined to reproduce a silver sauce boat of *c.*1750–60. Height 12 cm (4¾ in.).
V&A: C.141–1993.

commemorated on white salt-glaze with both mould-applied and slip-cast decoration, some teapots even cast in the shape of one of his ships. Although moulded decoration lacked the crispness of sprigs taken from metal moulds, if quality was to be subordinate to economy, there were big savings to be made in time and skilled labour by simply pouring slip into moulds and waiting for it to dry, rather than throwing and turning the pot before applying each sprig by hand. Once the use of plaster moulds made hollow wares possible, there was nothing to prevent the manufacture of elaborate tureens and sauce boats (plate 21), either slip-cast or, much more commonly, press-moulded. Thus the years around 1740 may be taken as the starting point for the salt-glazed dinner service, as complete as any porcelain imported from China but at a fraction of the cost, and moulded with a wide variety of decorated borders. Its wide appeal is confirmed by the survival of complete dinner services as far afield as Poland.

At first, the lack of three-dimensional models to copy must have caused difficulties, as shown by the rather desperate adaptation of seventeenth-century engraved illustration to bas-relief teapot moulds, such as the well-known 'Grand Tartar'.[26] However, the new trade of block-maker (the designer and maker of the positive stoneware block-mould from which any number of plaster moulds could be taken) soon grew, ultimately to be dominated by Aaron and Ralph Wood and their talented families. The range of cast forms encompassed pectin shells, tea chests covered with Chinese ornament, the gaunt great houses of master potters, exotic subjects such as camels, monkeys and chinamen, and national events, such as the capture of Portobello by Admiral Vernon in 1739 (plate 22). Evidently they were still a comparative novelty in 1747 when the *Daily Advertiser* of 24 August included the following:

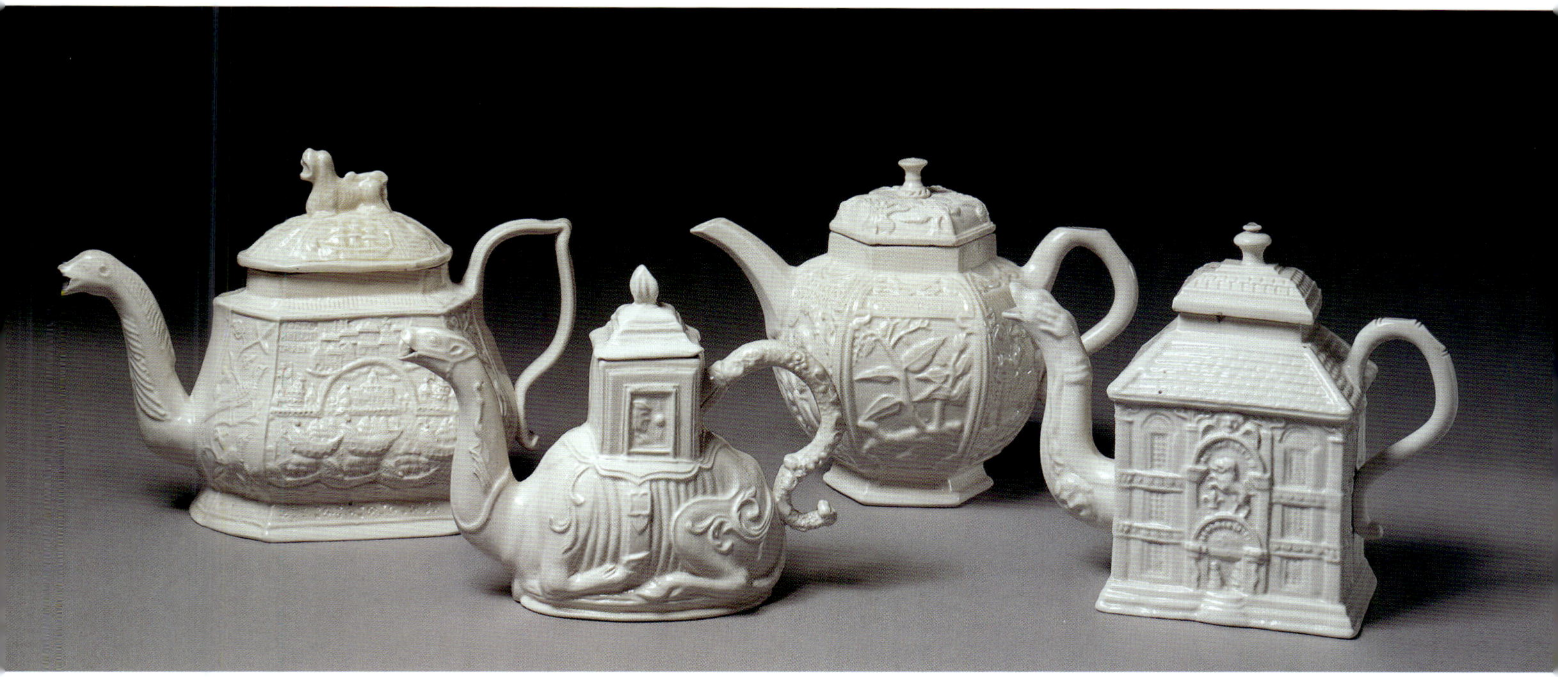

22

The invention of slip-casting with plaster of Paris moulds about 1740 made possible a huge variety of hollow forms. Designers of block-moulds were indiscriminate in their borrowings from exotic beasts, from local architecture, or from travel books already 80 years old.
Max. height 14 cm (5½ in.).

V&A: Sch.II 99, Sch.II 113, C.21–1999, Sch.II 111.

> Facing the Door of the Old London Spaw, in the Spau Fields during the Welch Fair. All Sorts of Welch Ware, Derby and Staffordshire fine Stone Ware, among which are great variety of curious Tea-Pots of all sizes, that far excel either Silver or China, both for Drawing or Pouring, and not inferior in make or beauty

Although prices were not given here, probably they were no different from an advertisement of 1753 for 'Staffordshire White Ware' at 1s 6d per dozen: so that a 1½ d might buy a plate or even, direct from the factory, one of Mr Warburton's White Ware teapots as observed by R. R. Angerstein on his travels in the years 1753–5.[27]

Other decorative features invented during the 1740s included the curly coated lion knop, the dragon and dolphin spouts, and bands of bread-crumb (crushed fired clay applied to a band of wet slip) as also found on Nottingham stonewares, and, of course, size-gilding, of which there are sometimes still traces trapped in the crevices of sprigged decoration. One of the leading potters of the decade was undoubtedly Enoch Booth, to whom the first cream-coloured earthenware with underglaze blue or 'resist' panels on a powdered background has been attributed. It is tempting to ascribe to him also the many teapots with lion finials whose front paws are secured to the lid by two parallel knife-marks, and some of which also have the innovative band of gilded bread-crumb decoration around their waist: but merely attributing the best potting to the best-known potter would be unwise. The same caution applies to the many knife-cut 'notched' handles that have been attributed to the most prolific producers of stoneware, John & Thomas Wedgwood of the Big House, Burslem, merely

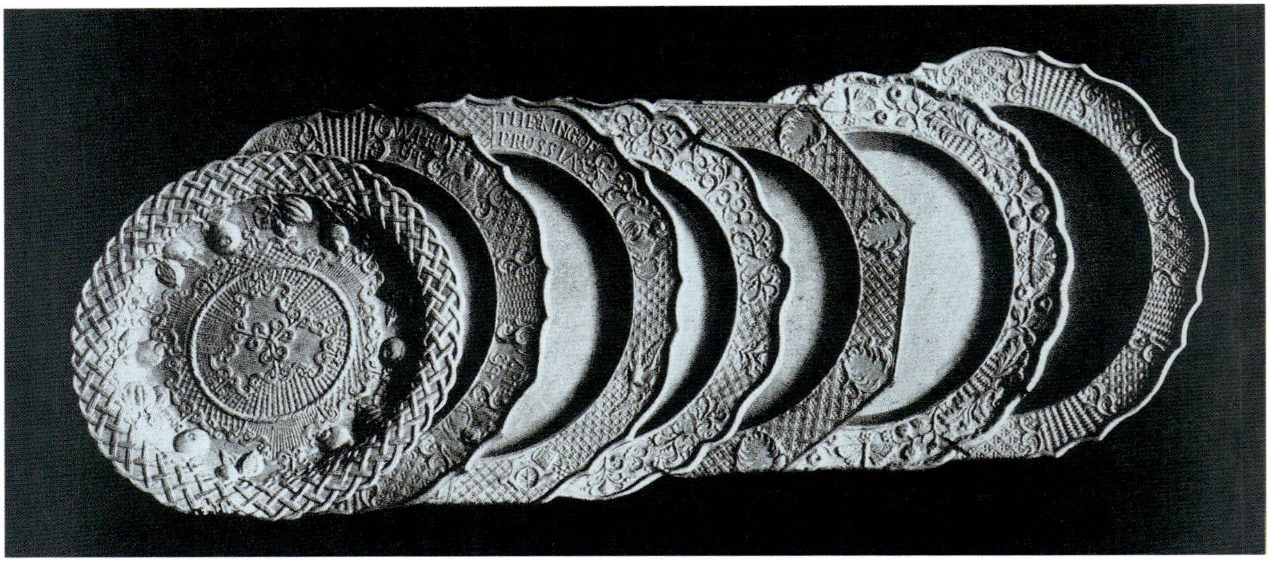

23
The number of basic designs for borders of salt-glazed plates was limited, but the individual variations many. Apart from rare commemoratives, such as 'Success to the King of Prussia' of the late 1750s, they are difficult to date accurately.

From Charles Luxmoore, *English Salt-Glazed Earthenware* (1924).

because 'notched' is mentioned in their surviving account-books:[28] it seems unlikely that, in the context of close-knit Staffordshire potteries, an essential design feature of this kind would be exclusive to a single maker, and indeed they have turned up at many excavated sites in Stoke-on-Trent.

As for moulded wares, in order to camouflage the slightly rough texture of salt-glaze it was evidently considered desirable to cover most of the surface with raised decoration – a technical problem that was later faced by manufacturers of pressed glass in the nineteenth century, and solved in exactly the same way. Of course, for plainer pieces it was possible to produce a smooth glossy surface by the use of more salt, as described by R. R. Angerstein, but this either added to the cost or diminished the profits. For plates, interesting borders were devised using variations on the seed and basket patterns – here again, almost certainly inspired by the Meissen porcelain factory, where the moulded *Ozier* pattern was introduced in 1732 and its successor the *Neuozier* in 1742. By the 1750s–1760s, and perhaps in order to compensate for the plainness of the material, a wide variety of different moulded edges and borders had been developed (plate 23), which, with one or two exceptions, enjoyed a long period of production and is extremely difficult to date: two references in the period 1755–7 to 'Mosaick' pattern undoubtedly relate to the fretted geometric design apparently copied from painted borders on Chinese export porcelain,[29] while those moulded with 'Success to the King of Prussia and his Forces' must date from the late 1750s when Britain's alliance with Frederick against the French was achieving some success. An apparently unique plate with moulded border commemorating 'W. Pitt Esq' is probably of similar date,[30] before his elevation to the peerage as Earl of Chatham in 1766. In order to increase the range of designs, the techniques of press-moulding, sprigging and piercing were successfully combined to make elaborate objects such as strawberry baskets, and the heavy but sharply defined press-moulding might even be combined with lightweight, but rather blunt slip-

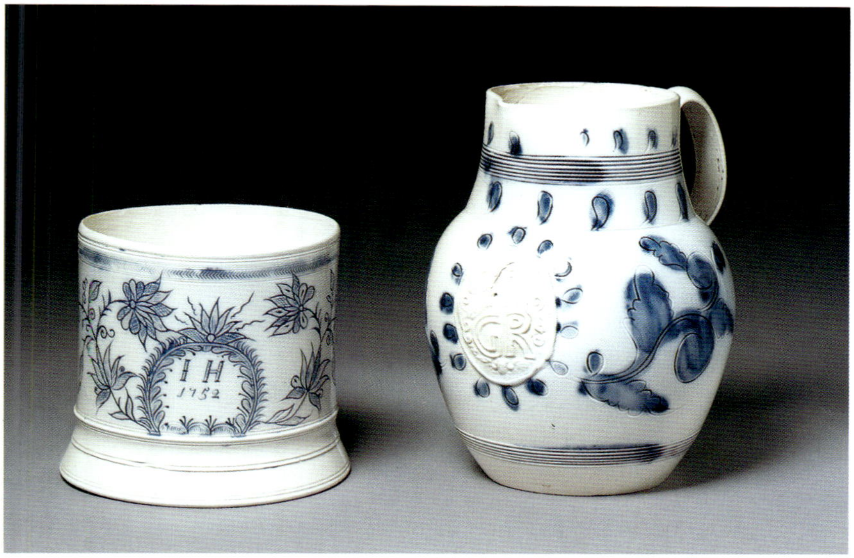

24
Decoration scratched onto white stoneware was invisible without cobalt-blue in the incisions. Appearing in the 1740s, it came into its own as export ware 'flowered' by women decorators using toothed combs, and survived as copies of Westerwald 'GR' jugs as late as the 1780s. The mug is dated 1752.
Max. height 19.7 cm (7¾ in.).
V&A: Sch.II 82, C.186–1933.

casting for objects such as sauce boats (plate 21), which closely followed the shapes of contemporary silver.

The early 1740s also saw the resurrection of *scratch-blue* technique (plate 24), perhaps by the innovative maker Enoch Booth of Tunstall, who in 1742 signed and dated a scratch-blue mug now in the Fitzwilliam Museum, Cambridge. The simple method was practised commonly on the reduced grey beer mugs imported from the Westerwald and had been used experimentally by John Dwight at Fulham;[31] but while the boldly painted Westerwald mugs had scratched outlines to prevent the volatile cobalt from running, the Staffordshire potters turned this inherent defect to their advantage by using the scratched line alone for finely drawn 'flowering' and inscriptions. Zaffre was used, an impure oxide mixed with sand, which could be rubbed into the incisions and the surplus scraped away. The prolific exporter John Baddeley of Shelton may conceivably have been responsible for a jug at Williamsburg inscribed 'ALE' in a cartouche and signed 'JB 1751' on the base, but such was the popularity of these ale jugs (and so speculative the interpretation of the initials) that individual makers almost always remain anonymous. Large numbers of fragments are found on most historic sites in North America, often with simple but highly effective patterns dextrously cut with a toothed metal comb – just possibly by the women 'flowerers' whom Simeon Shaw mentioned as being introduced to an otherwise male trade in order to meet the demand. Not surprisingly, the simple technique remained in use until white stoneware was finally replaced by lead-glazed Pearlware around 1790, as proved by an ale mug at Winterthur, based on a 'GR' mug but sprigged instead with the Great Seal of America designed in 1786.

Although enamelling undoubtedly began in the 1740s, allegedly introduced by two immigrant Dutchmen at the Warburton's factory in Hot Lane, Cobridge, it was not until the 1750s that it moved on from mere pattern to free painting of figures and landscapes. But the dating and attribution of enamelling

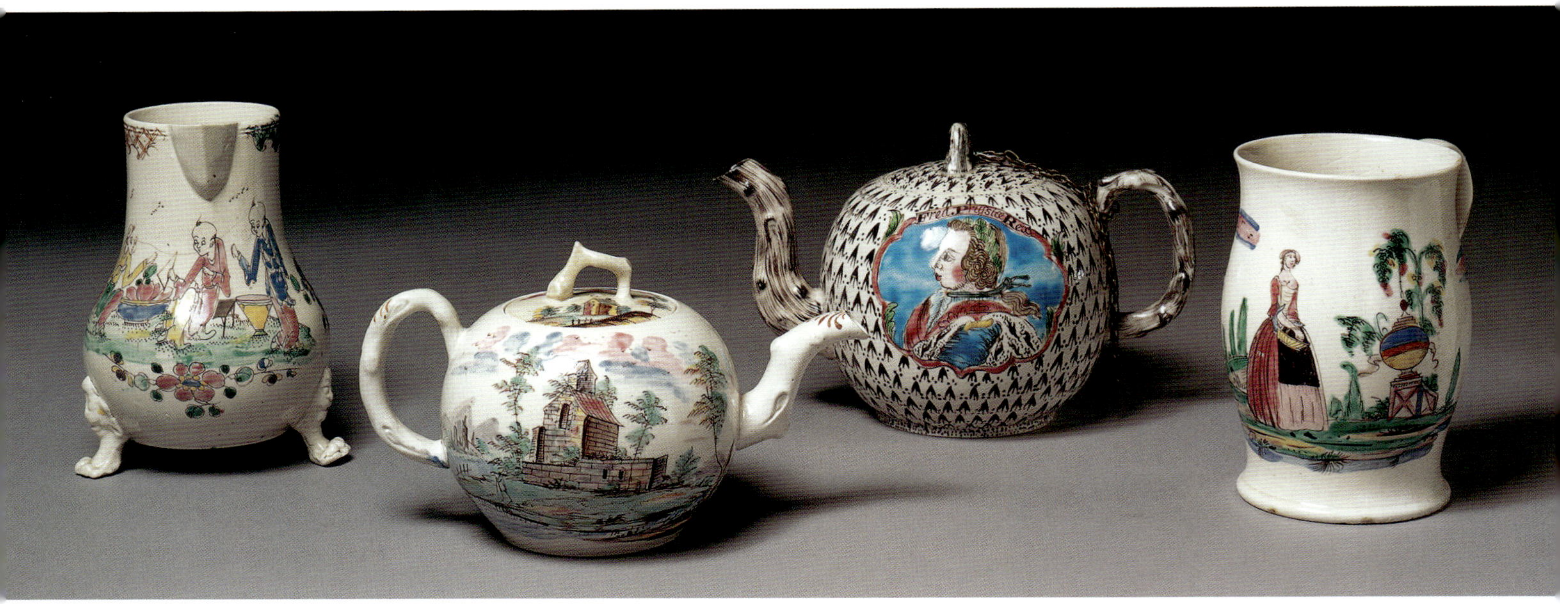

25
Some enamelling was carried out by painters at the salt-glaze factories, but the best was almost certainly executed by freelance decorators. Notable among these are the fantastic Chinoiserie of the 'Mekon Painter', the limited palette used by the 'Castle Painter', the images of Frederick of Prussia, Prince Charles Edward Stuart and others in the late 1750s, and the distinctive style used by Robinson & Rhodes at Leeds. Max. height 16.6 cm (6½ in.).

V&A: 2250–1901, C.27–1938, Sch.II 209, Circ.923–1926.

are made hazardous by the difficulty in separating first the earliest work of Dutchmen in the Potteries from that known to have been added by enamelling studios in Holland in the mid-eighteenth century, and secondly the unidentified factory house styles from those of equally unknown independent decorators, whose hand may sometimes be detected on opaque-white glass as well as porcelain from Longton Hall, Bow and Worcester. To add to these problems, J. F. Blacker noted the traffic in plain salt-glaze from England to Holland in the 1920s, soon to return newly clothed in bright enamels and with much enhanced value.[32] The supposition must be that the early factory enamellers were responsible for basic patterns, simple flower painting and the perfunctory colouring-in of moulded and sprigged wares (much of which is fairly crude), while the later more exotic and spirited decoration was done by freelance artists. For the latter, distinctive quirks of drawing and subject matter, as well as differences in the palette, offer the chance to isolate the styles of a few individual studios (plate 25):

Painter A specialized in tall Chinese women, notably one with a voluminous blue kimono and mop of black hair, sometimes holding a basket of flowers. This pattern is found on a Liverpool delftware water bottle with *petit feu* decoration and on a stoneware bottle and basin in the Schreiber Collection in the V&A, strongly suggesting Liverpool as the source.[33]

Painter B, the 'Mekon Painter', specialized in ultra-fine, spiky and very assured pen drawing of fantastical Chinese figures with light-bulb-shaped heads. The free drawing, surely the best draughtsmanship of all the decorators, was washed rather carelessly with translucent enamels.

Painter C, probably the 'Castle Painter' identified as the Longton Hall porcelain decorator John Hayfield, specialized in castles and towers, scratchily drawn in black and washed with juxtaposed stripes of contrasting colours, and clouds containing clusters of birds. A teapot of this group, painted with a naïve standing figure of Prince Charles Edward Stuart, is incised on the base 'Hannah Milns 1759 Aust seventeenth'.[34]

The Leeds Painters worked in the studio of Robinson & Rhodes of Leeds. Their exclusive contract to decorate Josiah Wedgwood's creamware from 1763 has enabled the studio style to be isolated. Most common is bold figure drawing of couples in landscapes, often taking refreshments at a tripod table, pink snail-like clouds with birds, a strong turquoise, and scrolly black trees washed in green, somewhat resembling the 'fried parsley' trees of Thomas Gainsborough. It is possible to isolate the work of Rhodes after his move to Wedgwood's Chelsea studio, and, depending on accurate dating, also therefore the work of his ex-partner Robinson, who carried on at Leeds. But their studio in Leeds must have employed a number of hands.

In addition, one must mention the many teapots painted with a stippled portrait of Frederick of Prussia in a cartouche on a background of black ermine, and also an occasional portrait of Prince Charles Edward Stuart, all dating from the late 1750s, when these subjects appeared as prints on Worcester porcelain. These portraits may well be the work of a native Staffordshire painter, very possibly the Revd John Middleton, partner of the potter Warner Edwards of Shelton, who signed the 'J. Walter de Checkley 1760' jug painted with a portrait in similar style.[35] A few other leading potters had decorating shops in their factories, such as the Warburtons at Cobridge and Enoch Booth at Tunstall, who are known to have enamelled pots on a sub-contracting basis.[36] But just as their pots remain anonymous, so it has never proved possible to identify their in-house styles, and it has further been suggested that Wedgwood's decision to send all his creamwares to Leeds to be decorated must indicate a poor opinion of his neighbours' work. As for other independent enamelling studios, the surviving account-book of William Duesbury's London decorating shop for 1751–3 shows that he was colouring stoneware figures rather than painting pots; and the ledger of 1762–97 of the Bristol decorator, gilder and sign-writer Michael Edkins shows just how busy such freelance artists could be, without however mentioning stoneware among the large quantities of glass that he enamelled.[37]

Using enamel in a different way, the partners Aaron Wedgwood and William Littler at Burslem made 'Littler's Blue' stonewares, providing a rich cobalt-blue ground colour suitable for gilded decoration (most of which has now rubbed away). References are few, but assuming that Aaron Wedgwood continued making them on his own while Littler was involved with porcelain at Longton Hall in the years 1749–60, then these rare products were probably the 'Blue' Staffordshire wares advertised in a clearance sale at King Street, London, in 1753, at 12s per dozen – or eight times the cost of plain white. John & Thomas Wedgwood bought blue wares from 'Cusen Aaron Wedgwood' in the years 1760–63, just before Littler moved to West Pans near Edinburgh, where he continued applying his 'Mazareen' blue and gilding to porcelain, creamware and, almost certainly, to his white stonewares during the period *circa* 1764–77.

Attempts to enhance the plain drab centres of stoneware plates by applying a range of sophisticated prints in pale manganese-purple or iron-red were

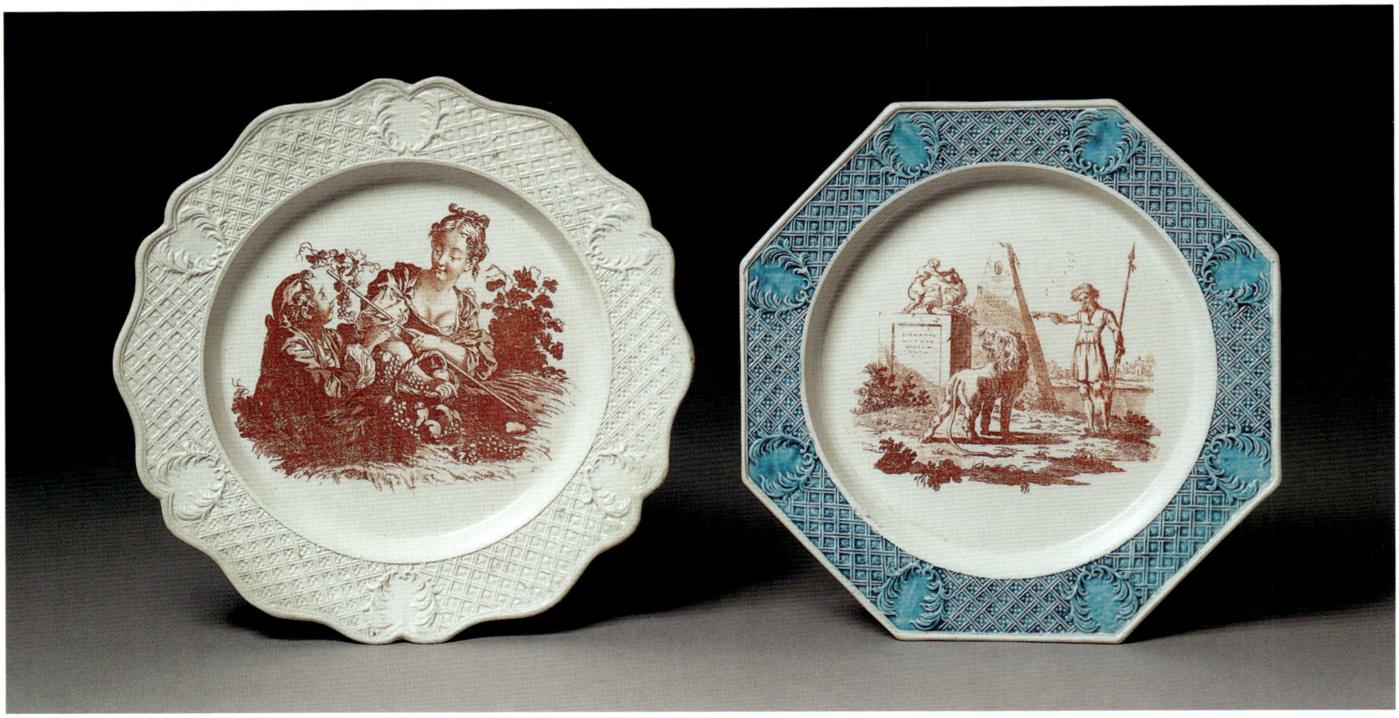

26

Although a salt-glazed surface was ill-suited to transfer-printing, when the technique was developed for porcelain in the late 1750s it was soon applied to Staffordshire stoneware. Sets of square prints of Aesop's Fables, including as here the 'Lion in Love', made no concessions to the circular form of a plate. Max. diameter 22.9 cm (9 in.).

V&A: Sch.II 229G, 2247–1901.

ahead of their time, and only after the perfection of smooth creamware was the technique of overglaze printing to achieve its spectacular success (plate 26). Their early date, which suggests either Birmingham or Liverpool as the source of the fine printing, is confirmed by an unambiguous advertisement for '400 Dozen of Stone Plates curiously printed' in the sale of the stock-in-trade of a London dealer, William Shaw, in 1757.

Josiah Wedgwood recalled that during his partnership with Thomas Whieldon in the years 1754–9 their main product was white stoneware, and Wedgwood himself may possibly have made some stoneware in his first pottery ventures at Burslem. Although Whieldon was probably the leading potter at this time, it is noteworthy that apart from some oddities, like the tiles moulded with Aesop's Fables (made in both coloured creamware and white salt-glaze), none of the fragments excavated on the site of Whieldon's pottery at Fenton Vivian appears to differ markedly from those of his neighbours. This apparent lack of creative ambition, however, may be explained by the fact that it was not only essential for commercial reasons for potters to have interchangeable wares, but that the whole supply and design of moulds were restricted to a few specialists makers like Aaron Wood, whose signature appears on several surviving block-moulds.[38] Popular models might run to several editions, perhaps by different block-cutters, but variants of borders such as 'gadrooned barley & basket' could easily be passed off to an undiscriminating public as matching 'sortable' wares stocked by all the earthenware retailers.

The period 1745–65 may be considered the heyday of salt-glaze, when foreign markets were being forged by enterprising potters such as the Baddeleys, the Warburtons, and John & Thomas Wedgwood, whose fascinating account-books for the period 1745–80 survive at the Potteries Museum in Stoke-on-Trent. This was the period when the technique spread to other areas, notably to Liverpool, where, in the absence of excavations, the extensive manufacture of salt-glaze remains unidentified. The same applies to the Chester White Ware Manufacture, which in 1757 advertised its wares as 'not inferior to any done in Staffordshire'. Right across the country in Yorkshire this new material was used to establish potteries that later became famous for their creamware: for example, the Swinton Pottery, where excavated material of the period 1768–75 has revealed, along with fine creamwares, a healthy production of traditional, rather old-fashioned stoneware. Further afield in Scotland, the Preston Pans pottery is recorded as making white stoneware from the mid-eighteenth century until as late as 1793, perhaps aiming at the export market like the very late production of Scottish delftwares. The Delftfield Pottery in the Glasgow area also made large quantities of white stonewares from the 1760s; in 1771, for example, it exported a total of 25,078 pieces to Virginia. Very little of this non-Staffordshire stoneware can be distinguished from the great bulk of anonymous 'Staffordshire' wares, for not only were most of these rival potteries established with the assistance of emigrant Staffordshire workmen, but the very success of their products lay in their anonymity.

When creamware, after a gestation period of twenty years, was finally perfected in the 1760s, the markets and trade routes were already in place, and the excellence of Staffordshire already well established throughout Europe.[39] White stoneware, in the way of many such technical advances, had not only paved the way but also made the ultimate sacrifice in lending its basic body, containing Devon clay and calcined flint, to its successor. But there was no sudden changeover, no immediate shift in public taste, for stoneware continued to play a useful, if more lowly, part until the arrival of cheap dry-bodied teapots and printed Pearlware in the 1790s stole its last tableware market. There was, however, a gradual running down, so that while mass-producers such as John & Thomas Wedgwood continued to supply the middle markets with vast quantities of miniature 'toys', spoons (expendable and now so rare), the tiny food-moulds called 'Starr pettys' and 'Turk's Caps', nests of bowls, pickle-trays and

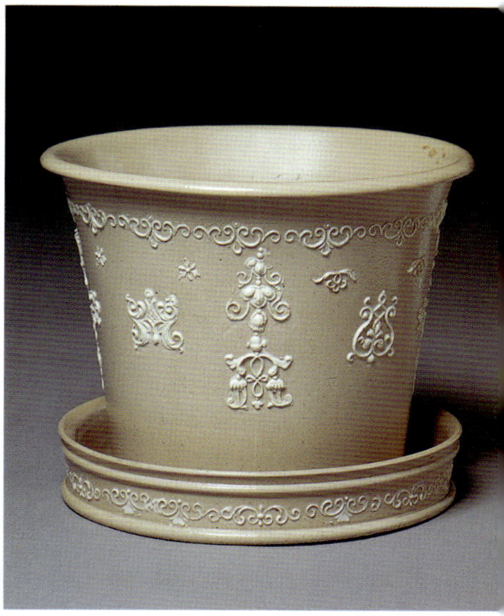

27
The use of fine white mould-applied sprigs on a drab-coloured body was a late attempt by Staffordshire salt-glaze potters to compete with red stonewares and other finewares after about 1770. This example must be similar to the 'Ash Flowr Pots & Stands' supplied by John & Thomas Wedgwood in 1772. Height 10.4 cm (4⅛ in.).
V&A: 2146–1901.

spoon-boats, the sales ledger of 1783–7 of John Wood, who set up as a salt-glaze potter very late in the day, includes 'Gallipots' (storage jars), stool pans and chamber pots, along with a surprising number of twiflers (small plates) and cups and saucers. Evidently these plates at 1d each and cups and saucers at a 1½ d still had a market, although by about 1800 it must be said that moulded 'Prattware' and blue-painted Pearlware were cheap enough for all to enjoy, and had the great advantage of being coloured.

Before admitting defeat, however, from sometime around 1770 makers of salt-glaze had had one last trick up their sleeve (plate 27). The latest fashion for red stoneware teapots and little flower pots on stands, with sharp delicate sprigging made in metal moulds, must have suggested an updated variant on the old coloured-ground sprigged earthenwares of the 1750s, now using a drab-stained stoneware body adorned with swags and bands of fine lace-like white sprigging: surely the 'Ash Flowr Pots & Stands' in John & Thomas Wedgwood's accounts for 1772.[40] Elegant miniature garniture sets for mantelpieces were even made for a smart market, copying those of porcelain or enamelled glass but very much cheaper. Unhappily, although it would be difficult to find fault with either the quality of workmanship or the design of these 'Ash' wares, by the 1780s they had shared the same fate as the unglazed red stonewares that they imitated, in succumbing to mass-produced Pearlwares and, of course, the ubiquitous Black Basalt. In modern parlance, for fashionable teapots, black was not only the new red but also the new white.

1. Blacker (1922).
2. Mountford (1971), Oswald, Hughes & Hildyard (1982), Gaimster, 'Regional Decorative Traditions' (1997). A monograph on white salt-glaze by Diana Edwards and Rodney Hampson is in preparation.
3. For details of these early London ventures, see Edwards (1974).
4. Pryor & Blockley (1978).
5. Haselgrove (1989, 1990).
6. Bimson (1961), Haselgrove & Murray (1979) and Green (1999).
7. The only two attributable pieces being the slip-cast teapot, with the blobby enamel floral painting sometimes found on Elers red stoneware, in the V&A: C.133–1938, and another recently discovered teapot that has passed through the auction rooms.
8. Johnson was last recorded in London in 1703 and first recorded in Bristol in 1715.
9. Full transcripts and analysis in Haselgrove & Murray (1979), pp.83–129.
10. Tait (1987), where it was still considered to be a Staffordshire product. Further examples illustrated by Green (1999).
11. The Woburn Abbey bills from the seventeenth century onwards provide many useful references to prices of household pottery and glass, published in part by Thorpe (1938); a transcript, catalogued as Literary Material No.338, in the library of the Ceramics Collection of the V&A.
12. Britton (1990), pp.61–92. None of these has been identified, though some may be masquerading as Staffordshire products.
13. Oswald, Hughes & Hildyard (1982), Appendices I–III.
14. For example, the patent for grinding lids taken out by R. B. Cooper in 1831 and utilized by John Wisker of the Vauxhall Pottery. These were held in place by a knurled screw on a metal crossbar engaging in slots in the rim, but later types made by other London potteries used iron claws twisted onto a coarse thread cut around the rim. Eight thousand hermetically sealed tins of bully beef, heavily contaminated by lead solder, were supplied to (and appear to have contributed to the demise of) the ill-fated expedition of Sir John Franklin to find the North-West Passage in 1845.
15. Howarth & Hildyard (2004). Figured jugs were listed by Messrs Jones, Doulton & Watts of Lambeth as early as 1818.
16. The signature of the modeller Thomas

Weatherill is found reproduced by several of these moulds, notably a 'Jim Crow' gin flask, illustrated in Oswald, Hughes & Hildyard (1982), pl.31.

17. Hume (1975), and Hume (2001), ch.XIV.
18. Bodleian Library, Oxford.
19. A sketch made by Josiah Wedgwood of a 'Nottingham ware kiln' (Wedgwood Archives) shows the square form and demountable arches
20. Jewitt (1878) includes comprehensive lists of the domestic and novelty products still being made at the various Brampton potteries. Jewitt, who was born in Derbyshire, was presented in 1871 with a contrasting pair of honey-coloured and brown Brampton loving cups, now in the V&A: C.2 &A–1982.
21. The huge globular sprigged jug with hunting figures at Williamsburg, inscribed 'The Flood Land Jug my Frend will be if Master Sam will lend ye key . . . Mr Sam Pirkin', must be the largest of these. There remains a possibility that the 'Group C' giant hunting mugs, listed in Oswald, Hughes & Hildyard (1982), Appendix II, may have been Bristol products: see Hamilton Foyn (2000).
22. *Victoria History of the County of Stafford* (1908), vol.I, pp.121–2.
23. Kansas City (1953), cat.no.123. Another loving cup, of more flaring shape, inscribed 'Martha Barlor Cornelius Toft hand 1727/8 WB CT', in Northampton Museum. Note that a thrower or turner John Toft signed the base of a salt-glaze teapot of *c.*1760 in the V&A: C.115–1980.
24. Hume (1969), figs 11–12.
25. For example, V&A: C.145–1991 and Bonham's sale of Fine British Ceramics, 10 December 2003, lot 32.
26. Grigsby ('Johann Nieuhoff's *Embassy*', 1993), pp.172–83. See also, by the same author, the articles of 1993 and 1994 on John Stalker and George Parker's *Treatise*, and George Edwards and Matthew Darly's *Chinese Designs*.
27. Angerstein (2001), p.340.
28. Mountford (1971), p.42. The Wedgwood brothers' account-books are held at the Potteries Museum, Stoke-on-Trent.
29. Bill of 1755 from Thomas Whieldon to the Earl of Bedford, and advertisement of 1757 for the sale of a stock of white stoneware at Red Lion Square, London. Two slightly differing examples of these plates, from the Enoch Wood Collection and transferred from the Museum of Practical Geology to the V&A in 1901, may be attributed to the modeller Aaron Wood, according to early records at the Potteries Museum, Stoke-on-Trent (information kindly supplied by Miranda Goodby).
30. Sotheby's sale, 15 October 1959, lot 119.
31. Dwight's recipe books for 15 March 1691 include 'a blew porcellane Cley to be turn'd into vessels or to spot and inlay pots'. One fragment of scratch blue drawn with the design of a shepherd was excavated at Fulham.
32. Blacker (1922), pp.97–8.
33. Fitzwilliam Museum, Cambridge, Glaisher no.1727, and V&A: Sch.II 177.
34. Sotheby's sale, 21 March 1967, lot 21.
35. The Potteries Museum, illustrated Mountford (1971), pl. 184. Simeon Shaw (1829), p.47, mentions that Werner (*sic*) Edwards made 'Pottery and Colours for the first Enamellers'.
36. Angerstein (2001), p.340, lists among Warburton's products in the years 1753–5 teapots 'White ware, enamelled' at 8s to 12s a dozen, as opposed to plain white at a mere 1s 6d.
37. Transcript in the library of the Ceramics & Glass Collection, V&A, Wallace Elliott Scrapbooks, vol.II.
38. A block-mould for a pectin shell cream jug signed 'RW 1749' (V&A: 3097–1852), for a spittoon signed 'Aaron Wood' (British Museum), for sauce boats signed 'RW 1748/9' and 'RW 1756' (Potteries Museum, Stoke-on-Trent) and for spouts signed 'RW 1748' (British Museum and Williamsburg). Others signed 'Ralph Wood' dated 1768 and 1770 (Potteries Museum).
39. Weatherill (1971)
40. This class of ware, because of its drab colour, was dated *c.*1730 by Mountford (1971). However, the range of shapes and delicate decoration shared with the later red stonewares suggest identification as the 'Ash' wares mentioned in the John & Thomas Wedgwood account-books of 1762–72. Presumably this trade-name was simply inherited from the earlier 'Ash colour tea pots with white flowers and glazed with lead', as noted by Angerstein (2001) in the years 1753–5.

CHAPTER THREE 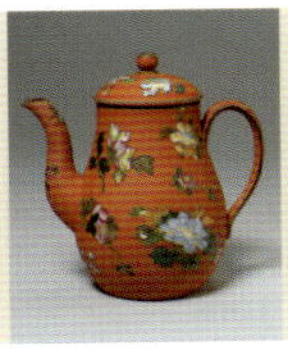

'Red China'

While most countries of Europe in the seventeenth and eighteenth centuries were making great efforts to produce white wares, either by covering red earthenware with slip or tin-glaze or by developing various types of porcelain, there flourished a ceramic type that boldly proclaimed its redness. For the colour identified the material, and the material identified the use – for brewing tea. The term 'red china', used in Britain throughout the eighteenth century, reflects both the origin of the ceramic body and the mistaken belief that it was merely a red type of porcelain. Actually a type of stoneware made from iron-rich clays by the potters of Yixing in Jiangsu Province, the material had long been highly regarded in China because of its ability to withstand the heat of a spirit lamp or brazier, so that tea leaves could be added to water boiled in the teapot itself. As early as 1533 a globular example with overhead handle was considered worthy of being deposited in the grave of Wu Jing, while a moulded hexagonal pot was discovered in another grave of 1616. Yet despite their early fame in their homeland, it was not until the establishment of tea-drinking in the West nearly half a century later that these expensive but utilitarian vessels were even considered as possible exports to Europe.

Tea, coffee and chocolate were, in fact, known in Europe in the sixteenth century, but, in the absence of regular trade between the West and China, Turkey and South America, they were regarded only as curiosities. With the founding of the British East India Company in 1600 and the Dutch Verenigde Oost-Indische Compagnie in 1602, however, followed by the public clamour that greeted the auction in Amsterdam of captured porcelain cargoes from Portuguese galleys, the *San Iago* in 1602 and the *Santa Caterina* in 1604, both the way and the means for profitable trade with China became clear. Yet it was not until Father Alexander returned from the Far East to Paris in 1653, and published his eulogy and first-hand account of the Chinese method of brewing tea, that the practice became known to Royalist exiles living in France and was thus conveyed back to Britain at the Restoration. But already by 1658 tea had been advertised as 'sold at Sultaness-head, a Cophee-house, in Sweeting's Rents by the Royal Exchange, London'.

Coffee, meanwhile, with its known stimulant properties, had already established itself as the drink for men of intellect and business, finding a natural home at Oxford, so recently Charles I's rival capital to Parliamentary London.[1] A certain Jacob opened the very first coffee house at the Angel Inn in 1651, followed by Arthur Tillyard's coffee-room at 90 High Street, where the architect Christopher Wren mixed with other notables who formed the nucleus of the

28
Other potters could make jasper and red stoneware of a quality equal to that of Wedgwood. Josiah Spode in particular made superb original red stonewares in the early years of the 19th century, such as this tripod pastille burner, as well as copies of Wedgwood's red and black teapots in the Egyptian taste.
Height 17.2 cm (6¾ in.).
V&A: 2609–1901.

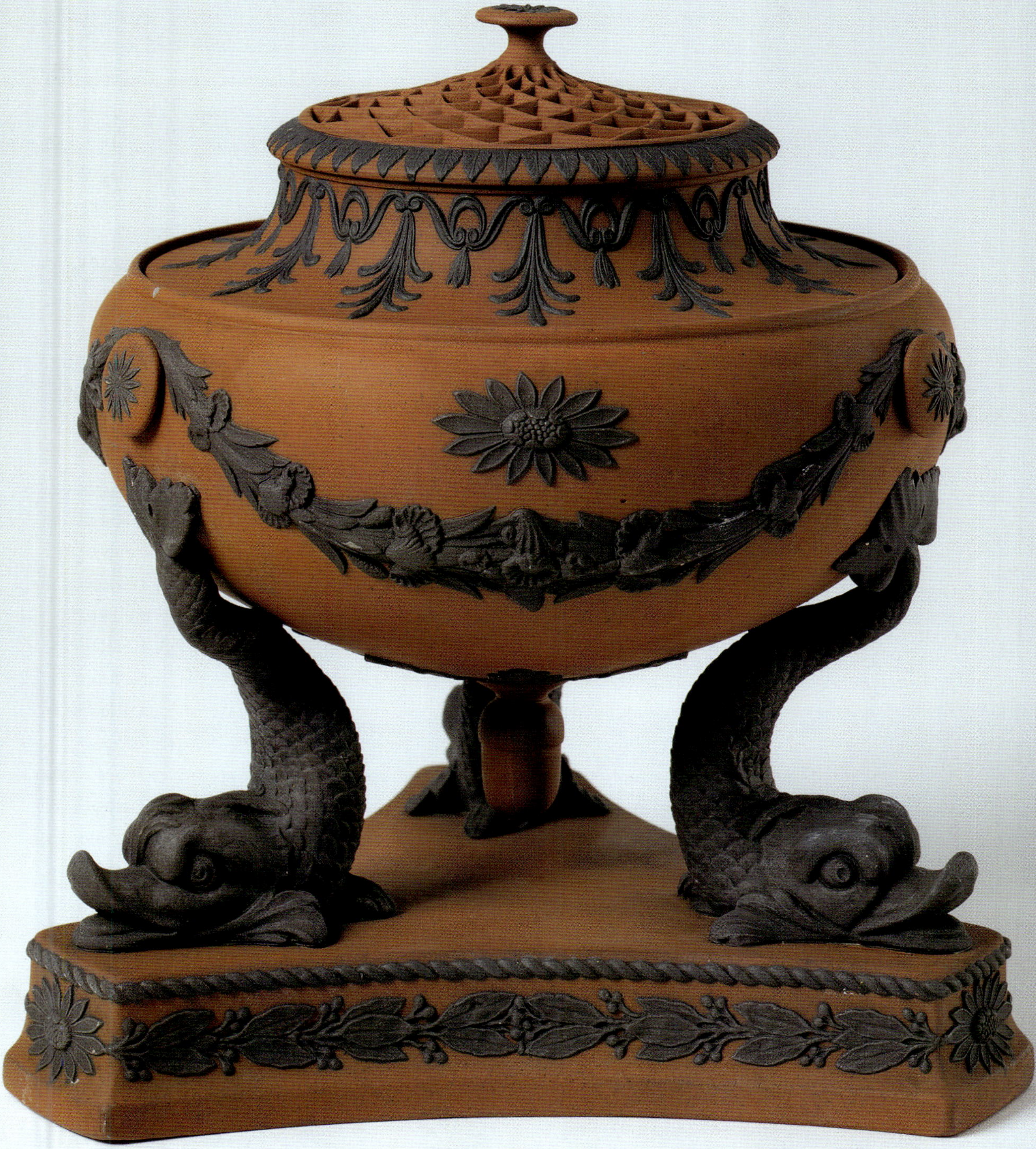

future Royal Society. In London, Pasqua Rosie opened a coffee house in St Michael's Alley, Cornhill, while in 1657 Thomas Garway advertised both tea and 'Spanish Chocolata in the Cake, from three shillings to ten shillings the pound weight'. Clusters of coffee houses – which, by 1675, numbered over 250 – around the areas of the Exchange, Lombard Street and Temple soon began to serve respectively London's stockbrokers, merchants and lawyers, while providing neutral territory where men of different professions and social backgrounds could meet on equal terms. It says much for its tenacious popularity that, whereas the beneficial medicinal properties of chocolate and tea were generally accepted, coffee drinkers were obliged to indulge their habit in the face of the malicious rumour that it led to impotence.

The 1650s witnessed not only the establishment of the trade in tea shipped from China, Turkish coffee transported from the Yemen to the port of Alexandria, and chocolate from South America, but also the establishment of regular supplies of refined sugar. Following the smuggling of live sugar canes in 1641 from Portuguese Brazil to the British West Indies, the first English commercial sugar refinery was set up in 1659. The rival seafaring nations soon picked suitable bases for their tea and porcelain trading activities in the Far East. Java was captured by the Dutch in 1682, Macao was used by the Portuguese for trading with Canton, and from the mid-eighteenth century the British established themselves at Amoy.

Unlike blue and white Chinese porcelain, which was avidly collected by wealthy aristocrats for their Porcelain Cabinets from the early seventeenth century onwards, the red stoneware of Yixing not only lacked obvious decorative possibilities but also had associations solely with the making of tea. Although the Dutch instructed all their ships to include casks of tea from as early as 1637, Europe was slower to adopt the specialist Chinese vessels for consuming tea. Thus the first unequivocal mention of a red stoneware Yixing teapot was an example seen by a visitor to the Danish Royal Cabinet of Curiosities in 1656. It is not altogether surprising that the Dutch, who made serious efforts to dominate the tea trade from the 1660s, should have also been the first to use the vessels especially favoured by the Chinese for their tea-making, and almost inevitable that Dutch potters, otherwise engaged in making tin-glazed earthenware copies of Chinese porcelain, should have also been the first to make copies of red stoneware. The Delft potter Arij de Milde later claimed to have been making red teapots from 1658, until his death in 1708, along with Samuel van Eenhorn from about 1674 and Lambertus Cleffius from about 1678. It is certain that de Milde and van Eenhorn were making them from 1679, when their guild ordered them to supply 'counterfeit East Indian teapots' – the same year that seven cases of red teapots were imported into Holland from China, followed the next year by 320 'figured red teapots'. It is tempting to think that these Delft potters may have been using English clay, perhaps the clay from Browne's Pit in the Isle of Purbeck, Dorset, 'being fit to make a sort of earthenware called Bastard China', for which Thomas Littleton petitioned the king in 1670 for a licence to transport. Such trade was not unusual: pipeclays from Southampton, Dorset and Kent were exported to Rotterdam as early as 1629, while Norfolk had provided clay for Netherlandish tin-glazed earthenware potters from the sixteenth century. But whatever the source of iron-rich clay, production of these Delft teapots must have been on a large scale since many survive, almost all with prunus sprigs originally decorated with gold leaf but now showing only traces of white gesso or gold-size in their crevices. The bases are marked with impressed seals containing animals, like the running fox of de Milde and van Eenhorn's rhebus of a unicorn.[2]

While tea drinking was firmly established in England at the Restoration of Charles II in 1660, both by returning exiles from France and by the tastes of Charles's Portuguese queen, Catherine of Braganza, the English were slow to begin importing tea directly from China, for the first official order by the East India Company for 4,713 lb occurred as late as 1678. Holland meanwhile dominated the market, supplying England also with red stoneware teapots of Chinese and Delft manufacture until at least the 1680s. So excellent for their purpose were these teapots that public demand was difficult to satisfy. A petition draft, undated but referring to a complaint of the potters in 1676 and an Order in Council of 1685 on behalf of the London delftware potters James Barston, William Knight and Thomas Harper, complained that the glass-sellers and merchants Samuel Eyre and John Bowles (owner of the Vauxhall glasshouse) had obtained authorization to import 'certain delph red wares, or counterfeit china wares, and galley tiles'. Further confirmation of the growing popularity of tea drinking in England, and, by implication, of the use of Oriental tea vessels, comes from the publication in 1685 of two specialist books about the subject: John Chamberlayn's *The Manner of making coffee, tea and chocolate as it is used in most parts of Europe, Asia, Africa and America*, a book translated from an anonymous French publication, and Dufour's *Traités nouveaux et curieux du caffé, du thé et du chocolat*, wherein appears the first mention of Yixing teapots: 'the Chinese use for their infusion teapots of a red clay with impressed designs which they claim are better than any others'. Two years later Nicholas de Blegny illustrated his *Le Bon Usage du thé, du caffé et du chocolat* (1687) with accurate engravings by the German court engraver Johann Hainzelmann of Yixing teapots and their braziers.

In this climate, it is not surprising to find the enterprising Fulham potter John Dwight adding 'opacous redd and dark coloured Porcellane or China' to his renewed patent of 1684, and to find in 1686 the first mention of the Dutchman David Elers practising as a silversmith at the Crown & Sceptre near St Clement's church in London. In fact, serious interest in red stoneware in England may be traced back further than the mid-1680s, for Martin Elers, father of David and John Philip, was recorded as dealing in 'East Indian rarities' in 1672, while their uncle dealt in expensive Oriental china and 'lackery ware' at his shop in St Mary-le-Bow and, more significantly, John Dwight's trial pieces of red stoneware at the Fulham Pottery derive from an archaeological context of 1672–5. But credit for the successful commercial exploitation of red stoneware belongs entirely to the Elers Brothers.[3]

John Philip (1664–1738) and David (1656–1742) Elers made such an enduring reputation that in the nineteenth century the term 'Elers Ware' was applied by collectors and authors indiscriminately to all red stonewares (plate 29). The Elers family were of German extraction, having first settled in Holland and then moved to England to trade in Oriental luxury goods in London, where from the mid-1680s David practised as a silversmith. From the evidence submitted in court during John Dwight's private prosecution in 1693 for infringing his red stoneware patent, much is known about the careers of the two brothers. From about 1690 David ran a pottery at Vauxhall, where, having already learned the secret of making salt-glazed stoneware from a stay at Cologne, he made 'browne muggs' and 'Red Teapotts'. Since David is recorded as going to Holland in that year, it is tempting to think that he might have familiarized himself with the manufacture of red teapots in Delft, although it seems unlikely, in view of his disastrously idiosyncratic manufacturing technique, that he would have recruited

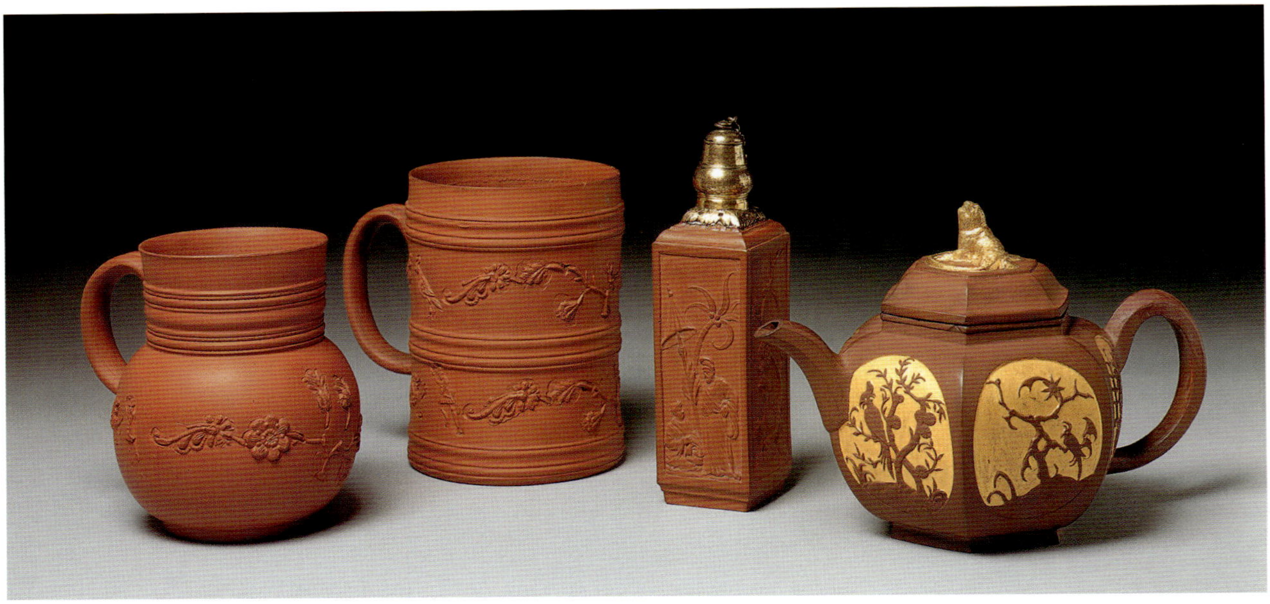

29
The brothers John Philip and David Elers made red stonewares at Bradwell Wood in Staffordshire from about 1690 to 1698, using a slow and labour-intensive slip-casting technique, but of an excellence never surpassed. Max. height 13 cm (5⅛ in.).
V&A: C.4–1932, C.275–1921, C.319–1951, C.100–1938.

a Dutch potter to assist him. Certainly, his products had been perfected by 1691, when the Corporation of Newcastle under Lyme ordered a presentation for a visit from Chief Justice Holt consisting of 'some of Mr David Elers earthen ware to the vallew of three pounds or thereabouts'. If Simeon Shaw is correct in estimating that the Elers' pots cost between 12s and 24s each, this gift would include only enough pieces for the barest tea equipage. The red teapots are also clearly mentioned by John Houghton in the *Collection for Improvement of Husbandry and Trade No.63* (1693):

> There is found near *Faux-Hall* in *Surrey*, a sort of *Clay* used to make all sorts of *Tea* pots, well approved of by most *Toy-Shops* about the *Exchange*, and are hardly discerned from *China*, and other Pots from beyond Sea, being very exact in Colour, Strength, and Shape, and lately applied to this use by two *Dutch* Brothers whose names are Eelers.

It is likely that David used his shop in the City as an outlet for their teapots, which, in the absence of fine red local stoneware clay, must have been either brought down from their pottery in Staffordshire or made at Vauxhall from Staffordshire clay – as in fact they admitted to Dwight. Since the lawsuit of 1693 was not followed through, there is strong circumstantial evidence that the brothers came to an amicable agreement with Dwight whereby they would cease making rival brown stonewares at Vauxhall and instead make only red stonewares under licence in Staffordshire. It is known that in the early 1690s John Philip took a lease on Bradwell Hall near Newcastle under Lyme, where he farmed and built a small pottery, taking advantage of the excellent and plentiful local seam of red haematite at Bradwell Wood, which presumably they had already been using, and it is surmised that David may have initially stayed in London to retail the teapots at his shop in the Poultry. That 1693 was the date when John Philip moved to Staffordshire is suggested both by Dwight's lawsuit and by Martin Lister's communication to the Royal Society in that year:

> I have this to add, that this Clay, Haematites is as good, if not better, than that which is brought from the East Indies. Witness the Tea-Pots now to be sold at the Potters in the Poultry in Cheapside which not only for Art, but for beautiful colour too, are far beyond any we have from China. These are made of the English Haematites in Staffordshire, as I take it, by two Dutchmen incomparable artists.[4]

Although neither the site nor the range of products of the Elers' Vauxhall pottery have been fully ascertained, the account of John Mountford, who demolished the remains of the Elers' kiln at Bradwell Wood around 1802, and of Enoch Wood and John Riley, who also examined it, together with trial excavations by Gordon Elliott, have shown that the small kiln, 5 ft wide with five fire-mouths, was used exclusively for red stoneware.[5] Thus, there can no truth whatsoever in the traditional story that the Elers introduced salt-glazing to Staffordshire.

The last decade of the seventeenth century saw increasing popularity of hot drinks and increasing interest in heat-proof vessels for their consumption. Delftware, soft-bodied with a loose-fitting thick glaze, could be as decorative as Chinese porcelain but without the strength needed for hot liquids, still less boiling water. Brown stoneware teapots, as well as capuchines for coffee or chocolate, were being made by Dwight at Fulham and, according to an inventory of 1699, also at the Pickleherring Quay pottery at Southwark.[6] In addition, there were regular shipments of Chinese porcelain and red stonewares by the East India Company, who held sales at their premises in Leadenhall Street to supply china dealers throughout Britain. What the Chinese did not make was red stoneware capuchines, tea bowls, tea bottles, and the vessels for drinking strong ale at home – small globular *gorges* with straight, ribbed necks and *canns* (cylindrical ale mugs) with two bands of lathe-turned ribbing. These were, however, all supplied exclusively by the Elers Brothers, whose products may be identified with those listed in an advertisement in the *London Gazette* for 14–18 February 1695 (by the modern calendar, 1696):

> At the Marine Coffee House in Birchin Lane Cornhill, on Friday the 1st March at 3 after Noon will be exposed to Sale by the Candle, fine red figured and flowered Tea Pots, Chocolate Cups, and other Curiosities, which are to be seen the 25th 26th & 28th Instant at Mr Elias Turner's, Merchant, in New Street next Devonshire Square, without Bishopsgate

This also raises the suggestion that David Elers, whose name disappears from the lists of inhabitants of the Poultry area between 1694 and 1696, may have given up his shop and perhaps moved to Staffordshire after 1693; and that, in any case, straitened circumstances may have obliged the brothers to resort to selling their wares by auction through a third party in London. At the same time, John Dwight, holder of the patent from 1684, is presumed to have continued his experiments, including recipes in his Notebooks for 'a bright red Cley wth Staffordshire red Cley' and 'red porcelane cley', and in 1695 to 'the little furnace where the last red Teapots were burnt' – presumably a muffle kiln. Without exception, however, all surviving pieces of this period may be attributed securely to the Elers for reasons set out below.

Nothing more is known of the Elers' activities until early 1698, when William Gilpen of Whitehaven recorded that one of the Wedgwood brothers, whom Dwight had also sued, had reported a 'Company of Dutchmen who (by Licence from Mr D.) make ye fine ware in Staffordshire'.[7] Later that year Lady Celia Fiennes recorded in her diary that she

> went to this NewCastle in Staffordshire to see the making ye fine tea potts, Cups and saucers of ye fine red Earth, in imitation and as Curious as yt which Comes from China, but was defeated in my design, they Comeing to and End of their Clay they made use off for yt sort of ware and therefore was remov'd to some other place where they were not settled at their work so Could not see it.[8]

It is certain that they left Staffordshire in that year, but certain too that it was not for lack of Bradwell clay, which still remains plentiful. Indeed, the expiry of Dwight's red stoneware patent in 1698 might be seen as a reason for continuing their manufacture there, but the stringent terms of the lease of Bradwell Hall to a new tenant in 1698, which included the demolition of the Elers' kiln and an embargo on digging pot clay, seem to indicate that the Elers departed under a cloud and may even have been evicted. Thus, returning to London they would have found themselves in the ironical situation of no longer having to pay royalties to John Dwight, but having at the same time lost their supply of Staffordshire red haematite with which to earn their living. Exactly what they did for the next two years is unclear, but having relied on a strictly limited production of very expensive finewares, they would have been ill-equipped to compete with the big Southwark potteries in the production of common brown salt-glazed stoneware. In December 1700 they were declared bankrupt and their pottery and equipment at Vauxhall sold up. Subsequently, they returned to the trade of their father and uncle, for in 1701 John Philip Elers was said to have been set up as a merchant by Lady Barrington in Dublin, where he was supplied with the quantities of Chinese porcelain bought by David Elers from the sales of the East India Company in the period 1714–22. It is worth noting that by this date Yixing red stoneware, though technically and artistically inferior to the Elers' products, was very much cheaper: the total of 978 'Red teapotts' purchased by agents of the East India Company in Canton on 13 March 1700 cost about

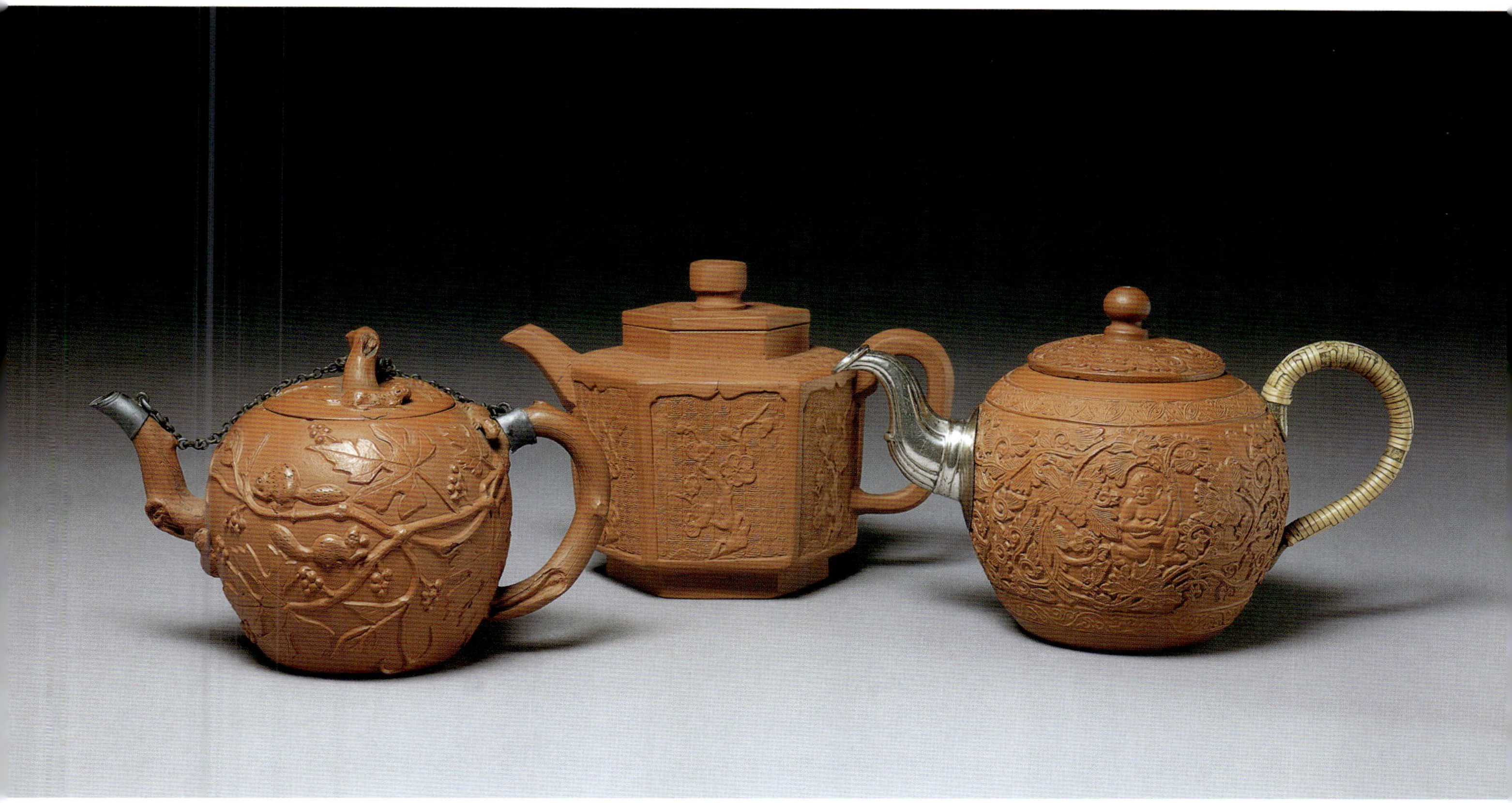

5d each, excluding transport and packing in the form of 'Sago to fill up ye chest' (plate 30).[9]

When considering the wares produced by the Elers, it should first be explained how they can be identified and distinguished from Yixing examples and those possibly made by Dwight. Fortunately, there is a foolproof diagnostic feature which concerns the technique of manufacture. In a Memorandum dated 1764, Josiah Wedgwood, repeating information supplied by an old inhabitant of Chesterton, Edward Bourne, and doubtless also depending on his own observation of Elers wares, stated:

30
The increasing numbers of Yixing teapots imported by the East India Company from the late 17th century onwards later provided models for Staffordshire teapots of the 1740s–1750s. Max. height 10.9 cm (4¼ in.).
V&A: FE.29–1970, C.27–1947, 729–1853.

> Turning, or the use of the lathe, we owe to them likewise for though they either could not find a hand capable of throwing Teaware, they therefore cast their ware in plaster moulds & turn'd it on the outside very neatly in a lathe . . . It is most probable we had also the art of preparing the alabaster, making it into moulds & casting the ware there in from these Foreign Potters.[10]

Improbable as this sounds (for many of the Elers hollow-wares are round), it has been proved conclusively by Gordon Elliott of the City Museum & Art Gallery, Stoke-on-Trent, that all wares plausibly attributed to the Elers are in fact slip-cast, as were all the fragments he excavated at Bradwell Wood in 1955. Despite the very fine particle size and natural smoothness of the Bradwell red clay, the slightly rough interior surfaces and the hollows where the slip has settled into every crevice in the mould are irrefutable signs of slip-casting. Conversely, the very few fragments of Dwight's red stoneware excavated at the Fulham Pottery were all wheel-thrown.

From its beginnings, the red stoneware of Yixing had included elaborately press-moulded hexagonal teapots, the sides having cartouches of fine bas-relief decoration. These wares, as well as the rather similar 'Blanc de Chine' teapots from Dehua, not to mention those Chinese silver teapots with cast panels that passed through the hands of the London Assay Office in the 1680s, would have been well known to the Elers family, and would have provided a wide variety of models for David and John Philip to imitate.[11] Having obtained access to a red clay with excellent casting properties, either by tapping into local knowledge or knowledge about red clays obtained from fellow potters in Holland, they began to use silversmithing techniques to produce hollow-wares, using plaster of Paris made from ground calcined gypsum. Although their lack of training as practical potters seems not to have prevented their making an effective stoneware kiln, the need for secrecy that precluded the use of skilled hired throwers was to prove disastrous: even plain globular teapots, which would take no more than a few minutes to throw on a wheel, had to be cast in stages in multi-part plaster moulds, which themselves would have been formed around a turned and carved wooden block-mould.

Perhaps partly due to the very slow speed of production, the Elers' red stonewares demonstrate not only superb craftsmanship but also inventive design. Many of the plainer wares, mainly teapots but also a few tea bowls and capuchines (coffee or chocolate cups), imitated the typical Chinese decoration of moulded prunus blossom, which the Elers applied as 'sprigs' in curved sharp-edged brass moulds directly onto the lathe-turned leather-hard pot, perhaps partly dried to allow separation from the mould and brushed with slip to make them adhere. The sprigs on some surviving pots, and on almost all the contemporary Dutch redwares, show evidence of having once been gilt. None of the Elers' tools or moulds survives, yet the finding of a set of John Dwight's brass sprig-moulds at the Fulham Pottery indicates exactly what these moulds were like, the style and size being so similar that it is difficult not to conclude that these may have formed part of a larger set made by the Elers and shared with Dwight as part of their arrangement. The sheer technical perfection of all these pots is astonishing, considering that they were the first true finewares to be made in Europe. The Bradwell clay, with its very fine particle size, not only became fully vitrified and impervious to water but also created a surface sheen – not unlike the lower-fired Roman Arretine or Samian Ware, although this was achieved by using a fine extra slip coating. With so much iron oxide in the body, kiln control was critical: thus the colour may vary between brick-red and purple, and could under reducing conditions easily have produced a fine black ware if the Elers had wished it. In fact, later writers such as Simeon Shaw took it for granted, with only scanty evidence since disproved, that they were the first to produce Black Basalt. Nothing now remains of the kiln used by the Elers, although we do have an account by Simeon Shaw of a visit to Bradwell Hall in 1808 by the potters Enoch Wood and John Riley, who discovered evidence of a small round kiln with an internal diameter of 5 ft and five fire-mouths, the whole standing some 7 ft high: in short, a wood-fired muffle kiln designed for high temperatures, which Simeon Shaw concluded was 'adapted to fire choice articles'.

The hexagonal teapots with oval panels of bas-relief ornament and lion finials, and the little square 'tea' bottles of the same type, are indeed 'choice articles' and undoubtedly the most important innovations of the Elers, with some importance for the future of the Staffordshire potting industry.[12] A combination of the styles of Yixing and of Continental metalwork, enhanced often by elegant gilt-brass chained mounts, and even, on at least one teapot, gold-leaf background to the ornament, sets these objects apart from anything produced in Europe at the time. The little 'tea bottles' may in reality have been intended as expensive bottles for toilet water, although their form derives from the very tall square jars with small necks made at Yixing and evidently intended for storing tea. The bodies of all these pieces are, of course, slip cast, perhaps using original block-moulds of metal to produce such sharp decoration, while the spouts and handles are of clay kneaded and worked to give them the tensile strength that cast clay notably lacks. Elegant design and much sure-handed fettling with a sharp knife – presumably carried out by the Elers with their own hands (in order to guard their secrets) – give these pots a concise vitality not to be seen again in Staffordshire until the ultimate perfection of reinvented red stonewares in the 1760s.

As well as their role as fineware manufacturing pioneers, the Elers may well have been responsible for introducing the first enamel decoration on ceramics into England. A class of enamelled pots has been isolated and published, all decorated in a limited palette and apparently by the same hand.[13] The group comprises a mixture of Chinese porcelains as well as brown and red stonewares of undoubted Elers manufacture, the most interesting of which are surely the two known slip-cast salt-glazed stoneware teapots that could have been made only at the Elers' pottery in Vauxhall. The introduction of enamelling to England has traditionally been credited to immigrants from Holland, where the art had been perfected by the end of the seventeenth century and where it continued to be employed in embellishing Chinese porcelain, Staffordshire salt-glaze and eventually creamware. But although there is little doubt that the technique appeared in Staffordshire around 1740 and that it was probably brought from the Low Countries, the group of somewhat crudely enamelled wares of *circa* 1700–10 may perhaps be attributed to an anonymous Dutchman mentioned by *The London Tradesman* in 1747:

> Some Years ago a Workman came over from Holland, and in a Pot-House in the Borough [i.e., Southwark] gave some Stone Wares the Colours common to the earthen, he succeeded so well that Cups and other vessels, even upon that first Essay, came little short of China-ware: But the Project was no sooner known to be in any Forwardness to become useful to the Public, than Ways and Means were found to send the Projector out of the Way, and with him the Scheme vanished.

The only dated piece, a half-pint tavern mug with 'AR' ale measure mark under the handle (see note 13), displays a much improved polychrome enamelling technique with the arms of Farmer and the date 1706. Assuming a degree of improvement after the first 'essays', for example, the Fulham 'AR'-marked tavern mug with the usual foliage sprays above a townscape most delicately painted in iron-red that was recently on the market,[14] and assuming that the Elers were in touch with their compatriots in the Netherlandish enclave of Southwark, it is quite possible that an immigrant enameller obtained both stoneware and Chinese porcelain from the Elers, and after their bankruptcy, brown stoneware from Fulham. Whether or not the Elers were closely involved with bringing this person to London is not known, but such a scheme could well have appeared an attractive proposition after their return to London in 1698 – exactly the period when the enamelled brown stoneware teapots were probably made. An intriguing reference in a London retailer's account-book of 1705, to 'painting Tea potts . . . 7.0d', must inevitably refer to Chinese porcelain (perhaps from the enormous quantity purchased by this dealer six months earlier for £447 5s 0d), but must also surely indicate enamel painting rather than 'cold' decoration in oil paints.[15]

After the departure of John Philip Elers to Ireland in 1701 and the death of John Dwight in 1703, the development of finewares in England suffered a setback. In London, the refined stonewares whitened with fine slip containing flint continued to be made at the Fulham Pottery under the management of Dwight's widow until her death in 1709, when, under her son Samuel Dwight, the pottery appears to have lost its pre-eminence and gradually declined to a basic level of technical and artistic competence indistinguishable from that of other stoneware potteries in Southwark, Lambeth and Vauxhall. In Staffordshire the hasty departure of the Elers was not followed by experiments by indigenous potters to recreate their superb red stonewares, but seems rather to have been ignored. The waters of ceramic history at this crucial point, however, are considerably muddied by the writing of Simeon Shaw, who, on the assumption that the

Elers' presence had inspired a steady progressive development of local potting skills in the early years of the eighteenth century, repeated a local myth that Joshua Twyford and Joshua Astbury had insinuated themselves into the Elers' pottery by feigning idiocy, after which they stole their secrets (including salt-glazing) and proceeded to exploit them for their own benefit and that of their fellow potters. Absurd though this story may be, it does beg the question of why the white stoneware of Dwight was so late in being reproduced in Staffordshire, why red earthenware was not made until the 1720s and in particular why red stoneware was not made again until nearer the middle of the eighteenth century. For the Bradwell Wood clay had been identified as eminently suitable for teapots; the local potters had the use of high-temperature stoneware kilns from at least as early as 1700; and they had potting skills that included lathe-turning and sprig

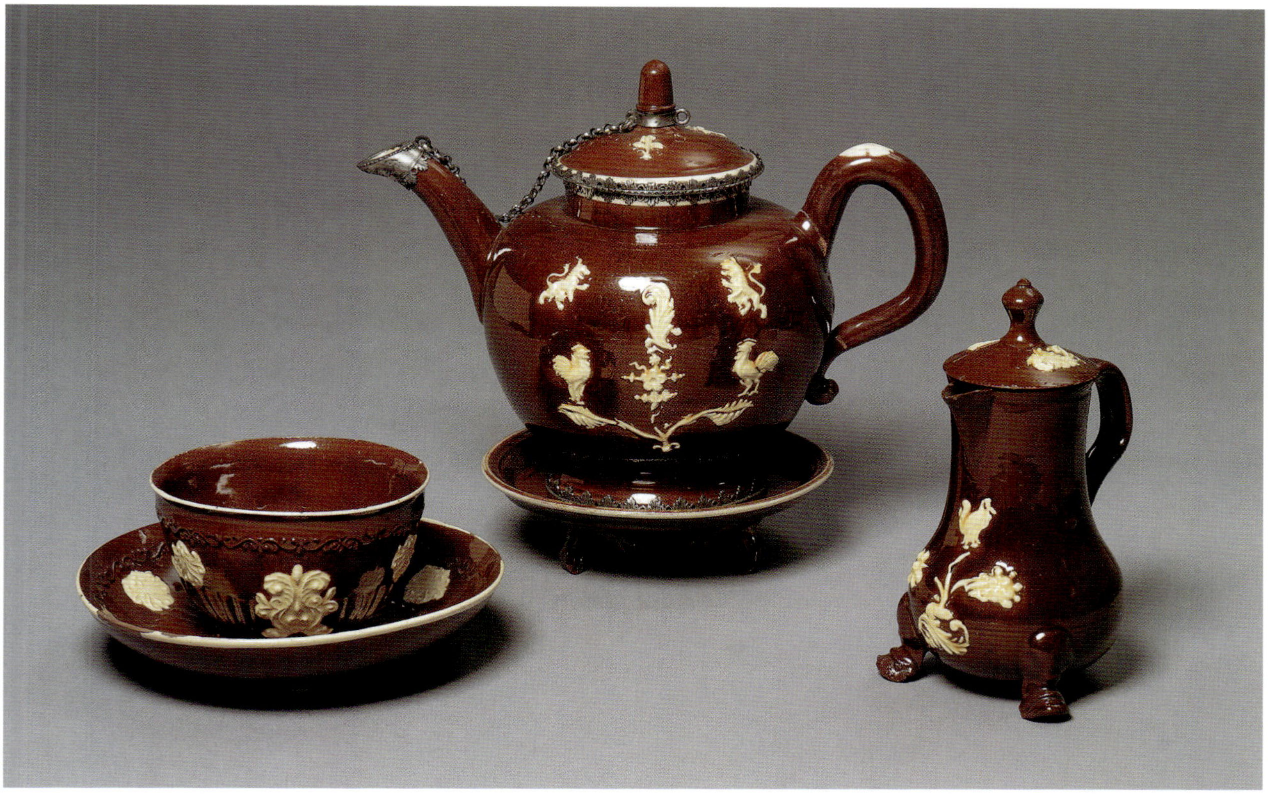

31
Lead-glazed red teawares were mass-produced by John Astbury of Shelton, Samuel Bell of Newcastle under Lyme and others in the period 1725–45. Max. height 16.2 cm (6⅜ in.).
V&A: C.26–1940, C.12–1967, C.13–1967, 2094–1901.

decoration. What they did not have, however, was the secret of slip-casting to enable them to make square or hexagonal pots with moulded panels, and no doubt they also lacked the confidence to manufacture a material that had already bankrupted the Elers. It is also likely that the increasing importation of Yixing stonewares had reduced their cost to a level at which English potters could not hope to compete: as mentioned above, the prime cost of Yixing teapots purchased in China in 1700 was about 5d.

All in all, the indications are that Staffordshire potters, with their high-firing stoneware kilns and excellent available red clay, did not lack the capability to make red stoneware teapots in the first two decades of the eighteenth century but simply chose not to do so. Instead, they competed with Nottingham in making the lustrous brown stoneware ale tankards that often bear 'AR' ale measure marks, as well as the lathe-turned speckled earthenwares with iron-manganese-lead glaze, and, from about 1715, the first white salt-glaze whitened with a fine engobe or slip containing calcined flint. The list of Burslem potters of the period 1710–15 compiled by Josiah Wedgwood from the memories of elderly local potters in 1765 includes a surprisingly early mention of 'dippt white' stoneware, but not a single mention of fine red earthenware or stoneware.

The Elers' legacy to Staffordshire was therefore more inspirational than practical, although it is also certain that a number of their products still remained in the district (both Wedgwood writing in 1765 and Shaw in 1829 were quite familiar with the Elers' red stonewares). One of the rare examples of direct influence may be seen in the white salt-glaze 'tea bottles', the press-moulds of which appear to have been made from an Elers' original: an example signed 'TW 1724' is in the Fitzwilliam Museum, Cambridge. And again, when moulding techniques were redeveloped around 1740, it was to the Elers' hexagonal teapots, already some forty or fifty years old, that potters turned for inspiration.

In the meantime, with the introduction of flint and Dorset clay and the opening of the River Weaver to navigation in 1733, Staffordshire potting skills were improving and their products becoming more widely available. Since the newly developed white stonewares offered very limited scope for decoration, and since red teapots were still very much in fashion, from the early 1720s Staffordshire potters tried a new combination of their native red clay and white pipeclay – both traditionally used for making slipware – to create an entirely new type of ceramic fineware that owed nothing to Chinese prototypes (plate 31). These elegant thinly potted red teawares and mugs, at first with lathe-turned raised bands fluted by hand with a gouge, and shortly thereafter decorated with scantily fettled white sprigs applied directly to the pots with metal moulds, were not only cheap to mass-produce, but proved capable of considerable refinement. Just as the early white salt-glaze teawares of the 1720s had the tips of spouts, neck rims and tops of handles evenly dipped in iron-brown slip, so the same treatment was given to red earthenwares, but with a trimming of white slip. This proved both aesthetically satisfying and practical, for the working extremities of the pots were thickened and protected. From the beginning, the major technical advance of double-firing was employed for all these pots: that is, the thrown, turned, handled and sprigged pots were biscuit-fired, and later dipped in liquid lead-glaze for the 'glost' firing at slightly lower temperature, thus avoiding heavy wastage of glazed wares while making a product of consistent quality with a thin lustrous glaze. At first, bodies were globular and generous enough to accommodate turning and fluting, but probably sometime around the mid-1720s rather austere but supremely functional silver shapes were copied and embellished with white sprigs, often consisting of the royal arms flanked by its supporting lion and unicorn.

According to Simeon Shaw (in this case with some truth), Shelton was the locality favoured for their manufacture; apparently for no other reason than that the pioneers of this new redware were already established there rather than in Burslem, the main centre of earthenware production. For Shaw states that Joshua Twyford and Joshua Astbury, having obtained all the Elers' secrets by deception and having thereby caused them to leave the district, overcame the technical kiln problems that had caused the copious 'smoke and flames' suffered by the Elers and 'commenced and carried forward, manufactories of Red Porcelain, and White Pottery glazed with salt, amidst many thatched dwellings in Shelton'. Further, that 'Mr Twyford commenced business near Shelton Old Hall, the seat of Elijah Fenton's family . . . Mr Astbury commenced also in Shelton, near Vale Lane, at first. And both these persons made Red, Crouch, and White Stone Wares; using lead ore glaze for some vessels, and salt for those of more value'.[16] Their names are mentioned in the *Victoria County History of Staffordshire* as partners at Shelton Hill Top in 1717, after which they may have conducted separate potteries, no doubt continuing to make a similar range of wares. Twyford died in 1729, while a John Astbury is recorded potting at Shelton in the years 1728–44. Again, as late as 1751 the traveller Dr Pococke described a visit to some of 'the Pottery villages . . . to Stoke, where they make mostly the white stone. I then went a mile north to Shefly where they are famous for the red china';[17] from his description of the geography, 'Shefly' is clearly Shelton, and since he makes a distinction between 'dry red china' and 'glazed', we may conclude that Shelton was still famous for its lead-glazed redwares.

In fact, Shelton's pre-eminence in the manufacture of lead-glazed red earthenware teapots is also abundantly confirmed by excavations in the area. In 1965 the laying of an electrical cable in Broad Street, Shelton, revealed a cache of biscuit red earthenwares, all over-fired to a point where the clay body would not accept a lead-glaze, and probably representing part of the waste from a single firing. These consisted of bowls with lathe-turned bands and hand-cut flutes, coffee or chocolate cups, sugar bowls, a lipped bowl with single handle, small thrown teapots with white slip bands and bodies either plain or fluted, hexagonal teapots moulded with panels of Chinoiserie, and tall coffee pots with side handles. The shapes and the very limited range of mould-applied white decoration were entirely typical of the period 1730–40, and, apart from their general proximity to the potworks of John Astbury and Joshua Twyford, offered no clue as to their origin. At nearby Shelton Farm in 1992, however, archaeologists discovered the site of a major redware-producing pottery that operated also in the 1720s–1740s period, which coincided with John Astbury's tenancy of his Shelton pottery from 1728 until his death in 1744.[18] Here were found the bases of circular coal-fired ovens with seven, and later eight, fire-mouths, and a good range of wares covering the life of the pottery: early white stonewares, red earthenwares with white slip and sprigged decoration, press-moulded wares, slip-cast hexagonal teapots, and a dump of 1750s wares including glazed red earthenware, agate ware, refined blackware, red stoneware, black-bodied stoneware, salt-glaze and tortoiseshell creamware, and some later engine-turned glazed red earthenwares. The red earthenwares presumed to have been made by John Astbury – well-potted but otherwise unremarkable – seem to bear out Simeon Shaw's assertion that Astbury, and probably his partner Twyford, introduced this pioneering material to Shelton.

That other makers in the closely grouped pottery villages made identical wares, even at this early date, is clear from excavations at Samuel Bell's pottery at Lower Street, Newcastle under Lyme, operating at almost exactly the same time as John Astbury, 1724–44. To choose to build his potworks in a well-to-do town with good markets and roads, well away from the cluster of thatched pottery villages, Bell must have been ambitious. The time must have seemed right for him to move on from his trade of saddler to that of entrepreneur. Assuming that fine red earthenware was a recent development of the early 1720s, he would have been confident of being able to offer a new successful product that could easily

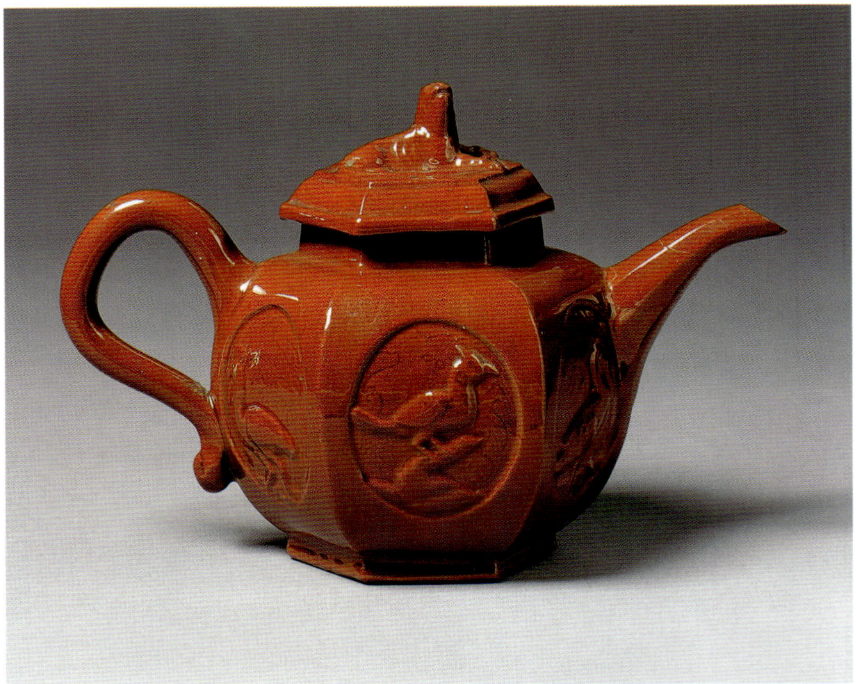

32
After about 1740s makers of red earthenwares such as Samuel Bell of Newcastle under Lyme attempted to adapt the material to the new technique of slip-casting, with results that were ill-defined and obscured by lead-glaze: this teapot matches excavated fragments. Red stoneware was developed in the late 1740s, almost immediately after this phase. Height 12.4 cm (4⅞ in.).
V&A: C.120–1980.

be exported from Newcastle under Lyme to wider markets; and it seems more than likely that he took advantage of the Elers' vein of red clay at nearby Bradwell. Certainly it may be presumed that he soon began the 'repeated experiments' that culminated in his patent in 1729 for

> red marbled stoneware with mineral earth found within this kingdom which being firmly united by fire will make it capable of receiving a gloss so beautiful as to imitate if not compare with ruby, that the stoneware may be formed into vessels for any necessary use or into ornaments for houses, gardens, such as flower pots etc.

In fact, although some thrown marbled wares – an age-old technique that could not be patented – were found in excavations, most of his manufacture seems to have been of plain redware sparsely ornamented with white slip. The actual subject of his patent seems to have been the curious novel technique of inlaying marbled bands of clay into the redware, usually around the lid and the belly of the pot – a technique that, though evidently not Bell's most prolific product, proved popular enough for Whieldon and others to make their own versions some years before the expiry of the 14-year patent in 1743. Whatever its merits, even when covered by a lustrous lead-glaze, these anaemic bands hardly 'compare with ruby', as claimed by the patent.

The excavation of Bell's pottery has been crucial for the interpretation of the development of red earthenwares.[19] Built of brick and tile and well-organized, with coal-fired kilns having eight fire-mouths, the works were designed for large-scale production of medium-quality wares. Apart from his high-quality red and marbled agate wares, Bell was probably one of the first potters to introduce slip-casting (plate 32) to enable manufacture of non-round teawares, in this case the familiar hexagonal teapots first made by the Elers (see note 12). His moulds, however, were made of low-fired biscuit earthenware with just enough porosity to act as a rather inefficient substitute for plaster-of-Paris.

33
Group of fragments from Fenton Low, Warburton factory, *c.*1751–60:
redware, V&A: C.97–1925; red stoneware, V&A: C.92–1925; Whieldon-type glaze, V&A: C.88C–1925; scratch blue, V&A: C.87F–1925; white earthenware, V&A: C.89A–1925; knife handle, V&A: C.242A–1925.

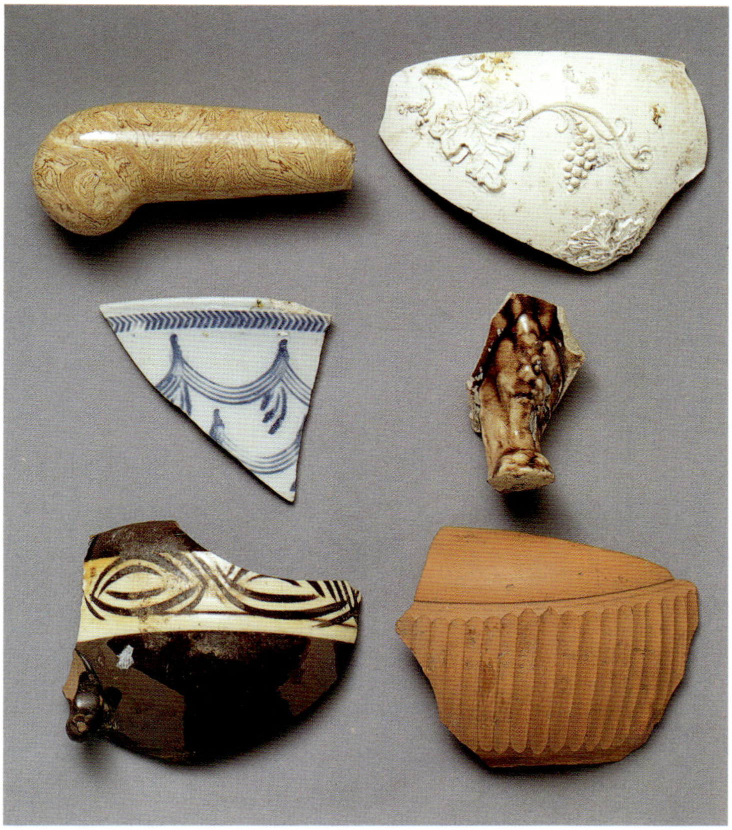

Potteries established in the 1740s still included red earthenware among their products. At Fenton Low, two excavations have revealed an impressive range of wares that for many years were considered to be products of Thomas Whieldon, whose pottery in reality lay at Fenton Vivian (or Little Fenton).[20] Red earthenwares with mould-applied white sprigging or with bands of white slip with sgraffito decoration were found, along with thrown agate wares, scratch-blue stoneware, blackwares and tortoiseshell wares and, significantly, red stonewares. Of the red earthenwares, the earliest would appear to be teapots with a central fluted band, of a type otherwise associated with the 1720s but here perhaps attributable to William Meir, who leased the factory in 1750–51, the rest almost certainly made by his successor Edward Warburton during the period 1751–61 (plate 33). As for Thomas Whieldon himself, he took over the Fenton Vivian pottery in 1747, at least a decade before the final decline of lead-glazed red teawares. Excavations have shown that, as might be expected, he manufactured the full range of contemporary wares, including thrown agate, red earthenwares with white slip and sprigged decoration, and all the blackwares, tortoiseshell wares and other early creamwares traditionally associated with him, particularly during his partnership with the young Josiah Wedgwood in the period 1754–9.[21] As at the neighbouring Warburton factory at Fenton Low, the introduction of unglazed red stoneware here in the 1750s must have heralded a new phase of fineware production.

If our view of ceramic history were based purely upon the evidence of surviving pots, as to a certain extent it has been in the past, we might be led to an assumption that the relative absence of early white stoneware – which later became such an important product for the development of the north Staffordshire potting industry – was due simply to the fact that it was undecorated, very cheap, absolutely ideal for its purpose, and therefore top of the list of expendable ceramics. There may be some truth in this, but the more one considers the evidence of excavated redware potteries such as those of Astbury and Bell, the more it becomes clear that the 1720s and '30s were indeed a period of redware supremacy, as the surviving number of pots would seem to indicate. Shaw tells us that Astbury and Twyford made white and brown stonewares as well as redware, but to judge from the excavated evidence Samuel Bell's highly productive pottery was founded in 1724 with the intention of making only redwares, and that nothing but redware was made until his death in 1744. The range of wares made by these potteries and by others in the vicinity was large: 59 individual designs were identified among the fragments excavated at the site of Bell's pottery. The need for affordable and practical teapots was surely the *raison d'être* for refined red earthenware in the early 1720s, but the material was soon adapted to other uses. For example, a substitute was needed for those lathe-turned brown stoneware and speckled lead-iron-manganese-glazed tavern mugs made from the early years of the eighteenth century, which was provided first by white stoneware and then by redware.

A range of tea and coffee wares was made, including cups, saucers and sugar boxes but surprisingly excluding tea canisters: it may be that the large number of surviving red teapots and coffee pots were always intended to complement Chinese porcelain cups and saucers, like their red stoneware successors. Some sort of development may be hazarded for the small lathe-turned teapots, in that the earliest seem to be those with raised bands fluted vertically with a gouge, while those with royal arms and either lion and unicorn supporters or little birds and squirrels may roughly be dated by comparison with white salt-glaze of the late 1720s. The derivation from salt-glaze, in fact, is suggested by a very rare class of teapot of brown-dipped white stoneware, having contrasting fine slip-trailed bands and the royal arms, the very use of which was probably inspired by those early eighteenth-century brown tavern mugs with an applied bust of Queen Anne flanked by lion and unicorn – in turn perhaps inspired by imported grey-and-blue Westerwald stonewares with 'AR' or 'GR' medallions. Some of these early wares exhibit an elegance and precision of form that betray more than a passing reference to metalwork: for example, the teapot and tankard in the Fitzwilliam Museum, Cambridge (Glaisher nos 618 and 623). Assuming that the quality declined as other alternative finewares became available, then the little teapots and much rarer tapering coffee pots with messily applied floral motifs should be late; and it is noteworthy that the raised decoration on slip-cast tea bowls was formed as part of the mould, crudely brushed with contrasting white slip to simulate applied sprigging.[22] The varying quality of the elaborate sprigging of ships, fortress and inscriptions that surround mugs commemorating the capture of Portobello in 1739 do suggest the onset of a gradual decline, while the introduction of moulded serpent teapot handles and spouts, as well as bird knops, suggests a date not earlier than the 1740s. Unusual forms with clumsy white sprigged floral decoration, such as the handled bowl with pouring lip and the wide-rimmed globular spittoon, also imply use of the material at an increasingly low domestic or tavern level. Other forms such as mustard pots are rare among survivals, but are well known from excavations.

As for the moulded wares, these would have begun after the new casting and pressing techniques were introduced around 1740, or perhaps slightly earlier depending on how we date Samuel Bell's efforts at using porous biscuit earthenware moulds. Most of the hexagonal teapots are of the type traditionally attributed to the Elers some fifty years before (see note 12), with a similar excellent sense of balance and proportion, while the low rectangular teapots with rounded shoulders were copied directly from early eighteenth-century Yixing wares – clear evidence that Staffordshire potters were familiar with even rare Chinese forms but often chose to ignore them. Many of the elaborate types, represented today by a surviving handful of camel and pectin shell teapots and gadrooned sauce boats of silver shape, were made in moulds primarily intended for white salt-glazed stoneware and must date from nearer the mid-eighteenth century, when red earthenware was losing its popularity. If in fact these soft earthenwares were attempting not only to imitate but also to compete with white stoneware, then they were doomed to failure: for not only was the fabric of these cast shapes often a light orange-red (possibly the result of blending clays to achieve good casting properties), but also the first appearance of white English porcelain at Chelsea and Bow in the mid-1740s must have fuelled a desire in the public mind for white teawares that only the thin and tough stoneware could satisfy. A further – and apparently desperate – attempt to develop the decorative possibilities of cast redware involved the application of pads of Samuel Bell's patented marbled inlay, as shown on a hexagonal teapot with marbled panels at Williamsburg, and a coffee pot in the Rosalie Wise Sharp Collection with moulded agate panels applied below the rim and around the lid. The late seventeenth-century design source for the Chinoiserie of the latter[23] links it chronologically with a hexagonal 'Grand Tartar' teapot, more commonly found in white salt-glaze and almost certainly dating from the early 1740s.[24] The extreme rarity of these ungainly pieces with inlaid panels, and the absence of excavated wasters at any site in Staffordshire, point to strictly limited manufacture. Additional colour on redwares was difficult to achieve, and oddly there are no signs of oil-gilding having been used on white sprigs, merely an occasional brush with underglaze cobalt-blue. A more successful development of lead-glazed red earthenware might have been the use of enamelled decoration, which was introduced and first applied to white salt-glaze from about 1740; but the teapot in the Harland Collection with sophisticated enamelled flowers and figures appears to be unique, and may even have been embellished in Holland rather than

Staffordshire.[25] When red stoneware emerged towards the middle of the eighteenth century, the rather severe cylindrical forms produced by the wheel and lathe were found better suited to sharp sprigged decoration than to enamelling in the *famille rose* style of some contemporary Yixing teapots.

Despite the addition of silver mounts and chains to some neatly finished – and probably therefore early – red earthenware teapots with well-defined mould-applied decoration, their absence from bills and inventories indicates a comparatively lowly status even from the beginning. The habit of tea drinking was indeed spreading to the lower strata of society, for whom these diminutive and inexpensive teapots would have been ideal. By 1721 a million pounds weight of tea was imported annually, and from the 1730s imports of tea began to exceed those of coffee: as Duncan Forbes wrote to Lord Tweedale in 1743, the practice was so common that 'at present there are very few Coblers in any of the Borroughs of this Country who do not sit down gravely with their Wives and familys to Tea'. In contemporary chinamen's bills, only the agate wares seem to have been distinctive enough to deserve an unambiguous description – for example, the '2 Marble Tea Potts' bought by the Duke of Atholl in 1744 from the dealer Hugh Jameson for 1s 4d, more than three times as much as white stoneware teapots in the same bill at 5d each. It is, of course, possible that these 'Marble' teapots were not thrown solid agate but had the bands of inlaid marbling as patented by Bell, or even bands of white slip with sgraffito decoration that may have been developed in order to by-pass the patent – all expensive and time-consuming additions to the manufacturing process.

Difficult though it is to be dogmatic about a subject whose history is charted only by sporadic clues, what evidence there is all points to a rapid decline of red earthenware after the mid-1740s, a time that coincided not only with the sudden development of moulded white stonewares, but also with the death in 1744 of two of the principal exponents of red earthenware, Samuel Bell and John Astbury (whose widow nonetheless continued operating his pottery until 1747). The finding of a single sherd of slip-cast red stoneware at Shelton Farm, matching the red earthenwares and almost certainly a late product of the Astbury pottery, suggests the introduction of the new material shortly before 1747, while also indicating minimal overlap, either chronological or stylistic, between the old and new types of redware. Thus, while wary of too-neat solutions, we are forced to conclude that during the decade 1750–60, after a production span of 25 years, the role of red earthenware began to change, in particular proving an ideal material for iron-and-manganese-glazed blackware: for example, in the years 1753–5 'Black painted tea pots' were being made at Hanley for 8s 6d per dozen, the unpainted pots selling for only 2s 6d,[26] and the inventory of 1761 of the porcelain and earthenware manufacturer John Baddeley includes 'Black & Red Warehouse . . . 80 Doz Red ware of sundry sorts at 12d. . . . 180 Doz Black ware at 2s'. Also generically known as 'Jackfield' because of its contemporary manufacture in Shropshire, this blackware formed an important product of many potteries during the 1750–80 period.

As for plain redware, its main role as a teapot material was made largely redundant when the Staffordshire potters finally decided to compete directly with red stoneware imported from Yixing. Although the exact dating of this is uncertain, the earliest known references to red stoneware are undoubtedly those in *Dr Pococke's Journey into England from Dublin* (1751), where it is implied that the manufacture was then in its infancy. Referring to Madely Hill in the Potteries (a brick-making area about six miles south-west of Stoke-on-Trent), he says:

> The red ware, in imitation of china, which they call the dry red china ware, to distinguish it from the glazed, is made of the red clay found here; but as it does not take among the common people, there is but little demand for it; they make garden flower pots of it, which are beautiful for the ladies' apartments.

This material, though refined and demanding a high degree of technical skill in its manufacture, had the great advantage of being once-fired and therefore comparatively cheap; and its association with expensive and fashionable 'china' gave it a status that may be deduced from its immediate appearance on chinamen's bills. For example, in 1751 the Duke of Atholl bought from James Carr a teapot of 'Red English Chenea' priced, like a tortoiseshell teapot in the same invoice, at 1s – which may usefully be compared with his purchase in 1753 of an imported 'Nankeen' porcelain teapot for 10s. A newspaper advertisement in 1753 advertised the clearance of a chinaman's stock 'under prime cost' next to the Blue Ball & Stag in King Street, Bloomsbury, with Red China at 5s per dozen, compared with Staffordshire White Ware at 1s 6d, which suggests that shops were buying at something over 5d each, to sell at about double. The chinamen Todd & Lamden of London supplied a 'Red Tea pott' for 1s in 1756, exactly the same price at which Wedgwood was willing to clear his stock of red china teapots in 1765.

If the making of red stoneware was inspired by a growing demand for teapots and coffee pots to be used with an équipage of Chinese porcelain, the discovery was not to be an immediate success. For Dr Pococke's visit of 1751 showed that the taste of the 'common people' was not susceptible to sudden change from its older ways, and that at first potters were compelled to adapt the material to make 'flower pots' for the mantelpieces and window ledges of elegant bedrooms. In fact, red stoneware, crisp, vitrified and impervious to liquids, soon proved considerably more adaptable than its predecessor, so that besides the many tiny teapots with applied prunus in the Yixing style that must have been affordable even by the poorest classes of tea drinker, enterprising potters devised a range of new forms that complemented their many types of lead-glazed earthenware. Of these, the earliest remained the most successful: as late as 1772 'Red China tea and flower pots' were listed as imports to New York.

Most of these forms owe nothing to China apart from the use of impressed imitation seal marks (plate 34),[27] which the potters would have found on imported wares as well as on any Elers products to which they had access. The sharp definition allowed by unglazed redware, first exploited on Roman Arretine

34
Apart from the similarity of Thomas Whieldon's press-moulded octagonal teapots to much earlier imports from Yixing, and some copies of more simple types, the red stoneware forms developed by Staffordshire potters from the late 1740s were wholly original and of superlative quality. It has been suggested that the seal on the cup and saucer was used by Josiah Wedgwood while at Burslem. Max. height 23.8 cm (9⅜ in.).
V&A: C.306–1951, C.25–1947, 2601–1901.

or Samian Ware through the use of detailed moulded ornament and the marking of potters' names with bronze stamps, also encouraged a revival of the Elers' technique of using fine brass moulds, which were applied to the surface of the pot. Exactly where these were made and by whom is unknown, for changing fashion has consigned them all to the foundries for re-cycling; but if the new trade of block-maker was advancing at great speed, so presumably were other skilled trades that supported the potting industry. Conventional Yixing overall ornament consisting of mould-applied flowers linked by hand-modelled trailing stems (the Chinese versions were actually fully moulded), which echoed the contemporary 'Whieldon' coloured earthenwares so often made by the same potters, was probably prevalent in the 1750s. With economy always in mind, potters appreciated that such decoration had the great advantage of being

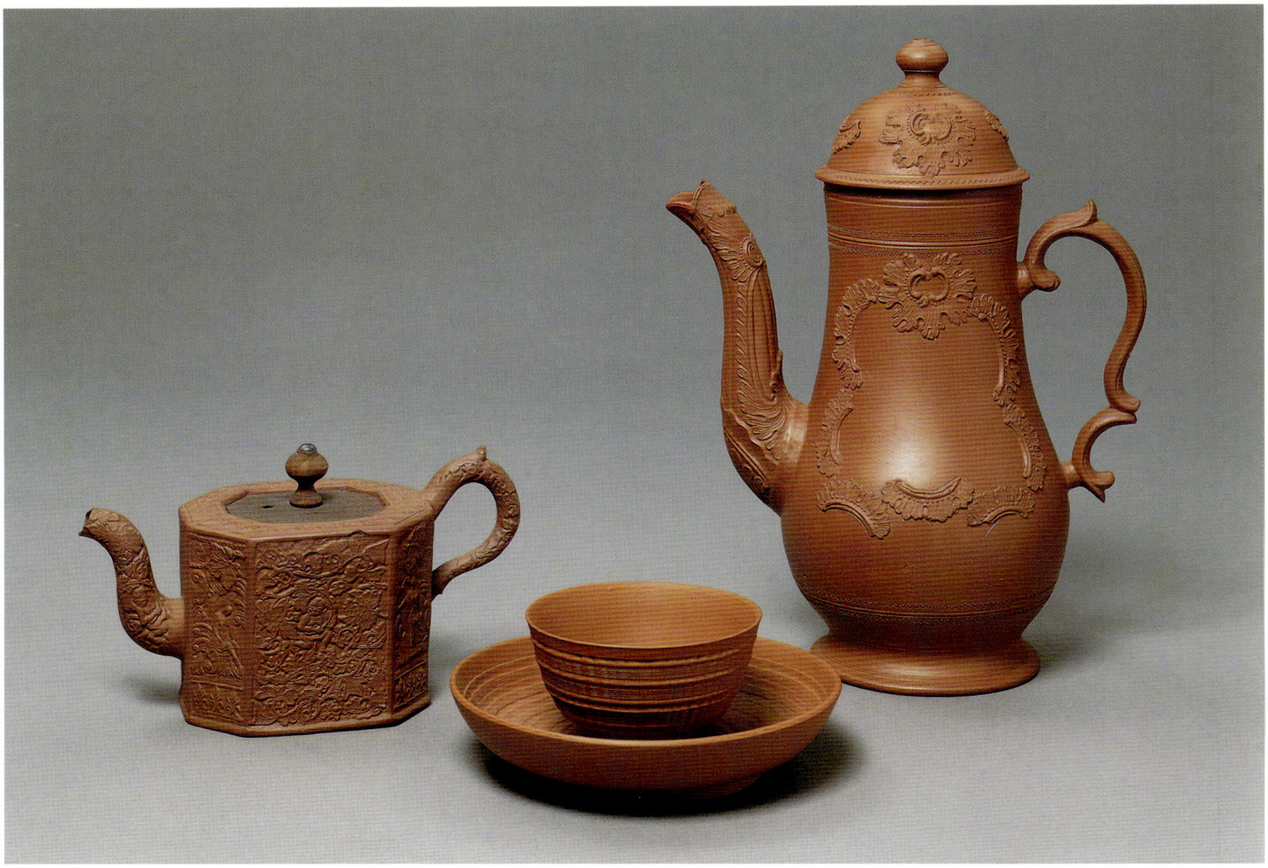

infinitely expandable, even to cover punch pots of great size. By about 1760, after the spread of English porcelain to a wider market and the establishment of transfer-printed decoration at Worcester in 1756, the tea-drinking public may well have expected up-to-the-minute crisp ornament in the fashionable Rococo style. The resulting range of finely executed mould-applied Chinoiseries, like nothing made in China, were used first on traditional globular teapot forms, but from the 1760s–1770s the barrel-shaped or cylindrical pots were found to be more suitable. Exact dating of these pieces is difficult since, with one exception, the pots themselves are never dated, and only two types of mould-applied sprig may be dated by virtue of being commemorative: the coronation of George III and Queen Charlotte in 1761, and the publication of Wilkes's no.45 edition of the *North Briton* in 1763.

Although the Elers had made capuchines and small *gorges* for beer, and although a few mid-eighteenth-century coffee cups and saucers survive, unglazed stoneware was generally considered an impractical material for drinking vessels. The Chinese themselves did not make red stoneware tea cups, and the cheaper grades of Chinese porcelain blue and white ('Nankeen') were freely available throughout England. Red teapots therefore predominated, with many cream jugs, miniature cream piggins and ladles, and very occasionally lidded sugar bowls and press-moulded square tea canisters. Press-moulded teapots had been made by the Chinese since the sixteenth century, exploiting the plasticity and fine grain of the material to reproduce every detail of the original mould: but apart from some early essays into the technique by Whieldon and others with their hexagonal pots moulded with Chinoiserie panels or with a traditional Chinese design of a boy among fruiting vines, comparatively little use was made of it. When fully developed, the material could be machined on the lathe with great precision, the blank areas filled with sharp mould-applied Chinoiseries and those delicate beaded swags more often seen on drab-coloured or 'ash' salt-glazed stonewares.

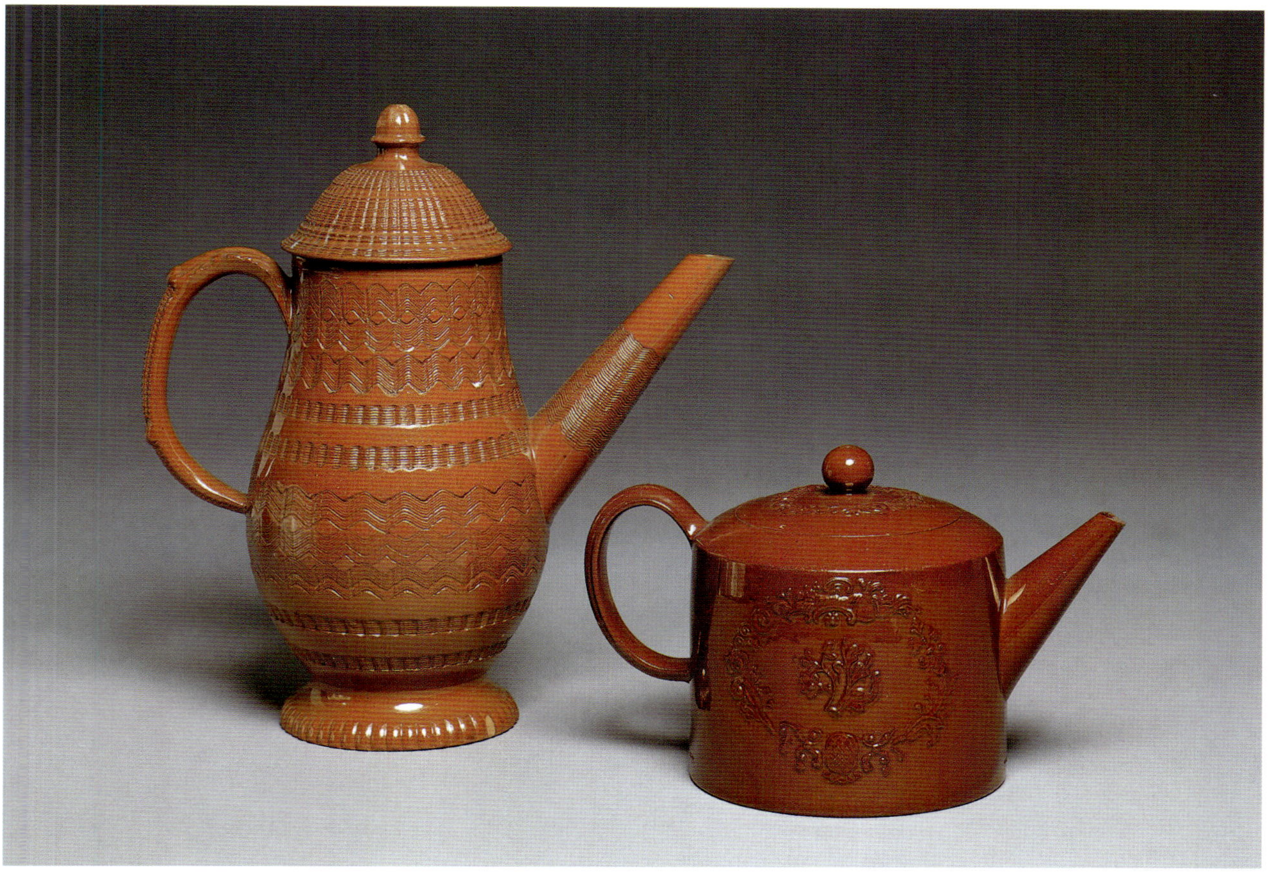

35
Simple cylindrical forms suited the age of Neo-classicism, and after Wedgwood's introduction of the engine-turning lathe in 1763, this extended the life of red earthenwares until the end of the 18th century. The teapot is marked 'MYATT'. Max. height 20.6 cm (8⅛ in.).
V&A: C.27–1940, C.15–1967.

It was, however, the machining capability of red stoneware that was to dominate its last phase, and finally to sever all links with its Chinese origin. Josiah Wedgwood, having witnessed the operation of an engine-turning lathe at Matthew Boulton's Soho factory at Birmingham, had obtained his own by 1763; and by 1769 the number had increased to three, which he moved along with their operators to the Ornamental Works at his new Etruria factory. At first applying it somewhat unsatisfactorily to lead-glazed creamware, he and his contemporaries quickly took advantage of the speed and ease with which a multitude of crisp wavy and zigzag patterns could be cut on the leather-hard clay by the action of the oscillating lathe headstock. Since the overall surface treatment rendered further decoration unnecessary, money was to be saved on making teapots that were already at the peak of their popularity. Nevertheless, outmoded Rococo sprigged and mould-applied ornament did continue in use for longer than might be expected, applied to the simple drum and elongated baluster shapes but matched with engine-turned spouts and functional basket-moulded handles. If the material's association with Chinoiserie was difficult to eradicate, at least the new engine-turned functional forms were devoid of extraneous ornament and not far removed from the late eighteenth-century potters' vision of Neo-classicism. So successful did this technique prove that it was soon applied to lead-glazed red earthenware, which enjoyed a new lease of life for the remainder of the century (plate 35).

The last quarter of the eighteenth century saw great upheavals in the importation and marketing of tea in England. Between 1770 and 1783, 5.8 million pounds of tea were imported and, after the tax that nearly doubled the price, offered for sale at an average of 8s per pound. Smuggling was rife, with captains of East Indiamen ships trading privately in the English Channel before landing their legal cargo, and high prices also encouraged merchants to defraud the public: legislation of 1776 forbad the adulterating of tea with, for example, sloe and liquorice leaves. Ironically, in view of the friction that resulted in the Boston Tea Party of 1776, this tax with its sliding scale was replaced by a flat rate in 1784, after which Thomas Twining was able to offer the popular Bohea tea at a mere 2s per pound. The subsequent huge expansion of tea drinking not only contributed to the success of new porcelain factories, such as Caughley and New Hall, but also ensured a future for the dry-bodied stoneware teapot. For even when complete sets of English porcelain teawares became widely available, the much cheaper and perhaps more durable red stoneware or basalt teapot continued to find favour.

For the later phase of redware production we may turn once more to the Wedgwood factory archive. Wedgwood himself saw red stoneware as an outmoded material that he disliked but continued to make for purely commercial reasons, as well as buying in stocks from his neighbours such as Sarah Meir from whom he ordered '19½ dozen red china teapots' in April 1763, or William Greatbatch, who supplied him with '9 doz China Tpts crooked spouts' at 4s per dozen in 1764, and in the following year with 58 dozen (though maybe not reckoned at 12 to the dozen) china teapots in three sizes at 4s per dozen. At the same time he was supplying dealers such as Robinson & Rhodes in Leeds in 1763 with '12 dry red teapotts some of them Crab tree sprouts [*sic*]', and a dealer called Hardy (perhaps Daniel Hardy, employed by Akerman & Scrivenors in London) with much 'red wrought ware' the following year. Although by 1765 he was referring to his red teapots as 'these falling stars', continuing demand compelled him to manufacture 'Engind red China' teapots in three sizes at 10s per dozen, coffee pots in two sizes, sugar bowls at 8d each and 'cream ewers' at 2d. As late as 1772 he wrote to his partner Bentley that he had made 'a quty of *common* red China Teapots to sell quite cheap' while also making a more expensive type of fluted pot: and it is tempting to identify his cheap teapots as those 'Red engine lath China tea pots of different sizes' imported into Philadelphia in 1771 or the 'Red China tea and flower pots' sent to New York in 1772. The successor to these excellent pots was finally launched by Wedgwood in 1776, when he reluctantly acquiesced in Bentley's proposal to develop a new type of red stoneware in the Neo-classical taste: 'I am afraid that where one spectator thinks of Antico Rosso an hundred will be put in mind of a Red teapot'.[28] Certainly, while the more popular market was supplied by cheap engine-turned red earthenwares until the end of the century, it was to be some years before red stoneware could satisfactorily be combined with Neo-classicism:[29] then, in the early years of the nineteenth century, the dense black of the popular moulded basalt teapots was most successfully paired with the new purple-red and covered with crisp geometric ornament in the Egyptian style.

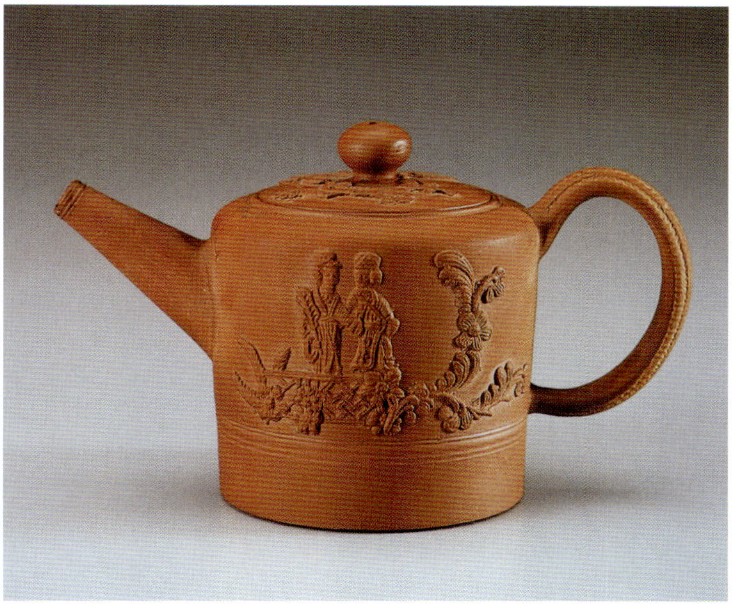

36
The modeller William Greatbatch established his own pottery in 1762, supplying other potters with both his moulds and his products. Excavations have proved that he never 'mould-applied' decoration from metal moulds, but always used the larger-scale sprigged decoration. Height 7.6 cm (3 in.).
Courtesy of Henry Weldon.

Identification of the huge number of surviving red stonewares remains hazardous despite the use by many makers of impressed seal marks on pots with mould-applied decoration or engine turning (but not, apparently, on sprigged wares). Even though the once-fired stonewares would have suffered relatively fewer kiln losses than twice-fired earthenwares, sites in Staffordshire and elsewhere have yielded many deposits of wasters, some of which may be tied to nearby manufacturers while others are clearly isolated groups dumped by contracted middlemen far from their place of manufacture. Where it has proved possible to form groups of pots bearing the same seal marks, it has also been possible to record large numbers of associated types of ornament or idiosyncratic detail, although the likelihood of independent mould-cutters supplying identical moulds to several potteries must cast an element of doubt upon attributions based on ornament alone.

As mentioned above, the Astburys at Shelton Farm were responsible for an early hexagonal slip-cast teapot, of which a few examples have survived, while a deposit of sprigged teapots and engine-turned red earthenwares – along with agate, refined blackware, salt-glaze and tortoiseshell ware – may be accounted for by later tenancies of the factory. At Fenton Low, fragments of teapots sprigged with trailing vines are attributable to Edward Warburton, who occupied the pottery from 1751 to 1761, and at Thomas Whieldon's factory nearby at Fenton Vivian, operating between 1747 and 1780, a good range of red stonewares was found, including the flattened octagonal teapot fully moulded with the Indian Boy, the lid having a knop in the form of a crouching rabbit, wares sprigged with trailing vines and roses, and hexagonal teapots with moulded panels containing Chinese figures of a type usually made in lead-glazed earthenware. Two seal marks were found on the site. At the Foley, the finding of a large waster dump of red stonewares with mould-applied decoration of the period 1765–70 has enabled some 40 pots to be identified as almost certainly the

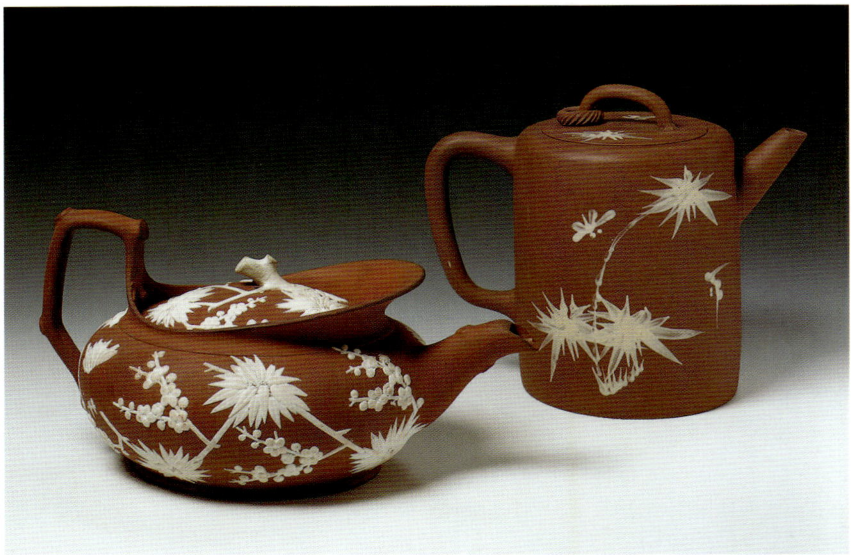

37
Wedgwood disliked red stoneware but developed this *Rosso Antico* colour to please his partner, Thomas Bentley. In the period 1800–10 Wedgwood & Byerley used this body to imitate contemporary Yixing wares with 'White Chinese flowers'. Max. height 10.8 cm (4½ in.).
V&A: 259–1870, C.33&A–1947.

work of Thomas Barker, who potted on the site from the 1750s to 1789.[30] Other sites such as Town Road, Hanley, yielded wasters that are attributable to the Church Works nearby, possibly made during the tenancy of Humphrey Palmer, one of the leading potters of his generation. Apart from the Barker site, the other major find of recent years has been the discovery of William Greatbatch's factory dump, the filling of which formed useful archaeological layers, and which spanned the period 1762–82.[31] Here were found Greatbatch's own products, many of which may also have been supplied to other manufacturers, notably Wedgwood as mentioned above. The many wares of Phases I to II (*c.*1762–70) were either decorated with Greatbatch's small repertoire of distinctive Chinoiserie sprigs (plate 36), Minerva and the Two Oriental Ladies predominating – or engine-turned. Phase III (*c.*1770–82) was represented solely by engine-turned stonewares, and these of a more everyday quality, which suggests a declining market. Since Greatbatch was himself a modeller, it is virtually certain that all the designs found were peculiar to his factory, and that the presence on some pots of his seal mark incorporating the disguised signature 'WG' would have been no obstacle to their being supplied, for example, to Wedgwood to fill urgent orders. It may well be that for this very reason the close-knit band of Staffordshire potters may have agreed to use complex Chinese-type marks that were identifiable only by themselves. The absence of mould-applied decoration on Greatbatch's pots does also support the theory that brass moulds could not be made on the factory premises, even by skilled mould-cutters, but were supplied by outside specialists in the metal trades.

The great salt-glaze manufacturers John & Thomas Wedgwood of the Big House, Burslem, also made red stoneware when white salt-glaze was losing popularity in competition with the new creamwares. References in John's account-book for 1762 to '6 Red China (tepots)' suggest limited production, but an intriguing mention in the same year to supplying their cousin Aaron

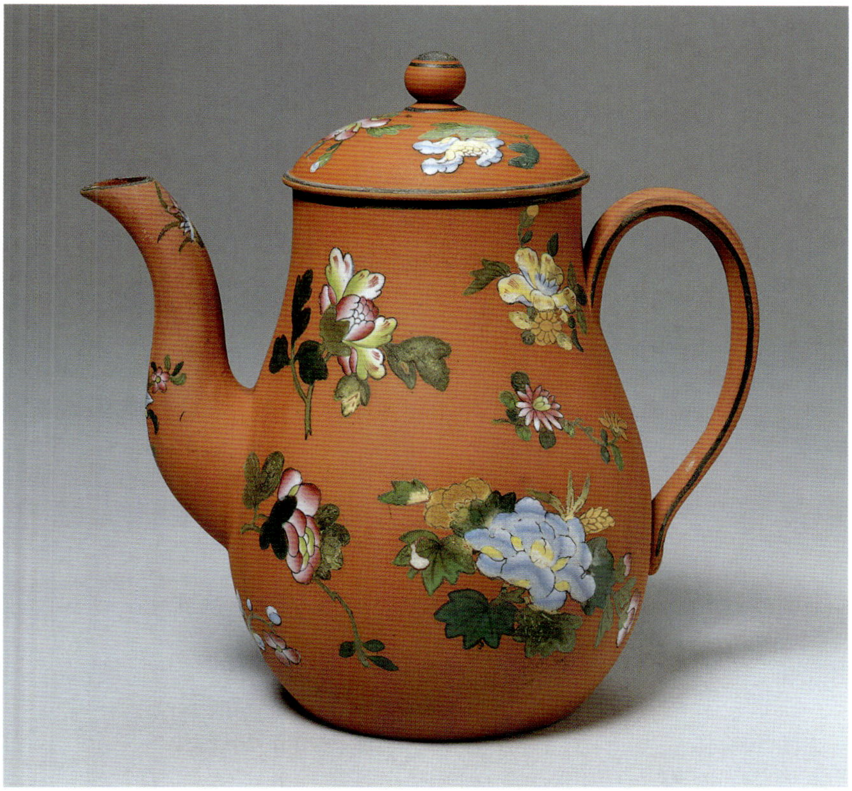

38
Lighter red stoneware became popular towards the middle of the 19th century, being made wherever suitable clay was found. At Lowesby in Leicestershire, Sir Francis Fowke, related to the architect of the original South Kensington Museum, operated a pottery around the years 1845–50 specializing in fine enamelling. Height 18.1 cm (7⅛ in.).
V&A: 2376 &A–1901.

Wedgwood with 'Ash & Red Teapots' could be taken to refer to a class of dark red cylindrical teapots closely copied from Chinese prototypes, on which the body was given a wide band of greyish slip as a background for large sprigged red dragons. As for Josiah Wedgwood himself, his rather disparaging views on the material are quoted above. None of his products was marked and it is not surprising that, although attempts have been made to link a seal mark incorporating 'W' with his name, none of his products at the Bell Works at Burslem or at Etruria has positively been identified. It is likely, however, that some of the red stoneware teapots and barrel-shaped cream jugs delicately moulded with a country house viewed across a park with sheep and cattle – similar to block-moulds in the Wedgwood Museum, which presumptuously have been identified with a 'landskip' pattern supplied by Greatbatch – were his products.

Engine-turned teapots did fill the gap between the decline of relief-decorated redwares from about 1770 until the great rise of Pearlware, cheap moulded wares with high-temperature underglaze colours, and especially Black Basalt at the end of the eighteenth century. Late examples include stoneware and earthenware pots marked 'ASTBURY' and made at Lane Delph by Joshua Astbury (1728–1780, son of John Astbury of Shelton), and similarly undistinguished pots marked 'MYATT' by Richard Myatt of the Foley, operating between 1781 and 1796 (and perhaps the same Richard Myatt who offered two potworks for sale at Lane End in 1771). They were also made outside Staffordshire. Excavated fragments of the period *circa* 1760s–1780 from the Indeo Pottery at Bovey Tracey were drum-shaped and unremarkable, though happily bearing a distinctive seal mark of a squared spiral. Invoices of 1790 for the Swinton Pottery in Yorkshire list 'Red China Tea Pots', which have not been identified and, in any case, would doubtless not be distinguishable from those engine-turned teapots 'en terre rouge' made at the Leeds Pottery at the same period. Many of these, of course, would have been intended for export to the Continent.

The public finally tired of the red teapot about 1800, when the popularity of smart black with its classical associations was given a massive boost after the discoveries resulting from Napoleon's Egyptian campaign in 1798. The late attempts by Samuel Hollins of Shelton to produce purple-red engine-turned teapots and jugs with experimental borders of silvering (now always tarnished to black, and preceding the reinvention in 1805 of non-tarnishing platinum lustre) were so dark as hardly to be called red. And the fact that no other manufacturers attempted to imitate them suggests a lack of commercial success. At the Wedgwood factory, however, the red and black Egyptian wares of the early nineteenth century were successfully copied by Spode (see plate 28) and others, to be succeeded by a new type of brick-red stoneware with bright enamelled flowers, or sprigged with spiky white Oriental flowers in imitation of the white-slip painting found on contemporary Yixing teapots (plate 37). After a lull the material was once again taken up with a vengeance by F. & R. Pratt, who applied colour-printed friezes in the revived classical taste of the mid-nineteenth century, as well as by other factories at Bishop's Waltham, Torquay, Swansea and other places where suitable clay was to be found (plate 38). Objects such as neatly turned tobacco jars and water coolers were mainly produced, although the clay did also attract the attention of the designer Dr Christopher Dresser, who recognized not only its superb moulding and lathe-turning characteristics but also the inherent possibilities for mass production. At the present day in China, the potters of Yixing, unaffected by the vagaries of changing fashion for types of 'Red China' acceptable to Europe, continue exactly as before to make extremely cheap thrown, turned, moulded or sprigged teapots of all sizes for the local market as well as for the West. Besides these commercial productions made for a pittance by anonymous potters, an elite class of 'designer' teapots are made by notable craftsmen who sign their work for collectors both in China and the West.

1. For the development of hot beverages in England, see Brown (1995).
2. Illustrated and discussed by Duysters (1998).
3. Elliott (1998).
4. *Royal Society Philosophical Transactions*, 17 (1693), p.699.
5. Shaw (1829), p.121; Elliott (1977).
6. Britton (1990).
7. Weatherill (1971), pp.160–81.
8. Morris (1947), p.177.
9. Godden (1979), p.38.
10. Wedgwood MSS, University of Keele: E.18772–25.
11. Valfré (2000).
12. Dr David Barker has doubts about these hexagonal teapots as Elers products, because of the excavation of a stylistically similar red stoneware sherd at Shelton Farm, and their general resemblance to white salt-glaze teapots of the 1740s. On the other hand, they are perfectly slip-cast, superbly finished and of a style quite consistent with a date in the 1690s. The slip-cast lid and lion finial with distinctive encircling tail are also found on the enamelled salt-glaze teapot of *c.*1700 in the V&A, attributed to David Elers's pottery at Vauxhall.
13. Rackham (1942).
14. Jonathan Horne Antiques, *English Pottery* (exhib. cat., March 2003).
15. Pulver (1985), quoting from the account-book of Captain Thomas Bowrey's china shop in Goodman's Fields, Mansell Street, in the parish of St Botolph, Aldgate.
16. Shaw (1829), pp.125–6.
17. Pococke (1751), p.7.
18. The pottery operated in the years 1720–21 by Fenton & Hill, 1721–8 by Machin & Fenton, 1728–44 by John Astbury, and 1749–63 by Thomas Taylor. For a brief account of the excavations, see Barker (1992).
19. Bemrose (1973, 1975).
20. Morley-Hewitt (1954).
21. Mountford (1972) and Halfpenny (1997).
22. I am grateful to Miranda Goodby for pointing out this unusual feature, which is clearly seen on unglazed wasters at the V&A.
23. John Stalker and George Parker, *A Treatise on Japanning and Varnishing* (1688), and also Croxall's edition of *Aesop's Fables*. Discussed by Grigsby, 'John Stalker and George Parker's *Treatise*' (1993) and 'George Edwards and Matthew Darly's *Chinese Designs*' (1993). The coffee pot is illustrated by Sharp (2002), p.40.
24. From the Luxmoore Collection (whereabouts now unknown), illustrated in Burlington Fine Arts Club (1914), pl.XLVII, no.45. The source of the Grand Tartar decoration is discussed by Grigsby, 'Johann Nieuhoff's *Embassy*' (1993).
25. Illustrated Burlington Fine Arts Club (1914), pl.XLVII, no.41.
26. Angerstein (2001), p.340.
27. Price (1957, 1962, 1963), and Barker (1996).
28. Wedgwood MSS, University of Keele: E.25–18578.
29. By the 1780s red stoneware was beginning to be associated, in terms of colour at least, with Greek red-figure vases. The Pompeian Gallery at Packington Hall designed by Joseph Bonomi in 1784 for the Earl of Aylesford included 60 Yixing red stoneware teapots: see Allen (1988–9).
30. Barker, 'A Group of Red Stonewares' (1991).
31. Barker, *William Greatbatch* (1991).

CHAPTER FOUR

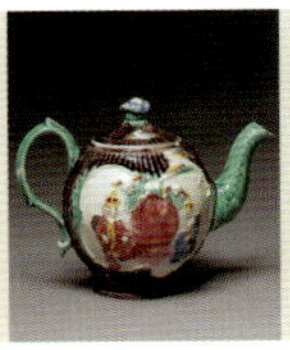

Cream Colour: The First 'Designer Pottery'

'A species of earthenware for the table, quite new in appearance, covered with a rich and brilliant glaze, bearing sudden alterations of heat and cold, manufactured with ease and expedition, and consequently cheap' perfectly sums up what we now call 'creamware', and shows the success of the young Josiah Wedgwood in achieving these aims, stated just before the start of his lengthy experiments at the Ivy House pottery in 1759.[1] But the importance of this statement, no doubt repeated by Wedgwood himself for the benefit of historians of the Staffordshire Potteries,[2] has since been inflated to the point where 'Cream Colour' has been considered as one of Wedgwood's greatest original inventions. This is far from the case, as recent authors have been at pains to point out (but the odds against historians making a fair assessment of developments in Staffordshire during the second half of the eighteenth century were always high).[3] For after Thomas Whieldon, by far the most successful potter of the generation before Wedgwood, had turned his back on the potting trade so completely as to demolish his factory in 1780 to make an ornamental garden, the way was clear for the ambitious Wedgwood to break with the familiar tendency for master potters to 'take the money and run' and, instead, setting an example to the later Spodes, Mintons and others, to found a major manufactory as a grand legacy for his children. The continuity of such an enterprise also ensured the survival of its archives,[4] which in the case of Wedgwood's factory at Etruria included not only moulds and pattern books, but also his copious personal correspondence upon which so much of our knowledge about this period is based. Thus the winner took all, to the historical detriment of his fellow potters, whose excellent products Wedgwood was happy to pass off as his own.

It was actually as early as the 1720s that the first glimmerings of the new material began to emerge, some forty years before the improvements of Josiah Wedgwood. This stemmed from the new white salt-glazed stoneware, refined by the addition of calcined flint and clay imported from the West Country, which was also to provide the basis for the creamware body, and for which the history goes back to sometime shortly before 1719, when the dealer John Akerman at the Rose & Crown in Cornhill was advertising 'white stone ware'. Simeon Shaw, apparently confusing the stories of the simultaneous development of early dipped white salt-glaze and lead-glazed redware, attributes the invention of 'Cream-coloured stone ware' using calcined flint to Thomas Astbury of Lane Delph around 1725, while describing only the typical 'Astbury' redware with white sprigs.[5] At this point, there is a 15-year gap in Shaw's story of the development of Cream Colour, probably because, as the number of surviving red earthenware

39
The excellent overglaze printing carried out by Sadler & Green in Liverpool perfectly complemented the smooth blank areas on thrown creamware jugs and mugs made in Staffordshire, Yorkshire or Liverpool itself. 'Commerce Revived' probably refers to the short-lived Peace of Amiens of 1802. Height 23.2 cm (9⅛ in.).
V&A: 3642–1901.

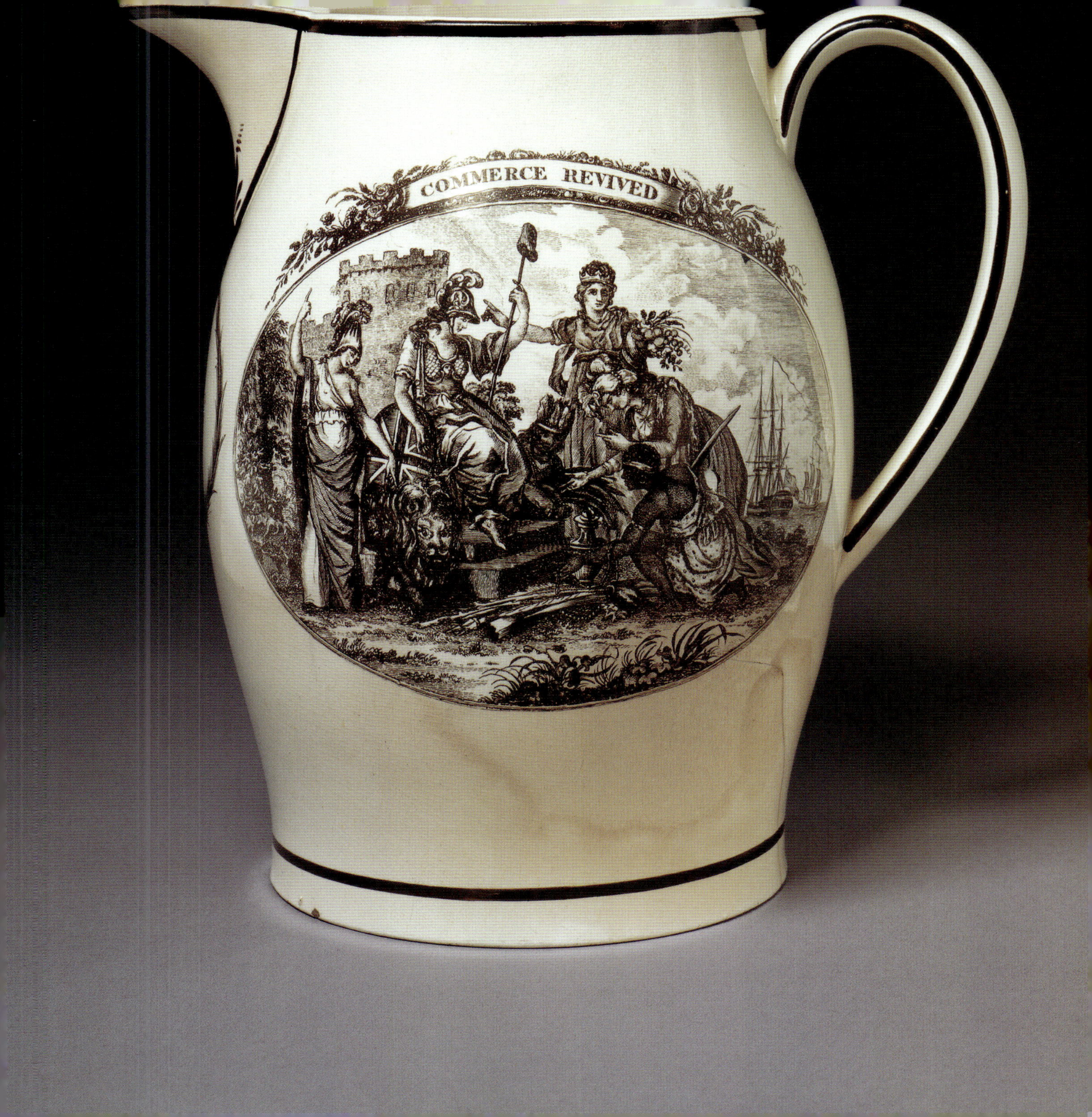
COMMERCE REVIVED

teawares would strongly suggest, production of these fine redwares, together with a limited range of white salt-glazed stonewares, kept potters fully occupied during the 1720s and '30s.

Later, Shaw picks up the threads with his statement that,

> About 1750, another introduction of fresh materials, or a different application of those previously employed, was beneficial to the person and to the whole district. Mr Enoch Booth, of Tunstall, first united the Clays of the neighbourhood carefully levigated, in union with those from the South of England (Devon, and Dorset) and a certain proportion of Flint, on Mr Astbury's method. This body he first glazed with lead ore; next he mixed it with one of the clays, and then added a little dry calcined flint in powder; and finally he used lead and flint in a liquid state, on Littler's method, but with this difference; Littler dipped the *clay* ware into his liquid; but Mr Booth fired his once, and dipped the Bisquet ware.

Some writers have taken this to mean that Enoch Booth introduced the use of both liquid lead-glaze and biscuit-firing, an interpretation that, in view of the fact that 'Astbury' wares from the 1720s onwards were biscuit-fired and glaze-dipped and that delftware had been manufactured in a similar way in England since the sixteenth century, is highly improbable.[6] A careful re-reading of the passage shows that Shaw was simply crediting Booth with *combining* two existing processes: the use of a blended clay/flint body previously developed for salt-glazed stoneware, and the liquid lead/flint/clay glaze invented for the 'Littler's Blue' stoneware, which he described on pages 168–9. He does clarify this by mentioning that Littler's once-fired stonewares were raw-glazed, whereas Booth's twice-fired earthenwares were dipped in lead-glaze.

Although many of Simeon Shaw's statements have been disproved, a surprising number of his opinions, culled from oral history and the fading memories of old inhabitants, have been shown to have at least a grain of truth; and where there is no other evidence, this can be of great value in determining who was responsible for making all the various crucial advances. His date of 1750 for Enoch Booth's improvements does agree with William Pitt's account in *Topographical History of Staffordshire* of 1817, in which he states that 'CREAM-COLOURED WARE, was first made in the year 1750, by Enoch Booth, of Tunstall, near Burslem'; but both dates may be taken as approximations since Booth's prolific potting activities may be charted through his signed pots to some years earlier, namely a scratch-blue mug signed 'Enoch Booth 1742',[7] a creamware punch bowl painted in cobalt-blue and manganese-purple signed 'EB 1743',[8] a large footed punch bowl with underglaze painted decoration inscribed 'WG 1743',[9] a teapot signed 'F. Morgan, Tunstall, Oct.20th 1743'[10] and a scratch-blue loving cup with 'EB 1754'.[11] Other unsigned pieces of early creamwares include three teapots (plate 40) and a tea canister.[12] All appear to be the work of one painter familiar with the painting of English delftware, the crucial piece being the teapot of 1743 in the Weldon Collection, whose decorator has been plausibly identified as Francis Morgan, apprenticed to a Liverpool potter in 1733 and recorded as a potter in 1741.[13] If we accept all these early creamwares as the work of Enoch Booth and his hired decorator – no doubt a tiny part of his vast production of salt-glaze – then we must also credit his pottery with introducing major advances in decorating techniques to the Staffordshire Potteries: underglaze painting in oxide colours, and the introduction of reserve panels on a powdered ground,[14] a technique copied from Chinese porcelain and much favoured by English delftware factories during the 1740s and '50s, and by the Bow porcelain factory around 1758–62. By the 1760s the enterprising Enoch Booth had become a major supplier of enamelled salt-glazed teawares.[15]

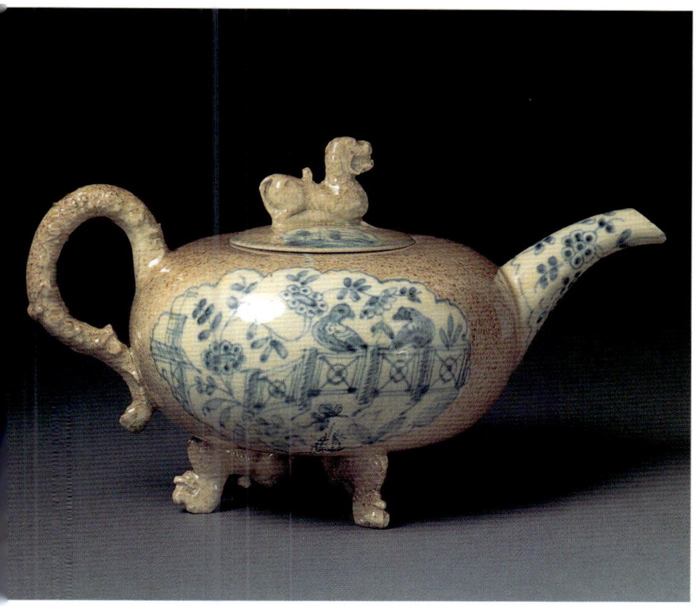

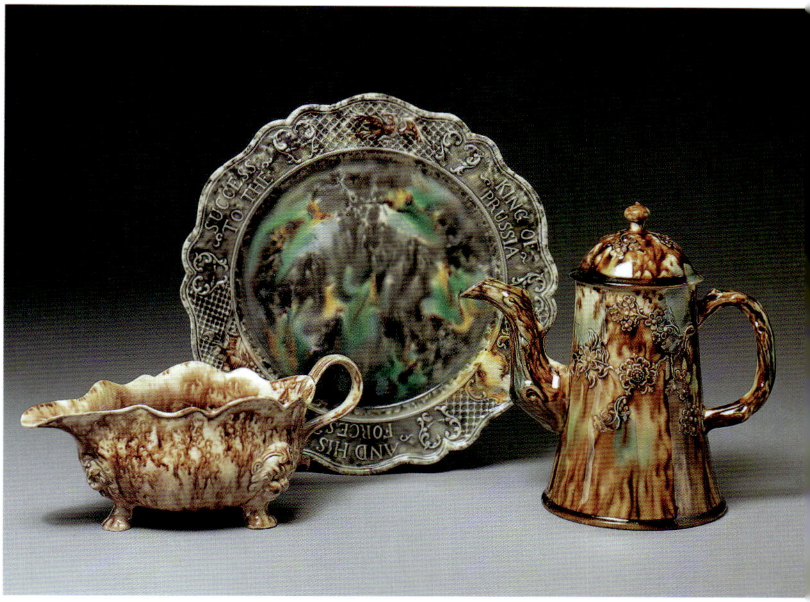

40 (ABOVE LEFT)
Enoch Booth has been credited with developing in the 1740s the first cream-coloured earthenwares, of which a closely related group survives. Height 10.5 cm (4⅛ in.).
V&A: C.66 &A–1989.

41 (ABOVE)
Before the improvements of Wedgwood in the 1760s, creamware was usually coloured, most commonly sponged underglaze with manganese and iron to imitate tortoiseshell. Max. height 17.8 cm (7 in.).
V&A: 2128–1901, 2123–1901, C.9–1940.

If Booth was the pioneer, then others were not slow to take up the baton. By 1749 we have the first mention of 'Cream Colour', as supplied by Thomas Whieldon in 1749 to Thomas Fletcher:[16]

1 Doz. plates Tor	8 0
2¼ Do [ditto] plane	2 6
2 2 dish	2 –
1 do [ditto] painted	2 –
1 do Creamcolr.	1 8
5 pails	2 6

There are several interesting points about this list. First, it shows that creamware was then considered mainly as a vehicle for overall coloured decoration, particularly tortoiseshell (plate 41), for which the price commanded was 8d each as opposed to just over 1d for a plain salt-glazed plate. Secondly, it lists enamelled two-dish (two-cup) salt-glazed teapots at exactly twice the price of the plain, which shows that (exactly like engraved wineglasses) any added decoration could double the cost. Thirdly, it shows how expensive was the plain twice-fired 'Creamcolr.' which could afford no imperfections in its manufacture. At the time, Whieldon was one of the leading potters of his generation, and there is no reason to suppose that his prices or range of wares were any different from those of his fellow potters.

Apart from Thomas Whieldon of Fenton, in the two decades before the final improvements achieved by Josiah Wedgwood, production of creamware seems to have been mainly associated with two dynastic potting families, the Warburtons and the Baddeleys, one of Shelton, the other of Cobridge. While Burslem – and in particular John & Thomas Wedgwood of the Big House – produced most of the common white stonewares, it was particularly Shelton that fostered major advances during the second quarter of the eighteenth century, from the red earthenware of the Astburys to the first creamwares of Enoch Booth. Unfortunately, although scattered references by early writers like Simeon Shaw suggest the relative importance of these potters in the local hierarchy, comparatively little corroborative evidence survives. With neither marked pots nor excavation reports, we may only guess at their early products on the basis that these were almost certainly interchangeable with those of their neighbours, notably Whieldon, whose range of products is now known from excavation.

Writing less than eighty years after the event, Simeon Shaw recorded of the Warburtons and Baddeleys that 'In 1751, were made the last improvements of Cream Colour. (prior to those of the late Mr Wedgwood,) by Mrs Warburton, of Hot Lane . . . and also by Mr Baddeley, of Shelton, a good potter and very worthy man'.[17] Elsewhere Shaw claimed that it was at Warburton & Co. that 'the first Cream-Colour Pottery was manufactured on the improvement of Mr Enoch Booth's fluid glaze'.[18] As for the products, an invaluable guide to these is given by the journals of R. R. Angerstein made during his travels in England in the years 1753–5, in which he visited the Potteries and purchased samples:

> Sales Prices of embossed and tortoise-shell ware.
> Tea pots from Joh. 'Worverton' [Warburton]. Each dozen
> consists of 12, 18 or 24 according to size.
> Tea pots, white ware 1s.6d.
> Cream colour ware with lead glazing 6s.
> Bush [Ash] grey colour with lead glazing 6s.
> Orange colour with lead glazing 6s.
> Red China, not glazed 5s.
> Agate colour, lead glazed 6s.
> White ware, enamelled 8–12s.[19]

This list comprises the whole repertoire of Staffordshire fine earthenwares of the mid-eighteenth century, including the new red stoneware of which the Warburtons appear to have been pioneers. Securely identifiable surviving products are limited to a rather undistinguished globular creamware teapot with crabstock handle and spout, covered with hastily applied sprigged foliage and birds brushed with green and brown glazes, incised on the base 'Warburton Ann': this may probably be dated shortly after 1761 when Ann Warburton succeeded her husband as Master Potter, and is entirely typical of the mass of anonymous creamwares made in Staffordshire during the third quarter of the eighteenth century.[20] A letter from Burslem, reproduced in the *Virginia Gazette* of 30 June 1768, does not mention Wedgwood, but instead states that 'Though our stone ware has been universally used, yet until our turnpikes were made few people ever saw our manufactures, but now they are gazed at as a novelty. The Ladies go to Warburton's to buy the Queen's sets of cream coloured ware'.[21] Besides specializing in the enamelling of salt-glaze and creamware, Ann Warburton and her sons had many dealings with Josiah Wedgwood from 1762 onwards, supplying 'Wedgwood' wares for resale.

Much is known about John Baddeley, mainly through his financially disastrous involvement with Messrs Reid & Co. in porcelain manufacture.[22] After Baddeley's partnership with John Mare was dissolved acrimoniously in 1749, he continued making pottery, forming a partnership with William Reid in 1755 to make porcelain, for which in the following year he began to build a new factory at Shelton. For business reasons, he then leased this to Reid & Co. in 1759, making 'Flint Ware, Biscuit China Ware, Red & Black Ware' until the bankruptcy of William Reid and all his partners in 1761 put an end to the china-making branch. Now in some financial distress, he immediately found a compatible partner in Thomas Fletcher. The factory thrived, employing as many as 40 persons in 1762 and supplying during the period 1753–67 as many as 100 crates every two months to the agent Alexander Parks in Amsterdam. By April 1771, the year John Baddeley died, Wedgwood could refer to 'Mr Baddeley who makes the best ware perhaps of any of the Potters here, and an ovenfull of it per diem, has led the way' in cutting creamware prices to those of white salt-glaze in order to survive a trade recession, from which it was hoped that the new Russian trade would rescue them.

John Baddeley's wares were never marked, for he supplied many other potters including the Warburtons, Booths, Daniels, Josiah and Ralph Wedgwood. Besides regular shipments of wares to Holland, in 1766 he is recorded as supplying the Liverpool delftware manufacturers John Dunbibin & Co. with 'Crates by Sea', presumably destined for their warehouse at Southwark in London. Some details may be gleaned from surviving records (see note 22), for example, an undated reference to '[Wi]cker Work Baskets & Stands', in 1761 '40 Doz: Tortoiseshell plates of sundry sorts', the purchase of block-moulds from Greatbatch in 1761–2, exchanging pineapple ware for Wedgwood's printed ware in 1762, bartering 'Coly Flowr Blocks' with Wedgwood in 1766, only to sell back to Wedgwood a month later '6 Doz Coly cups & saws'. This all confirms the healthy working relationship that existed among these interrelated potteries, which faced common problems and shared a common market; and it raises questions not only about the credibility, but also about the importance, of identifying similar wares made by different potters from shared block-moulds.

While the Warburtons and Baddeleys were building up their businesses by making a full range of creamware-based products, during the period 1754–9 Josiah Wedgwood was in partnership with Thomas Whieldon, the leading potter of his day. Whieldon, like Enoch Wood some years later, was content to mass-produce unadventurous wares for general consumption, supplying the demands of the market without seeking to create markets by introducing new products. This made him an exceedingly wealthy man, no doubt providing his partner, the much younger Wedgwood, with an object-lesson in how to acquire wealth with the minimum of risk, while enabling him to pursue his experiments into clays and glazes. He later stated that white salt-glaze was the backbone of the business, and that he improved both the colours and the glazes of Whieldon's creamware and agate ware. However, to complete the story of the development

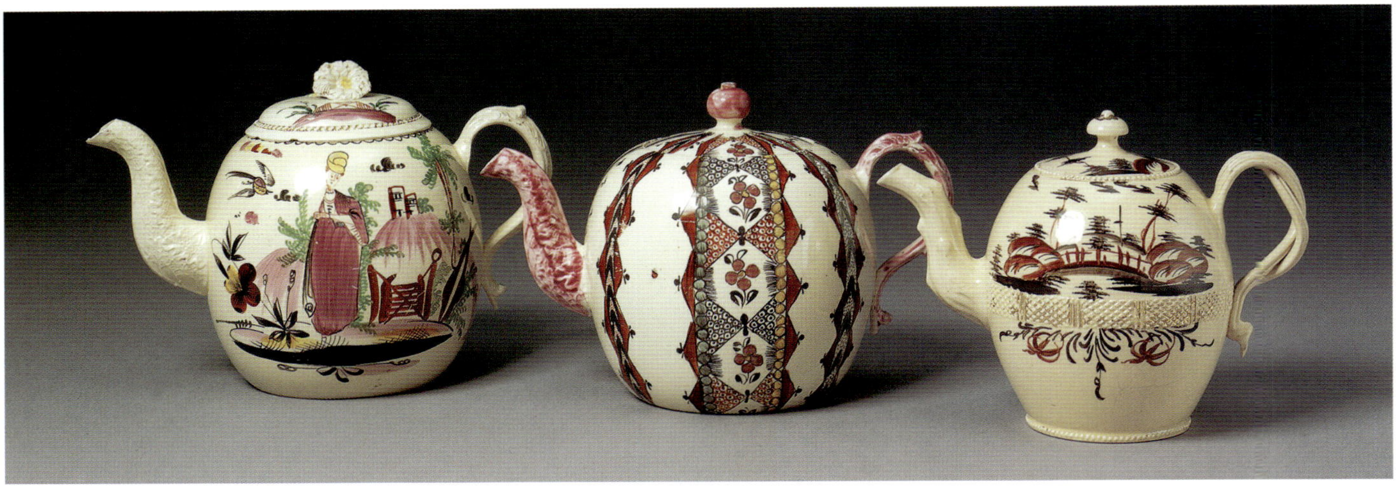

42
The firm of Robinson & Rhodes of Leeds was responsible for distinctive styles of decoration, both landscapes with figures and wild abstract patterns. Many Leeds Pottery wares and Wedgwood (middle) passed through their hands. Max. height 3.7 cm (5⅜ in.).

V&A: C.1407–1924, C.203–1926, 2281–1901.

of creamware, it is necessary to start at the Ivy House pottery where Wedgwood established himself in 1759 after parting from Whieldon. For it was here that he began his Experiment Books with the aims stated at the beginning of this chapter, making full use of the clay bodies and glazes that he had developed during his partnership.

The story of Wedgwood's success in refining creamware and its carefully matched glaze has been told many times.[23] The breakthrough point came when the material was considered capable of displaying its beauty naked, thus enabling it to imitate the elegant Neo-classical boat and urn-shapes of Sheffield plate made at Matthew Boulton's fashionable Soho factory in Birmingham – well known to Wedgwood and the source of the engine-turning lathe that he purchased in 1763. As the two materials had common links, both being impostors in the sense that they were cheap mass-produced substitutes for silver and porcelain, it is likely that even at this stage Wedgwood may have set his heart on building a model manufactory to which fashionable society ladies would flock. He realized almost immediately the possibilities of his refined material for plain tableware, which, quite unlike the dimpled grey surface of salt-glazed stoneware, also offered a smooth shiny ground for decoration. As early as 1761 he was corresponding with Sadler & Green in Liverpool about adapting their tile-printing process for use on his new creamware by adding topical overglaze prints (see plate 39), beginning a mutually beneficial trade that escalated from a modest £30 per month in 1763 to £600 by 1771. In 1763 he acquired an engine-turning lathe from Matthew Boulton, and in the same year he engaged the services of Robinson & Rhodes of Leeds (plate 42) to enamel his creamwares, eventually establishing his own decorating studio in Chelsea in 1768 and persuading David Rhodes to run it for him.

In order to create a lucrative market for his creamware among the 'Middling Classes', Wedgwood first needed to have his common earthenwares accepted at a high social level: in his words, to 'begin at the Head first, & then proceed to inferior members'. Having sent a parcel of engine-turned samples to Queen Charlotte in 1765, shortly afterwards he was offered by her agents a commission for a Staffordshire tea and coffee service for 12 persons, an order that he was quick to accept, safe in the knowledge that the future benefit of royal patronage would greatly outweigh any financial loss incurred in fulfilling the special order. Alas, the 'complete Sett of tea things, with gold ground & raised flowers upon it in green, in the same manner as the green flowers that are raised upon the mehons [melons]' has not survived, but Wedgwood's astuteness paid huge dividends, culminating in his appointment as Potter to Her Majesty on 9 June 1766, the naming of his product 'Queen's Ware' and the addition of the sign of the queen's arms to his London showroom. Having met the urbane and cultured Thomas Bentley in 1762, the building of his new Etruria Works in 1769 enabled him to take him as partner in the Ornamental branch, in which capacity he proved an indispensable asset, expertly steering the Wedgwood factory through the changing whims of London fashion and maintaining the steady rise of its reputation through the social hierarchy.

Despite the growing production of luxury objects such as vases and medallions, however, Wedgwood's interest in adjusting the colour of his creamware to the fickle public taste never waned. As early as 1768 he was experimenting with a lighter cream body, hoping to satisfy a new demand for 'white' that encouraged the potters of Staffordshire to develop their 'China Glaze' – what we now know as Pearlware – and which probably indicated that although traditional buyers of Chinese blue and white were turning to Staffordshire creamware, they were loathe to lose completely the familiar greyness of porcelain. In fact, although the public expected Wedgwood to lead this new fashion, it was the fear of his products being compared unfavourably with porcelain – whether Chinese or Worcester – that held him back from launching too soon a type of white ware that he considered less than perfect. In 1770 he outlined in a desperate letter to Bentley the difficult choices he faced: first to continue as before with his new whitened wares; secondly to accentuate the colour further by making it straw-coloured (which would greatly please the Russian and German market); and thirdly just to follow the fashion and develop a new white ware. In the event, he continued his experiments to perfect a new body while hoping, perhaps, that the fashion would fade. Having referred in 1775–6 to his

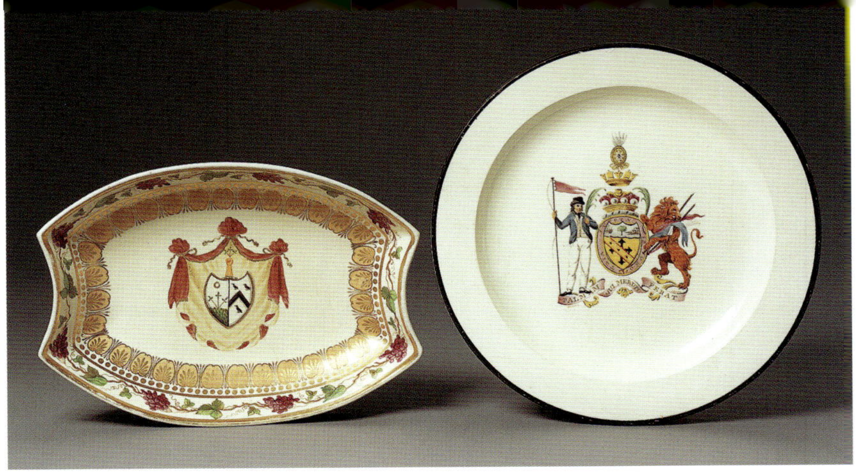

43
Armorial decoration on creamware was offered by Wedgwood and his contemporaries, as well as by many independent decorators, as a substitute for the unobtainable Chinese armorial porcelain. J. Eaves of Bristol signed this plate enamelled with Nelson's arms, while Wedgwood's Chelsea decorating studio specialized in fine armorials, often now unidentified. Max. diameter 25.1 cm (9⅞ in.).

V&A: 3135–1901, 2321–1901.

'good old Creamcolour, painted & varied in every way we can invent . . . I cannot at present find it in my heart to relinquish my good old Creamcolour', it was not until 1779 that he was finally satisfied with the new 'Pearl White' body, which incorporated added Devon clay and flint with a cobalt-stained glaze. Nevertheless, he considered this merely 'a change rather than an improvement'. This body, though never used for the cobalt-blue Chinoiserie decoration that Wedgwood much disliked, at least provided a good substitute for Chinese porcelain and for the armorial creamware services decorated at his Chelsea studio (plate 43).

The subsequent history of creamware and Pearlware can also be followed through the archives of the Wedgwood factory. Long after Josiah Wedgwood's death, the production of blue transfer-printed Pearlware finally began in 1805 under the partnership of Josiah Wedgwood II, John Wedgwood and Thomas Byerley; but three years earlier a fully whitened version of creamware described as 'something like the French Fayence' had been developed to bring the factory into line with current trends. With a much tougher body requiring a higher firing temperature, this could only with difficulty be fired with the old creamware; and, later, it formed the basis of the 'Granite Ware' dinner services and washstand sets exported to America and elsewhere in such vast quantities by many Staffordshire potteries from the 1840s onwards.[24]

Having followed the thread of creamware development from its roots in the 1720s to its transmutation into 'White Ware' in the early nineteenth century, it is necessary to return to the 1740s to explore the many other important applications of this most versatile material. The main sources of information on these are Simeon Shaw, the *Travel Diary* of R. R. Angerstein dating from 1753–5, and excavations of the factory sites of the prolific potters Thomas Whieldon and William Greatbatch.[25] Apart from the white salt-glaze that was a staple product of most potteries, and wares made from red clays, the range of products around the middle of the eighteenth century consisted of Tortoiseshell, Agate, Ash Grey, Orange, Green and Gold, Moulded Wares such as cauliflower and pineapple, and Melon Ware.

As we have seen, tortoiseshell with sponged oxide decoration beneath a lead-glaze was first mentioned in 1749. It was used for the popular plates moulded with 'Success to the King of Prussia' of the late 1750s, and remained popular even during the 1760s alongside fully developed plain and printed creamwares. The decoration was simple to make, relying on the melting glaze to mix and spread the randomly applied iron and manganese during the firing, so that it could be applied to any form or any size of pot, from plain teapots to pierced and sprigged baskets, not to mention some early figures (plate 83). Other colours could be added, and a brush might be used to apply these to the biscuit-fired pots in a consistent way.

So-called Agate Ware was apparently developed even earlier, and perhaps specifically for cutlery (plate 44), paving the way for the fashionable Chelsea and Bow handles of the 1750s; for Nathaniel Jeffreys of the Strand advertised in 1740 that he 'has had the Honour of serving a great many Gentlemen of the first Rank in the Army, with the fine new fashion Staffordshire-Handle Knives and Forks for the Camp . . . at the lowest prices'. Simeon Shaw stated that agate handles were one of the important products of the Whieldon-Wedgwood partnership of 1754–9, and indeed as early as 1749 Thomas Whieldon was recorded as supplying '32 dessert handles'. The technique of making Agate Ware allowed for great flexibility in the design, colour and scale of the veined patterns. It could be made up into blocks, then rolled or squeezed to reduce the size of the original pattern, then cut into slices and rolled into a sheet. It could also be thrown on the wheel,

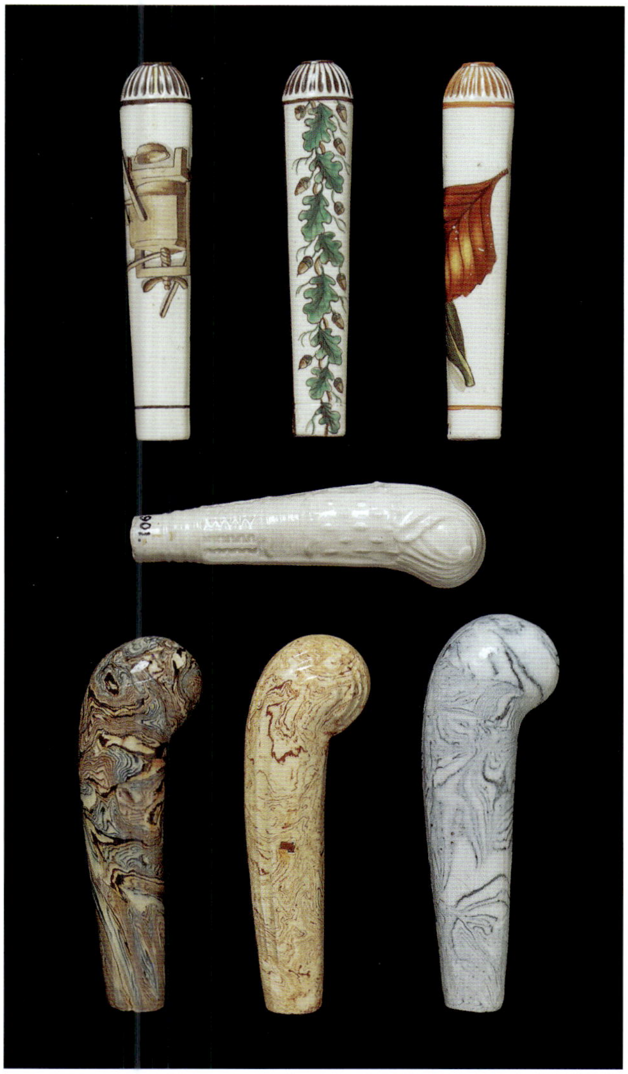

44
The fashion for both earthenware and white porcelain knife-handles flourished in the mid-18th century, agate handles forming an important product of Whieldon's pottery during his partnership with Wedgwood in the years 1754–9. Later, Wedgwood produced finely painted creamware handles for dessert knives.

Three from a set of samples, V&A: 2332 to E–1901, the others, V&A: 3168–1853, 2114 &A–1901, 2229–1901.

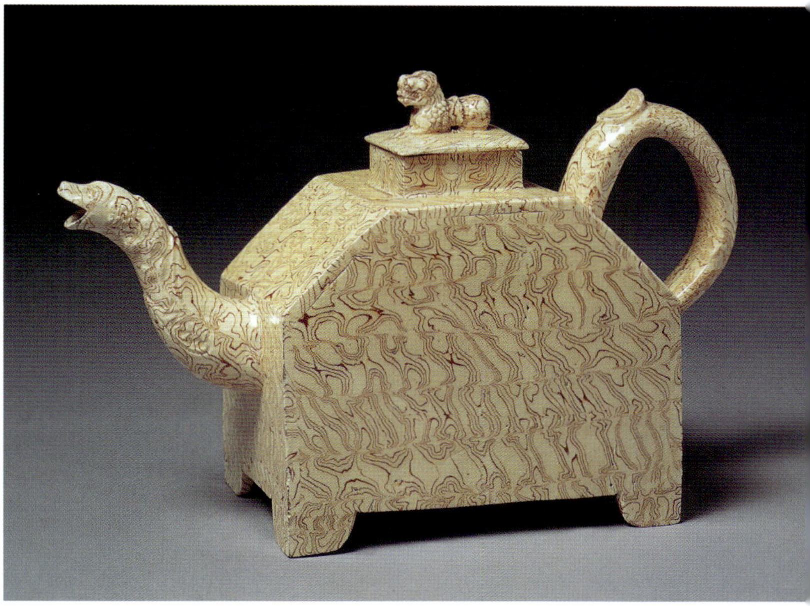

45
Cream-coloured earthenware could be stained or simply given coloured surface decoration. In the 1750s–1760s sheets of agate clay lent themselves particularly to slab-built forms. Height 13 cm (5⅛ in.).

V&A: . CIRC.427-1967.

with perhaps some risk of stretching the pattern: cruder traditional thrown pottery using red and white clays generally display a striped spiral effect. To a certain extent, the agate technique may be said to have influenced design, for example in the highly decorative slab-built teapots (plate 45); but for shapes like spoon trays and sauce boats it could be pressed into open moulds, while for globular teapots two moulded hemispheres could be expertly (and almost invisibly) joined around the girth. Surprisingly, the few surviving price lists show that it was quite cheap, with teapots costing only about 6s per dozen in the 1750s. Fairly sophisticated and like no other type of ceramics, it remained popular at least until the 1770s, when 'cream colour'd ware, red china tea pots . . . cream, aggit, delf, black and white stoneware, and crates of flat and hollow ware for country consumption' were still being imported into America.[26]

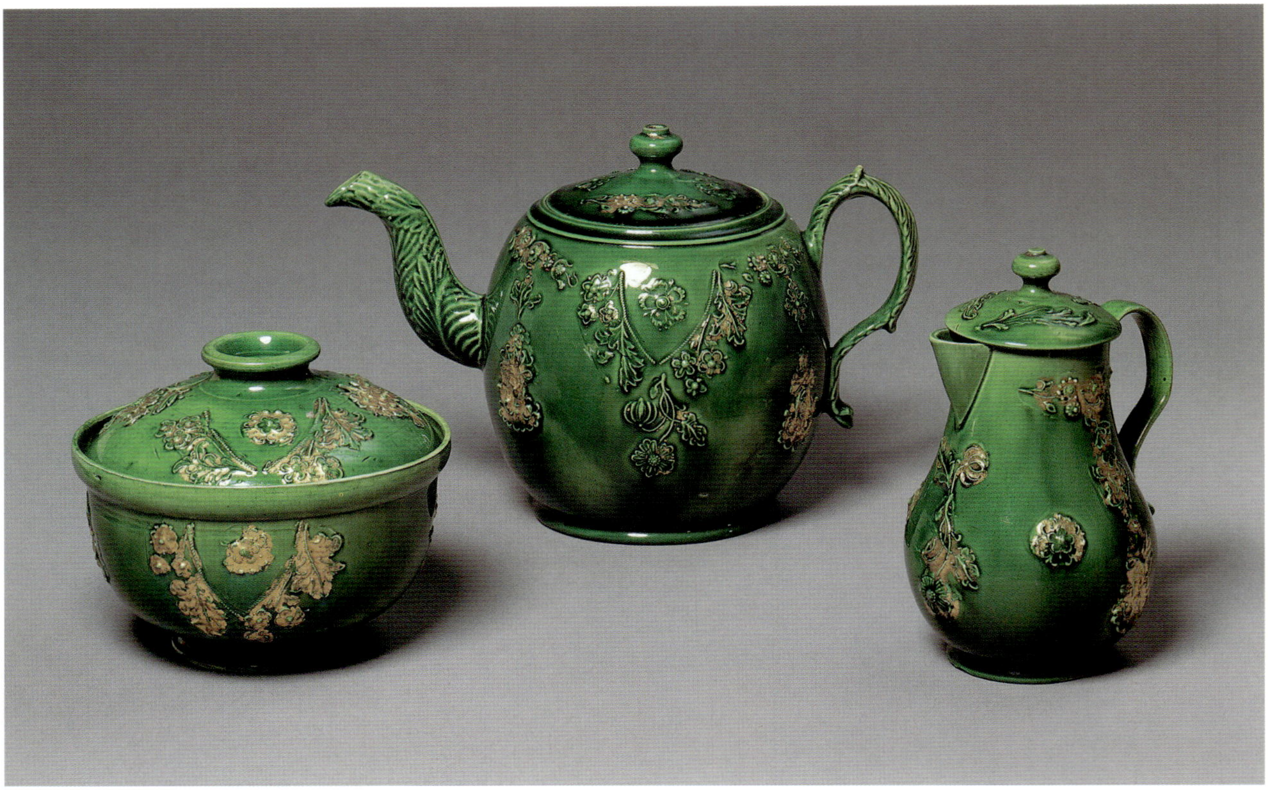

46
The bright copper-green glaze developed by Wedgwood during his partnership with Whieldon was used to good effect with 'cold' gilding. But by 1766 Wedgwood was dumping his old stock onto the export market. Max. height 3.3 cm (5¼ in.).
V&A: 891, 892, 894–1905.

The various types of creamware with white or oxide-brushed sprigs on a coloured slip ground were made by most potters, and it is only the account of 1753–5 by R. R. Angerstein that enables us to identify what may well have been their 'trade' names: for example, the grey 'ash' that is no doubt similar to the salt-glazed stoneware version with delicate white sprigs made by John & Thomas Wedgwood in the 1760s and '70s.[27] The 'orange' must surely be the apricot-coloured ware that has survived in some quantity, and which seems to have been popular as late as 1782, when it is found on ale mugs commemorating the victories of Admiral Rodney. As for sprigged creamwares dipped in coloured glaze, it was Josiah Wedgwood's experiments during his partnership with Whieldon that perfected these translucent copper-green and iron-yellow glazes. Although Queen Charlotte specified a tea and coffee service with gold ground and green sprigs, the striking combination was more usually, and much more easily, produced the other way around. It has been suggested that Wedgwood himself made green and gold wares at his Ivy House Works in the early 1760s, as proved by a tea canister with what appears to be his signature.[28] The fashion was short-lived, however, since by 1766 Wedgwood was dumping his surplus stock on undiscriminating markets: 'Pray sell all the green and gold for Pensecole, the new discover'd Islands, or where you can, for I never will make it again . . . I am quite clearing my Warehouse of Colour'd ware, am heartily sick of the commodity' (plate 46).[29] By 1774, in a reflective mood, he would comment rather disparagingly that

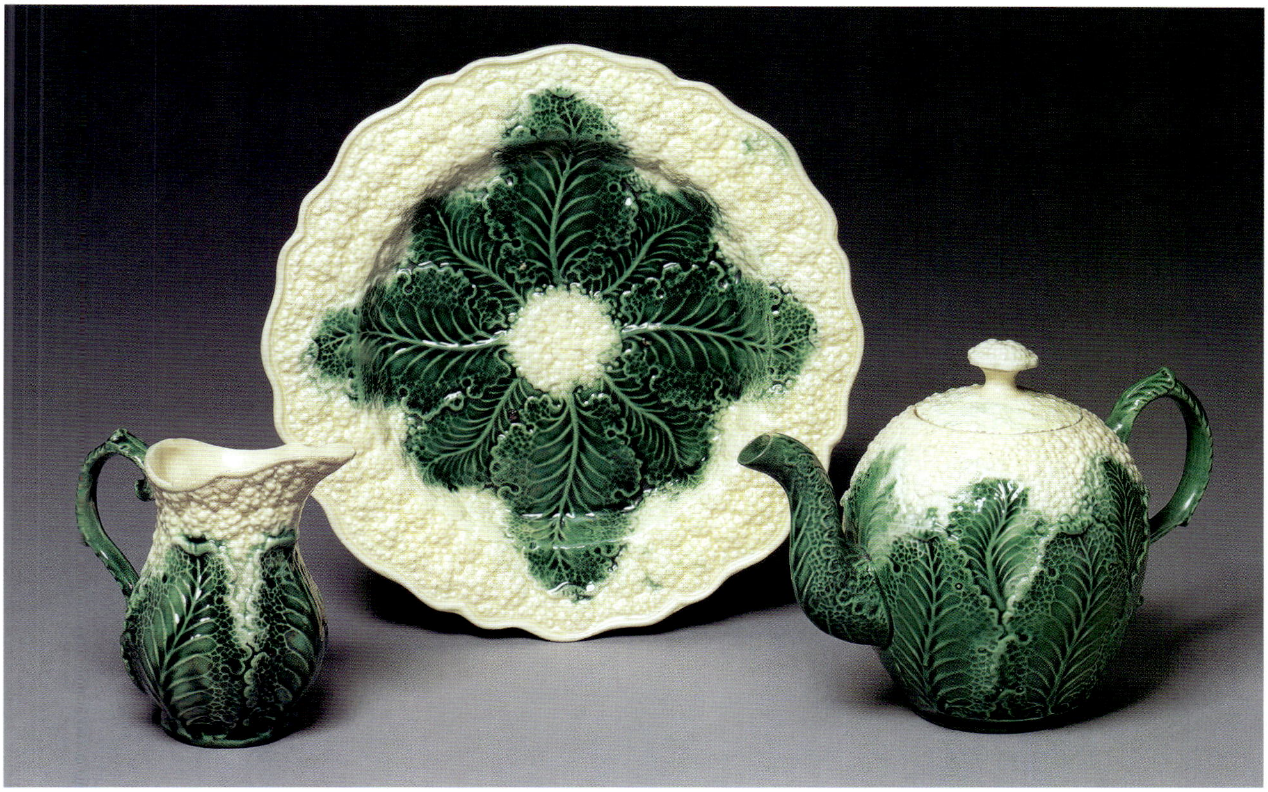

> the Agate, the Green & other colour'd Glazes have had their day, & done pretty well, & are certain of a resurrection soon, for there are, and ever will be a numerous class of People, to purchace *shewy* & *cheap* things. The Creamcolour is of a superior Class, and I trust has not yet run its race by many degrees.[30]

47
Innovative Cauliflower and Pineapple Ware cleverly combined the block-making skills of William Greatbatch with the coloured glazes developed by Wedgwood in the 1750s. Max. height 19.7 cm (7¾ in.).
V&A: 2272–1901, C.1242–1919, C.23–1940.

The invention of moulded creamwares decorated with coloured glazes (as opposed to underglaze sponged oxides) was a phenomenon wholly in keeping with Rococo taste of the mid-eighteenth century, while its great technical and artistic success was due mainly to the emergence of a generation of talented

Staffordshire block-cutters, whose products were perfect vehicles for the bright translucent green and yellow glazes developed by Wedgwood in the 1750s (plate 47). The related Melon Ware, necessarily round because of its lathe-turned rouletted background, was embellished with applied leaves under striped yellow and green glazes. The principle figure involved in this wholly original Staffordshire creation was William Greatbatch (*c.*1735–1813), who had worked for the Whieldon-Wedgwood partnership during the 1750s. By 1762 he had established his own pottery, which sold block-moulds to Baddeley and Wedgwood during the 1760s, for example, and supplied Wedgwood during the period 1763–4 with 200,000 pieces of pottery. An exhaustive analysis of the finds excavated from his pottery site at Fenton has shown that the cauliflower, pine-apple, pineapple-and-basket and melon wares made throughout the life of the

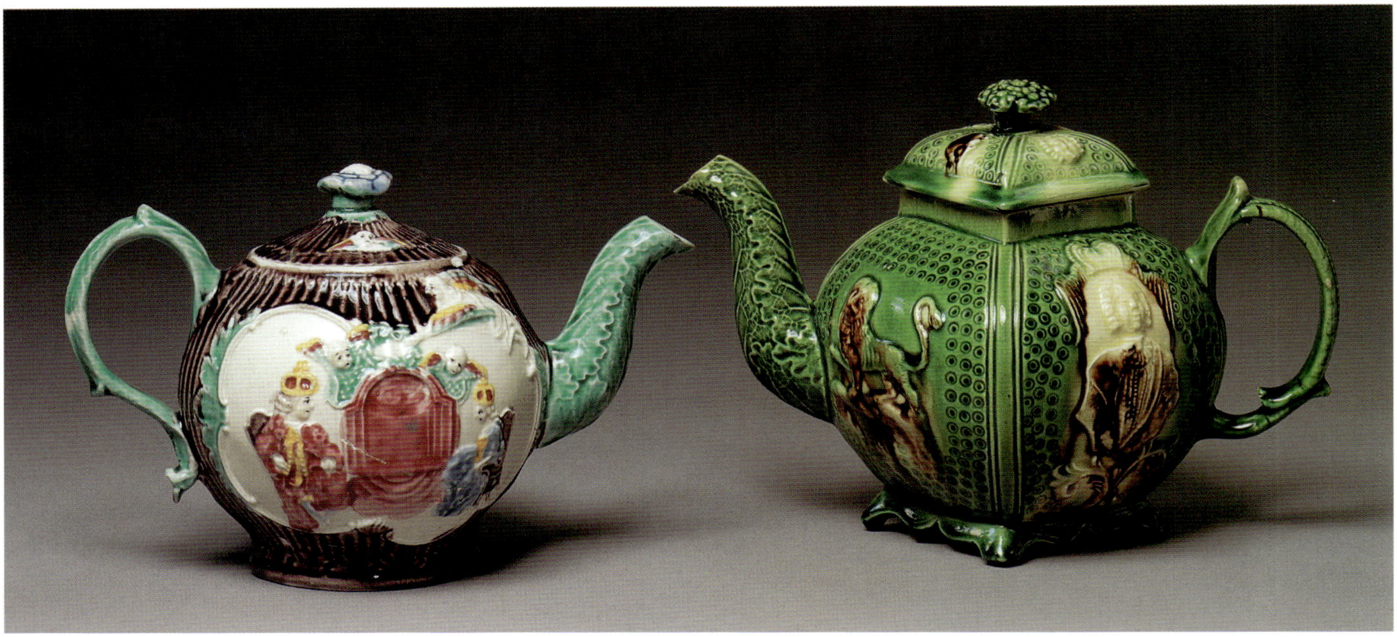

48
Creamware proved highly adaptable, and capable of quickly commemorating important events, such as the coronation of George II and Queen Charlotte in 1761 and the alliance with the King of Prussia in the late 1750s. Max. height 24 cm (5½ in.).
V&A: Sch.II 187, C.19–1938.

factory from 1762 to 1782 were manufactured from a recognizable set of block-moulds, and that this holds true for other factories whose sites have been excavated. Small but significant differences in factory moulds have been isolated and published for the potteries of Thomas Whieldon at Fenton Vivian, William Meir and Edward and William Warburton at Fenton Low, and William Greatbatch of Fenton.[31]

While these popular coloured applications of the creamware body remained the staple product of many Staffordshire potteries during the third quarter of the eighteenth century (plate 48), Josiah Wedgwood led the way in establishing his more refined Queen's Ware as a suitable background for over-glaze printing and enamel painting, which ultimately undermined the demand not only for fragile tin-glazed earthenware at home and abroad, but also for pewter. After a serious trade slump around 1770, the opening of the Russian market ensured that creamware would maintain its popularity in Europe, especially after the enormous interest excited by the display of Wedgwood's huge Frog Service at his London showrooms in 1774. Here the 952 pieces destined for Catherine the Great's palace of La Grenouille were displayed, according to Mrs Delaney, in 'three rooms below and two above . . . laid out on tables, everything that can be wanted to serve a dinner'.[32]

Such was the success of creamware at this period as a superior substitute for both delftware and pewter that in 1776 about a hundred Cornish tin miners, distressed by this double disaster to their trade, marched on Redruth bent on destroying as much creamware as they could find, and thence to Falmouth, where they were narrowly prevented from burning the Town Hall, which housed a 'large parcel' of Staffordshire earthenware. They were finally dispersed only by promises and the placing of a large order for pewter by a local alderman. The effect on Continental faience factories must have been even worse, particularly after 1786, when, much to the joy of the Staffordshire and Yorkshire potters, the French agreed to the import of English earthenware at a reciprocal flat-rate tariff of 12 per cent. The spread of creamware throughout Europe was unstoppable: for by the 1780s Wedgwood was exporting as much as 80 per cent of his output, and by the 1790s had agents in Amsterdam, Antwerp, St Petersburg, Italy and the German States.

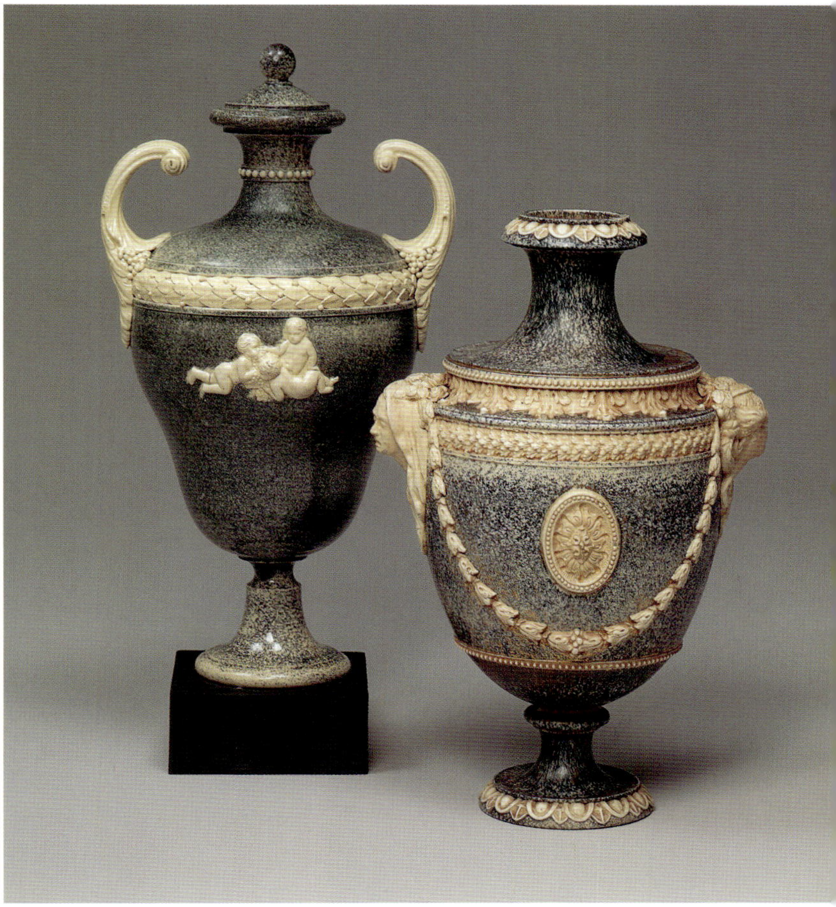

49
The 'Vase Mania' that gripped fashionable society in the 1770s produced memorable examples from Wedgwood and his contemporaries, in this case Neale & Co (right). Max. height 31.8 cm (12½ in.).
V&A: 2386–1901 and 304–1869.

While Wedgwood solved the conflicting demands of lucrative mass-produced tableware on the one hand, and exclusive but non-profit-making ornamental wares on the other (plate 49), through having separate wings at his Etruria factory managed respectively by his cousin 'Useful' Thomas Wedgwood and the Wedgwood & Bentley partnership, many other factories simply took up creamware manufacture without any such grand ambitions. But the leading makers, such as the partnership of John Turner and Andrew Abbott, who became Potters to the Prince of Wales in 1781, and the various partnerships between Humphrey Palmer, James Neale and Robert Wilson,[33] were deeply involved in the London retailing trade, dealing in all kinds of porcelain, earthenware and glass, as well as making successful alternative versions of coloured Jasper ware after its introduction in 1775, and caneware and Black Basalt of excellent quality. The symbiotic and incestuous relationship of all these potters and dealers was inseparable from their trade, both in Staffordshire and in London: Neale was actively trading with Wedgwood in the 1780s, to the extent of Neale creamwares being decorated at Wedgwood showrooms in Greek Street. At the same time, rivalries flourished, fuelled by Wedgwood's artists and modellers, who unwillingly continued to provide models for plagiarists: as early as 1768 he complained that major London retailers were sending his new designs back to other Staffordshire factories to be copied. John Carravella of Oxford Street was supplied with pirated Wedgwood designs by Humphrey Palmer, while Robert Fogg of New Bond Street had similar dealings with Bagnall & Baker. While the Wedgwood wares supplied by their showrooms were consistently marked after 1771 and deliberately priced higher than their contemporaries, other fashionable dealers such as Carravella were supplying a wide range of creamwares made by other makers, sometimes listed on surviving bills such as the cream bowls, custard cups, green enamelled flower pots, jelly moulds and bin labels for the Duke of Gordon in the period 1768–74. Most of

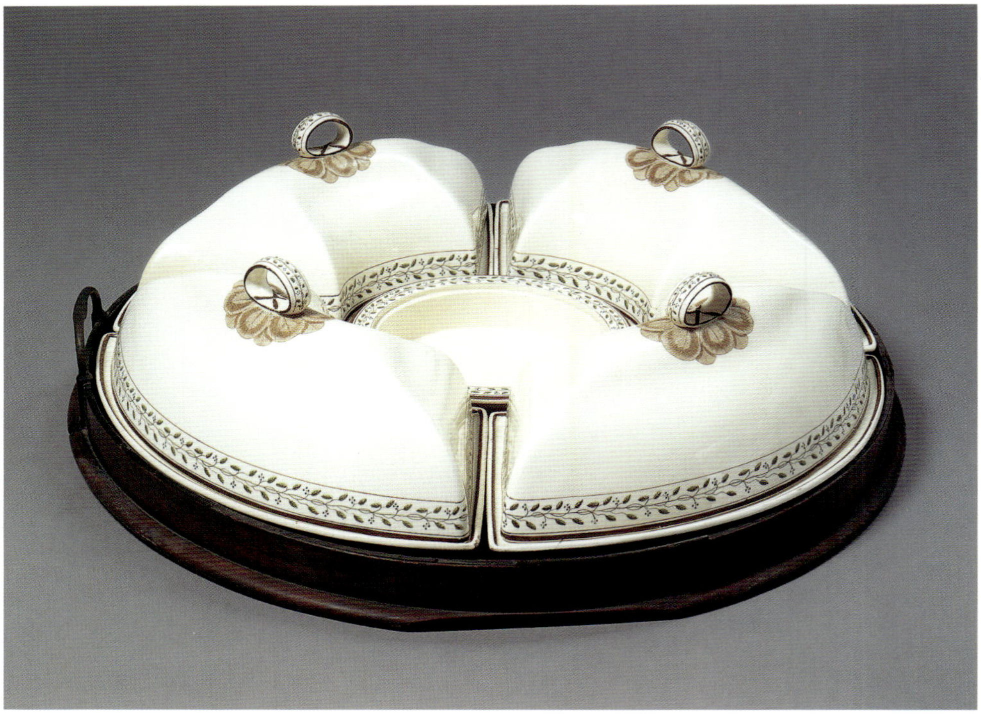

50
Creamware quickly responded to changes in eating habits in the late 18th century. For those returning home after the theatre, a cold supper of sandwiches or a large hors d'oeuvres could be left by the servants in one of Wedgwood's fashionable Supper Sets. For an intimate meal, it could be carried anywhere on its own tray. Diameter of tray 53.3 cm (21 in.).
V&A: Circ.279–1910.

Wedgwood's ambitious and innovative range, which introduced the most up-to-date designs to the dining tables of the 'Middling Classes' at a fraction of the cost of porcelain or Sheffield plate (plate 50), may be seen in the illustrations of the first Queen's Ware catalogue of 1774, which significantly carried a French translation and for which Wedgwood specified the inclusion of

> Terrines 4 or 5 sorts, oval and round, particularly the round ones we have in *Dead stock* . . . Sa[uce] Bowles, & boats – Sallads, Epargne Pickle stands, Casters & that for Oil & Vinegar . . . Ice pails for Bottles – Do for Single Glasses – Monteiths. Salts . . . Candlesticks, Egg Baskets, Egg cups with covers & without. Pouch'd Eggs cups, Entre Dishes, Covered Dishes Argyles. Root dishes.

Many of these types remained in production for long periods, as may be seen from the catalogue of 1790 and the masterly one of 1817, mostly engraved by the artist and visionary William Blake. A selection of creamwares was still available in *The Wedgwood 1880 Illustrated Catalogue of Shapes*.

Throughout the nineteenth century, however, while Wedgwood's luxury products were admired and avidly collected, Queen's Ware itself was simply known as 'Old Leeds Ware'. For when the market for refined earthenwares had been developed by the close-knit potteries of Staffordshire, the West Riding of Yorkshire found itself well placed to follow their example, lying above rich coalfields and with access to the major port of Hull, from which exports of earthenware rose from 645,215 in 1751 to the colossal figure of 13,287,000 by 1783.[34] Although the production of fineware was established some decades later than in

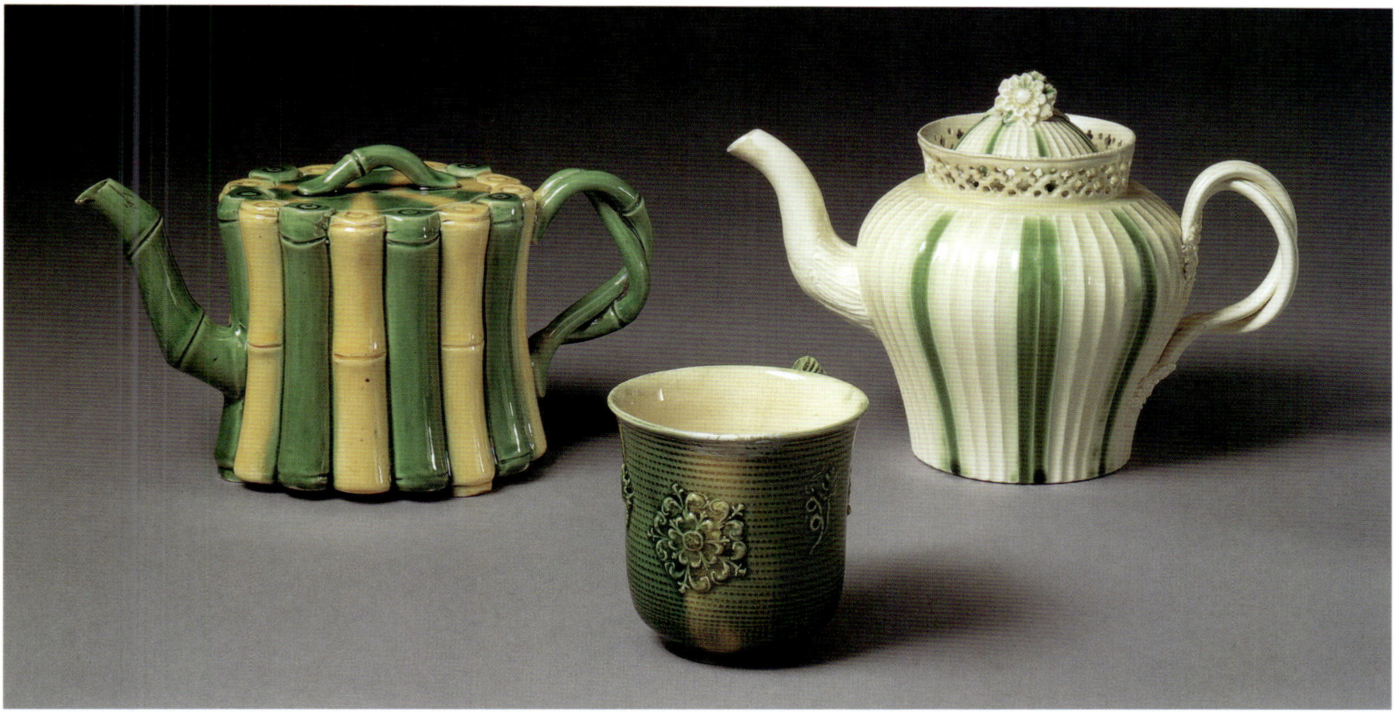

51
Vegetable forms, and stripes in particular, enjoyed great popularity during the 1760s; the Melon Ware cup Staffordshire, the striped teapot Leeds. Max. height 12.4 cm (4⅞ in.).
V&A: C.99–1911, C.327 or A–1951, 158–1874.

Staffordshire, by the 1760s both salt-glaze and creamware were being mass-produced by interrelated potteries with the aid of potters from Staffordshire and Derbyshire. In contrast to the mass of anonymous Staffordshire potteries, whose individuality was submerged for the sake of a homogenous, interchangeable product, some of these Yorkshire factories, though making almost identical salt-glaze and creamware, were sufficiently independent from each other to merit serious study by ceramic historians. And because their owners were not master potters but local entrepreneurs seeing a chance to expand their interests from textiles or iron into the new, potentially highly lucrative, fine pottery trade, much is known about their activities and complicated inter-relationships. The big Leeds Pottery at Hunslet, though by no means the first fineware pottery venture, has inevitably overshadowed the others to become the generic name for the type of pottery that they all shared. Established on a grand scale in 1770 by a consortium of businessmen, the pottery ran through several changes of partners until 1781, when the firm became Hartley, Greens & Co., surviving until its bankruptcy in 1820. Various proprietors carried it on until its final demise in 1881, after which the large stock of factory moulds was used for making rather dingy reproductions, notably by William Slee just before the First World War.

The Leeds Pottery is justly famous for its grand centrepieces and elaborately pierced tablewares, as shown in their catalogues of 1783 and 1794.[35] Rarely marked, these creamwares can often be identified by comparing the shapes in the catalogues and several surviving factory pattern books,[36] as well as the distinctive sprigged handle-terminals and, perhaps to the trained eye, by the subtleties of colour that Donald Towner stated to have been Deep Cream until about 1775, and then 'primrose yellow'. The interlaced double handle was in use from the beginning, as well as the beaded rouletting around rims and feet, which imitated contemporary silver while avoiding comparison with the fine lathe-turned edges of earlier salt-glazed stonewares: both are found, for example, on an enamelled creamware jug of Leeds type inscribed 'Thos:Stonier 1769'.[37] The bulk of production was robust creamware tablewares, including tortoiseshell, but salt-glaze, red earthenwares and basalt were also produced. An effective innovation perhaps made at Leeds, and certainly at other Yorkshire potteries, consisted of enamelled or underglaze-blue flowers painted within wax-resist cartouches on an iron-brown ground colour,[38] imitating 'Batavian' teawares imported from China much earlier in the eighteenth century. Most pieces that survive are, of course, those with attractive decoration, notably those with overglaze printing, which date from after about 1780, the striking fluted teapots with copper-green stripes echoing contemporary Staffordshire Melon Ware (plate 51), and the bright enamel decoration added by the Leeds decorating workshop of Jasper Robinson & David Rhodes, which had been established in 1760, ten years before the Leeds Pottery.[39] The distinctive style of this firm – bold iron-red and black decoration, red monochrome designs of a fashionably dressed lady and gentleman taking tea or drinking and smoking in a park, and fleecy scrolled pink and blue clouds with black birds in silhouette – may be seen on earlier salt-glaze as well as on the creamwares sent up by Wedgwood. Subsequently Rhodes was lured away in 1768 to run Wedgwood's Chelsea enamelling studio, leaving Robinson to continue in Leeds until 1779; but by that time the Leeds Pottery had their own decorating and printing shops. By the early nineteenth century local competition was much stiffer and the range of old-fashioned creamwares was joined by coarser wares such as dipped teapots with lathe-turned chequering (plate 98), of a type also made by the Castleford Pottery around 1805–10.

At Rothwell, four miles from Leeds, a redundant glasshouse was converted to a fineware pottery in 1767 by John Smith and John Pullen, 'for the making of Pots, such as are made in Burslem in Staffordshire and the trade is now very briskly carried on'.[40] By 1772, however, it was running at a loss and never recovered, though struggling on till about 1790. An apparently more promising rival pottery nearby started by a potter from Staffordshire, Samuel

Shaw, did not outlast his death two years later. Further down the River Aire, an existing fineware pottery was re-founded in 1790 as the Castleford Pottery by David Dunderdale and John Plowes, who were soon trading with America and Spain.[41] Their first and only printed catalogue of 1796 shows that their range of creamwares was similar to, sometimes identical with, that of the Leeds Pottery, and interestingly it was titled only in French and Spanish. But having survived the total embargo on European exports during the Napoleonic Wars – making, incidentally, at least some of the felspathic stoneware teapots to which it has given its name – the Castleford pottery was unable to withstand the trade recession that followed Waterloo and ended in bankruptcy in 1821.

Another pottery on the River Aire was established at Ferrybridge by Tomlinson & Co. in 1792, and is notable for having taken the compulsive inventor Ralph Wedgwood (Josiah's nephew) as partner after the bankruptcy of his Burslem pottery in 1796. Despite the obvious advantages of trading as 'Wedgwood & Co.', the partnership collapsed in 1801, leaving the original partners to carry on until 1834. It is fortunate that this factory has left behind a hand-drawn pattern book of 1799, which somehow found a home in the Wedgwood archives, and it is likely that the full range of the Wedgwood & Co. products was similar to those at the closure of Ralph Wedgwood's London shop in 1794, viz. 'plain and ornamented Wedgewood [*sic*] Table and Dessert Services, Water-Plates, Broth Bowls Oyster Barrels, Blancmange-Moulds, Ice Pails . . . Jasper Vases, Tea and Sugar Boxes, Terra Tersia Bouquetiers . . . enamelled and black Figures . . . blue printed Wares, black Egyptian Tea Pots'. Enough marked pieces exist to demonstrate that the quality was superior to that of many major exporters, such as Enoch Wood at Burslem.

In the south of Yorkshire several potteries sprung up on the River Don, using the abundant local coal and skilled labour imported from Staffordshire and Derbyshire. At Rotherham, the mason-architect John Platt entered a partnership with a local glassmaker, William Fenney, to build a pottery in 1765, Fenney dropping out two years later, to be replaced by an iron-founder, Samuel Walker. Messrs Platt & Walker's trade card includes 'White Stone Ware, Black, Tortoise Shell, Agate, Cream Colour & Gilt & Enamel Ware for Tea & Table Services', much of which is thought to have been exported, particularly to Russia. A 'muffle or kiln for ye painted or enamel ware pottery' was constructed in 1767, resulting in finely decorated lathe-turned stonewares, such as the 'John Platt 1767' jug in the Victoria and Albert Museum.[42] By the following year the traveller Arthur Young noted 22 or 23 men and 40 boys at work making salt-glaze, creamware and tortoiseshell, evidently in such quantity that John Platt felt obliged to become a signatory to the important Price Agreement of 4 February 1770. Walker bought out Platt's share in 1772, when it is assumed the pottery ceased production.

The Swinton Pottery, though founded as early as 1745, only began making salt-glaze and creamware after 1768, when it was taken over by the partnership of William Malpass & William Fenney, becoming Bingley, Wood & Co. in 1778. Excavations have revealed a range of stonewares and creamwares, including dinner plates, sauce boats, mugs and teawares, unremarkable though having certain identifiable characteristics.[43] In 1785 John Green of the Leeds Pottery partnership took a 21-year lease, after which the Swinton Pottery became an unwilling, though prosperous, satellite of the much larger pottery. A now-lost document of 1796 owned by Jewitt mentioned 'all sorts of Earthen Ware, viz. Cream-coloured, or Queen's, Nankeen Blue, Tortoise Shell, Fine Egyptian Black, Brown China etc. Also the above sorts enameled, printed or ornamented with gold or silver' – the 'silver' evidently not platinum lustre, the secret of which was not unravelled until ten years later. All these types made during the partnership with Leeds from 1785 to 1806 have been excavated at the pottery site, some proving identical to Leeds Pottery products but others peculiar to Swinton. Interesting oddities such as the creamware tiles enamelled with vine-leaves ordered by one of Earl Fitzwilliam's guests at Wentworth House in 1789 were perhaps attempts by the manager, John Brameld, to cater for the more aristocratic tastes of customers introduced by his noble landlord.

In the years before the lease expired in 1806, the Leeds Pottery deliberately ran down the Swinton side of the partnership, leading to a crisis that only an injection of capital by the paternalistic Earl Fitzwilliam could resolve by enabling John Brameld and his sons to re-establish the pottery. Happily he proved amenable to supporting the pottery, and as early as 1807 the Prince of Wales became a customer, buying a number of the tall baluster-shaped teapots with the streaky iron-manganese 'Rockingham' glaze. Two years later the pottery was completing three biscuit and four glaze firings per week, all for the domestic market via the port of Hull: these included sprigged canewares, finely enamelled creamwares, transfer-printed Pearlwares, and later the green-glazed moulded dessert wares made in quantity by firms such as Wedgwood and Davenport. But even after the factory renewed its exporting activities after Waterloo, the general depression of trade and in particular the difficulty of extracting payment from clients as far afield as Russia led to a further crisis, resulting in the Bramelds' bankruptcy late in 1825. Once more, however, Earl Fitzwilliam came to the rescue and the restored Rockingham Works of 1826 began to make the soft-paste porcelain for which it is justly famous, as well as continuing a range of superior earthenwares such as the 'Cadogan' teapots handled by Mortlocks, the London retailer, 'The Only Warehouse for the Oeconomical Rockingham & Cadogan Tea & Coffee Pots'.

Swinton was also the site chosen for the Don Pottery in 1801, built and managed by John Green with the aid of Staffordshire workers. Although not perhaps the best time to start a pottery, the brief Peace of Amiens in 1802 may have offered the prospect of an early return of the export trade. Manufacture of cheap salt-glaze had finally come to an end by this time, but the good range of products shown in the catalogue of 1808 proves the popularity of creamware well into the nineteenth century, mainly perhaps for the benefit of the middle-market customers they served in Russia, France, Belgium, the German States, Denmark and South America. Coal was readily available from Earl Fitzwilliam's Elsecar Colliery, while Dorset clay and Suffolk flint came by sea and the waterway system through Hull. Again, it is the brightly enamelled pieces that have survived in disproportionate numbers, but the entire range of run-of-the-mill wares has now been reconstructed: these include blue transfer-printed tablewares, caneware, Black Basalt, copper lustre, Rockingham-glazed wares, and even drab stoneware.[44] The bankruptcy of 1834, caused in part by the damage inflicted by the earlier bankruptcy of the closely linked pottery of the Bramelds in 1825, was followed in 1839 by the transfer from the Green family to the less-ambitious Barkers. Like the Leeds pottery, their heyday as creamware manufacturers was past.

After the pioneering creamware ventures of Wedgwood and his contemporaries in the 1760s, a second generation of prolific manufacturers soon sprang up in Staffordshire. The more prosperous acquired outlets in London, while the others were content to supply the export market and remain almost anonymous: for example, Charles & James Whitehead of Shelton, whose products are known only through their catalogue of 1798, translated into German, Dutch and French.[45] Among these new efficient and well-capitalized firms, Josiah Spode must rank as the most successful,[46] initially building up his business through making creamware and blue-printed Pearlware of the highest quality, which both sold through his London warehouse from 1778 and through Liverpool for the American market, adding the new bone chinas after he had perfected these in the late 1790s. Another success story was that of John Davenport, a Liverpool dealer in pottery and porcelain who bought a factory at Longport in 1794.[47] Having a Liverpool outlet and existing links with America, he built up a thriving business in 'export quality' wares, including creamwares that were already old-fashioned. About the same time, in 1793 Thomas Minton established his pottery at Stoke, from the first setting a very high standard which ensured that his goods would be in demand not only by the London trade (including his brother Arthur, whose shop in Swallow Street took more than £12,000 of his wares between 1796 and 1804), but also other manufacturers, notably Wedgwood & Byerley. Rarely marked, the cream colour and edged wares listed in an inventory of 1806 are now difficult to identify, although the printed patterns can be matched up with lists of wares supplied to others.[48] But at this period some of the older firms found it hard to compete with these upstarts: Wedgwood & Byerley went through a lean patch in the early nineteenth century, and the sons of John Turner at Lane End became bankrupt in 1806, despite all the up-to-date products listed at the sale the following year: 'Cream Colour, China-Glazed blue edge, China glazed printed and painted, Egyptian Black, Cane, Stone, Jasper, Pearl and Patent China Goods'.[49] The remnants of this once-important factory were sold off in 1829.

Elsewhere in Britain, their example was followed by entrepreneurs who could see good profits to be won by exploiting some inherent advantage such as proximity of clay and coal, or access to the export market. The Cockpit Hill factory at Derby, founded in the mid-eighteenth century, produced creamwares of the highest quality until the unrelated bankruptcy of its partners forced its closure in 1779.[50] The decorated wares evidently benefited from the proximity to the Derby Porcelain Works and its many talented enamel decorators, but the principal aid to identification of Cockpit Hill products lies in their transfer-printed decoration, which was practised after 1764, when the partners acquired the process from Richard Holdship of Worcester. A more shadowy factory at Melbourne, for which the only hard evidence is a newspaper advertisement of 1776 and a deposit of wasters, has been accredited by Donald Towner with a homogenous group of creamwares, both enamelled and printed. Although it is possible that the missing factory site may now lie under a reservoir, Towner's statement that 'the Melbourne Pottery must have been one of the most important eighteenth-century factories in this country, producing wares of superlative quality' may well be an over-statement.[51]

In the North-West, an obvious choice for creamware manufacture was Liverpool, through which port so many Staffordshire earthenwares had passed

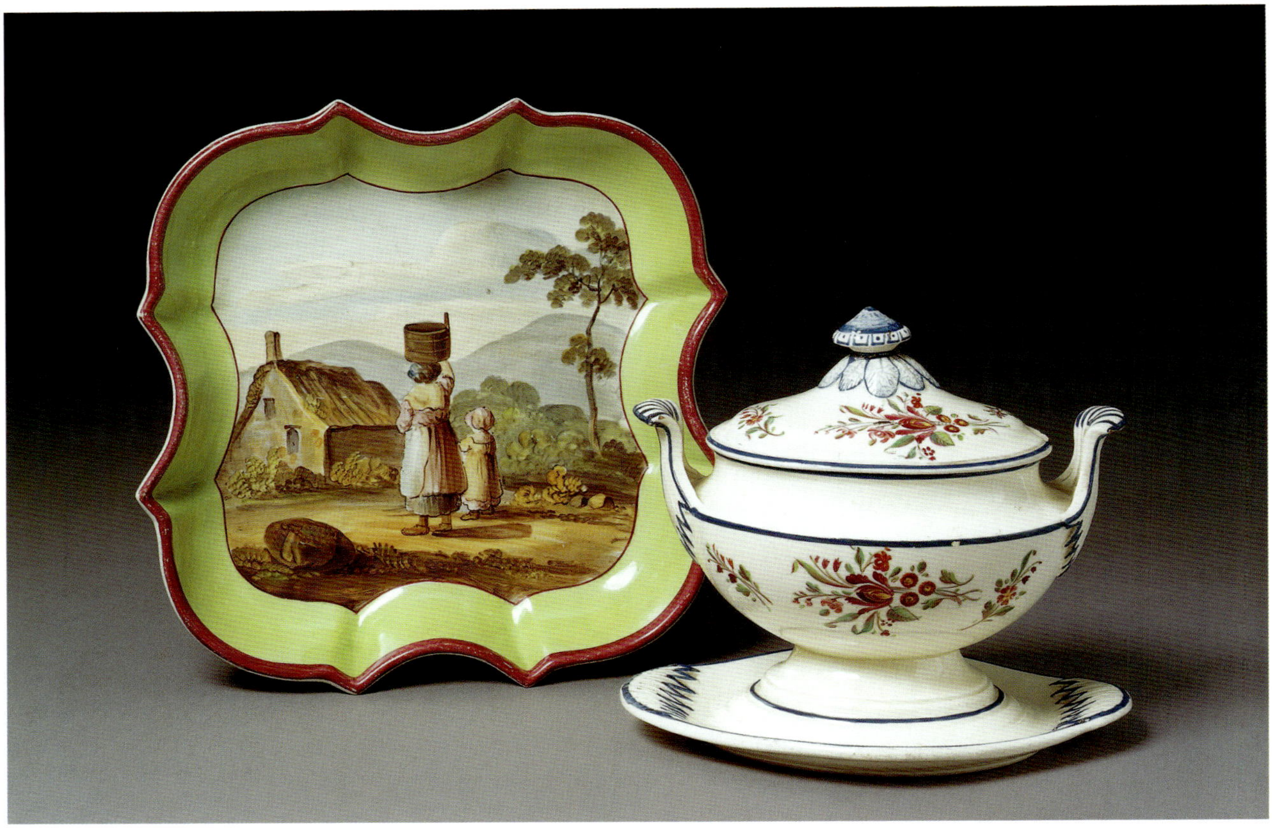

52
By the early 19th century, creamware had become almost white, giving it a new lease of life particularly outside Staffordshire. At Newcastle upon Tyne, Sewell & Donkin made fine-quality tablewares until at least the 1840s, while earlier the Herculaneum Pottery (left) was noted for its enamel painting. Max. height 20.3 cm (8 in.).
V&A: C.47–1967, C.33–1968.

on their way to America: in 1770, for example, a total of 492,980 pieces. Although by the 1780s the native delftware industry had become extinct and Liverpool porcelain manufacture was in decline, the existing potteries and the pool of skilled pot-painters were retained on a reduced scale in making popular painted Pearlware and banded wares. But it was not until 1796 that a new factory was started as Samuel Worthington & Co. in a former copper-smelting works at Toxteth, to be called the Herculaneum Pottery (plates 52, 73).[52] Forty potters and their families are said to have migrated from Staffordshire to join the enterprise, which, having a warehouse in Duke Street and its own dock, was also able to export vast quantities of pottery on behalf of other major makers such as Josiah Spode. Much of the output, which included bone china from about 1800, was aimed directly at the American market, but even this could not keep the competition at bay later than 1840, when the valuable site was redeveloped.

Other ports fully exploited their potential for export or, in the case of Yarmouth, a ready market for local decoration, such as the green monochrome landscapes of William Absolom. At Hull the Belle Vue Pottery was founded about 1802, at Stockton-on-Tees the aptly named Stafford Pottery was established by William Smith around 1825, and at Newcastle upon Tyne[53] various partnerships between Sewell and Donkin managed the St Anthony's pottery between about 1780 and 1878, leaving behind a comprehensive catalogue around 1825–40 showing old-fashioned creamwares including the popular baskets and stands, either pierced or plaited from strips of clay. In the South-West, Bristol had lost most of its delftware industry by the 1770s, and increasingly turned to making salt-glazed stoneware bottles, which were essential for transporting cider, vinegar, oil and, of course, rum for the army and navy. But the tradition of fine painting lingered on, and was successfully grafted onto the new creamwares, such as those of the Bristol Pottery started by Joseph Ring in 1785. The enamelling by Thomas Pardoe's decorating studio in the early nineteenth century was outstanding, as was the flower-painting signed by William Fifield, father and son, on luxury presentation objects such as miniature barrels. The pottery was later run by the Pountneys under various partnerships, surviving until the very end of the twentieth century. In Wales, the Cambrian Pottery was operated by the Dillwyn family from about 1783, making excellent creamwares and transfer-printed Pearlwares, of which the dessert wares finely enamelled with botanical specimens must rank as superior to any produced in Staffordshire. Later, between 1814 and 1838, Messrs Baker, Bevans & Irwin at the Glamorgan Pottery[54] made good-quality plain and shell-edged creamwares as well as transfer-printed Pearlwares. In south Devon, at Bovey Tracey – despite the dismissive remarks made by Josiah Wedgwood in 1775 – excavations have revealed some good-quality creamwares closely imitating Staffordshire and Leeds, replaced in the 1790s by Pearlware, white domestic earthenwares and a wide range of banded and 'Mocha' wares to be exported via Teignmouth.[55]

Further afield, a cluster of potteries on the east coast of Scotland made both salt-glaze and creamware.[56] The Prestonpans Pottery of the entrepreneur William Caddell was set up as early as 1751 expressly to make fine earthenware of Staffordshire type, and by 1764 William Littler had moved from Staffordshire to make pottery and porcelain at West Pans. A bill-head of 1766 lists his porcelain and 'all kinds of Stone Ware, such as fine Gilded and Japand Black and Tortoise Shell Ware', which presumably includes plain creamwares, and, in addition, some striking creamware plates and pierced baskets with 'Littler's Blue' glaze and gilt decoration have been identified as his work. After these pioneering attempts to found a native industry, by the mid-nineteenth century Scottish potteries, particularly on the west coast around Glasgow, were major exporters of painted, sponged and printed pottery. As for Ireland, until recently it was assumed that the end of delftware manufacture had not been followed by attempts to produce its natural successor, creamware.[57] In fact, new owners of Delamain's defunct World's End China Manufactory at Dublin began experimenting with creamware in 1769, eventually resulting in success, albeit short-lived, in 1771 with the help of two Staffordshire 'flint-ware manufacturers', Edward Ackers and Thomas Shelly. After further attempts to revive manufacture creamware in the 1780s, the mantle passed to Belfast, where the purpose-built Downshire Pottery was established by a consortium of three wealthy entrepreneurs. Although the problem of finding suitable local clays, in the face of an export prohibition from England, was overcome, and although excavations show that a good range of plain, black-printed, slip-decorated, rouletted and enamelled creamware was produced, trade restrictions conspired to reduce its profitability until the inevitable closure in 1796. Once again, the might of Staffordshire interests had suppressed the local competition.

It is difficult to make a balanced assessment of the relative importance of all these potteries, some of which never attempted to rise above the lower or middle markets and others of which simply used creamware as a stepping stone towards branching out into more prestigious porcelain manufacture. The matter is complicated also by the fact that so many important Staffordshire factories remain buried and un-researched, while others outside the Potteries, begun as commercial enterprises by wealthy industrialists, have not only left behind copious documentation but also pottery sites available for excavation. But it is abundantly clear that the cream-coloured earthenware as perfected and popularized by Wedgwood in the 1760s was the *raison d'être* for all these potteries, and that this undeniably useful product was the key to the major expansion of Staffordshire-type pottery and its world trade in the second half of the eighteenth century. If the commercial success of the British may be sometimes attributed to their ability to single out a versatile product for mass production and development, using advanced technology and cheap labour to make profits while undercutting the competition, then cream-coloured earthenware must provide a shining example: for while the great aristocratic porcelain factories of Europe exhausted themselves in the pursuit of extravagant forms and rich decoration, British potters quietly prospered by flooding the markets of Europe first with utilitarian white salt-glaze and eventually with an earthenware so refined and so inexpensive that it rendered meaningless the old social divide between earthenware and porcelain. It was, in fact, the perfect egalitarian material for an age of revolution and new-found liberty.

1. Contained in the First Experiment book, beginning 13 February 1759, Wedgwood MSS, University of Keele: E.11–19115.
2. For example, Aiken (1795), which states that 'Josiah Wedgwood . . . invented a species of earthenware for the table, of a firm and durable body, and covered with a rich and brilliant glaze'.
3. Halfpenny (1993).
4. Traditionally, and for wholly unsentimental, strictly commercial reasons, most changes of pottery ownership were accompanied by wholesale destruction of moulds and pattern books. This practice continues: for example, many Susie Cooper designs were destroyed when her

employment at Wedgwoods ended, and within the last few years the stock of original engraved copper plates from the Mason factory has been sent for scrap.

5. Simeon Shaw (1829), p.141.
6. Shaw further confuses the issue by his statement on p.18 that 'Mr Enoch Booth first introduced that most important improvement in the manufacture of pottery – the fluid glaze'. Since he later claims that Booth copied his fluid glaze from that already in use by Aaron Littler, and since red earthenwares of the 1720s are clearly liquid-glazed, this statement does not bear scrutiny.
7. Glaisher Collection, no.507.
8. British Museum, illustrated in Towner (1978), pls 1A, 1B.
9. Potteries Museum, 117P1989, illustrated in Grigsby (1990), p.202, Halfpenny (1993), pp.19–20.
10. Weldon 631.
11. Potteries Museum, Stoke-on-Trent, illustrated in Mountford (1971), pl.166.
12. Teapots at Colonial Williamsburg, 1975–178, Victoria and Albert Museum, C.66&A–1989, and Grant-Davidson Collection. The tea canister, Weldon Collection 369.
13. Williams & Halfpenny (2000), pp.164–6.
14. The V&A teapot shows the lines of the string that was wrapped around the pot to secure the cut pieces of masking paper when it was powdered with finely ground pigment.
15. Mountford (1971), p.57, quoting from the Thomas & John Wedgwood papers at the Potteries Museum.
16. Possibly Thomas Fletcher, later the partner of John Baddeley.
17. Shaw (1829), pp.177–8.
18. Shaw (1829), p.36.
19. Angerstein (2001).
20. Phillips, 13 June 2000, lot 174.
21. Quoted by Hume (1969).
22. Mallet (1966, 1967).
23. See note 3 above. Recent accounts include Blake Roberts (1995).
24. Ewins (1997).
25. Fully covered by Halfpenny (1997), and Barker, *William Greatbatch* (1991).
26. Announcement in 1772 by the retailers Davies and Minnitt of New York, as quoted by Hume (2001), p.231.
27. Mentioned in the Thomas & John Wedgwood account-books from 1762 onwards: 'Ash Flowr Pots & Stands, Ash Pint and Qut. Jug' were among items sent to America in 1772, quoted by Mountford (1971), p.45. Angerstein described the earthenware colour-ground wares as having a 'yellow, brown, speckled or black glaze with litharge, red lead, white lead, galena and magnesia, according to the colour desired'.
28. Victoria and Albert Museum, see Young (1995).
29. Letter of 18 July 1766, Wedgwood MSS, University of Keele: E.18123–25.
30. Letter of 7 March 1774, Wedgwood MSS, University of Keele: E.18521–25.
31. See Halfpenny (1997) and Barker, *William Greatbatch* (1991).
32. See M. Raeburn and L. N. Voronikhina, *The Green Frog Service* (1995), and Young (1995) for a full account.
33. For monographs on these important factories, see Hillier (1965) and Edwards (1987).
34. My thanks to John Griffin for drawing my attention to this statistic from Gordon Foster, *Hull in the Eighteenth Century* (Oxford, 1972).
35. Towner (1963) and Walton (1976)
36. These pattern books at the Victoria and Albert Museum and Temple Newsam House, Leeds, are shortly to be published in their entirety by John Griffin.
37. V&A: C.14–1952.
38. Perhaps the 'Brown China' mentioned by Jewitt (1878) as a product of the Swinton Pottery. Examples illustrated by Walton (1976), p.248.
39. Towner (1974), pp.134–9.
40. Undated document, Leeds Reference Library, quoted by Lawrence (1974), p.40.
41. Roussel (1982).
42. V&A: C.67–1971. See Mallet (1973), pp.111–14.
43. Cox & Cox (1983).
44. Griffin (2001).
45. J. & C. Whitehead catalogue, 1798 (reprinted Milton Keynes, 1974).
46. Whiter (1970).
47. Lockett & Godden (1989).
48. Godden (1968).
49. Hillier (1965), p.74.
50. For the history of this factory, see Towner (1978), pp.90–104.
51. Towner (1971), p.30.
52. Smith (1970).
53. Blakey (2001).
54. Hallesy (1995).
55. Adams & Thomas (1996).
56. McVeigh (1979).
57. Francis (1995).

CHAPTER FIVE

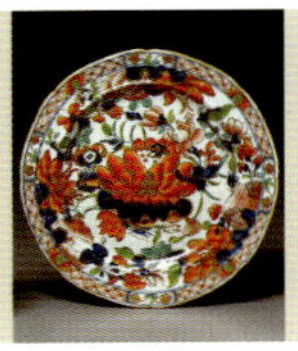

Harnessing the Exotic: Britain and the Orient

'Our tea and coffee set were of common India china, our dinner service of earthenware, to which, for our rank, there was nothing superior, Chelsea porcelain and fine India china being only for the wealthy. Pewter and Delft ware could also be had, but were inferior'.[1] This journal entry of 1783 by Mrs Papendiek, Assistant Keeper of the Wardrobe to Queen Charlotte, confirms that, although Chinese porcelain was still preferred for teawares, by this time 'Queensware' was unreservedly accepted by the gentry; but, more importantly it also places delftware firmly into its eighteenth-century context, as a locally made substitute for the cheapest imported blue and white porcelain. By the 1780s, of course, many of the factories in Lambeth, Bristol and Liverpool had already closed; but the terms 'Delft' or 'delftware', the last names by which the material was known before its demise in the face of competition from Staffordshire, were to remain in use as defining a type of pottery that, until the arrival of creamware and cheap bone china towards the end of the eighteenth century, played an essential role in providing the poorer social classes for more than 200 years with inexpensive but attractive hand-painted tableware. It is one of those ironies of history that at the present time, because almost any sort of hand-painting is considered superior to that produced by mechanical means, the refreshing simplicity and direct appeal of delftware has achieved among collectors an iconic status unimaginable in the seventeenth and eighteenth centuries.

The history of tin-glazed earthenware, from its invention in Mesopotamia to its subsequent spread via Moorish Spain to Italy, from thence to neighbouring France, up to northern Europe and across from the Low Countries to England, has been told many times. Like many successful inventions, the technique was simple, effective and adaptable. Calcium-rich and local clays were blended, thrown on the wheel and fired at a relatively low temperature to produce an absorbent biscuit body, which could be dipped into liquid glaze consisting of calcined lead ore mixed with tin oxide to make it opaque white, and then re-fired at about 1,000 °F to melt the glaze and – with varying success – fuse it to the open-grained clay body. As compensation for the expense of the extra firing, provided that the underlying clay was uncontaminated by iron oxide, this process could produce a milk-white surface that offered obvious possibilities for decoration, the simplest of which was found to be the painting in copper lustre practised exclusively in Spain under Arab rule. While this did much to popularize the material in a late medieval Europe just awakening to the possibilities of luxury tablewares, the effect that it had upon the future development of tin-glazed earthenware in the North was minimal. Far more important was the technique

53
The subtle *bianco sopra bianco* decoration was developed to a high point during the period 1760–70, notably at Bristol (as here). Diameter 22.5 cm (8⅞ in.).
V&A: Sch.II 11.

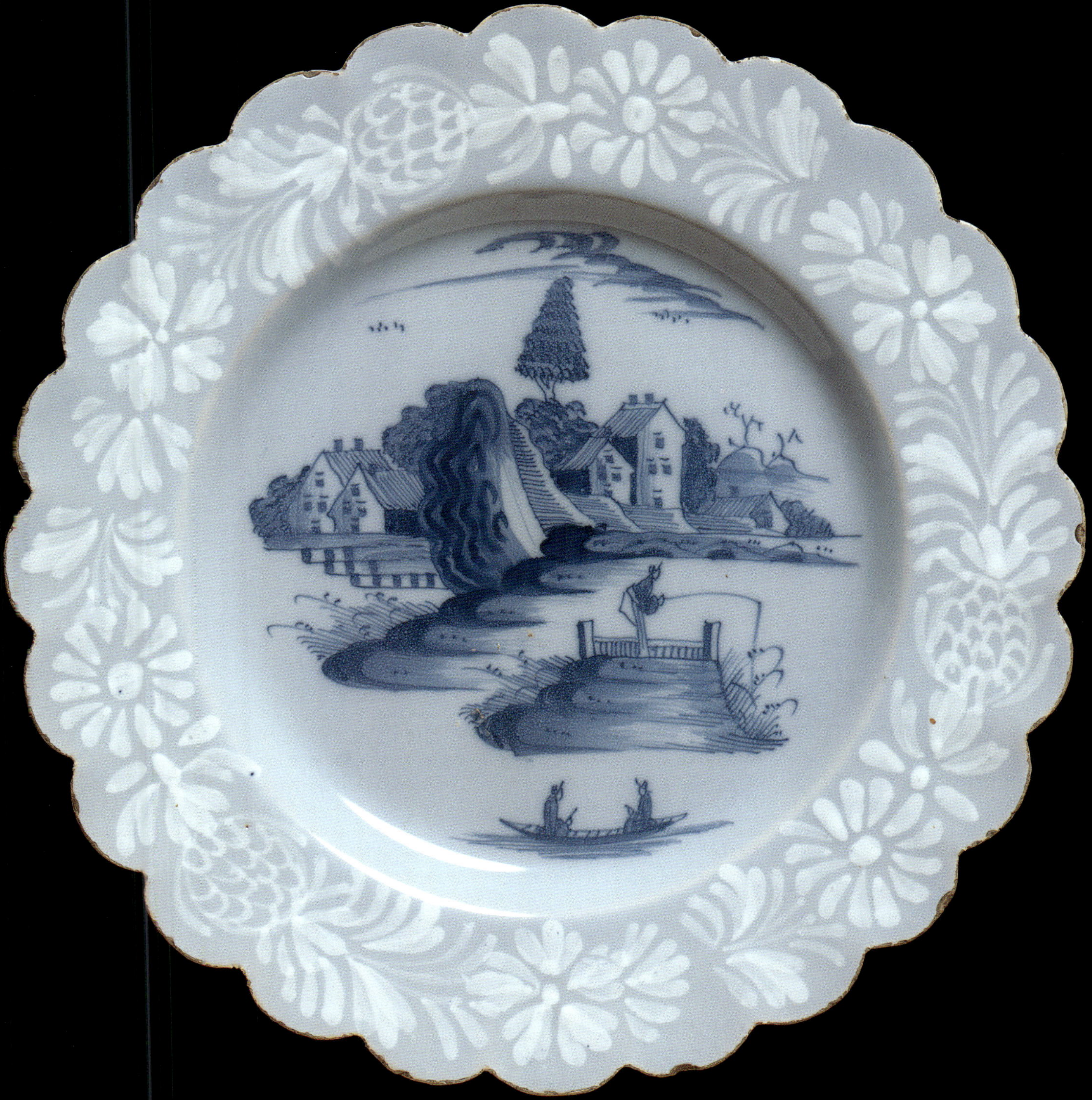

of painting the raw glaze with colours that would fire 'in-glaze', at first using the common metallic ores of cobalt-blue, iron-brown, manganese-purple and copper-green, and later the rarer colours of antimony-yellow and iron-red. The much more sophisticated technique of low-temperature enamel decoration, generally known today as 'petit feu' after its successful development by eighteenth-century French faience makers, is discussed elsewhere, notably in the Glossary. But of all the decorative techniques available to the tin-glazed earthenware potter, it was the simplest and cheapest that is now almost synonymous with the material: cobalt-blue designs painted on the raw glaze with swift and sure brush strokes, derived directly or indirectly from Chinese Export porcelain of the seventeenth and eighteenth centuries. It is worth repeating here that the original creation of blue and white porcelain and its subsequent worldwide popularity were not so much an example of brilliant design created by Chinese potters, as happy accidents necessitated by the technical limitations of the material: of all the metallic oxide colours that might be painted onto a biscuit-fired body, it was cobalt-blue alone that proved capable of withstanding the subsequent glaze-firing without detriment. Although obviously these high-temperature considerations did not apply to low-fired tin-glazed earthenware, nevertheless the very convenience of being able to use semi-skilled artists to render bold, effective patterns in a single colour made it not only highly economical, but also ensured a scale of mass production that belied the obvious drawbacks of a soft clay body loosely clad with a brittle glaze.

The growing prosperity of England under Elizabeth I provided a fertile ground for immigrant Netherlandish craftsmen, notably weavers, to establish manufactures of luxury goods. Of these new skills, the secrets of making painted maiolica and decolourized *cristallo* glass reached England via Italian workers who had first settled in Antwerp; so that when the manufacture of delftware, or 'galleyware' as it was then known, took root in England sometime in the 1560s, it came, like crystal drinking glasses, imbued with the stylistic influences of its immigrant promoters. Here Jaspar Andries (whose father, Guido di Luca Savini, had moved to Antwerp from Castel Durante) represented the Italian polychrome maiolica tradition, while Jacob Jansen represented the cobalt-blue and manganese-purple tradition of Antwerp. As with most other types of ware, this new English product had a definite place in the hierarchy of utilitarian ceramics, in this case the 'Galley pavinge tyles and Vessels for potycaries' for which they petitioned Queen Elizabeth for a patent to manufacture about 1570, enclosing a chest of their handiwork as proof of their abilities. In the event their petition was unsuccessful, for in that year another group of applicants was granted a patent for various products involving alien craftsmen, including 'erthen woorke after the manner of Turkye Italye Spayne and Netherlond with purtraict and coloures'.[2] There is no evidence that the group of gentlemen from Lincolnshire and Northamptonshire who received this ambitious patent ever made use of it, and its very failure reinforces the assumption that it was functional pottery – tiles and pharmacy pots – that English consumers required. Moreover, circumstances were favourable to the manufacture of these wares in England. Tiles were heavy and expensive to import from abroad,[3] whereas the tin and clay needed for their manufacture could be easily supplied by sea from Cornwall and from the clay-beds of Norfolk and Suffolk, both of which sources were already in regular use by the potters of Holland. As for drug pots and storage jars, these were simple to throw on the wheel and, even before the seventeenth-century potters' innovation of 'labelling' the contents in cobalt-blue, were so ideal for their purpose that pharmacies in Italy and Spain continued to use their locally made tin-glazed earthenwares until well into the nineteenth century. Even in Britain, the pharmaceutical pots made at Vauxhall in the 1840s were the very last delftwares to be made.

In 1571 Jacob Jansen moved to London, where he continued to use Norfolk clay to make the same range of wares at his pottery at Aldgate, assisted by six other Flemish potters. This, the first delftware pottery in London, survived until about 1615, after which the centre of the fledgling industry moved across the river to the established Flemish quarter in the parish of St Olave's at Southwark, where it consolidated itself and began to leave behind its Antwerp roots.

It was, however, something of an accident that led to the founding of the most famous Southwark pottery, at Pickleherring Quay, for it represented very much a second choice of career for its founder, the Protestant entrepreneur Christian Wilhelm. He had come to London in 1604 from the Rhenish Palatinate expressly to manufacture smalt (a blue dye derived from cobalt, also known as 'blew-starch'), but when a rival smalt maker Abraham Baker applied for a monopoly in 1605, Christian Wilhelm agreed not to oppose him on the condition that he should be allowed to continue his own manufacture for a period of 21 years. When Baker obtained his patent, he promptly reneged on his part of the bargain, leaving Wilhelm no choice but to find another trade. Fortunately for him, it was at exactly this time that the first large cargoes of Chinese porcelain tablewares reached Holland through the capture of the Portuguese galleys *San Iago* in 1602, and in 1604 *Santa Caterina* with a cargo of 30 tons of porcelain: the distribution of these through public sales in Amsterdam helped to create a demand for blue and white that only the addition of locally made copies could satisfy. Thus Christian Wilhelm, after a period of using his furnaces for distilling vinegar, and shortly after James I renewed in perpetuity the charter of the East India Company in 1610, soon realized the advantages of combining his cobalt-blue with the manufacture of fashionable blue and white tableware. Although it was not until 1618 that he was first described as 'galley pott maker' and 'aquivtay styller', he later claimed to have been making pottery as early as 1612, at a time when experienced potters working at the old Aldgate pottery might have provided some degree of continuity.[4]

At about the same time, in 1613 Hugh Cressey and Edmund Bradshawe managed to obtain a 21-year patent to make pots, dishes and tiles 'of all fashions after such manner as used in Fiansa and other parts beyond the Seas' at a pottery in Montague Close in London on the pretext that they were the inventors – a claim later weakened by the evidence of Christian Wilhelm and Samuel Sotherne whom Cressey sued for infringement. While never tiring in his efforts to resume making smalt, Christian Wilhelm's pottery venture meanwhile succeeded so well that in 1628 a document mentions his 40 employees making wares that 'shews as faire as China dishes'. Having by this time discredited Hugh Cressey's patent, in 1628 he himself obtained a 14-year patent for making the full range of contemporary tablewares, viz 'Bottell[es] of all Colo[urs] basons & ewers salt[es] dishes of all sort[es] drinkinge pott[es] paving tyles Apothecaries & Comfittmaker pott[es]', in competition with the 'galleyware . . . now made beyond the Seas and in great abundance brought over & imported'. Although Wilhelm lived to enjoy the freedom of his new patent only for two more years, the pottery that he had founded continued to flourish in the hands of his son-in-law, Thomas Townsend.

In the first two decades of the seventeenth century, therefore, the establishment of the delftware industry was accomplished only after fierce competition between four separate potteries, of which Montague Close and Pickleherring Quay were to survive until well into the eighteenth century.[5] To build a working pottery, import trained potters from the Netherlands and locate reliable supplies of raw materials in a foreign country represented no small investment, and it is some indication of the possible wealth to be generated from these ventures that these early entrepreneurs – not themselves practical potters – were prepared to risk large amounts of venture capital.

The changes on the dining table brought about by the introduction of delftware were so radical that one might be forgiven for comparing it – in reverse – to the 1960s tableware revolution, when the tureen was abandoned in favour of oven-to-table ware and the cup and saucer gave way to the ubiquitous coffee mug. Before northern Europe awoke to the existence of Chinese porcelain plates in the early seventeenth century, wooden trenchers or pewter plates were the most commonly used tablewares, supplemented by tough German brown salt-glazed stoneware ale mugs or locally made earthenware copies. To study what has survived is to see but half the picture, for the many ashwood mugs and trenchers quickly turned up on the lathe by country craftsmen have long perished, leaving behind only the cherished ceremonial vessels like silver-mounted hardwood mazers (small bowls for ceremonial drinking) and lignum vitae wassail bowls, while examples of ordinary pewter, so easily damaged and almost invariably recycled, survive hardly at all. But pewter was very widely used and expensive to purchase, so that from the sixteenth century at least it was the practice for households to hire from the pewterers their set or 'garnish' of tableware, which consisted of three dozen plates and a dozen saucers, and thereafter to part-exchange them every few years.[6] At the same time, wooden trenchers continued in use at a lower social level, for example the 12 dozen bought by the Dean of Salisbury in the 1620s for 13s (just over 1d each), presumably for some local entertainment, and those wooden trenchers and earthen pitchers that Samuel Pepys noted with distaste at a Lord Mayor's feast. Of these two rivals for delftware, by the middle of the seventeenth century the wooden trencher had been relegated to use by the rural community, while in the 1650s the durability of pewter was greatly increased by the addition of antimony, named 'French Pewter' after its immigrant inventor. This improved material was to remain a superior but more expensive alternative to delftware tableware until the end of the eighteenth century.

Chinese porcelain was almost unobtainable and hugely expensive in the early years of the seventeenth century,[7] at least until the first official East India Company cargo of chinaware in 1637; but on the sparsely furnished dining table of the thrifty urban family, besides the traditional set of pewter plates, these new fashionable blue and white delftwares of the type listed by Christian Wilhelm's patent were cheaper than any imports, and notably more sophisticated than the functional lead-glazed earthenware chafing dishes (cooking pans with handles) and other vessels made by potteries on the Surrey-Hampshire borders. They complemented perfectly imported goods such as Rhineland stoneware ale mugs, moulded colour-glazed wares from Saintonge, trailed slipware bowls from North Holland and fine sgraffito plates from the potteries along the River Werra in Germany. And their inherent fragility was offset to a large extent by their exotic Chinese blue and white idiom, which immediately offered possibilities for display, as well as by other advantages such as cheapness and the ability to adapt to almost any form besides basic tiles and storage jars. Thus was born a taste for blue and white that was nurtured for the succeeding three centuries, and which embraced porcelain, Pearlware and finally transfer-printed Staffordshire wares typified by that great survivor, the Willow Pattern.

Christian Wilhelm has been credited with being the main innovator in the London delftware industry,[8] so that while Montague Close and other later potteries were to concentrate on the plainer blue and white tablewares, the Pickleherring Quay pottery was instrumental in helping the industry to break away from dependence on its Netherlandish roots and on Chinese porcelain prototypes. Certainly, the series of spectacular polychrome chargers – dishes intended for display – which began in the 1620s are all attributable to his factory, as well as a series of inscribed pots dated in the years 1628–35 decorated by one unidentified painter.[9] But the starting point for the success of the pottery at this period was surely the bird-on-rock pattern copied from Chinese export porcelain of the Wan-Li period, which, though old-fashioned by 1630, nonetheless remained popular for some twenty years and was easily produced by comparatively unskilled painters (plate 54). Common also in Holland in the 1620s, it may well have been introduced to Southwark by potters migrating to London as a result of a slump in the industry at home – ironically caused by the huge increase in the importation of Chinese porcelain.

As excavated wasters of these have shown, to avoid kiln debris settling on the decorated surface they were stacked upside down in the kiln, separated by three-pronged trivets that left the characteristic three scars in the glaze.[10] Other simple patterns, consisting of similar compartmented borders of Wan-Li type enclosing geometric designs, completed the repertoire of basic tablewares. As for shapes, elegance was sacrificed to solid construction, the heavy flanged rims and thick handles compensating for the soft clay body with thick brittle glaze. Globular serving bottles ('sack' bottles') took their form from imported Frechen stonewares; porringers with a single ear handle followed the similar pewter examples; the posset pots with sucking spout were adapted from smaller silver versions of the late sixteenth century; while barrel-bodied mugs followed the form of Border Wares – all of these tablewares complementing rather than attempting to compete with what was readily available from abroad. Since the use of steel forks, with their sharp prodding and scratching action, did not become common until the late seventeenth century, the soft delftware dishes or shallow bowls must have provided a perfectly satisfactory, and infinitely more decorative, substitute for the traditional pewter or wood.

Polychrome chargers, made for display and painted in manganese-purple, copper-green, iron-red and cobalt-blue, represented a new departure for the English ceramic industry, and one to which the Pickleherring Quay pottery has a strong claim. For apart from an isolated dish inscribed 'The Rose is Red the

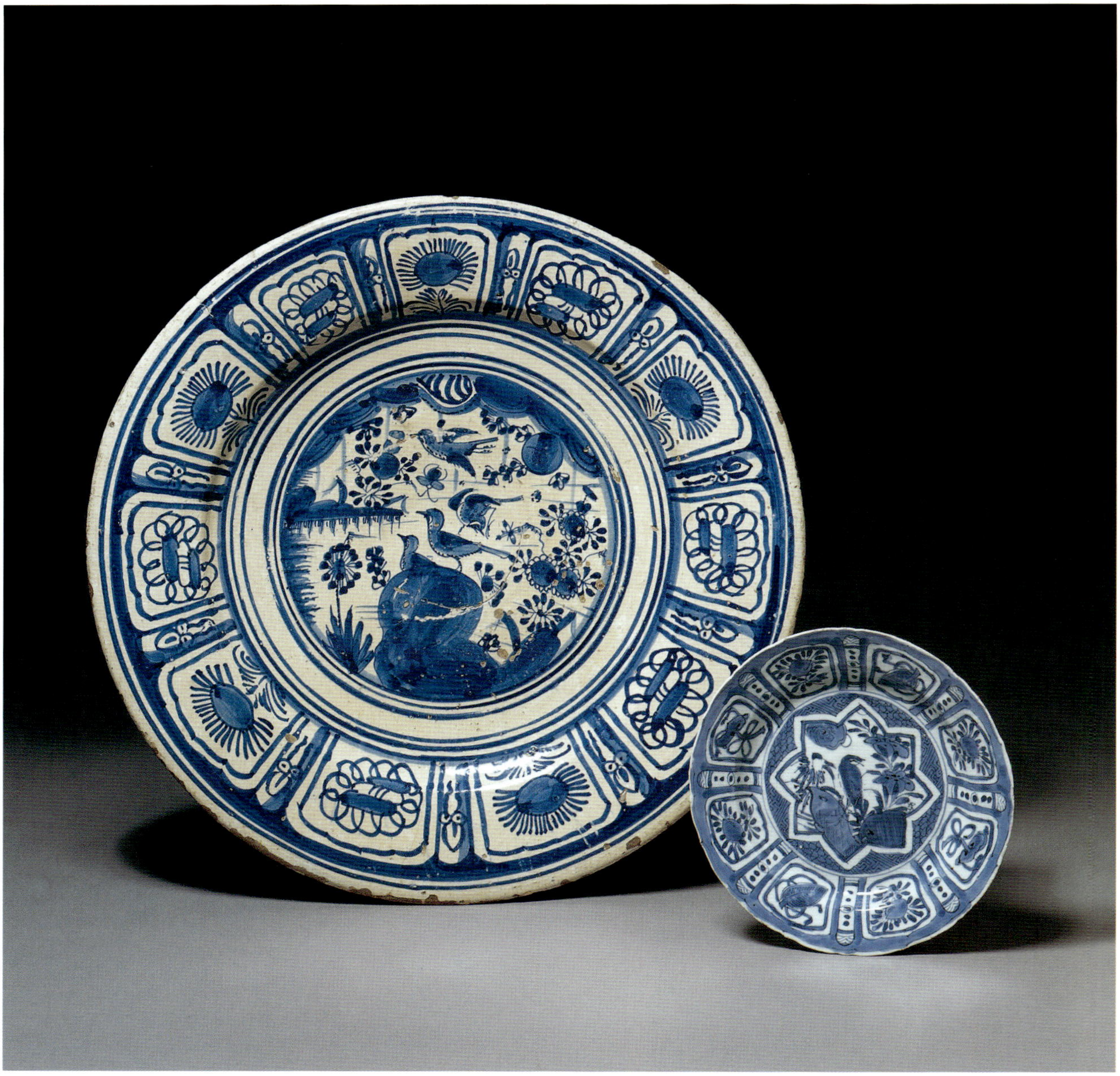

54
By the 1620s the Chinese bird-on-rock decoration (right) was already an old design, but its direct appeal and simplicity to paint made it extremely popular among the London delftware potters. Max diameter 49.5 cm (19½ in.).
V&A: C.588–1922.

Leaves Are Grene God Save Elizabeth Our Queene 1602',[11] which was almost certainly a product of the Aldgate pottery, the series begins with a dish dated 1620, vigorously painted with leaves and fruit in the manner of contemporary Netherlandish or Italian maiolica. These dishes with exotic fruit and flowers, species known in England mainly through imported Turkish rugs and Iznik pottery, became a staple product, with the well-known design of three tulips introduced shortly after the bursting of the 'Tulip Mania' bubble in 1636/7, which had ruined the entire Dutch economy. A further development, perhaps stimulated by the prospect of commercial success attending Christian Wilhelm's successful application for a 21-year patent in 1628, and at a time when it is known that eight other Netherlandish potters were employed at the Pickleherring Quay pottery, encompassed a completely new type of pictorial charger. The earliest

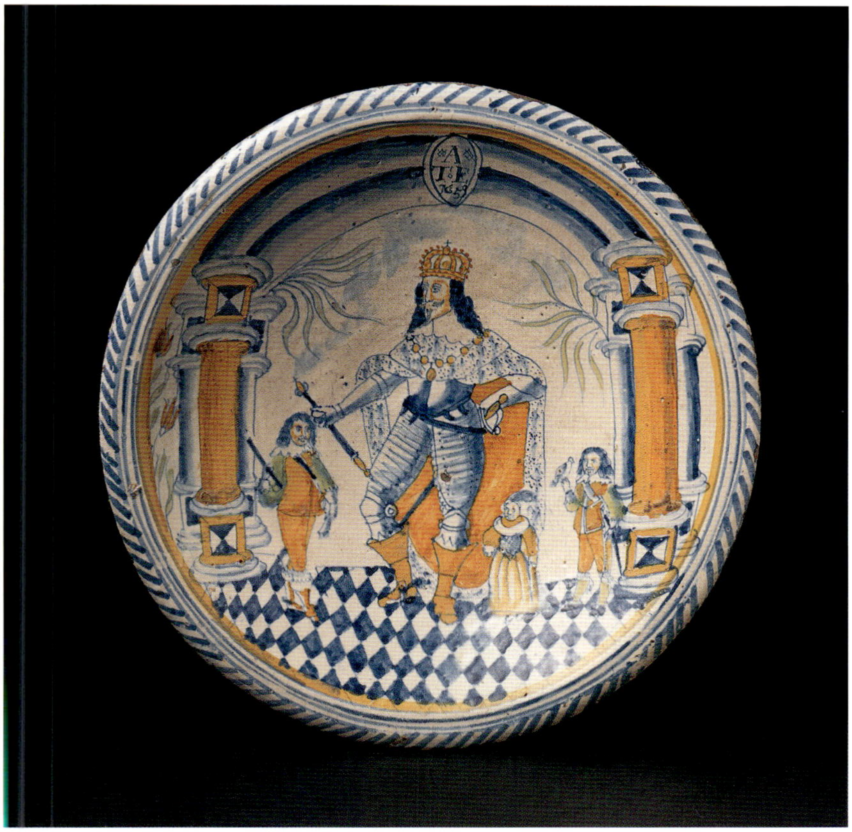

55
No doubt specially commissioned, this dish showing the entire Stuart succession, including the future Charles II and James II, was made boldly in London in 1653 during the Commonwealth Period, copied from a Dutch print of several years earlier. Diameter 36.5 cm (14⅜ in.).
V&A: C.71–1998.

survivor of this series shows the King of Bohemia and his family after a print by Willem van de Passe, bearing a commemorative date, 1614, but securely datable to around 1627.[12] Thereafter, the number, quality and variety of these dishes escalated, notably after the first of the popular *Temptation* chargers of 1635.[13]

Though now surviving in fairly large numbers, these specially commissioned pieces originally must have formed a miniscule proportion of the total output of the potteries where they were made, at Pickleherring Quay and Montague Close in Southwark, and at Rotherhithe (plate 55). From the beginning, the inscribed initials show that they were ordered by, or for, local City tradesmen, often members of the various Livery Companies whose arms appear so regularly on seventeenth-century London delftware. For this specialized market – the very backbone of Puritan London just before and during the Civil War – it is hardly surprising that the decorators chose to copy readily available prints by fellow Netherlanders, selecting mainly religious subjects sometimes extracted from contemporary Bibles. Apart from versions of *The Temptation* mentioned above, which were loosely copied from prints by Crispin van de Passe and Hendrik Goltzius, other notable subjects include *Mary Salome* after Marten Vos dated 1637,[14] *The Garden of Eden*[15] and *Susanna and the Elders*,[16] both dated 1648, *The Nativity* dated 1652,[17] *Christ on the Road to Emmaus* dated 1653,[18] *Mankind Awaiting the Last Judgement* of 1657[19], and *The Prodigal Son among the Swine* dated 1659 after an unsigned Netherlandish print.[20]

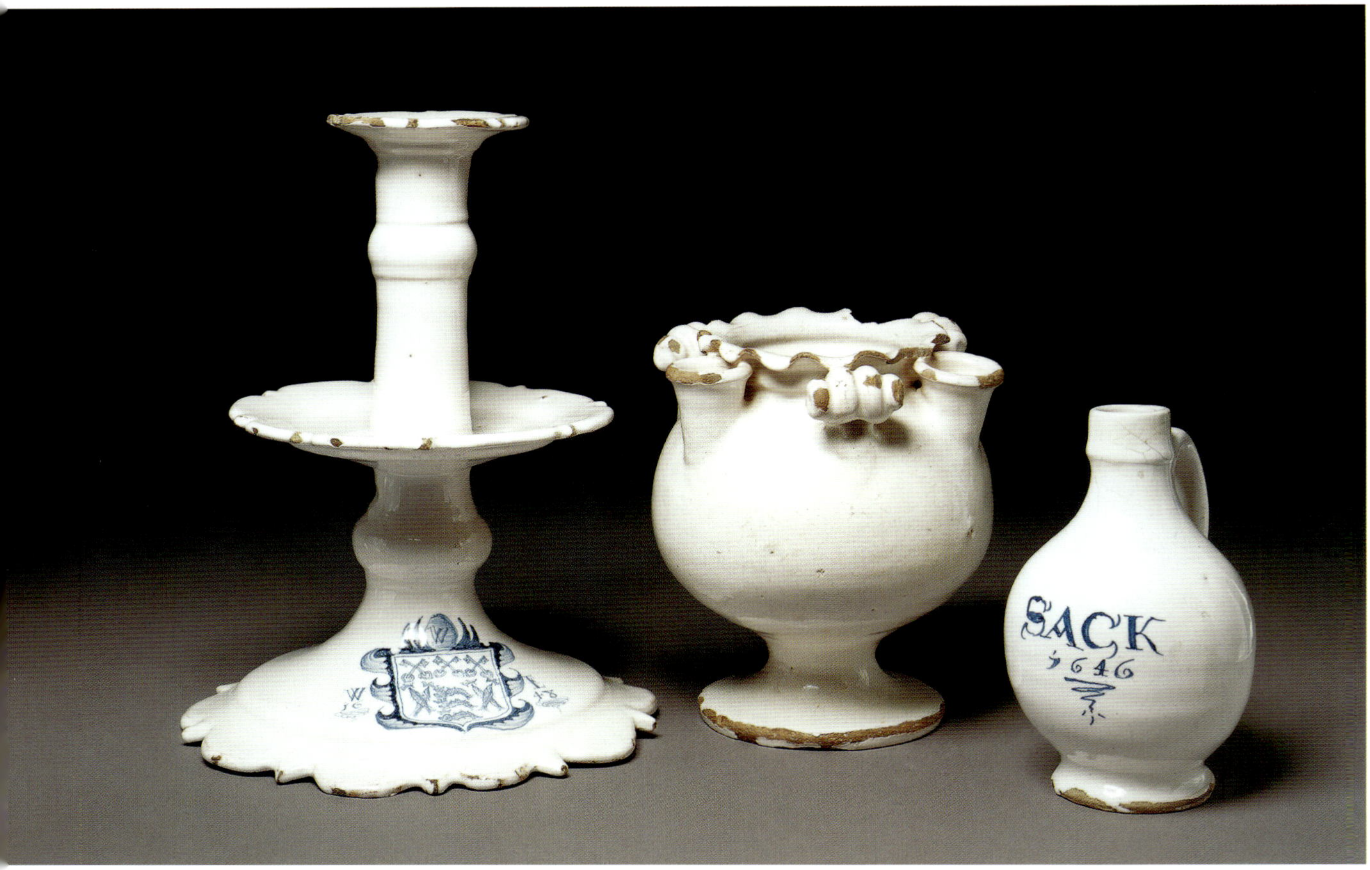

56
Although plain white delftwares were made in vast quantities, it is almost entirely the decorated examples that have survived: the relative plainness of these pieces being consistent with a mid-17th-century date. 'Sack' bottles were given as gifts at New Year. Max. height 27.3 cm (10¼ in.).

V&A: 4752–1901, Circ.98–1952, Sch.II 3.

Sometimes drawn with an unsure hand, with the figures unintentionally rendered as caricature, these bright, highly decorative polychrome display dishes were of a wholly new type invented for the English market. At their best, for example, the spirited and dextrous drawing of *St George*, closely based on a Netherlandish print after Raphael,[21] they could so easily have been adopted at a much higher social level as either display pieces or as armorial tableware. Yet the perfect opportunity for this to happen, the advent of the English Civil War in 1642, followed by the fall of the Ming Dynasty in China, which entirely halted the export of porcelain from 1647 to 1683, was apparently lost to the London delftware industry: for the materialistic and uncertain political climate was unsympathetic to display objects of no intrinsic value, and by the time that Royalists were compelled to cut up their silver plate to make emergency currency ('siege pieces'), London was in the hands of the Roundheads, while the king and his court were in Oxford. By contrast, when the War Chests needed to be replenished in Spain in 1601, and in France when a harsh royal edict of 1709 compelled the aristocracy to surrender their plate, the faience industries of both Talavera and Rouen stepped into the breach by producing highly decorated armorial tableware, with great long-term benefits for their respective pottery industries. But in England, although one City Livery Company is recorded as replacing its plate with delftware, this worthy example of self-sacrifice was not followed by other potential delftware patrons.

Apart from a definite plainness about mid-seventeenth-century delftwares (plate 56), the effects of the Civil War, while the rival armies joined battle in Oxfordshire, Warwickshire, Leicestershire and Worcestershire, seem to have been minimal. Already by the 1630s the potteries were making moulded dishes copied from the work of the earlier French potter Bernard Palissy,[22] which required only rudimentary decoration, as well as most of the basic types that were to form the potteries' repertoire for the remainder of the century: posset pots (vessels with spouts and lids) for communal drinking in winter months of curdled spiced ale, dated 'sack' bottles to be given as New Year gifts, porringers, barrel- and cup-shaped ale mugs, and many other forms. The occasional use of speckled powdered manganese-purple as overall decoration indicates an awareness of, and perhaps even competition with, contemporary Rhineland brown stoneware. But if the Civil War, and particularly the austerities of Oliver Cromwell, which included the banning of the celebration of Christmas, may have been responsible for arresting their natural development at this period, the London potters were not slow to seize upon the mass jubilation that greeted the Restoration of Charles II in 1660. This single event led to the invention of popular commemorative ceramics in England, employing to the full delftware's unique advantage of being able to record personal or popular events. From as early as 1660, the year before the coronation took place, until at least 1682, the health of the king could be drunk from beer mugs adorned with his bust or figure, initials and date. Display dishes, too, were made with full-length figures of Charles II, missing the unpopular James II but continuing on to include William and Mary, Queen Anne and George I in increasingly debased form.

The Restoration of 1660 also unleashed a rapid expansion in the London delftware industry, with the establishment of the Hermitage pottery at Wapping in 1665, the Bear Garden at Southwark sometime before 1671 and Gravel Lane in 1694, and with a tendency for the industry to move eastwards, first with the Rotherhithe pottery moving to Still Stairs, Southwark, in 1663, followed by the founding of the Vauxhall Pottery in 1683, the Norfolk House pottery in Lambeth in 1680, and the Putney pottery in 1680.[23] To put this expansion into context, one should not overlook the simultaneous activity in other areas of ceramic production, all of which indicate great financial rewards to be obtained from manufacturing, rather than merely importing, either well-tried or completely new products for the kitchens and dining tables of newly prosperous consumers. These activities include the granting of a royal charter to the Glass-Sellers' Company (the official body that maintained centralized control of the trade in ceramics and glass) in 1664, the lucrative patent for mirror-glass manufacture obtained by the Duke of Buckingham in 1663, the experiments of John Dwight at Wigan in the 1660s, which resulted in his patent for salt-glazed stoneware in 1672, and the patent for 'a perticuler sort of Christaline Glasse resembling Rock Cristall' granted in 1674 to a wealthy importer of Venetian glass, George Ravenscroft.

Yet despite the revival of delftware after the Restoration, its place in the hierarchy of tablewares remained unaltered. Even though production and export of porcelain was not resumed in China until 1683, well after the establishment of the new emperor Kangxi in 1662, the English delftware potteries seem to have failed to make inroads into the growing number of customers for Chinese porcelain. New forms were made, often innovative and whimsical such as puzzle jugs, jugs moulded as sitting cats, hand-warmers, and elaborate covered posset pots for the ceremonial consumption of warm spiced ale curdled with milk. Sets of inscribed and dated plates inscribed with six verses, latter-day versions of those painted wooden trenchers of the sixteenth century and somewhat reminiscent of the pious inscriptions on so-called Metropolitan slipwares, were produced in quantity, both in London and in Holland, remaining popular from the 1680s to the 1740s. The most common of these read: 'What is a Merry Man; Let him do what he can; To entertain his guest; With wine and merry jest; But if his wife does frown; All merriment goes down', or alternatively, 'When thou sit down to meat; Give thanks before thou eat; Unto him that does give; The mercies thou receive; That such favours may be; Repeated unto thee'. Such things, without any pretensions to become smart tableware, were aimed at consumers of the middling or lower ranks; and although influence from Delft raised the standard of painting on tablewares considerably in the last quarter of the seventeenth century, it was the market for Oriental porcelain that offered by far the greater scope for expansion. Peace with Holland from 1674 reopened the supply, first from Japan and later from China; and from 1699 the English East India Company was able to bypass the Dutch and deal directly with China from their trading station at Canton. Along with this explosion of trade came tea from China, coffee from Turkey and chocolate from South America, together with a demand for heat-resistant vessels for hot drinks. Here the delftware industry could offer little, and even their production of bowls for the newly invented punch, dated examples of which start as early as 1681, was rapidly overtaken by Chinese porcelain copies, which, given the use of boiling water to heat the contents, immediately proved more durable. Nonetheless, the fragile delftwares of London supplied a small proportion of the market for vessels for hot drinks,[24] in competition with the Elers brothers' red stoneware capuchines and the brown salt-glaze of John Dwight at Fulham. As early illustrations of coffee houses show, coffee and chocolate were usually brewed in metal pots by the fireside, from which the drink might be decanted into ceramic serving pots well below boiling point. But when the fashion for tea began to dominate the market after about 1700, it was natural that the established range of imported Chinese porcelain or red stoneware vessels should be preferred to softer local substitutes.

It might be thought that ceramic importers and manufacturers at this time were locked in deadly rivalry. Appearances, however, are highly misleading; for the closer one looks at the range of vessels offered by different makers, the clearer it becomes that each branch of ceramic manufacture had its own specialities with its own niche in the wider market, and that direct competition between them was minimal. A brief study of the invaluable list of delftware and stoneware products prepared by Mr Bateman for taxation purposes in 1696 shows that delftware

57
Towards 1700 the increasing import of Chinese porcelain began to have an impact on the delftware industry. Although tablewares now had competition, there were still exclusive forms such as ale mugs, traditional polychrome 'chargers' and storage jars. Dish and mug London or Bristol *c.*1690, jar probably London. Max. height 33.6 cm (13¼ in.).
V&A: C.27–1963, C.323–1914, Circ.468–1967.

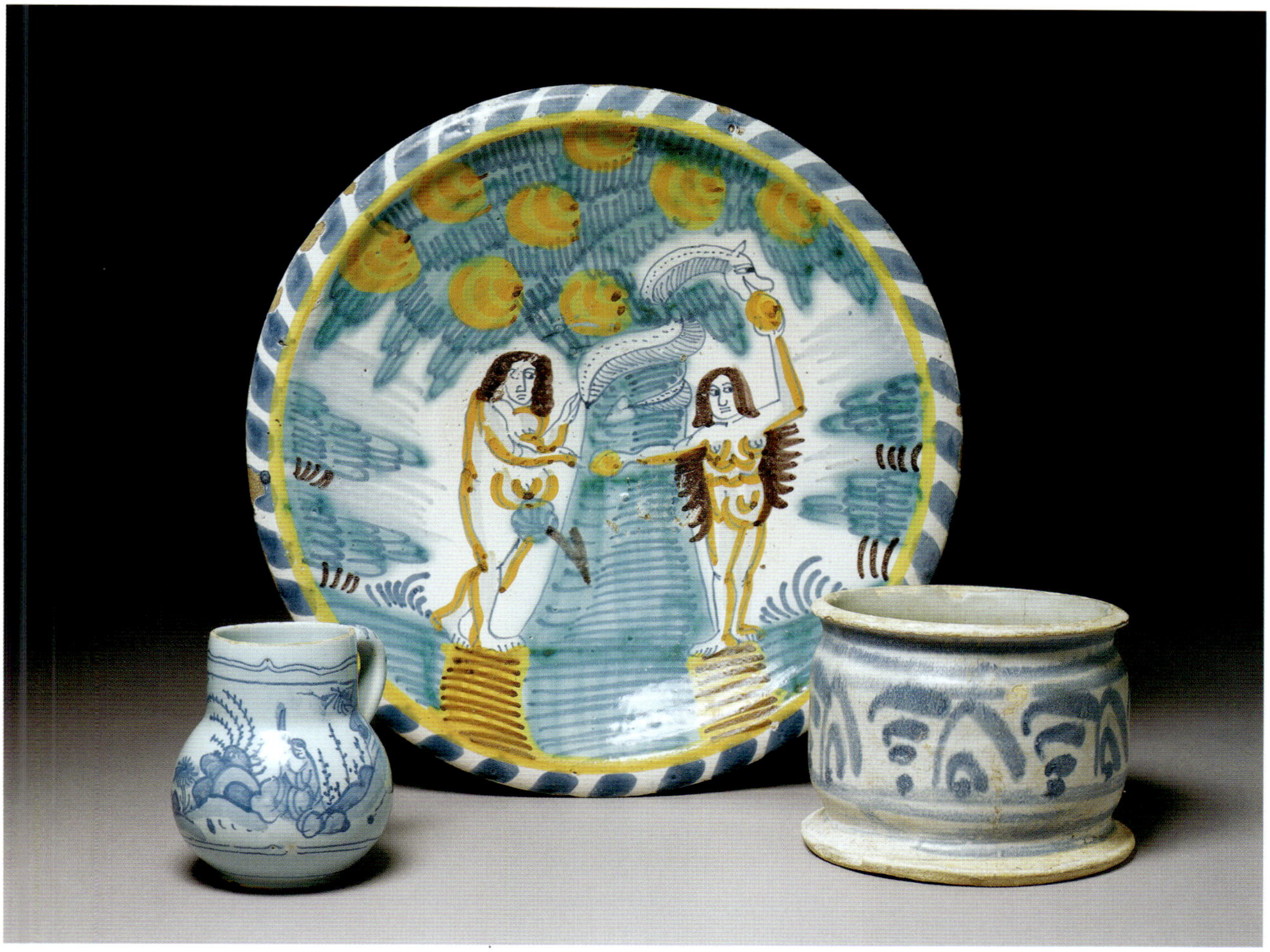

factories were offering a wide range of both utilitarian and obscure products (plate 57), such as, for example, 'Pigeon-Potts, Cawdell Potts, Marmalet Potts, Blood porringers, Chamber Potts',[25] few of which would have interested the multitude of anonymous Chinese potters whose profitability depended entirely on the mass production of a limited range of standard products for annual shipment to Europe.

But if the delftware manufacturers missed out on the new craze for hot drinks, and if they were further handicapped by the taxation imposed in 1696 when Jonathan Chilwell of the Vauxhall Pottery stated that 'there has been no Work at Foxhall for seven weeks', at least they could fall back on products for which there was absolutely no competition: pharmacy jars and tiles. From the 1650s cylindrical *albarelli* for dry preparations, and globular spouted jars on a spreading foot for medicinal syrups, had been made in increasing numbers by London potters, exploiting their unique capability for permanent fired-in labels. This was a product that not even Wedgwood's creamware could threaten in the 1760s, although it was eventually to be made redundant after the mid-nineteenth century by the development of glass for medical purposes, in particular the mould-blown medicine bottle. Useful though delftware potters found the continuing demand for pharmaceutical wares to be, it was tiles that offered a much greater opportunity for expansion. As early as 1634 Sir William Brereton records the purchase in Holland of 'four-score painted stones for one chimney', issuing very careful instructions about the arrangement of these 80 tiles painted with soldiers, officers and drummers.[26] Fifty tiles with birds and another 50 with flowers were also purchased. Unfortunately for English delftware potters, although the demand for tiled fireplaces was well established in the seventeenth century, both the skilled painters and the method of successfully firing thin squares of clay without warping proved elusive. In an age when dependency on foreign imports was actively discouraged, this deficiency was pointed out in a Bill before the House of Commons in 1673/4; but when, as a consequence, Jan Ariens van Hamme obtained a patent 'to exercise his Art of Makeinge Tiles and Porcelane and other earthenware wares after the way practised in Holland' and settled in Lambeth in 1676, this promising venture ended prematurely with his death three or four years later. Meanwhile, in the absence of English competition, large quantities of Dutch tiles continued to be imported, until shortly before 1718 the enterprising Thomas Oade of the Gravel Lane Pottery, declaring that 'Galley tiles for Chimneys, being a very beneficial part of the Trade, and not a Man in the Kingdom to be got, that could make them to any purpose', journeyed from Harwich to Holland to bring 'a Person well skilled in that Art', whom his father Nathaniel then engaged for six years.[27] From this time onwards English delftware potters were equipped with the technical expertise to mass-produce thin tiles for wall and chimney, even if, as has been estimated, usually only 25 per cent of tiles survived the firing in a state fit to be used. As for decoration, they seldom surpassed the Dutch, whose fluently painted products remained in demand, for those who could afford them, throughout the eighteenth century.[28]

By 1700 the growing fashion for hot drinks was firmly linked with tough, elegant Chinese porcelain, soon to be accompanied by a huge demand for tablewares. For example, in 1705 the East India Company's *Dashwood* carried 15,979 blue and white plates,[29] which sold for 1s 6d each, as against the delftware 'fine painted plates' on Mr Bateman's list of 1696, which were valued at between a 1½d and 1s each. At the same time, a general increase in living standards during the early years of the century fuelled a demand at every social level for blue and white, which, for the poorer classes, could be entirely supplied by the delftware factories.[30] Thus the industry saw a period of great expansion, riding on the back of the highly popular but more expensive Chinese porcelains, which culminated in the establishment of branches in Bristol, Liverpool, Glasgow and Belfast – all ports with good facilities for importing all the raw materials combined with a vigorous export trade to the New World and elsewhere. But with the price of Chinese porcelain falling steadily as the number of East India Company shipments increased, this expansion could not be maintained beyond the middle of the eighteenth century: by this time, the average price of a Chinese plate had fallen from 1s 6d to 1s, 'fine earthen [i.e., delftware] plates' were 6d, the same price as Staffordshire tortoiseshell, and white salt-glaze plates were a mere 1½d.

58
Competition between the London potteries by the 1760–70 period had produced some unusual forms and bright but simple decoration. The material, however, was ill-suited to the *veilleuse* with its spirit lamp. Max. height 22.9 cm (9 in.).
V&A: C.50–1939, C.732–1923.

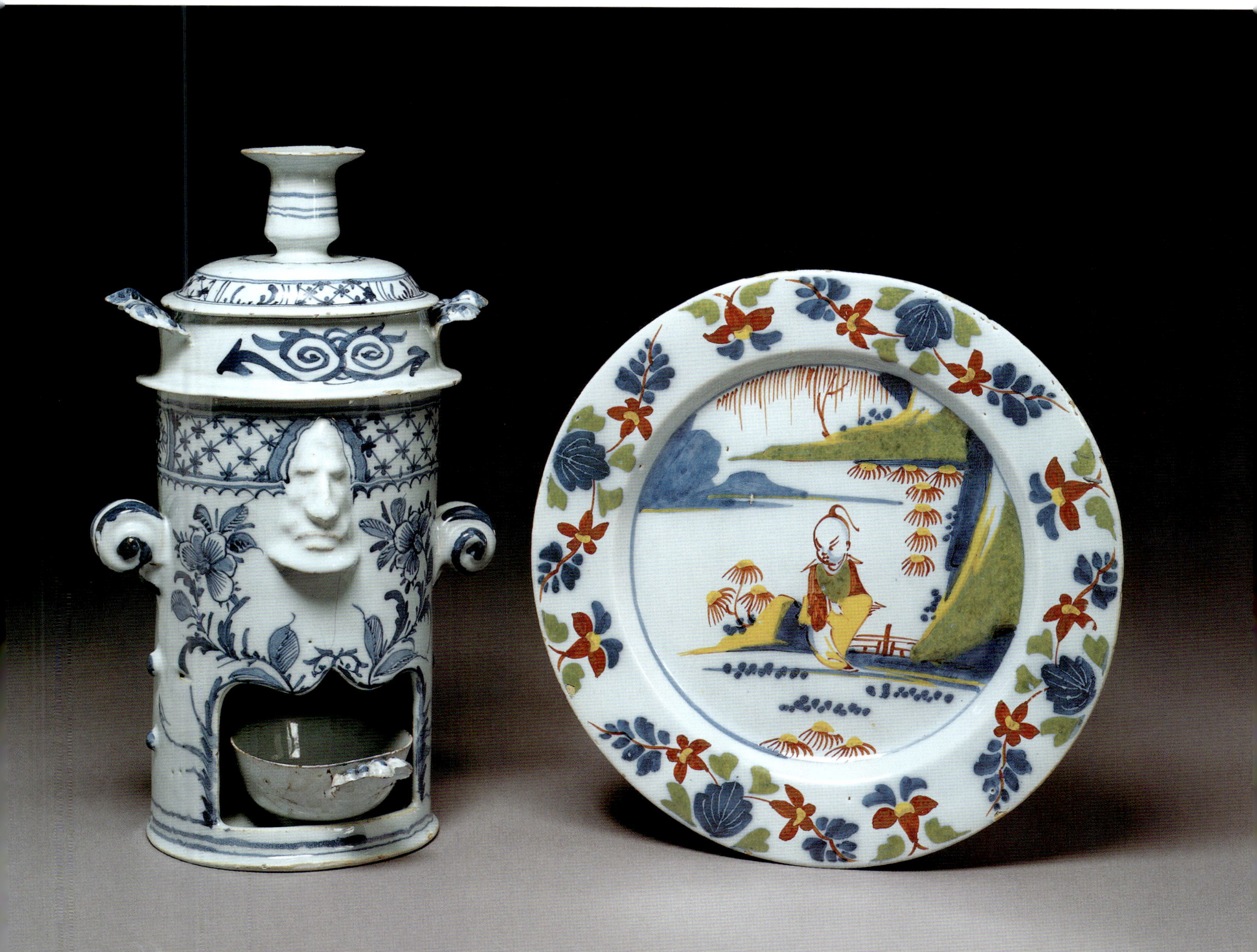

Given the fact that delftware was easily damaged, while porcelain and white stoneware were extremely tough, it is not surprising that delftware, prettily and fashionably painted though it might be, was bound to lose ground. Meanwhile, pewter retained its popularity at a middle-class level throughout this period.[31]

The history of the major eighteenth-century British delftware factories and their products, in many cases backed up by archaeological evidence, has been comprehensively covered by recent literature.[32] Nonetheless, having already looked at the origins and the wider context of the industry, it is necessary to complete the story by repeating brief accounts of delftware production in different parts of the British Isles. For although delftware had always relied on Chinese porcelain for its decoration, when manufacture spread from London to Bristol, Liverpool, Scotland and Ireland (and even apparently to Biggleswade on the River Ouse, where a pottery is recorded as operating in the years 1736–43), distinctive local styles and shapes evolved, which today form the main basis for attribution. In London, the headquarters of the East India Company and its trade, Chinese influence naturally remained strong, with marked similarities (perhaps from shared painters) between patterns on delftware tablewares and on the porcelains made at the mid-eighteenth-century factories in Bow, Limehouse and Vauxhall. Apart from a few innovative bright polychrome patterns, such as a Chinese boy in landscape and a parrot with tree stump, most blue and white patterns were fairly humdrum but competently painted. Even where new techniques were attempted, these all derived from Chinese porcelain: powdered ground colours with masked reserve panels, and *bianco sopra bianco* decoration where pure white tin-enamel was used to produce border patterns on the slightly bluish or greenish ground. Late attempts to abandon Chinoiserie and adopt symmetrical Neo-classical designs with swagged borders, as on the 'Ann Gomm' plates of the early 1790s, proved a vain gesture. For those who could afford it, the New Hall factory did it so much better, and with tough hard-paste porcelain.

At Bristol, the first pothouse was established in 1683 as an offshoot of the pottery at Brislington. Perhaps because of its distance from London and its great trade with the New World and elsewhere (notably in slaves for the West Indies and the fruit of their labours, sugar and rum), by the second half of the eighteenth century the delftware, stoneware and creamware factories of Bristol achieved a high technical and artistic standard. Here ceramic historians have been able to ascribe certain painting styles to talented individual painters who signed their work, including John Bowen, Michael Edkins and Joseph Flower. The *bianco sopra bianco* technique (see plate 53) is thought to have been introduced at Bristol by Magnus Lundberg, a Swede from Rörstrand, who in the 1760s may have been the manager of Richard Frank's pottery at Redcliff, which at that time he recorded as having 42 employees. In general, the painting of Bristol tablewares ranged from pedestrian 'export quality' to the finest Rococo fantasies, and a period of exuberance in the third quarter of the eighteenth century was followed by a sharp decline in the 1770s.

The Liverpool potteries began in 1710 as an offshoot of the London industry and continued to run along similar lines. The painting, however, was exceptional, perhaps inspired by the more discerning Irish and American market cultivated by the Staffordshire potteries whose products passed through the city. The Pennington factory is known to have specialized in handsome punch bowls painted with named ships, while other Liverpool specialities included puzzle jugs, flower bricks, vases, cornucopia wall-pockets and, of course, tiles. The proximity of porcelain factories with their wider technical expertise also encouraged attempts to improve the basic material – without, however, achieving anything comparable to the situation in France, where the aggressive dominance of the royal porcelain factory at Sèvres forced faience makers to employ skilled porcelain painters to embellish their highly refined body with fine enamelling and gilding. Nevertheless, a limited amount of *petit feu* enamelling was practised by freelance decorators at Liverpool, while the pioneering printing firm Sadler

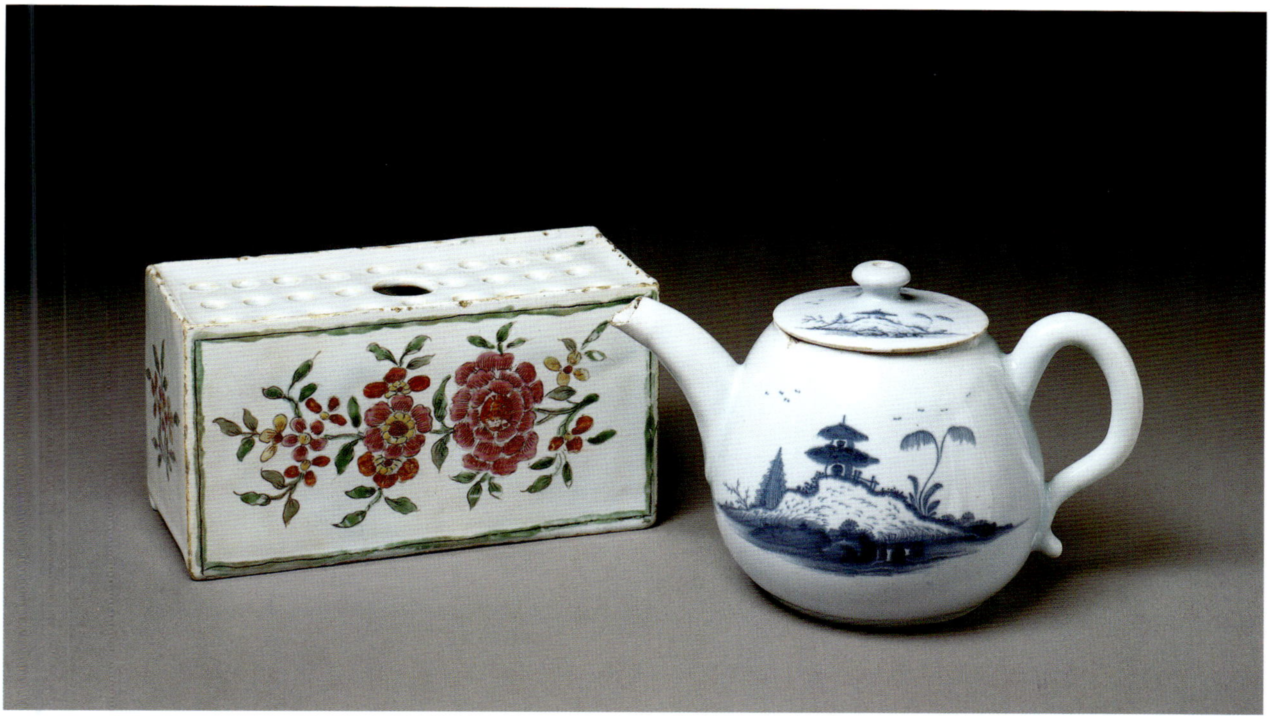

& Green were quick to apply their method of transfer-printing to tiles, with great commercial success, representing a rather typically British triumph of technology over artistry.[33] An innovation just as promising, but apparently hardly exploited, was the tin-glazing of salt-glazed vitrified stoneware, whereby, at the cost of an extra firing, teawares could offer resistance to boiling water while still retaining the soft blue in-glaze delftware painting. Little is known about this experimental technique, which would surely have brought delftware into direct competition with the fairly unsophisticated blue and white porcelains made by neighbouring Liverpool factories (plate 59). None of these improvements to the basic delftware technique, however, could insulate them against competition from the mass-produced creamwares of Staffordshire, so that by the 1780s almost all the Liverpool potteries had closed.

59
At Liverpool in the 1750–60 period, the presence of porcelain factories inspired some unusual experiments, including low-temperature enamel decoration and, in order to make teapots heat resistant, tin-glazed stoneware. Max. height 10.2 cm (4 in.). V&A: C.66–1979, C.88–1967.

In Ireland, the first delftwares were made around 1688 at Belfast where suitable clay was identified at Carrickfergus – so suitable that it supplied not only the Dublin factories established around 1735 but also the Delftfield Pottery at Glasgow and the entire Liverpool delftware industry. Much is known about the important factory on the Strand in Dublin under the proprietorship of Henry Delamain *circa* 1752–7, whose fortune was entirely expended on perfecting his manufacture. With the prospect of halting the huge import trade of faience from Burgundy and Rouen, he successfully applied for large grants from the Dublin Society which enabled him to continue, while adding stoneware clays to resist thermal shock and developing a successful method of coal-firing, which he offered to impart free to any other manufacturer. Despite a strong export trade to the West Indies, the excellence of the wares (plate 60), the skill of the painters

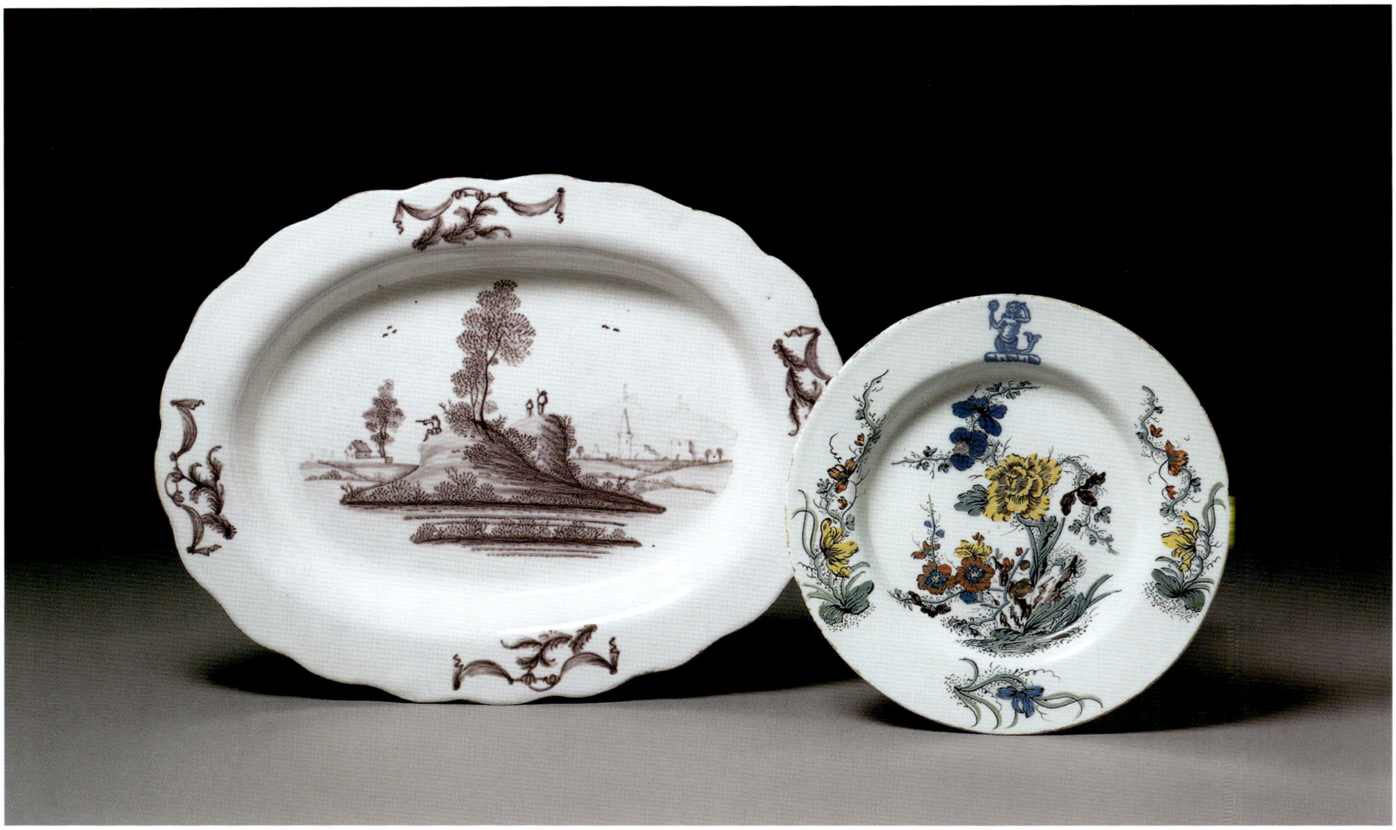

60
Offshoots of the English delftware industry developed their own characteristics, such as the spiky painting found at Glasgow (here with the Murray crest) and the soft 'watercolour' style found at Delamain's Dublin factory *c.*1753–60. Max. height 10.2 cm (4 in.).
V&A: C.103–1965, C.4–1928.

and a limited production of armorial services for wealthy patrons, after Delamain's death in 1757 the business lost its driving force, passed through several hands and folded up around 1771.

Scotland, with restricted access to imported luxury goods, appeared to offer good entrepreneurial opportunities. Its inhabitants were perhaps less critical than those spoiled by the feast of riches in London, and furthermore the port of Glasgow had a thriving export trade. Thus a partnership of local businessmen set up the Delftfield Pottery in 1748 (plate 60), relying on the services of a potter called John Bird (perhaps of the well-known Staffordshire potting family) to establish the major enterprise with potters and painters hired from London. There were immediate set-backs when the melting of saggars caused the loss of the first firing, leading to the dismissal of Bird, who promptly sued the directors.[34] Thereafter the pottery flourished, and figures for the export of pottery from Scotland show that it continued long after the potteries at Lambeth and Bristol had closed: for example, 6,794 dozen pieces were exported from Glasgow as late as 1791, no doubt mostly bound for America and Canada. So it may be inferred that the entire remaining markets for cheap delftware were eventually inherited by the last factory to survive. An interesting parallel may be drawn here with the 18 factories at Rouen, which, during this same period, continued to export huge amounts of outmoded faience to far-flung outposts of French culture, including Canada. The fact that William Littler's attempts to make porcelain and Staffordshire-type pottery at West Pans in the years 1764–7 met with so little favour, while the humble mass production of delftware was rewarded with great success, also reveals much about the commercial climate of Scotland at this period. A few delftware objects with a distinctive spiky painting style, mainly armorial plates, have been attributed to Delftfield; but as for the general quality of their output, it may be significant that when the Duke of Buccleugh decided to purchase a massive dinner service of tin-glazed earthenware in 1765, he went shopping with his £150 to Marseille rather than Glasgow.[35]

Thus by about 1790, apart from a continuing supply of tiles, pharmaceutical wares made at the Vauxhall Pottery (plate 61), and the late-flowering manufacture at Glasgow, production of delftware tableware had all but ended in the British Isles. By this time London had been deserted by the last of its porcelain makers; the glassmakers were establishing themselves near sources of refractory clay and coal in Stourbridge and the North-East; and along the banks of the Thames the making of coarse salt-glazed stonewares had largely supplanted that of delftware, with which it had been made in tandem for a hundred years. In other centres the winding down of delftware was more gradual, since the more direct access to sources of coal and West Country clay offered redundant potters a chance to switch to creamware at Bristol, and to blue and white porcelain and Pearlware at Liverpool. Even on Pearlwares apparently made in Staffordshire, it is sometimes possible to detect the practised hand of the delftware painter. But the decline of the thriving delftware industry, inexorable and final though it was,[36] might have been predicted decades before, as a close look at the complex wider context will show.

The English taste for blue and white, well-established by the early eighteenth century, received further stimulus during the 1740s not only with the founding of the first English porcelain factories at Chelsea and Bow, but also with the hotting-up of the trade in Chinese porcelain, accompanied by demands from London for ready-sorted dinner and tea services and by the dispatch to China of the first patterns for objects designed expressly for the English market. Both documentary and archaeological evidence demonstrate that the mid-eighteenth century was, in fact, the high-point of the blue and white fashion, when a 43-piece 'Nankeen' tea service cost no more than about £3 from a retailer. In

England the new porcelain factories, unable to compete on cost, were at least able to offer a wide range of new and imaginative patterns: the Bow factory, styled 'New Canton' and modelled on a large Chinese porcelain factory, initially made only blue decorated ware from 1747, while at Liverpool it was made in large amounts from the 1750s, at Lowestoft from 1759 to the closure of the factory in 1799, at Worcester from the 1750s, and from 1772 at Caughley by a former Worcester employee, Thomas Turner, whose 'Salopian' products were widely advertised by London chinamen during the period 1784–95. But whereas the lucrative blue and white market had led the Worcester factory in the period 1757–60 to crack the secret of fusing cobalt-blue transfer prints onto the biscuit body to make them immune from the liquid glaze, the Staffordshire pottery manufacturers, busy developing their novel cream-coloured alternatives at this

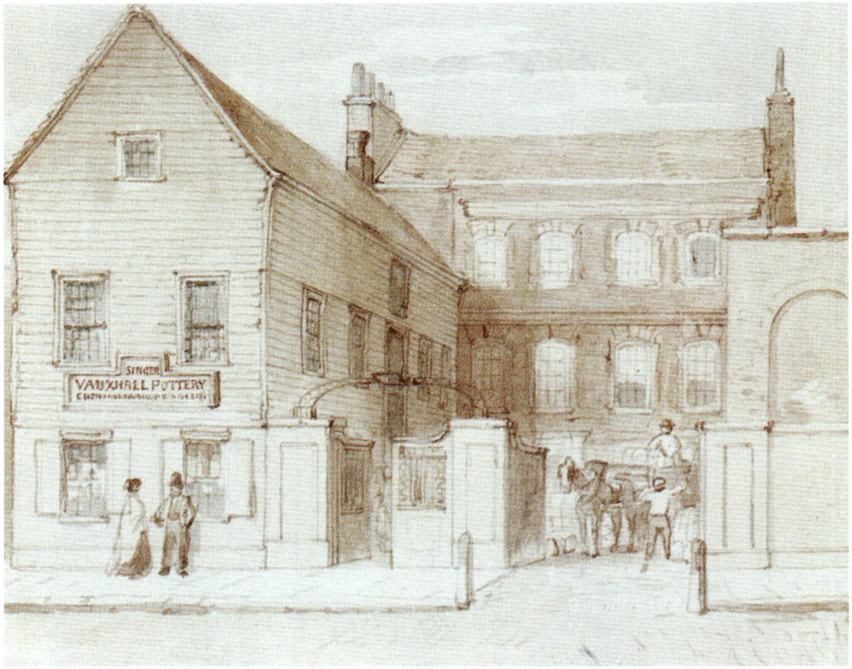

61
The Vauxhall Pottery made delftware continuously from the late 17th century until the early 19th, adding stoneware to its production about 1715. The artist Findlay recorded much of the Lambeth area in the 1840s, well before the building of the Embankment.
V&A: D.56-1904.

time, were entirely uninterested in underglaze-blue Chinoiseries, either painted or printed. For the cheap pottery market was still adequately served by delftware.

However, the introduction and expansion of English blue and white porcelain must be seen as one of the main causes of the simultaneous steep decline in imports by the East India Company after the mid-eighteenth century. Although English dealers attempted to enhance the jaded product by having gilding added by decorators of the calibre of Humphrey Chamberlain of Worcester, the Company, for their part, did little to promote their porcelain, ordering no more than four different patterns for their last shipments around 1790. Perhaps in order to correct this imbalance, at this period the Chinese potters even produced hand-painted copies of printed Caughley and Worcester patterns, including fake marks. But for the East India Company, the profitability of the product (only one, after all, among many of their regular imports, the greatest of which was tea) was further reduced by three factors: first, poor packing and careless, or perhaps deliberate, mismatching of sets in the consignments from China; secondly, a ruinous duty of 47.5 per cent imposed in 1787 in order to subsidize the wars with France, increasing to over 100 per cent in 1799; and thirdly, the unscrupulous conduct of the London chinamen who formed 'combinations' (now known as 'rings') to defraud the auctioneers at the East India Company sales. But it is clear that the demand remained for some years after the Company resolved to cease importing porcelain in 1791, for in 1795, at a time when old stocks of porcelain must have been completely cleared, the London chinaman Miles Mason requested that the Company resume importation, but acting directly on behalf of the dealers themselves. They refused. Mason promptly took Wolfe as a partner in making blue and white porcelain at Liverpool in the years 1796–1800, and then moved to Staffordshire, where he abandoned blue and white in favour of more fashionable polychrome bone chinas.

By about 1800 the English porcelain manufacturers had simply moved on: Worcester had long since given up blue and white, Lowestoft had closed in 1799, while the 'Salopian' china made at Caughley ceased to be advertised by London chinamen after 1795, and in 1799 succumbed to a takeover by John Rose, who moved to Coalport, soon to become famous for its colourful bone chinas. Porcelain makers now concentrated on developing enamelling and gilding on the austere shapes copied from the hard-paste porcelains of Paris, the existing demand for which immediately increased after 1789, when it was made unobtainable by the French Revolution. For traditional porcelain customers, the fashion for Chinese grey now gave way to French white, in the form of the chalky white bone china body developed in the 1790s; for this proved to be an ideal background for the polychrome Chinese and Japanese styles rapidly adopted in Staffordshire by the ambitious new generation of makers like Spode and Minton, as also at Derby and Worcester.

Not surprisingly, earthenware potters lost no time in feeding this revived interest in the Orient, taking as models the popular Japanese polychromes made at Arita (and generally known as 'Imari', from whence they were exported). For in the wake of the expiry of Champion's Patent for hard-paste porcelain in 1796, the development of new ceramic bodies became an immediate possibility, using porcelain ingredients to produce bone china and various types of felspathic stonewares. But neither of these new bodies could replicate the toughness of Oriental hard-paste porcelain, and it was only the ingenuity of 'Turner's Patent' of 1800 that finally provided a tough grey body using Tabberner's Mine Rock. This excellent material might have enjoyed wider success but for the bankruptcy of John and William Turner in 1805. However, the concept of using an extra tough earthenware body to imitate grey Oriental porcelain and bright polychrome decoration had been planted in the minds of makers and public alike, and whether or not it was Josiah Spode who succeeded in purchasing the patent in 1805–6, the Spode factory launched its perfected 'Stone China' in 1813, the same year that Charles and James Mason obtained a patent for their 'Ironstone China' (plate 62). Both names represented a brilliant marketing ploy, since the material itself was neither stoneware nor china.[37] Masons combined their very grey dense body with transfer-printed 'Japan' patterns, hand-coloured and gilt, to produce initially a fine material which, apart from its greater weight, it is sometimes difficult to distinguish from porcelain. But if we are to believe Thomas Byerley, writing from the Wedgwood showroom on 19 March 1814, the huge Spode factory was aiming even higher: 'Every one enquires for the stone china, made by Spode and Mason and it has a very great run – I presume you know what it is, it is a thick coarse china body, not transparent, with china patterns, but in texture similar to old stoneware'.[38] In fact, Spode's Stone China was so good that Queen Charlotte bought a service from their showroom in 1817, after which copies and pastiches marked with variations on 'Stone China', 'Opaque China' and 'Semi-Porcelain' began to flood the market, eventually undermining

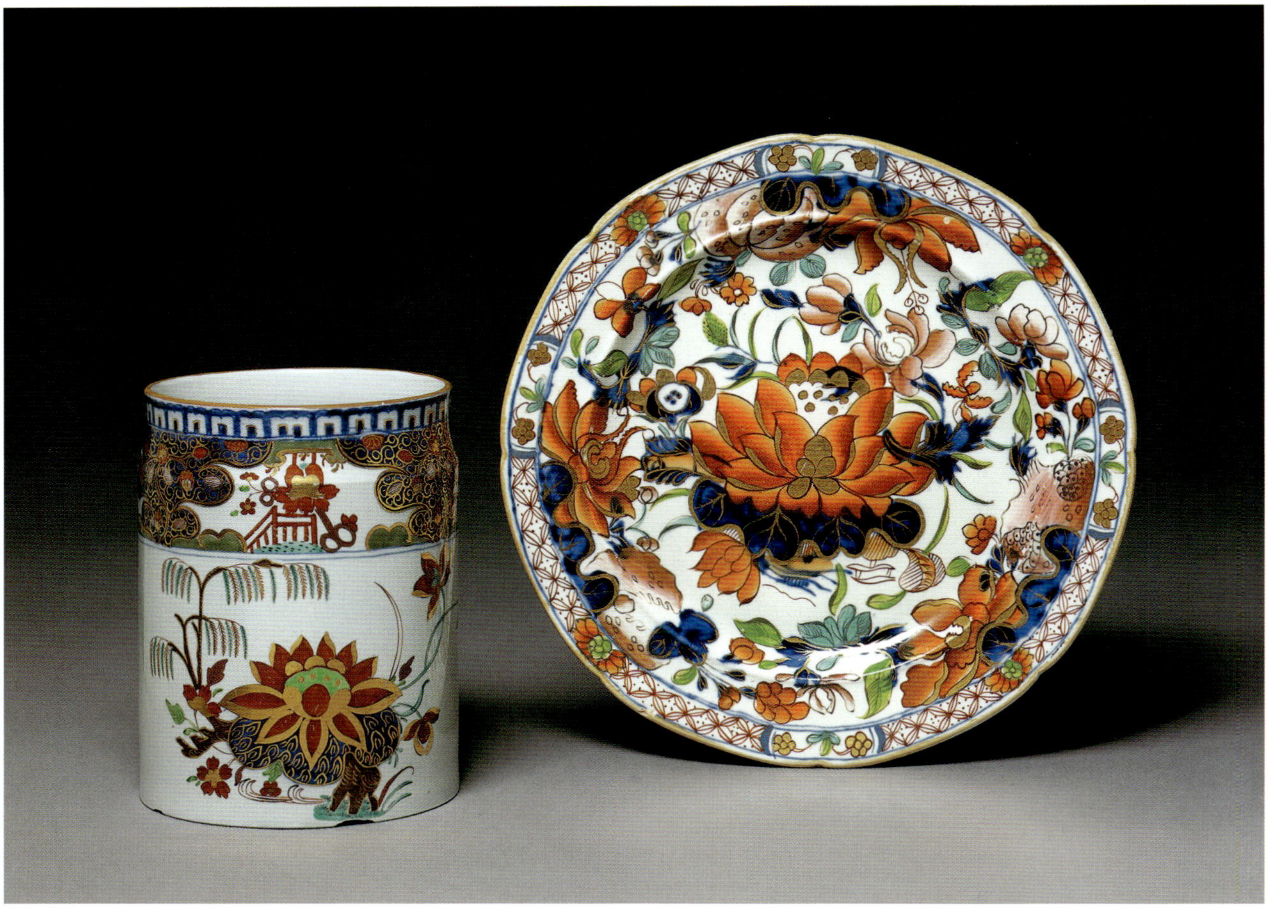

62
The grey body and Oriental-style decoration of Turner's Patent, as shown on this mug, had much in common with C. J. Mason's patent for 'Ironstone China' (right) obtained in 1813. Diameter of plate 23.8 cm (9⅜ in.).
V&A: C.55–1964, 1472–1870.

Masons' market and doubtless contributing to their bankruptcy in 1854. Nevertheless, it was Masons' product that, adapting to market trends while aiming at a more popular level than Spode, became the famous name to which their successor Ashworth soon reverted. It is still made, now under the umbrella of the Wedgwood group.

Meanwhile, the market for blue and white shifted its position in the ceramic hierarchy but did not wane. During the last two decades of the eighteenth century the gradual whitening of fine Staffordshire earthenwares ran parallel with the final phases of blue transfer-printed porcelain manufacture. Eventually, having put the makers of delftware out of business through the undisputed superiority of its body and glaze, by a clever process of assimilation it also succeeded in taking over the entire market not just from delftware but also from English and Chinese porcelain. It has commonly been supposed that Josiah Wedgwood was responsible for almost every important ceramic development and change in fashion from about 1760 until his death in 1795 – a belief actively encouraged by Wedgwood himself. But with blue and white, this is not so. Nevertheless, inevitably the starting point for charting the history of this period of change must be the correspondence between Wedgwood and Thomas Bentley.[39] From these letters, it is clear that, though a hard-headed business man, Wedgwood was not immune to human frailty, an example of which was his over-protective attitude towards creamware, the perfection and marketing of which formed the bedrock of his fortune and reputation. And like an anxious parent, at the same time he was fearful of launching an under-developed new type of whitened body into direct competition with the big porcelain makers. Always experimenting, as early as 1768 he was attempting to lighten his creamware body by adding Cornish clay and stone, and by the following year he was deliberating whether to continue as before, do radical changes to make his creamware straw-coloured, or continue whitening his creamware body to the point where it would compete with porcelain. He vacillated, but continued to experiment until the clamour from the public for a whiter product overcame his scruples. Yet as late as 1775 he was referring to 'good old Creamcolour, painted & varied in every way we can invent . . . I cannot at present find it in my heart to relinquish my good old Creamcolour'.

Other circumstances, however, now focused his attention, for in that year Champion attempted to renew his patent for hard-paste porcelain, to which Wedgwood and his fellow potters reacted with such fierce and well-argued resistance that Parliament restricted the patent to porcelain only. The way was now open for potters to bring their earthenwares even closer to porcelain by adding china clay and china stone to the clay body. Although Wedgwood was ostensibly uninterested in porcelain, he was very well aware of the possibilities that these ingredients offered, so that within days of the patent renewal he and his fellow potter John Turner journeyed to Cornwall to acquire mining rights. Breaking Champion's monopoly did, in fact, have far-reaching results, both for earthenware and, in the 1790s when the patent was near expiry, for the development of bone china. But more immediately, with the fashion turning away from yellow and towards cooler colouring, as early as 1775–6 Messrs Wedgwood & Bentley in London supplied the Duke of Atholl with a huge service of 'Blue Ivey' pattern, and in 1777 they supplied the Duke of Gordon with 'pearl white green shell edge'.[40] By 1779 Wedgwood himself considered his new body, after the addition of white clay and flint to the body and cobalt to the glaze, perfect enough to suggest that his partner Thomas Bentley should name it – the unsurprising choice being 'Pearl White'. More used to the role of innovator, or to copying only rare marble and hardstone rather than rival ceramic bodies, he grudgingly called this 'a change rather than an improvement . . . the pearl white being considered as an imitation of some of the blue and white fabriques, either earthenware or porcelain'. By this time other potters had developed their own versions of what we now call Pearlware, briefly termed 'China Glaze' in the 1780s but then, common as it rapidly became, allowed to lapse into anonymity, often simply under the name 'shell edge' (plate 63).

Even at this point, Wedgwood could surely have taken over the market with his 'Pearl White'; but his innate dislike of Pearlware, together with a consuming interest in developing more prestigious ornamental wares such as Jasper and Black Basalt, militated against it. Instead, since the new material was generally considered to be unattractive in an undecorated state, from the 1770s he produced plain tablewares with a moulded 'shell edge', the edges painted in blue,

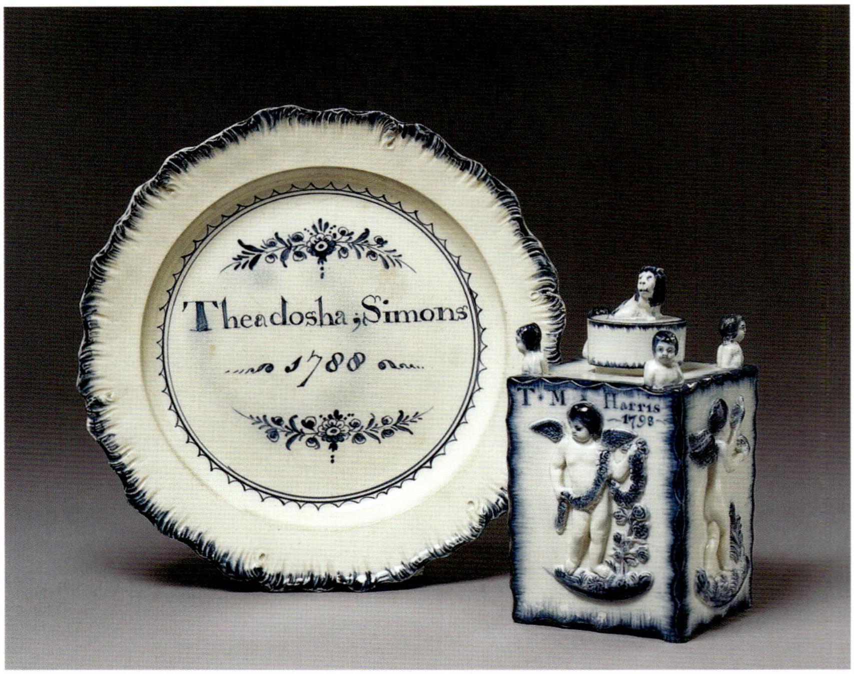

63
Pearlware became a major product of potteries outside Staffordshire, particularly those with access to the export trade. Both this Swansea plate of 1788 and the Bovey Tracey tea canister have been identified from excavations on the pottery sites. Diameter of plate 23.4 cm (9¼ in.).
V&A: C.148–1984, 127–1874.

green or brown. Dismissing the commercial opportunities offered by underglaze-blue transfer-printing in the Chinese idiom,[41] he continued having his creamwares overglaze-printed at Liverpool and using his Pearl White either for tablewares with non-Chinese blue decoration or for armorial services with bat-printed, hand-coloured crests or arms, which were intended to replace the traditional grey Chinese Export armorial porcelain.

Until the 1780s, Pearlware manufacturers were content to reproduce standard blue patterns by 'pouncing' finely ground pigment through a pricked paper design, doubtless employing redundant delftware painters to give life to the resulting dotted image, but the increasing demand for Pearlware made some more efficient form of mass production essential – and what better than to take a leaf from the porcelain manufacturers' book and learn how to fix a print to the biscuit body by mixing the cobalt with oils and firing it onto the biscuit body before dipping in glaze, as first developed at Worcester shortly before 1760.[42] Simeon Shaw tells us of Josiah Spode that

> about 1784, he introduced the manufacture of *Blue Printed* into Stoke; on the improved methods successfully adopted by Mr Ralph Baddeley, of Shelton. The Patterns were – for Table Services what is now called the *Old Willow*, with a border of a willow and a dagger; and for Tea Services the *Broseley*, from the Pattern used at Caughley. The engraver was named Lucas, and his first printer was named Richards, from Caughley.[43]

This account of the birth of underglaze transfer-printed pottery, though not necessarily accurate in every detail, is fairly plausible: Ralph Baddeley was one of the leading potters of his generation, while Josiah Spode, a former apprentice of Thomas Whieldon, was ambitious enough to open a London showroom in Foregate Street, Cripplegate, as early as 1778 and went on to become the major maker of blue and white. It is almost certain, too, that both the printing technique and the earliest patterns were introduced to the pottery industry by engravers from Caughley. Following the discovery of cobalt deposits in Cornwall and the establishment by Roger Kinnaston of a cobalt-refining furnace in the Potteries around 1772, as well as improvements in the transfer-printing process whereby the print was laid on to the biscuit body via an intermediary piece of fine tissue paper that could be dampened and peeled off, the way for major expansion lay open. By 1797 William Adams had built the first mill for making the fine transfer paper at Cheddleton, and soon engravers, designers and makers of printing machinery were drawn to the Potteries to supply the growing local needs.

By the 1790s simple standard patterns, such as the infinite variations on the Chinese House with its trees, rocks and fence, were being made not only in Staffordshire but in the potteries of Yorkshire, notably the Leeds, Don and Swinton Potteries, at Liverpool, Bristol, Swansea and Bovey Tracey in Devon. It was widely exported, excavations at Williamsburg showing that from about 1790 Pearlware was already more common than creamware, much of it bearing variations on the Chinese House pattern. Like its predecessor delftware, it was very rarely marked, the exceptions being an impressed 'IH' for Joshua Heath of Hanley, 'Wedgwood & Co' for the Ralph Wedgwood partnership at Ferrybridge of 1796–1801, 'ASTBURY' for Richard Astbury and 'TURNER' for John & William Turner, both of Lane End. As the techniques was refined, so the early coarse prints were eventually brought up to the high standards set by Josiah Spode and his major contemporaries, whose products created such a demand that Wedgwood's London showrooms were compelled to buy it in from other manufacturers. Apart from the technical merits of the product and its low price – effectively an earthenware parallel to the new bone china – its success was assured by the fact that the leading makers such as Spode had direct feedback from the fashion-conscious customers of their London showrooms. The latest designs soon filtered down to other manufacturers, who, long before the coming of Design

Registration in 1842, could note the success with which new patterns were received by the public and then immediately copy them with absolute impunity. Thus, for example, exactly contemporary with the Greek Revival movement in the arts, Spode introduced its *Greek* pattern in 1806, already made by Wedgwood & Co. of Ferrybridge but now quickly copied by the Herculaneum Pottery. Similarly, Spode's inspired *Indian Sporting Series*, based on engravings in Captain Thomas Williamson's *Oriental Field Sports: Wild Sports of the East* of 1807, was copied in its entirety by James & Ralph Clews of Cobridge to feed their flourishing export market. Apparently at random, some patterns like Spode's *Italian*, based on a drawing by the seventeenth-century Dutch artist Frederick de Moucheron and introduced around 1816, caught the public imagination and have remained in production ever since.

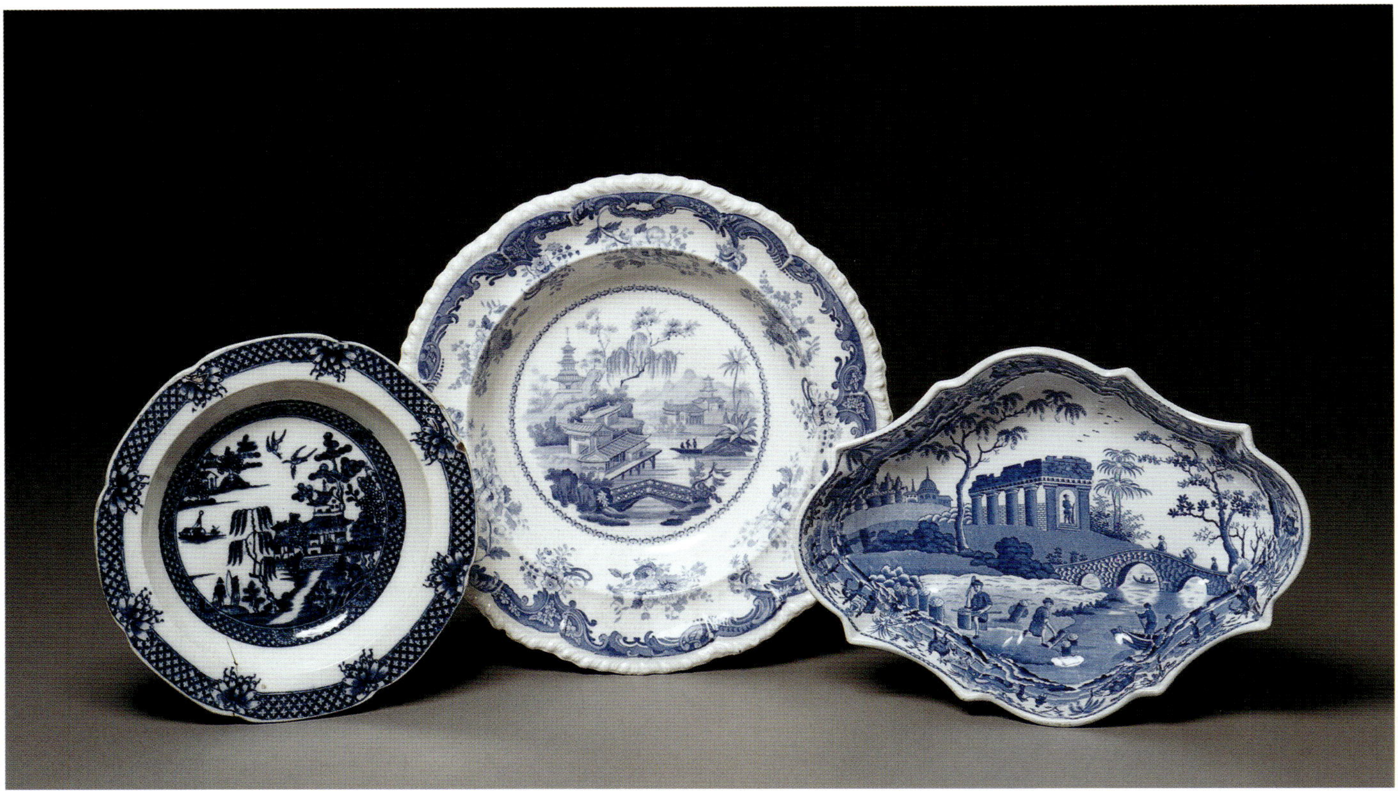

64
An early inky-blue 'Harrison' plate of *c.*1800 is contrasted with a Spode dish of *c.*1810 with classical ruins and a light blue Minton plate of *c.*1830. Max. diameter 25.7 cm (10⅛ in.).
V&A: C.110–1917, C.89–1945, C.39–1969.

By 1806 the late Josiah Wedgwood's son John, after much deliberation and technical development, had finally launched his first blue-printed earthenware, beginning with *Chinese Vase* and soon turning to botanical specimens culled from William Curtis's *Botanical Magazine*.[44] With exceptional printing quality and lightness of potting, and trading on an established reputation, late in the day the firm managed to claim a stake in the market, which by 1810 was attracting the envy of major rivals such as Spode, Henshall and Minton, who copied their patterns.

Essentially an egalitarian material that suited the mood of the times, blue and white pottery encompassed a very wide variety of standards and styles. While the major manufacturers invested the basic Pearlware material with cleverly designed collages taken from travel and botanical books in order to attract sophisticated customers, the original patterns that launched it, such as *Willow* and other pseudo-Chinese designs,[45] were firmly established among a less discriminating market, who appreciated the advantages that it was easily replaceable and still touched by the glamour of its recent descent from Worcester and Caughley porcelain. Although at first it was not cheap, but rather priced on a level with enamel decorated wares, both the rapid increase in mass production and the coarsening of the product itself soon made it almost universally available. At a basic level, major provincial potteries such as William Smith of Stockton-on-Tees continued making vast quantities for the export market until past the middle of the nineteenth century, paralleled in Staffordshire by Enoch

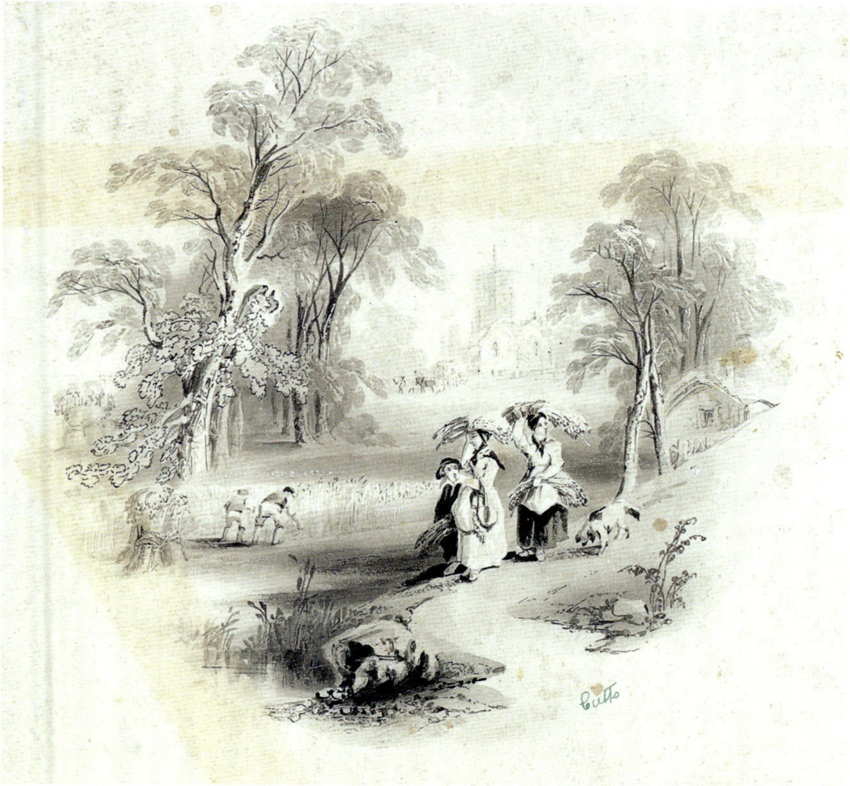

65
Vignette by John Cutts, former manager of the Pinxton porcelain factory, for engraved decoration on blue-printed tableware. From a volume of more than 900 drawings, many signed by James Parr.
V&A: E.1068–1973.

Wood of Burslem, whose export trade in utilitarian pottery made him a very rich man. George Phillips of Longport and William Adams of Stoke also mass-produced wares of similar quality. For more discerning customers, major producers such as Davenport channelled vast amounts of blue and white to North America via their Liverpool warehouse, while comparable firms such as John & George Rogers of Longport and Thomas Minton of Stoke flourished by concentrating on a product for which the demand was apparently insatiable.

The market was driven by regular small changes (plate 64), either devised by the makers themselves or occasioned by the quirks of the public. From the Wedgwood archives, we learn of a preference in the north of England for a lighter shade of blue and a partiality among country customers for rustic scenes, neither of which predilections could easily be deduced from a study of the subject two centuries later. Cobalt-blue, indeed, was capable of many subtle variations, and these were selected with great care, both to suit the taste of the moment and to match the changing subject matter and the delicacy or boldness with which the engravers might choose to interpret it. Through demands from present-day collectors, the subject has acquired such a comprehensive literature that here a rather brief overview may suffice to tell the story.[46] Well before the 1820s the old inky blue had largely been replaced by a new pale colour, in line with the pale lavender ground colour found on contemporary Staffordshire bone chinas, and English views began to appear after about 1810. Floral decoration became popular, the less formal designs in keeping with the Rococo Revival of the period. After about 1830 a vogue for fantastic Continental castles and watery vistas held sway (plate 65), combining the spirit of the old Chinoiserie with a wild romanticism, as demonstrated by the hundreds of designs for copper plates produced by professional engravers like John Cutts, who is said to have employed as many as 40 workmen at his Stoke workshop. Following this phase, the prints grew coarser, the blue grew stronger and by 1840 Wedgwood and their contemporaries were using the 'flowing blue' favoured by the American market, whereby saggars were washed with salt, lime and white lead to encourage the dark cobalt to smudge and run. This found little favour in the home market, but huge quantities of tablewares with American views were made for export, representing the most extreme form of this type of decoration and typifying the general decline in quality that took place in the 1840s.

As for direct influence from the Orient that had played such an important part in English ceramics for nearly 250 years, it could be said that, apart from the continuing popularity of debased versions of the Willow Pattern,[47] by the 1840s it was a spent force – at least until the purer Japonism of the 1870s, but that lies outside the scope of this book.

1. Northern Ceramic Society (1986), p.11.
2. Public Records Office, quoted by Edwards (1974), p.8.
3. But note that much of London at this period is said to have been built from Dutch bricks and roof tiles imported as ballast in trading vessels. Painted maiolica, however, could well have suffered in the damp conditions, like the vessel glass and mirror plates imported from Venice packed in damp salty seaweed.
4. See Edwards (1974), pp.120–22, for transcripts of all these documents.
5. Britton (1987). The Pickleherring Quay pottery closed in 1723, Montague Close in 1755.
6. The role of pewter is discussed by Meteyard (1865–6), pp.78–80. See also Museum of London (1989) and North (2002).
7. For example, at one of the first East India Company sales (India Office Records Court Book, vol.IV, folio 156) in 1618, when 'it was resolved to sell away some . . . of China ware', several 'greate deep basons' were sold, one for as much as 13s 6d.
8. Tait (1960, 1961).
9. Hildyard (1990).
10. Fully discussed by Hume (1977), pp.38–42.
11. Museum of London, Museum Number c.84. Illustrated in Lipski & Archer (1984), p.17. Recent tests on the clay body have shown it to be a London product.

12. V&A: C.38–1928, illustrated in Archer (1997), pl.1, no.A1.
13. V&A: C.26–1931, illustrated in Archer (1997), pl.10, no.A13.
14. V&A: C.278-1919, illustrated in Archer (1997), pl.32, no.A53.
15. Burnap Collection, B.189Y, William Rockhill Nelson Gallery, Kansas.
16. British Museum.
17. Colonial Williamsburg.
18. V&A: 3861-1901, illustrated in Archer (1997), pl.34, no.A55.
19. Liverpool Museum.
20. British Museum.
21. Longridge Collection (Grigsby & Archer 2000, vol.2, no.D63), the dish inscribed 'John Ayers 1637', the underside with initials of the three decorators involved, including 'IL', almost certainly the artist of the central scene. The recipient, a member of the Drapers' Company, identified by Britton; the print source, an engraving of 1627 by Lucas Vorsterman the Elder, by Hildyard.
22. Britton (1989, 1991).
23. For full details of all these potteries, see Britton (1987).
24. For the 1699 inventory of the Pickleherring Quay pottery, see Britton (1990, 1993). The delftware totals were: coffees 7,192, chocolates 4,034. For salt-glazed stoneware: coffees 734, capuchines 634. For Chinese imports, see Godden (1979), p.119. The East India Company specified for their shipment of 1700–01 that 'coffee, tea and chocolate cups sell best without saucers, therefore buy up fewer saucers'; the reason given for this was that (before the development of the intimate tea party) these drinks were served on salvers like wine.
25. Wills (1967).
26. Brereton (1844).
27. A partial transcript of one of the three tirades issued by Thomas and Nathaniel Oade reproduced by Britton (1987), p.48.
28. Many dealers offered 'fine Dutch tiles' during the eighteenth century. In 1760 John Dunbibin, proprietor of a Liverpool delftware factory, advertised 'Galley Tiles . . . in every respect equal to the Dutch' available at his warehouse in Southwark, as well as transfer-printed tiles: see note 33 below.
29. For a radically different interpretation of the facts, see Archer (1997), p.7, which states that 'in the first half of the eighteenth century . . . oriental exports, although widely owned, were generally used only as decoration'.
30. For the archaeological evidence, see Gaimster (1994).
31. For example, the 1773 inventory of Thomas Wedgwood, which listed no ceramic tableware, but only 44 pewter plates and 24 dishes. His warehouse, however, contained 295 dozen cheap white stoneware plates.
32. Ray (1968), Garner & Archer (1972), Britton (1982, 1987), Lipski (1984), Austin (1994), Archer (1997), Grigsby (2000).
33. As early as 1760 the Liverpool potter John Dunbibin advertised at his warehouse in Southwark 'Copper-Plate printed tiles, of which they have got upwards of forty different Patterns, which are the neatest Tiles ever made in England or Holland for Workmanship before'.
34. The case heard before Lord Erskine in the Court of Session in Edinburgh, 1748–9.
35. Noted by Lady Mary Coke, who expressed surprise at the duke's choice of faience since 'the finest doesn't come up to porcelaine'.
36. Weatherill (1986), p.451, table A1–7, estimated that the number of workers in the delftware industry declined from 640 in 1760 to a mere 55 in 1785.
37. Godden (1980, 1999).
38. Quoted by Reilly (1989), p.583. After several years of experiment, Wedgwoods began regular production in 1821.
39. Wedgwood (1965, 1973).
40. Horn (1995).
41. Simeon Shaw (1829), p.193, quotes Wedgwood, out of loyalty to his enamellers, declaring: 'I will give you my word, as a man, I have not made, neither will I make any Blue Printed Earthenware'. This flattering hearsay account is unsubstantiated by his letters, which show a personal distaste for the technique.
42. For discussion of the evolution of Pearlware, see Lockett (1996), Miller & Hunter (2001) and Hume (2001), pp.224–56
43. Shaw (1829), pp.210–15.
44. Des Fontaines (1983).
45. See Copeland (1980).
46. Little (1969), Coysh (1972), Coysh & Stefano Jr (1981), Coysh & Henrywood (1982–9), Blake Roberts (1998).
47. By the mid-nineteenth century it was associated with low life. Lydgate, in George Eliot's *Middlemarch*, when considering the style in which he might expect to live with his new bride, had a horror of a home with 'the children in soiled pinafores, and lunch lingering in the form of bones, black-handled knives, and willow-pattern'.

CHAPTER SIX

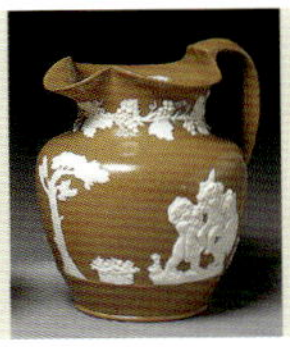

Stoneware Meets Porcelain: A Marriage of Refinement

It was to the potters of Yixing that Europe owed the concept of a pot that was fully vitrified and covered with decoration in bas relief, yet wholly without glaze. For the Chinese in the seventeenth century, however, the importance of these red stoneware teapots lay not in their capacity as vehicles for decoration but as vessels that would stand the heat of a spirit lamp for brewing tea – a consideration that did not apply to the British, who preferred to add water already boiled. Nevertheless, the material of these pots was hailed in Europe as having almost magical properties, enabling the brothers John Philip and David Elers in the 1690s to charge exorbitant prices for their own, superbly executed versions. As described in chapter Three, when 'red china' was once again made in Staffordshire from about 1750, its immediate success and the appeal of its ultra-sharp applied decoration must have suggested further development if only one major obstacle could be overcome: the fact that the rich red colour derived from a high concentration of iron oxide, which was inseparable from the material. But if a white body could not be created from red, potters well knew that, should there be any public demand, a dense black surface could be obtained by depriving iron-rich clay of oxygen in the kiln.

In the decade when creamware was perfected, however, it may have seemed unlikely that matt black stoneware would ever find a market. But the 1760s was also the decade when the colourful Rococo style was losing ground to cool and sober Neo-classicism, fuelled by excavations at Herculaneum and Pompeii, and the publication of Sir William Hamilton's collection of red-figure and black-figure Greek vases by Baron D'Hancarville as *Antiquités étrusques, grecques, et romaine* in 1766–7. Not surprisingly, the first potter to exploit this shift in taste was Josiah Wedgwood, who, along with his partner and cousin 'Useful' Thomas Wedgwood, was conducting experiments at his Burslem works by at least 1769, shortly before his move to his new factory at Etruria, where the new body was fittingly named 'Etruscan Ware'. Wedgwood ignored the rare and expensive local red stoneware clay and chose instead to colour an ordinary body with 'carr' – a slurry rich in iron oxide, obtained from drainage of the mines – combined with manganese to produce a body with the same basic constituents as the shiny black lead glaze already in use. Since these were not difficult to obtain, almost immediately the secret was stolen by a perfidious employee, Jean Voyez, and passed to the potter Humphrey Palmer, who lost no time in exploiting it. Rather than attempting to protect a material that his fellow potters would have described as an improvement rather than an invention, Wedgwood responded by patenting the rather staid 'Encaustic' painting with which, in

66
Because of the survival of pieces marked, as here, 'DD & Co. CASTLEFORD' for David Dunderdale, the name 'Castleford' has lent its name to a whole class of felspathic blue-edged stoneware made by many potteries in Yorkshire and Staffordshire. Height 15.5 cm (6⅛ in.).
V&A: 3581–1901.

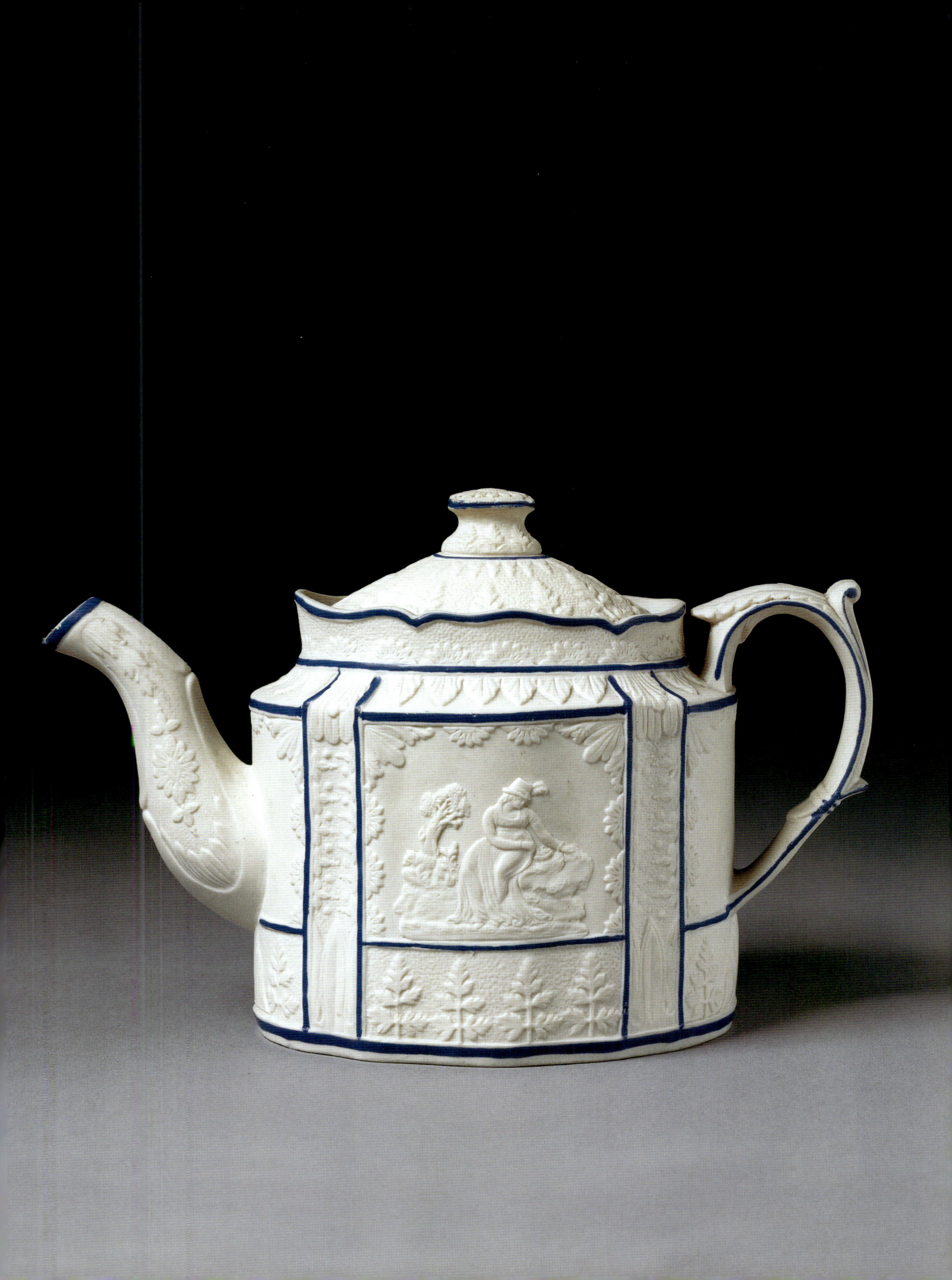

ignorance of the Greeks' cunning method of producing both black and red from a single oxidizing/reducing kiln firing, he attempted to imitate the Greek vases then thought to be Etruscan. This anglicized polychrome 'improvement' on Greek vase painting, executed at Wedgwood's Chelsea decorating studio, immediately found favour with an aristocratic clientele, including George III and Queen Charlotte. When adapted to useful wares, the simple boldly painted borders were certainly effective, but much of Wedgwood's basalt was plain, consisting of portrait medallions, seals and sets of 'gems' made for a wealthy antiquarian market.[1] By 1773 Wedgwood considered his black stoneware sufficiently refined to merit inclusion in his *Ornamental Pattern Book* under a new name, 'Black Basalte', designed to link it in the public perception with that monumental tough Egyptian marble. By the following year, he could confidently claim that 'The Black is sterling & will last for ever'.[2]

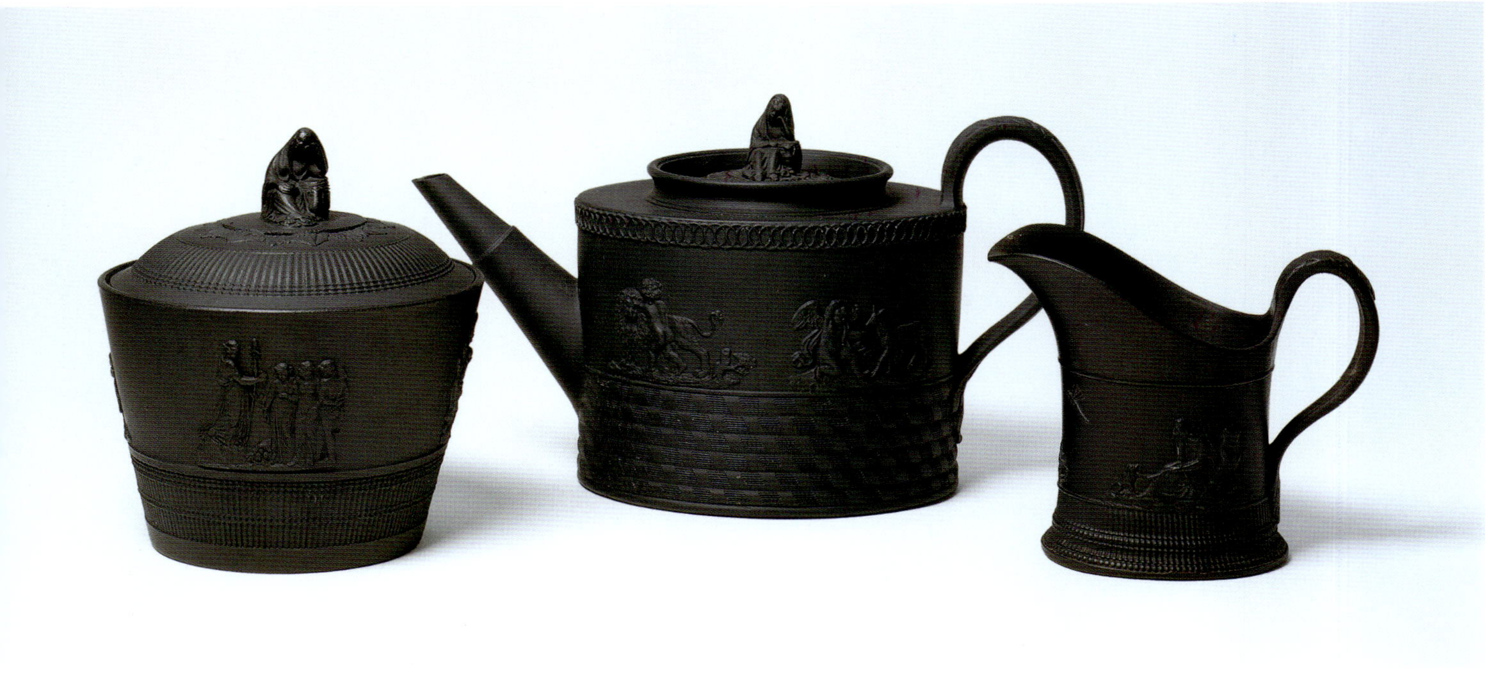

67
Since Black Basalt was never patented, Wedgwood's contemporaries soon produced their own high-quality teawares, usually copying silver shapes. The unmarked sugar box by P. & F. Warburton, the teapot marked 'Mayer', the helmet jug 'Wedgwood & Co.' of Ferrybridge, all 1790s. Max. height 11.5 cm (4½ in.).
V&A: 38&A–1899, 452–1903, C.53–1967.

As for the wider use of black stoneware, other potters soon invented their own recipes for 'Egyptian Black' and saw a chance to fill the gap left by the declining popularity of Chinese-inspired red stoneware with their novel Greek-inspired black teapots (plate 67). It could also be thrown and engine-turned or lathe-turned almost to the thinness of the silver that it copied, and as technical expertise among Staffordshire potters such as Neale, Turner, Mayer, the Warburtons and Birch became ever more refined, their basalt wares achieved a satisfying combination of mechanical and artistic perfection. Fortunately for the smaller factories, Black Basalt not only had good casting properties but also had the great economic advantage of containing enough ferrous oxide to act as a flux, which considerably reduced the required firing temperature. Soon it assumed a wide variety of contemporary silver shapes, entirely covered with raised Neo-classical ornament,[3] but, according to the Price Agreement of 1795, at a cost of no more than 2s each for 'Oval pressed Tea-pots' with or without sliding lid. The fact that teawares, especially cream jugs, needed to be lined with glaze in order to avoid staining proved no deterrent to manufacture by some fairly minor Staffordshire potteries, and at the end of the eighteenth century it was taken up in Yorkshire, where the creamware factories already had an established trading network with northern Europe and Russia via Hull. The Leeds Pottery's *Drawing Book for Black Ware* of 1800 forms an invaluable aid to identification of unmarked pieces,[4] while pieces marked 'DD & Co CASTLEFORD' for David Dunderdale, and 'S & Co' for Sowter & Co. of Mexborough shared identical moulds with the much more numerous white 'Castleford' wares.

Despite, or perhaps because of, its obvious origins as stylish teaware of the late eighteenth century, Basalt remained popular at a declining social level

68

Wedgwood's cane was also known as 'Bamboo' ware, from which it clearly drew its inspiration. Here, his Bamboo vases flank a Neo-classical vase of similar quality by Elijah Mayer, both made about 1800. Max. height 31.1 cm (12¼ in.). V&A: 2135&A–1899, 2492 &A–1901.

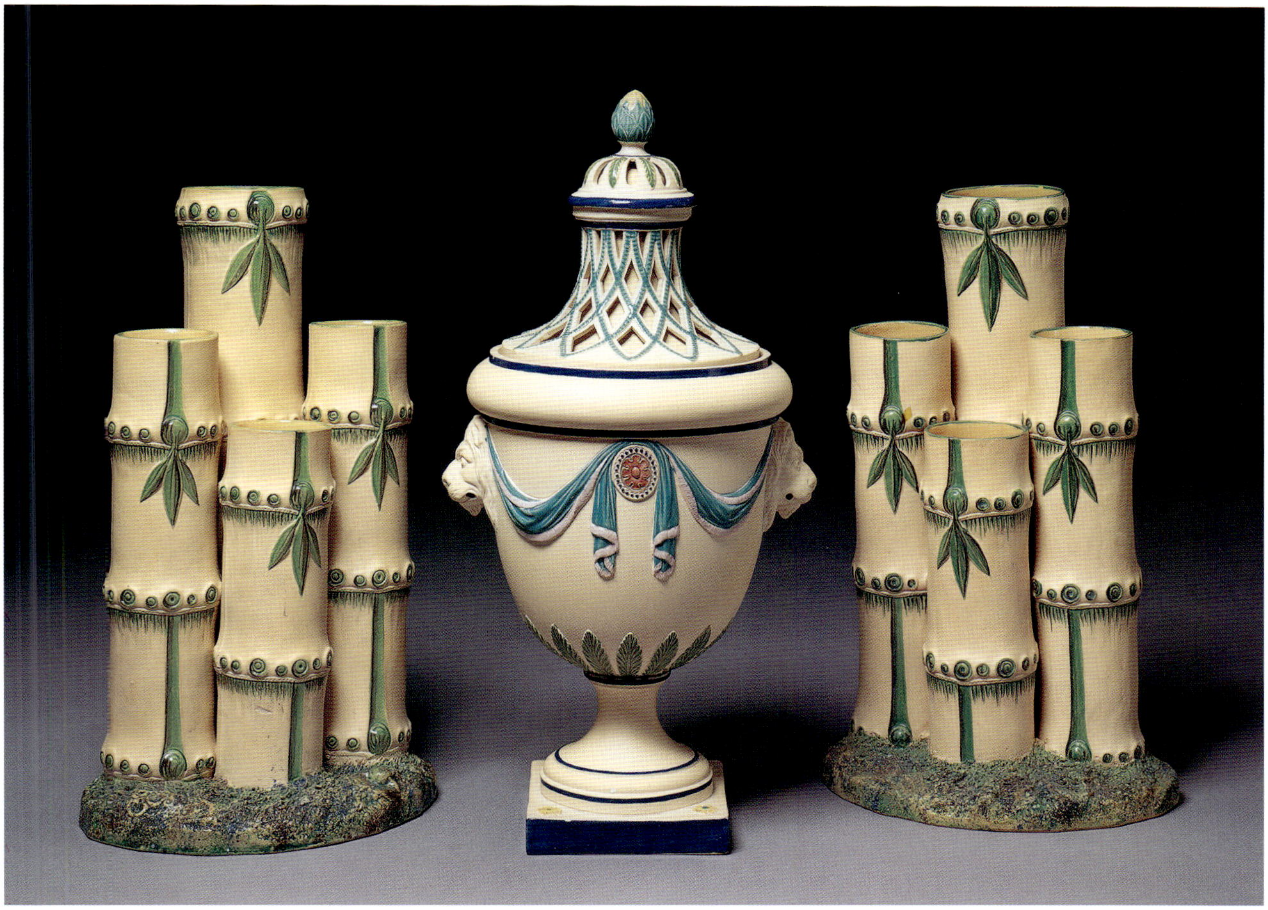

until at least the 1820s, when the general softening and thickening of forms that accompanied the Rococo Revival dictated a change from dry-body to the more practical smear-glaze or lead-glaze. The many surviving small Egyptian Black teapots, merely red-bodied with a shiny black glaze, made by firms such as Cyples and Hackwood during the 1830s, bear witness to this extended life among the impecunious or thrifty. The fashion for black teapots never quite died, but

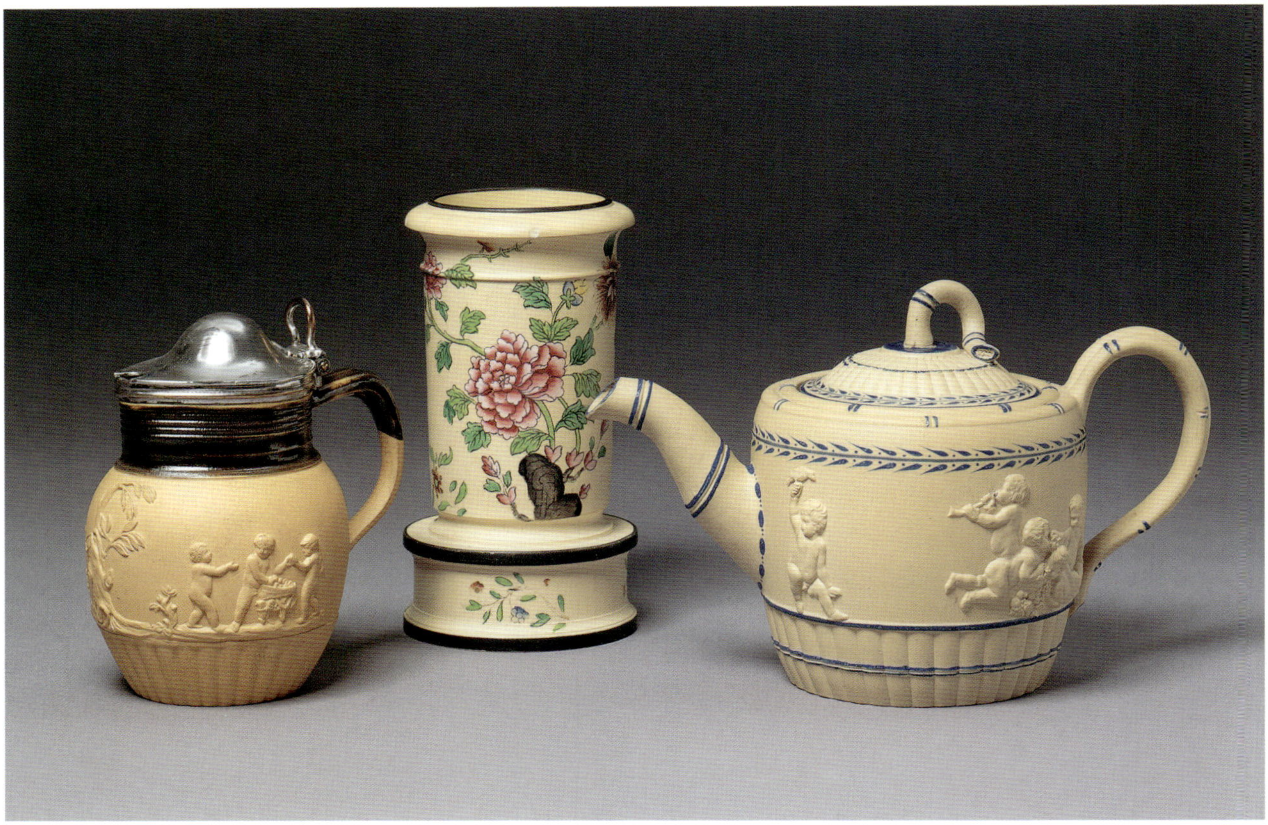

69

Caneware, lined with a glaze to make it hygienic, proved suitable for a wide range of objects made by many of the leading manufacturers: for example, a mustard pot marked 'Adams', and a Spode spill vase, both about 1800–10, with a diminutive Wedgwood teapot of about 1790. Max. height 11.1 cm (4⅜ in.).

V&A: C.148–1912, 425–1901, 1505–1855.

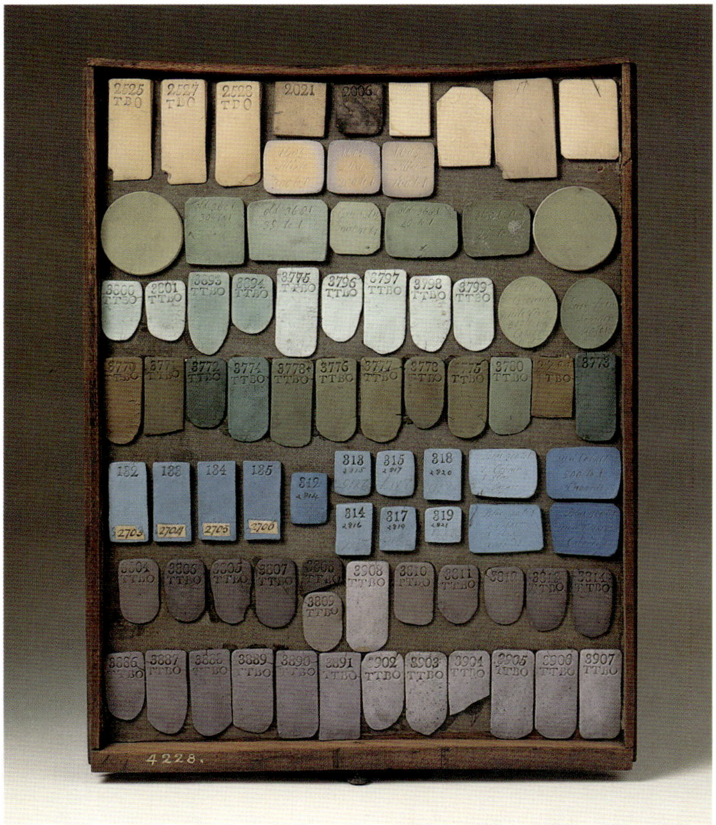

70

Josiah Wedgwood applied both scientific principles and great patience in his quest for the perfect colours for Jasper ware – his only original invention.

Courtesy of the Wedgwood Museum.

enjoyed a considerable revival in the last quarter of the nineteenth century.

Following shortly after the invention of Basalt, by 1771 Josiah Wedgwood was attempting to develop a new body from local marl clay which he called 'Fawn'. The pride that he expressed in this new product, however, proved premature since it was both unstable in use and also resisted vitrification, so that it was not until the mid-1780s that he considered it satisfactory. As with Black Basalt, he announced and named this perfected material in the next edition of his catalogue, in this case 1787, where he described it as 'BAMBOO or cane-coloured biscue porcelain' (plate 68). Anticipating the Regency love of bamboo furniture by a decade, he led the way in making a variety of canewares, usually strikingly edged with blue or green enamel, with other leading potters such as Turner and Spode making their own successful versions almost from the start. In the mid-1790s he also added a range of covered pie-dishes in 'pastry ware', imitating a pork or game pie but having an inner liner of creamware to contain the cooked meat, the popularity of which is said to have been enhanced by the acute shortage of flour during the wars with France.[5] Caneware, though never as widely manufactured as basalt, and never made to a standard formula, remained fashionable until the 1820s, and achieved a high standard in the hands of manufacturers such as Spode, Elijah Mayer, Adams and William Baddeley (plate 69). After its spread to Yorkshire, in the 1820s the Swinton Pottery added an effective range of intense blue sprigs, under a thin smear-glaze so typical of local 'Castleford' stonewares.

Of all the pioneering experiments and ceramic improvements of Josiah Wedgwood, the only one to become inextricably associated with his name was, appropriately enough, both his greatest labour of love and his only truly original invention: Jasper ware (plates 70–72). Always seeking new manufactures for the Ornamental Works at his new Etruria factory, by 1771 he was working simultaneously not only towards perfecting his black stoneware but also towards creating 'a white body susceptible of being colour'd and which shall polish itself in burning Bisket'. In 1774 he was lamenting the unstable experimental bodies, which either fired an off-white or melted, perhaps due to the flux required to melt or 'polish' the surface. Later that year his perseverance was rewarded by 'an excellent white body', and by New Year's Day 1775 he was already beginning to develop the colours, telling his partner Thomas Bentley that 'the blue body I am likewise *absolute* in of almost any shade, & have likewise a beautiful Sea Green, & several other colours, for *grounds* to Cameo's, Intaglio's etc.' (plate 71). Having now established a reliable basic body, the range of forms and colours could easily be expanded to keep abreast of every changing whim of fashion. It was no wonder, therefore, that other leading makers, such as Turner, Neale, Adams and Spode, set about developing their rival versions of this versatile and lucrative material, using whatever materials they could. Turner, for example, did not use the ingredient barytes, but instead made the type of semi-porcelain that Wedgwood had carefully avoided for fear of infringing the existing hard-paste porcelain patent. Neale was also quick to follow Wedgwood's lead, as shown by a superb blue pot-pourri vase commemorating the Treaty of Vergennes of 1786,

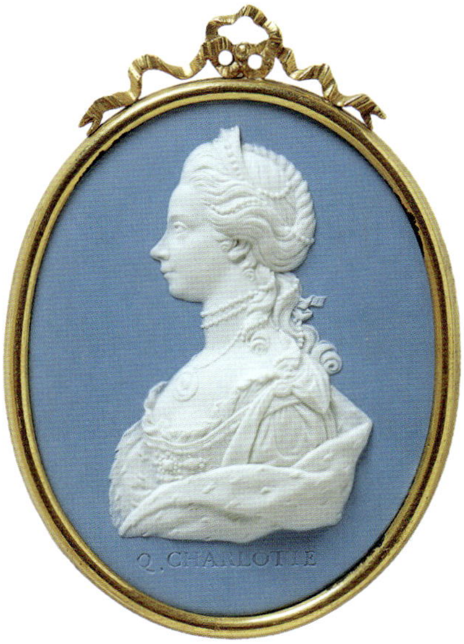

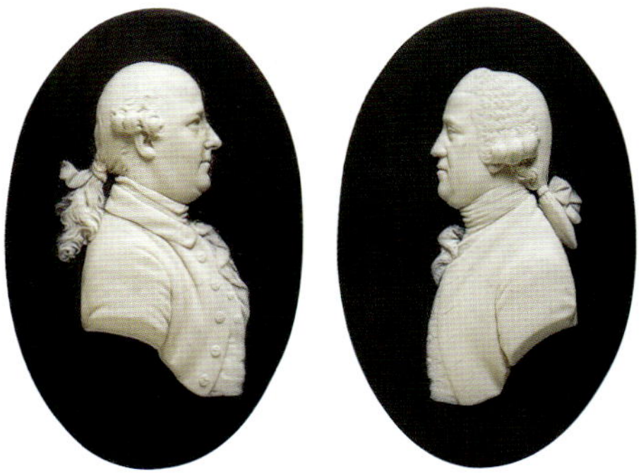

71
Jasper proved ideally suited to portrait medallions, which could be collected in sets, mounted individually or even applied to furniture. Without Thomas Bentley's guidance and the patronage of Queen Charlotte, the career of Josiah Wedgwood would have been very different. Queen Charlotte *c.*1780, Wedgwood and Bentley 19th century. Max. height 8.2 cm (3¼ in.).
V&A: 453,454–1890, Sch.II 517.

which finally opened the doors of the French to the mass-produced pottery of Staffordshire.[6]

The complete story of Wedgwood's Jasper has been told many times.[7] Having created his basic white or coloured material, he systematically set about finding artists to design the applied decoration, besides his resident modeller, William Hackwood, who had been employed since 1769. Hackwood himself became increasingly proficient, playing a vital role in adapting the designs of borrowed classical gems and converting to bas relief the sentimental drawings by Lady Diana Beauclerk and Lady Templetown of genteel domestic life. By 1775 Wedgwood was commissioning work from the younger John Flaxman, of whose genius he had been aware since 1771 when the child prodigy was considered 'a coxcomb, but . . . not . . . a bit the worse for it, or the less likely to be a great Artist'.[8] Without Flaxman's many rather austere designs for busts, figures, portrait medallions and applied reliefs, it is extremely doubtful whether Wedgwood's Jasper would have enjoyed such instant, and continuing, success. Wedgwood was indefatigable in scouring England for designs, copying objects from great collectors such as Sir Roger Newdigate, Sir Watkin Williams Wynn, the Duke of Bedford, the Duke of Marlborough, Lord Lansdowne and the Earl of Bessborough, but he also maintained a studio in Rome, where modellers such as Pacetti would copy and adapt antique reliefs. His Jasper was so perfectly in tune with the Neo-classical movement that it was applied to a multitude of sizes and uses, from châtelaines and sword-mounts mounted in polished cut-steel to furniture and mantelpieces. Carefully designed to harmonize with the work of leading architects like the Adam brothers, James Wyatt, Sir William Chambers and 'Athenian' Stuart, and firmly linked with aristocratic patrons and royalty, the material and its colours (plate 72) immediately gained a permanent place in the repertoire of great English design.

Having developed basalt, cane, and the blues, greens and pinks of Jasper, Wedgwood was extremely reluctant to introduce an improved form of the despised red stoneware. His partner Thomas Bentley, however, insisted on a purplish-red body that might reflect, in a more tasteful way, the brash colours of Roman terracotta and *terra sigillata*. In 1776 Wedgwood wrote to Thomas Bentley: 'I will try to imitate the Antico Rosso from your description, but when I have done my best I am afraid where one spectator thinks of Antico Rosso an hundred will be put in mind of a Red teapot'. It was not until after 1798 that the material came into its own, however, with the craze for Egyptian motifs that followed the French invasion of Egypt. Crisp and linear matt black sprigs in the Egyptian taste well suited the dull red body, which was made by others, notably Spode (see plate 28).

In keeping with the political turmoil of the decade, the 1790s also brought many changes in the world of English ceramics. The beginnings of the French Revolution in 1789 brought a sudden end to trade with France, both export and import, and put a stop to the supply for Paris porcelain, which was rapidly becoming fashionable. Following this, the sudden decision by the East India Company in 1791 to cease importing Chinese porcelain must have provoked instant reactions from both potters and dealers, on the one hand giving a massive boost to the new blue-printed tableware, and on the other hand depressing the china trade enough to drive the prominent London dealer Miles Mason to set up his own manufactory in Staffordshire. In the face of cheap mass-produced Pearlware, porcelain factories such as Caughley were soon forced to abandon their expensive blue and white, and embraced first French and then German styles. In 1795 the death of Josiah Wedgwood ended 45 years of domination by his Etruria factory, and heralded a period of decline under John Wedgwood and his partner Thomas Byerley until, in a highly competitive world, it managed to override the inherited prejudices of its creator and regain its pre-eminence by adopting printed Pearlware and other new bodies. After Champion's patent for hard-paste porcelain expired the following year, there remained no obstacles to

72
Complementary and harmonious, Wedgwood's original choice of Jasper ware colours, particularly blue, green and pink, have always remained popular. Max. height 21 cm (8¼ in.).
V&A: 1275–1855, 2134–1899, 3472–1855.

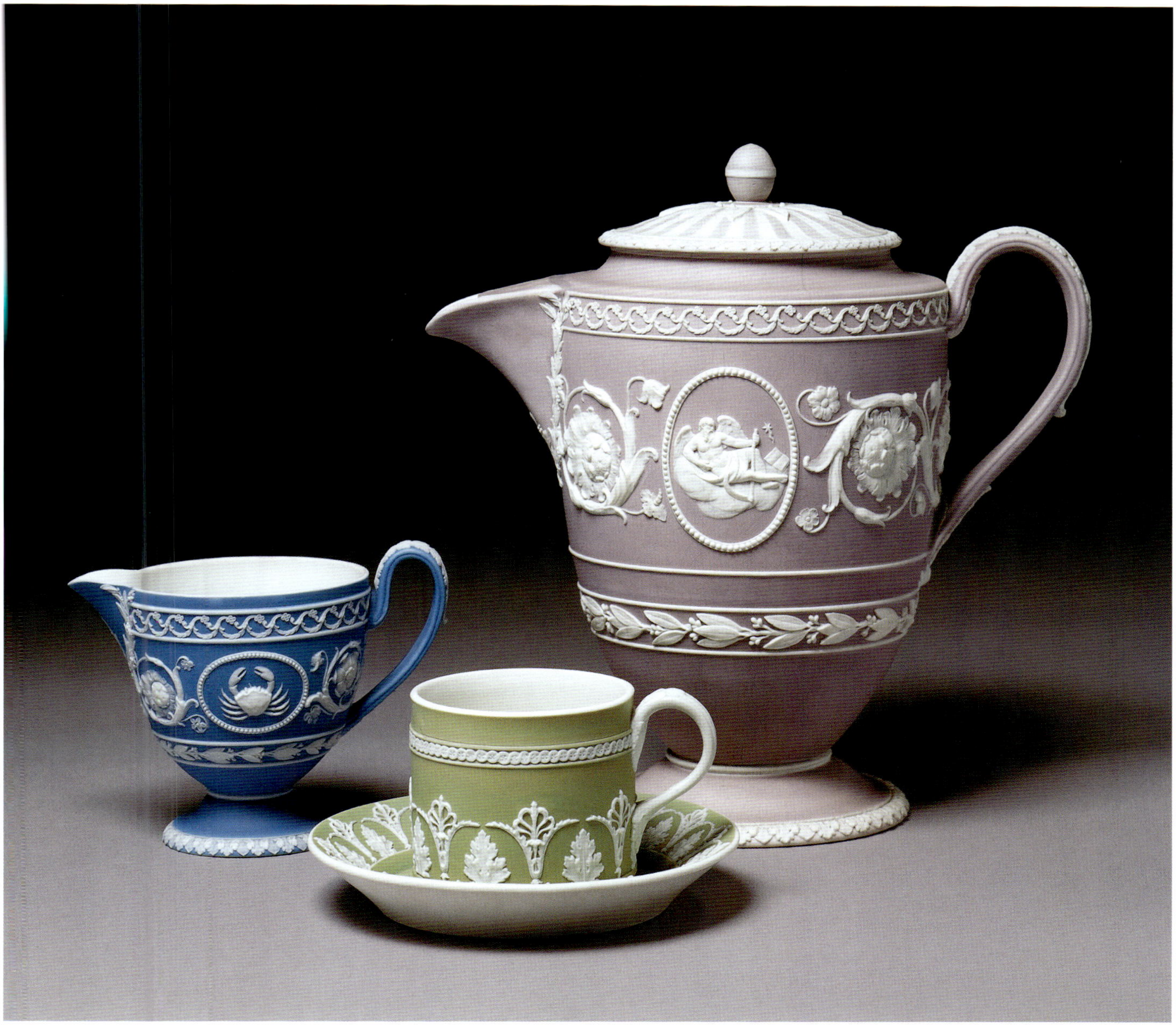

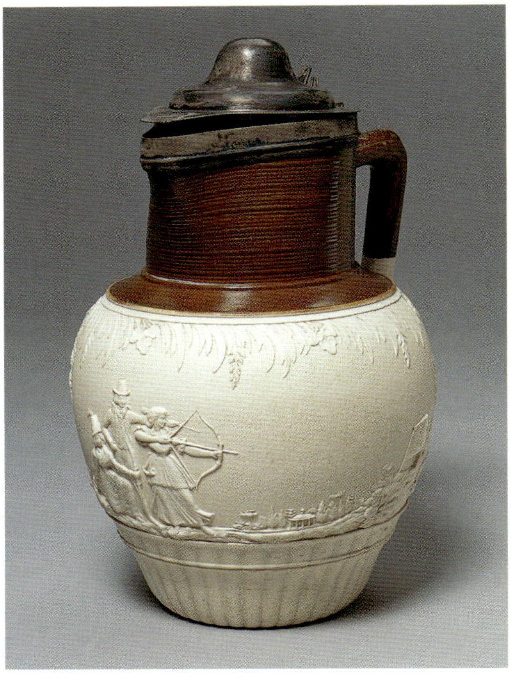

the development of new ceramic bodies containing large quantities of hard-paste porcelain ingredients: namely, bone china and semi-translucent stoneware.

The white so-called felspathic stoneware was no doubt inspired by John Turner's discovery of a seam of cream-firing dense stoneware clay, said by Simeon Shaw to have occurred about 1780, but, to judge from his jugs with hallmarked silver lids, probably nearer to 1790 (plate 73). These jugs, with their ribbed brown-glazed necks and sharply modelled sprigs, immediately became highly popular and were soon copied by leading potters such as Neale, Adams, T. & J. Hollins, Wedgwood, Spode, Davenport and the Herculaneum Pottery at Liverpool (plate 75). The products of Adams are, if anything, finer than Turner's, and with contemporary scenes such as the skittle match introduced a pleasing satirical element to their decoration.[9] The unexpected bankruptcy of John & William Turner in 1805 resulted in a sale of factory equipment the following year, including an array of wares absolutely typical of Staffordshire factories of the period: 'Cream Colour, China-glazed, China-glazed blue edge, china glaze printed and painted, Egyptian Black, Cane, Stone, Jasper, Pearl, and Patent China Goods'. Many of the moulds, acquired by the Spode and Adams factories, are now at the Spode Museum in Stoke-on-Trent and include a variety of subjects from Neo-classical mythological scenes to hunting and contemporary scenes, such as the popular Archery Lesson.[10] The body of these beer jugs and mugs – which surely inspired the Kisheres of Mortlake to invent the brown salt-glazed hunting jug – was a true vitrified stoneware, lined nonetheless with frit glaze to avoid the possibility of staining, but completely opaque. Unless William Turner refined his stonewares immediately after the bankruptcy, he could not have been responsible for any of the fine semi-translucent stonewares (of the type sometimes marked with the name of the London retailer Mist) so often attributed to him, even though his final sale in 1829 included, among the great bulk of blue-printed earthenwares, some 'ditto stone (teapots & cream ewers) and ornaments, beautifully figured etc.'. These are discussed below.

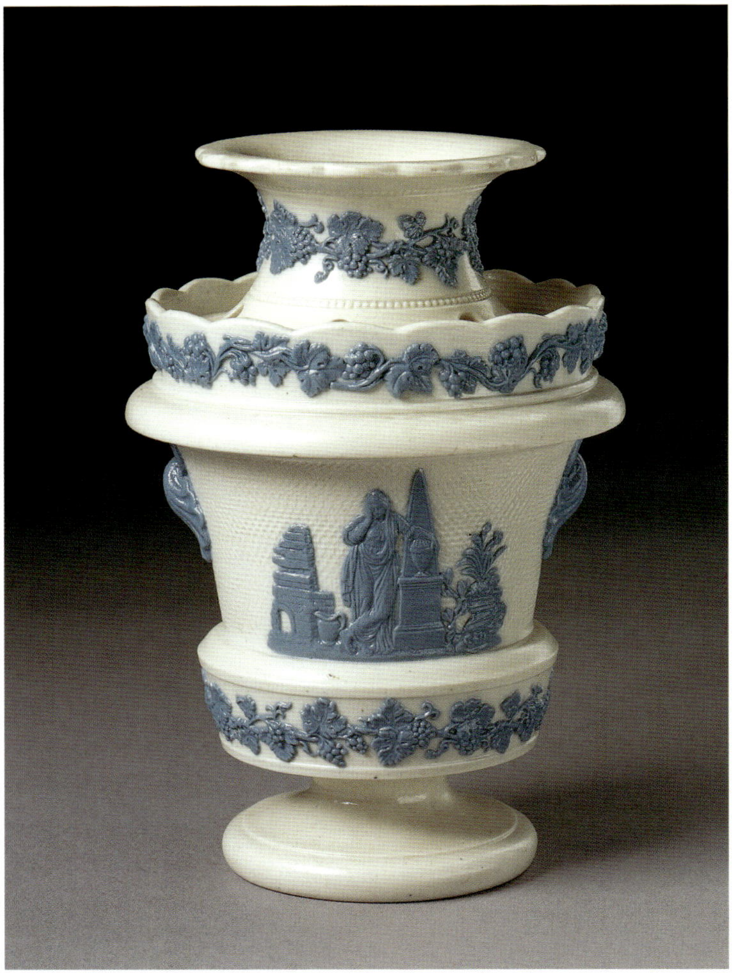

An experiment that, to judge by the few surviving pieces, was not a commercial success was made by William Pratt at Lane Delph, in business *circa* 1781–99, and under his widow until 1806. Marked pot-pourri vases (plate 74), Dutch jugs and porter mugs of grey, lightly salt-glazed stoneware, with sharply modelled blue sprigs on a textured background, demonstrate excellent workmanship and show how deeply embedded was the fashion for Staffordshire salt-glaze.

While production of Turner-type creamy stonewares, basalt, caneware and Jasper continued unabated in the period 1790–1820, other potters were exploring ways to take advantage of their new freedom to use porcelain ingredients, especially the felspathic china stone from Cornwall, which could make stoneware translucent. The result was what we know as 'Castleford Ware', named by collectors purely on the grounds that some pieces are marked, like their basalt counterparts, 'DD & Co. CASTLEFORD' for the firm of David Dunderdale (see plate 66),[11] while others have 'S & Co' for Sowter & Co. of Mexborough, or the enigmatic number '22'. But since so few are marked, it is difficult to determine whether this type of ware was first developed in Staffordshire (by, for example, Ralph Wedgwood, who moved from Burslem to Ferrybridge in 1796), or whether the economy-minded Yorkshire potteries simply discovered a white material that could be cast in the same moulds as the basalt. At any rate these

73 (OPPOSITE TOP)
The sprigged decoration on Turner's white stoneware of the 1790s was sometimes copied from contemporary prints, such as this archery contest at Hatfield. Lid hall-marked 1796/7. Height 17.1 cm (6¾ in.).
V&A: C.106–1971.

74 (OPPOSITE BELOW)
The rare smear-glazed stonewares made by William Pratt around 1800, comprising pot-pourri vases, porter mugs and jugs with hunting frieze, demonstrate a skill equal to any of his contemporaries. Height 14.6 cm (5¾ in.).
V&A: 2545–1901.

75
In the early 19th century the Herculaneum Pottery at Liverpool achieved a high standard of potting and decoration, as this unique dry-bodied and enamelled stoneware punch-bowl shows. Diameter 44.2 cm (17⅜ in.).
V&A: C.30–1982.

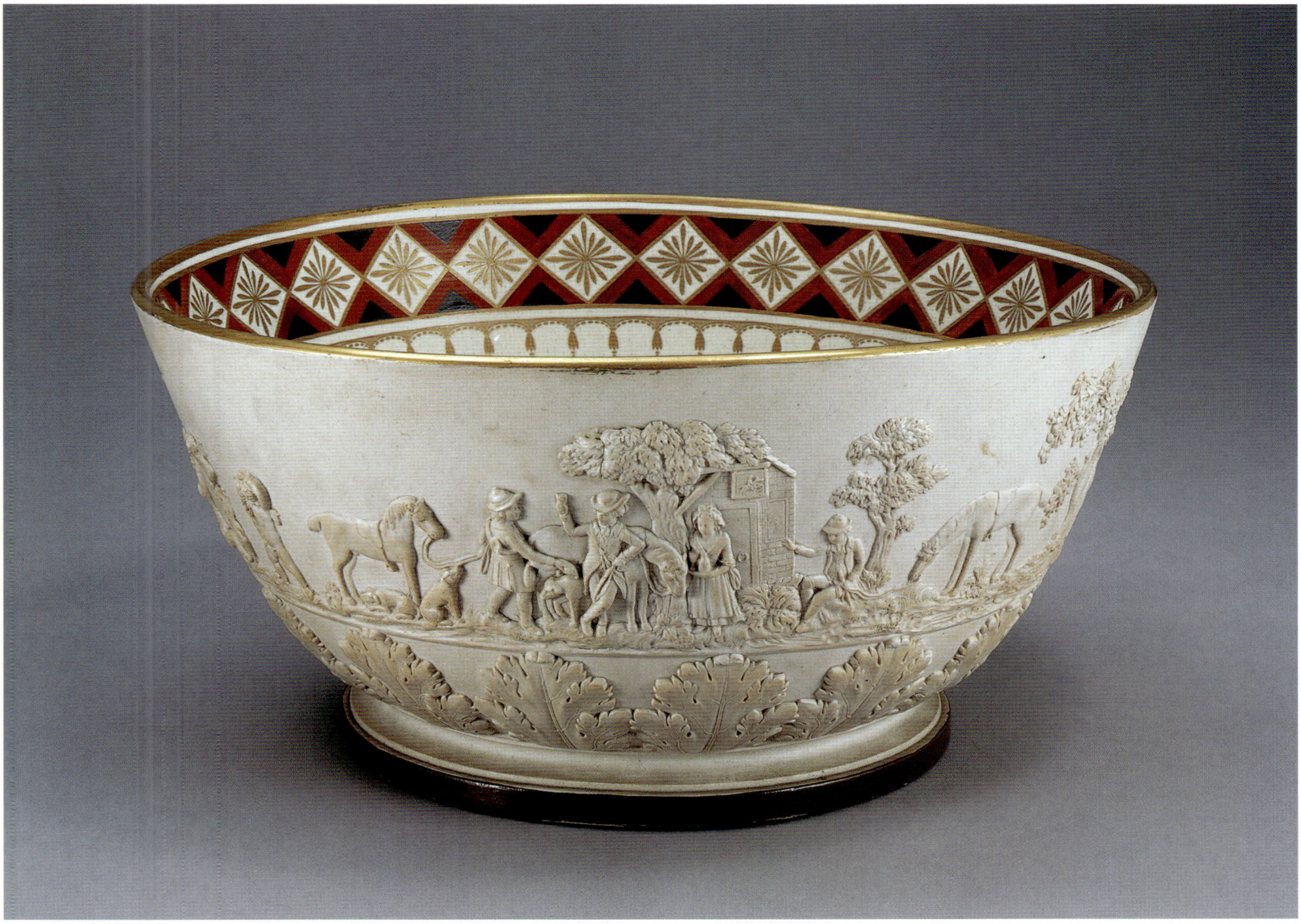

teawares, which contain enough feldspar to be highly translucent and were often cast almost to eggshell thinness, appeared around 1795 and, with smart blue edging, silver shapes and modest price, not to mention novel hinged or sliding teapot lids, instantly became popular, to be mass-produced by factories in both Yorkshire and Staffordshire. Their serviceability as teawares was further enhanced by the recently developed smear-glaze, formed by the vaporization of salt deliberately applied to the inside of saggars before the firing. While not obscuring the raised decoration, this glaze effectively protected against staining.

The technical expertise of many Staffordshire factories, which by about 1800 was in no way inferior to that of Wedgwood, was soon directed towards this new porcellanous material. Skilled hands and precision machinery combined to create a product that was flawless in design and execution. Outstanding among

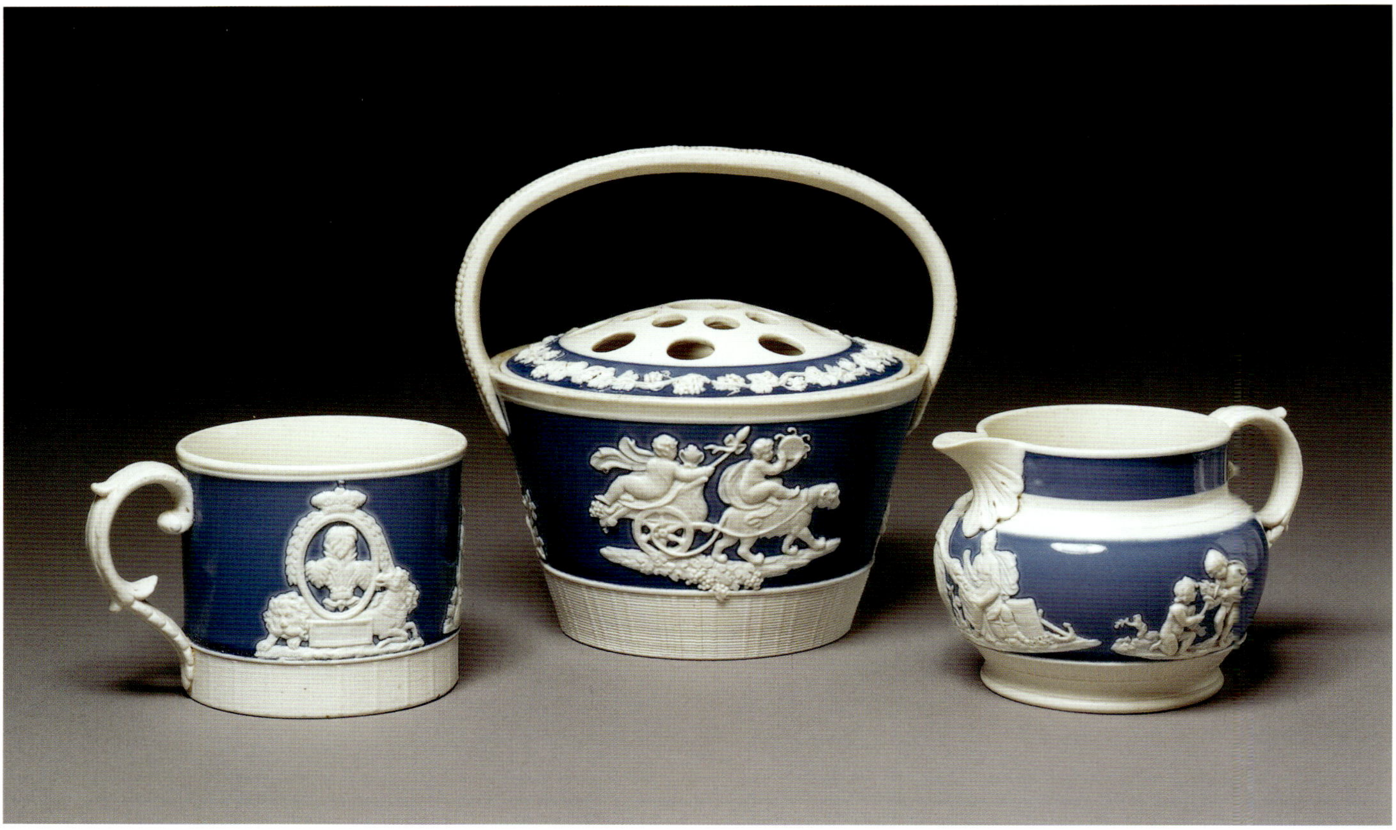

76
Various types of porcellanous stoneware became popular in the first decade of the 19th century. One of the most prolific maker of jugs and porter mugs seems to have been Chetham, to whom this class of stonewares has been attributed. Max height 14.6 cm (5¾ in.).
Private Collection.

these is a group (plate 76) of jugs, mugs, teapots, inkwells and small decorative objects made of unglazed pure white stoneware, having engine-turned bottoms and crisp sprigged decoration, usually over a dip of glassy lavender-blue or nut-brown, which were made from about 1800 until at least 1815, when the victory at Waterloo was commemorated. The body of these is little less translucent than that of, say, Paris porcelain, and although the only mark to be found on these is that of the retailer James Mist, operating at 82 Fleet Street in London from 1809 to 1815, all the indications are that they are products of the Longton potters Chetham & Woolley (1796–1810), Ann Chetham (1810–18) or Richard Woolley

(1809–14). Other pieces of equally high technical standard are sometimes marked 'J. Lockett', a family of potters in business at Lane End from 1802.[12] As with so many other Staffordshire developments, documentary evidence for the new body is provided by the Wedgwood archives, which record about 1810 the introduction of 'White porcelain' or 'White Bisque porcelain' with blue-edging and 'basketwork' shapes – presumably a trade name for the familiar engine-turned bases.

Apart from the white body, a range of coloured stonewares was also made by leading potters such as Wedgwood, Spode, David Wilson and Ralph & James Clews, often made as sets of three graduated beer or milk jugs with white sprigged Neo-classical or hunting decoration under a frieze of vine-leaves. As if to reinforce the classical decoration, the elegant 'Antique' shape was often used, having a rim formed as a spout between two swelling lobes. Despite the close working relationship of these makers, the various distinct shades of buff, ginger (plate 77), chocolate or French grey seem to have been peculiar to each factory. Until as late as the 1830s coloured stonewares poured out of many lesser factories, often bearing tantalizing applied pad-marks containing an impressed pattern number, which, apart from the known Ridgway lozenge mark and the 'Angels & Banner' mark now attributed to Hicks, Meigh & Johnson of Shelton operating in the years 1822–35, have defied identification.[13] Some idea of the popularity of these jugs, both at home and on the Continent, may be gleaned from the very exact copies of Ridgway models made by David Johnson at Bordeaux in the 1830s.

Resisting the French influence that pervaded porcelain manufacture in the first decade of the nineteenth century, many of these cheaper dry-bodied and smear-glazed stonewares relied for their applied or moulded decoration on a repertoire of earlier Neo-classical ornament entirely borrowed from the Wedgwood factory. These occur so frequently that it is worth mentioning a few, such as: 'Group of Three Boys' from an engraving by Bartolozzi after Lady Diana Beauclerk; 'Silenus and Boys' and 'Boys Playing with Goat' after François du Quesnoy; 'Sportive Love', 'Charlotte at the Tomb of Werther', 'Poor Maria' with her dog and 'The Bourbonnais Shepherd' from Laurence Sterne's *Sentimental Journey*; 'Domestic Employment', 'An Offering to Peace', all after Lady Templetown and mostly modelled by Hackwood; figures from 'Blind Man's Buff' and the 'Borghese Frieze', and the harp-playing 'Terpsichore', all after Flaxman; figures from 'The Marriage of Cupid & Psyche' after the Marlborough Gem, modelled by Hackwood; 'Endymion on the Rock Latmos' asleep with his hound, after Pacetti; and many others, including 'Hope' leaning on her anchor, 'Ganymede and the Eagle', two cupids igniting the fire of Love, and Cupid with lion as 'The Force of Love', often paired with 'Cybele' with her cornucopia.

These plagiarized motifs also became common currency among the makers of popular bone chinas, although it must be said that the soft material with its glassy glaze was much less suited to applied relief decoration. The old boundaries between makers of pottery and porcelain became increasingly blurred from the beginning of the nineteenth century, as porcelain ingredients

77
Ginger-brown, no doubt inspired by the new popular brown stoneware hunting jugs, was much favoured on Staffordshire stonewares in the period 1800–20, each factory having its own distinct colour. Here a Wilson dish and cover is contrasted with a Spode jug. Max. height 14.6 cm (5¾ in.).

V&A: 2564–1901, C.54 or 55–1971.

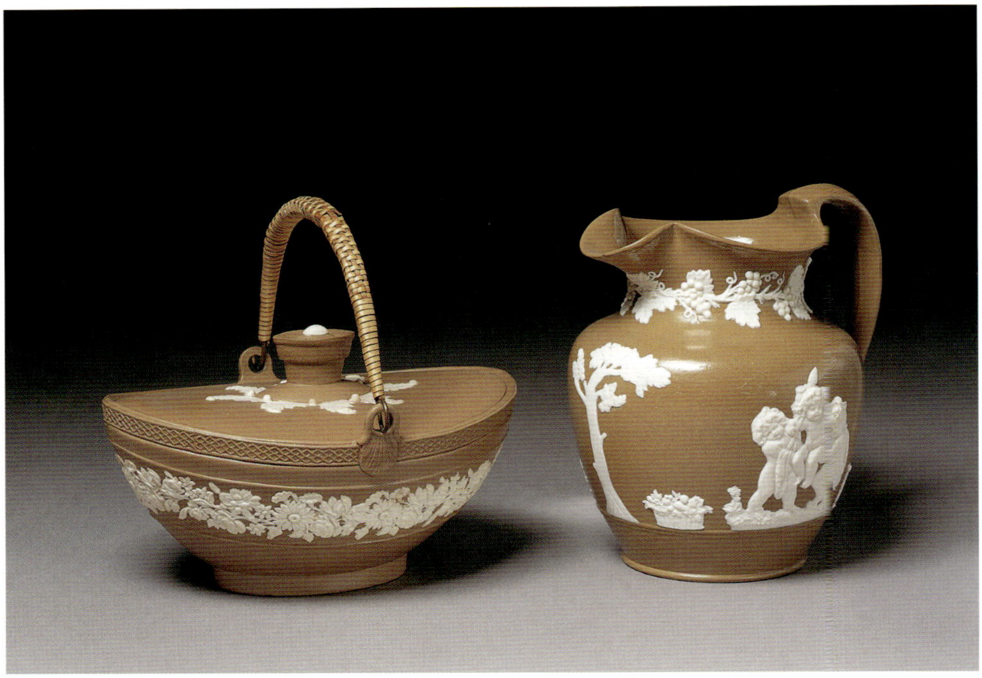

78
Drab-coloured stoneware became fashionable after about 1810, along with other colours. The quality was high, as on this 'Brameld' cup, the snake-handled jug with unidentified 'chrysanthemum' pad mark, and the crisply finished Ridgway lidded jug. Max. height 17.8 cm (7 in.).

V&A: 3176–1901, C.107–1971, 34 &A–1904.

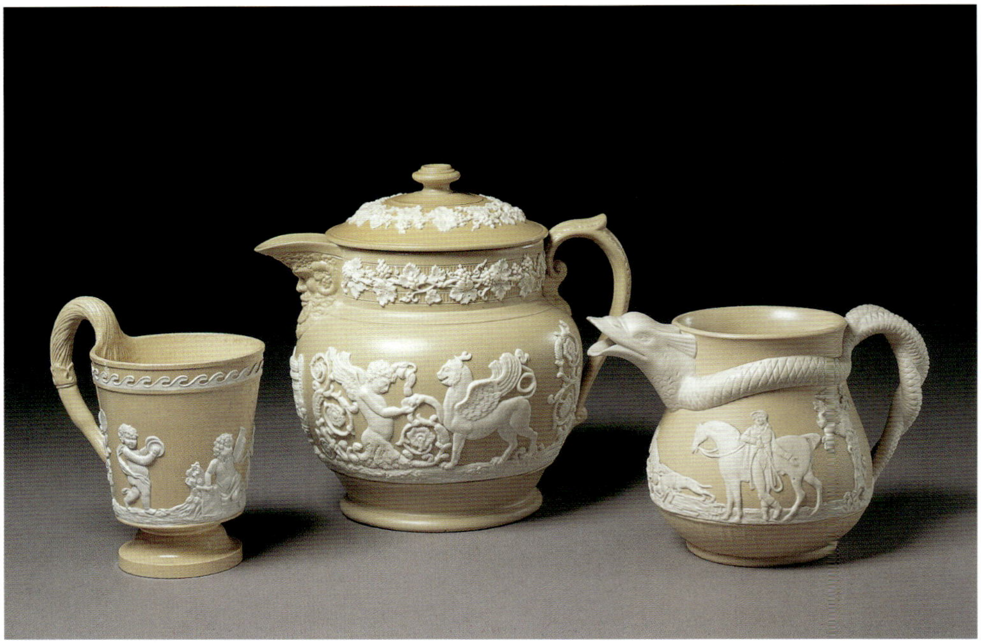

were added to stoneware and the new generation of makers such as the Ridgways, Davenport, Minton and Spode made a full range of both. There were also anonymous sub-contractors, such as the shadowy firm of Dudson of Shelton, which is recorded as supplying teawares to the New Hall factory in 1819, just possibly some of their 'blue figured jugs' and 'dipt mugs, jugs and bowls'.[14] But Dudson is more famed for its continued manufacture of excellent sprig-decorated smear-glazed stonewares throughout the nineteenth century, comprising jugs, mugs, candlesticks and especially the huge cheese bells.

While the legacy of Wedgwood's Jasper ware designs became ever more dissipated, to be taken up by mass-producers of cheap export wares such as Enoch Wood (see chapter Eight), the peace that followed Waterloo in 1815 brought a wave of French influence that is discernible in both bone chinas and in these stonewares. The old sentimental Neo-classicism of the late eighteenth century was gradually replaced by a range of stylish linear motifs, such as the griffins, dolphins and festoons favoured by Napoleon's architects Percier and Fontaine, whose designs were freely available from engravings. A successful adaptation of a Roman frieze in this general style was also made by the Ridgways at their Bell Works, Shelton, sometime around 1820, bringing an element of sophistication to their putty-coloured drab stonewares (plate 78).[15] But such skilled and labour-intensive methods of manufacture were uncompetitive, and would soon be ousted by the use of two-piece press-moulds with integral decoration, the technique that gave drabware and other single-colour stonewares a new lease of life while opening the doors for a huge range of designs, which, in their combination of eclecticism and practicality, were truly Victorian.

1. Wedgwood's rival Jean Voyez also exploited the fashionable market for seals, advertising in the *Bath Chronicle* on 10 October 1776, 'Black Cypher Seals. Upwards of 7000 names in cypher on seals are now ready to deliver at 2s. only, and neatly set at 3s/6d'.
2. Wedgwood MSS, University of Keele: E.25–18521, letter to Bentley, 7 March 1774.
3. Grant (1910), Northern Ceramic Society (1982), Edwards (1994), Miller & Berthoud (1985).
4. On deposit at Leeds City Art Gallery and Library.
5. Recorded by Captain Jesse, *The Life of George Brummel*, 1844, quoted by Hillier (1965), p.19.
6. V&A: 2496 &A–1901, illustrated in Hildyard (1999), pl.113.
7. For example, Reilly & Savage (1973, 1980), Reilly (1986), Young (1995), Edwards & Hampson (1998), Herman (2003).
8. Wedgwood MSS, University of Keele: LHP, 7 September 1771.
9. From the print, *View of Skittle Ground at Hampstead*, by Woodward, engraved by Cruickshank, published by Allen & West, 1796.
10. *Archery at Hatfield* by Corbold, engraved by Cook, published by J. Wheble on 1 December 1792. For details of the moulds at the Spode Museum, see Leese (1987).
11. Roussel (1982).
12. A large porcellanous stoneware brandy barrel surmounted by a figure of Bacchus, on wooden stand, marked 'J.Lockett' in the V&A: 388 &A–1872. Of the several Locketts working around 1800, this is likely to be John Lockett of Lane End.
13. Fully discussed by Henrywood (1997).
14. Dudson (1985).
15. 'Baccanalian frieze. A fragment from the Forum of Trajan, now on the principal front of the Palace Aldobrandini at Rome', illustrated by C .H. Tatham, *Ancient Ornamental Architecture* (London, 1803), pl.8. See Hildyard (1997), where the source was identified.

CHAPTER SEVEN 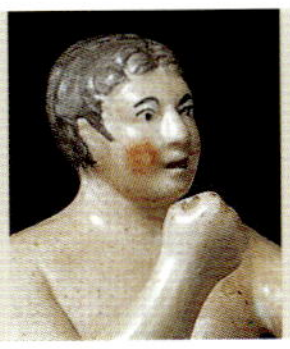

Figures: 'Images' of their Age

Although the pottery figure now appears as an essential and timeless constituent of English ceramics, it was by no means always so. Its birth and early progress were obscure and at first so slow as to be hardly traceable; for it was neither steadily honed to perfection from humble beginnings, nor did it spring fully modelled from the hands of the Wood family at Burslem in the 1770s. In fact, if we disregard for the moment those private and unique masterpieces made for John Dwight at his Fulham Pottery in the 1670s, it is evident that the fashion for ornamental figures in England took some decades to emerge, and gathered pace rapidly only after the mid-eighteenth century.

It might well be asked why it took so long for these small decorative objects to appear in seventeenth-century homes, when the art of modelling in terracotta and wax, not to mention mould-making, was already well developed. To which the answer must surely be that while the technology was already in place, the market was not. In an age noted for its austerity, there was little demand from a thrifty population for luxuries that were both frivolous and without any intrinsic value. Besides this, the wide log-burning hearths of the seventeenth century provided neither shelf above nor alcove at the side for the display of such small-scale objects. The only ceramic objects considered suitable for display in a prosperous urban middle-class home of the mid-seventeenth century were huge delftware dishes, and perhaps at a farmhouse level those massive slipware chargers whose early history and purpose remains largely obscure; images of such interiors are rare, but at least one (on a delftware charger dated 1638, no. D64 in the Longridge Collection in Milwaukee) shows an unmistakably ceramic dish with segmental border of Wan-Li type on a high shelf above a window. Yet figures were certainly available from this period onwards in the form of white porcelain from Dehua, for long known to collectors as 'Blanc de Chine', and it is likely that the introduction of these inexpensive knick-knacks – crudely pressed into two piece-moulds with extra pieces attached, much like the Thuringian 'fairings' of the late nineteenth century – into the domestic setting occurred only when the smaller hearths and projecting chimneybreasts of compact new houses could offer opportunities to build a 'mantle piece' with flanking shelves for display.

As the seventeenth century progressed, and as the hearth that symbolized the home became smaller, the mantelpiece above the fire came to be regarded as a domestic altar, whereon secular 'altar furniture' could proclaim the owner's wealth and taste.[1] The supposition that if the householder could not afford to display silver, then cheaper but exotic imported porcelain or locally made substi-

79
But for the rare Staffordshire figures of Polito's and Wombell's menageries, these travelling shows would now be almost forgotten. Polito's is thought to have been lost in the Irish Sea in 1836.
Height 32 cm (12⅝ in.).
V&A: C.128–2003.

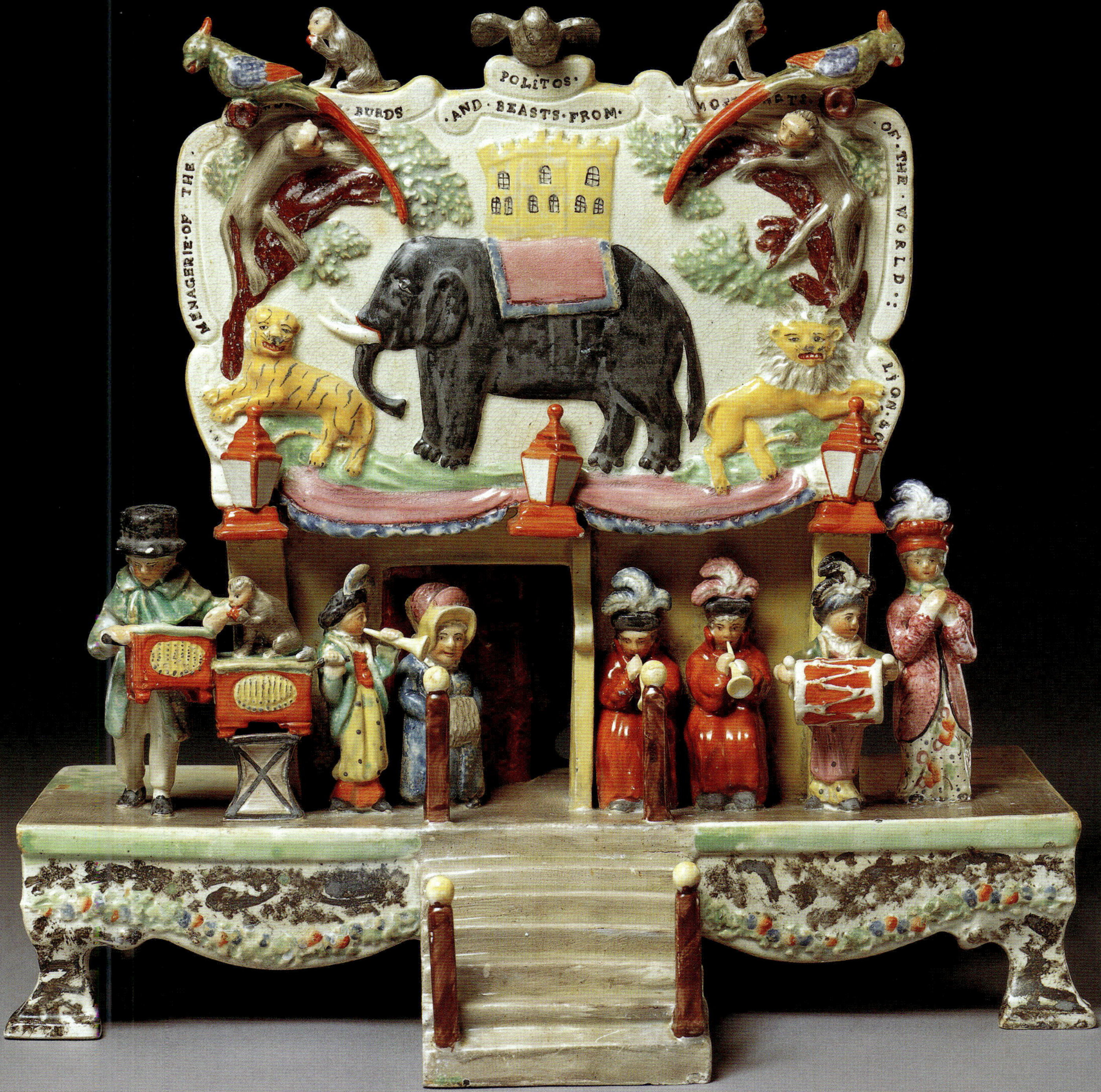
POLITOS
AND BEASTS FROM
BURDS
MENAGERIE OF THE
OF THE WORLD

tutes might suffice, is well supported by references from early inventories.[2] For example, the widow of a shopkeeper in Leicester in 1692 had 'Figures for the Chimneypiece'; in 1702 the Steward of the Choristers at Lincoln had in his Best Chamber 'Earthen Ware and Toys on ye Chimney' valued at 6s 8d, and in the Parlour, 2s worth of Toys 'on the chimney'. A gentleman at Barwell in Leicestershire in 1703 had 'China figures, Stone figures', while a Lincoln woollen draper in 1713 had 10s worth of 'Toys' on his dining-room chimneypiece. More specific references to Dehua figures include '2 images of White China 2s 6d, 2 Jappann'ed China Images 2s 6d, 10 small China Bottles and Two China Lyons' in the Best Parlour at Northill Manor, Bedfordshire, in 1731; '2 China Images 6d . . . 1 pair White Lyons 6d' owned by a gentleman at Stratford-upon-Avon in 1734, and '4 small images in my Lady's room; 5 Images on the Chimney £1 5s 0d in the Long Gallery; 3 images in the Best Parlour; in the Hall, ye 2 lions' at the house of a baronet at Long Ashton in Gloucestershire. As late as 1754 the probate of a draper and china seller John Sainthill records 'a large pr of China Swan or Bird 15/- . . . 4 dozen small images @ 6d', while in the same year the chattels of a prosperous London wire-drawer James White included '3 small Lyons china'.

Although it is likely that a taste for decorative figures was evolving in the last quarter of the seventeenth century, serious importing of Dehua figures only really took off after the British were allowed to use Canton as a trading station in 1699, from which time onwards there are detailed records of these figures imported by the East India Company (plate 80), as described below. We might also expect to find evidence of native manufacture at this period, following the general rise in national wealth and living standards after Charles II's return from exile in 1660. This was, after all, the period when native industries, such as the lead glass of George Ravenscroft, the mirror glass of the Duke of Buckingham's glasshouse at Vauxhall and the salt-glazed stoneware of John Dwight, were being developed in a scientific and commercial way, and when immigrant Huguenot craftsmen were transforming the products of British weavers, silversmiths and furniture makers. But although certain types of pottery figures were made, we may look in vain for any indication that these formed the starting point of what was to become, by the second quarter of the nineteenth century, a major production of popular 'images' in Staffordshire. Figures that were made during this period may be divided into either cheap 'toys' or expensive hand-modelled miniature stoneware sculpture – which strongly suggests that the middle market for figures had not then emerged.

The least well-known seventeenth-century figure is that made of pipeclay, solid but made in a two-piece mould, no doubt similar to those used for confectionary and gingerbread of the period. These unglazed white figures, comprising fashionably dressed young men and cupids with bow and arrows, have turned up in excavations, and are surprisingly sophisticated in their modelling, some having surface deposits that may be the remains of painted decoration.[3] Although widely distributed, their original purpose is not entirely clear. The possible themes of youth and love, however, militate against their being children's toys, suggesting rather that they were perhaps love tokens, or in the case of the male figure holding a scroll, presentation pieces to mark some academic or family occasion. The use of pipeclay and the addition of clearly impressed but unidentified maker's initials 'PB' on a figure found at Aldgate suggest that these were not made by London potters, but represent a sideline product of clay-pipe makers. There is, however, at least one example of overlapping between these two distinct trades, either by copying or through sharing of common moulds: for another pipeclay figure, unprovenanced but thought to have been found at Exeter, shows a pair of young sentimentally entwined lovers wearing exactly the same type of French dress fashionable about 1670–85 (coat buttoned front and back, jabot at the neck, loose hair, the woman with open petticoats pulled back and pinned behind), which is essentially the same model as delftware versions

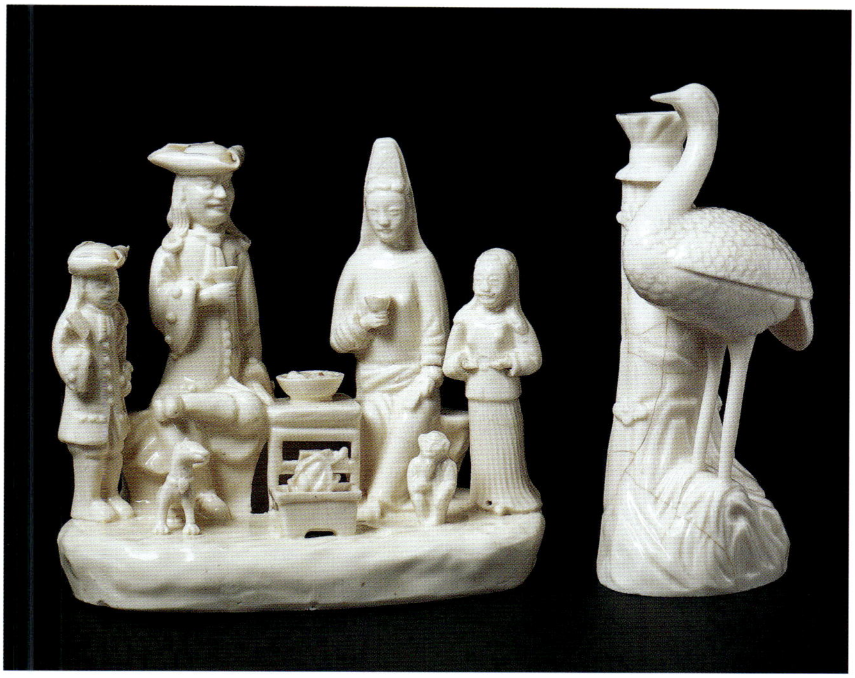

80
The glassy porcelains imported from Dehua, such as 'Admiral Duff' and the crane candlestick, provided inspiration for the earliest Staffordshire salt-glaze figures. Max. height 13.7 cm (5⅜ in.). V&A: C.108–1963, 1453–1853.

made at Southwark or Lambeth.[4] The delftware figures are true figures, in that they have bases, are fully moulded front and back, and were evidently intended to stand as ornaments on a narrow shelf.

No doubt these figures were copied from popular engravings, as were probably the few other known delftware figures, such as the flatback bust of King Charles I and a figure of Apollo. Certainly there is absolutely no influence from imported Chinese porcelains to be detected, although as might be expected there are links with the Continent: a fragmentary delftware figure of a boy stealing puppies in the Museum of London has been shown to derive from a French model produced at Avon in the early seventeenth century,[5] entirely consistent with the borrowing from Bernard Palissy of the design for relief-moulded *La Fécondité* dishes. Most of the other figural London delftwares of the period, for example the series of dated sitting cats, had a primary function as pouring vessels or money boxes, with only a secondary role as ornament. There may, however, have been some small 'fairings', if these are to be identified with the 'Toys' listed for taxation purposes by Mr Bateman in 1698.[6] None of these 'toys' has been found even as excavated fragments, and the extreme rarity of any type of delftware figure cannot be explained merely by the passing of three centuries. For tin-glazed earthenware can never have been thought suitable for moulded forms with projecting corners, and charming though the naïve press-moulded figures may be to the eyes of the modern collector, any finesse in the modelling is almost entirely hidden by their thick brittle glaze, while their sparse decoration in a limited range of oxide colours places them firmly into the category of ephemera. Since the costume worn by the pairs of lovers is no later than 1685, it may be suggested that the London delftware potters' brief excursion into figure-making ended with the coming of the first imports of porcelain figures from Dehua – many of which, as we shall see below, were naturalistically painted and always very much tougher than delftware.

From an art-historical perspective, the well-known stoneware figures made at the Fulham Pottery in the last quarter of the seventeenth century would naturally eclipse all the unpretentious commercial offerings made of delftware and pipeclay. If viewed as part of the history of ceramic figures, however, their complete lack of either antecedents or later derivatives must inevitably diminish their significance. They were, quite simply, brilliant oddities, an inspired but short-lived attempt on the part of John Dwight to raise his patented salt-glazed stoneware to the level of art, in much the same way as the ambitious Josiah Wedgwood was to perfect by 1775 his new Jasper ware as a medium for finely modelled sprigs and portrait medallions.

When John Dwight sold his appointments as ecclesiastical legal advisor to the bishops of Chester and invested everything in building the first commercial stoneware pottery in England, he had high hopes not only of making a fortune but also of breaking into the market for expensive luxury goods. While his first patent of 1672 covered the making of stoneware and (somewhat optimistically) porcelain, it made no mention of the form of the vessels that he intended to make. By the time of his second patent in 1684 he sought to protect the many experimental applications for his material, including the 'Statues and Figures' that his modellers had made around 1673–5 (see plate 11), and which impressed Dr Robert Plot, who in 1677 praised Dwight's figures 'of the said transparent Earth (as a thing not done elsewhere, for China affords us only imperfect mouldings)' – surely a perfect description of contemporary crudely press-moulded porcelain figures from Dehua.[7]

The story of Dwight's figures has been told many times and will be covered only briefly here.[8] After the death at the Fulham Pottery of Dwight's last descendant, Charles Edward White, in 1859, a collection of stoneware heirlooms was discovered and acquired by a Fulham antiquarian, Thomas Baylis, who published them and immediately sold them on to C. W. Reynolds, who in turn lent them to the Special Loan Exhibition of 1862 at the South Kensington Museum. With their importance now fully understood and their value enhanced, they were sold by Christie, Manson & Woods in 1871 and divided more or less equally between the South Kensington Museum and the British Museum. In 1961 Mavis Bimson gave a paper to the English Ceramic Circle in which she established most of the identities of the busts and divided up the whole group as the work of four modellers: Group One consisted of the life-size bust of Prince Rupert, a small bust of King Charles II and the two figures of the dead Lydia Dwight; Group Two included Jupiter, bronzed Neptune, Mars, bronzed Meleager and Saturn; Group Three consisted of the busts of John Dwight and his wife Lydia; and Group Four contained a white Meleager, Flora, Boy with Dog and Girl with Sheep. These groupings have not been challenged, although neither have their characteristics proved distinctive enough to provide plausible attributions to their modellers, despite attempts to link them with the sculptors John Bushnell, Caius Cibber, Grinling Gibbons and Edward Pierce. We are simply left with the supposition that Dwight hired comparatively unknown but competent English, Italian or Netherlandish modellers to experiment with his new material. There is no doubt that these pieces were made either as highly personal portraits of his family or as demonstrations of the use to which stoneware might be put, and were never made commercially. The simple fact that their existence was unknown for nearly two centuries, from 1673–5 to about 1860, precluded them from having any influence whatsoever on the development of English pottery figures in the eighteenth and nineteenth centuries.

As mentioned above, the import of Dehua porcelain figures began to accelerate rapidly around 1700. Not only was the market hungry after the recent hiatus in the supply of porcelain from Holland caused by the Dutch Wars, but the beginnings of direct trading with the Chinese at Canton now brought shiploads of tea and porcelain into the warehouse of the East India Company in Leadenhall Street, London.[9] Records for 1699 list from the *Nassau* 32 large gilded lions valued at 7s each, 56 small painted women at 2s, 37 large painted children at 4s, several small images at 6d, 45 'Tartarian women' at 3s 2d, 10 'Sancta Marias' at 5s 2d, 38 white or painted cocks at 3s 2d, and 40 very small images at 1s 8d. The following year the *Northumberland* and *Dashwood* brought new models, such as 144 parrots sold at auction for 5s 3d each, 7 'pulpits and padries' at 2s 9d, 200 men on monsters at 1d each, 2 others (presumably a much larger size) at 2s 6d, 134 lions at 2s, 156 wrestlers at 4d, 500 dogs at 2d, 160 rabbits at 2d, 276 'Buffeloues' at 1d, and 510 horses. From 1703 there are mentions of 'Dutch Families', that well-known group depicting a European family grouped around a table, sometimes erroneously known as The Duff Family: these came in three sizes, at 3s, 2s 6d or 1s 6d. The few scant records that survive show that these figures were being snapped up by London china dealers, for example Henry Tombes, who in 1703 bought 30 men on antelopes at 1s 6d, 123 men, 8 cranes with candlesticks at 1s, 14 dolphins, 88 birds at 1d and 46 lions at 3d, all from the *Dashwood*. In 1705 the stock of another retailer, Captain Bowery, included '660 small lions' valued at a total of £5 10s, or 2d each.

No doubt in the early eighteenth century Dehua figures were appreciated for their glassy white porcelain body, but the fact that almost all survivors are white is misleading. The cold paint and gilding that was applied to those examples listed as 'painted' would have long since begun to flake off the shiny porcelain surface, to the point where subsequent owners decided to remove it entirely. One might draw parallels with the removal of thick gaudy vegetable colours from the white marble sculptures of ancient Greece. The '2 Jappann'ed China Images' at Northill Manor in 1731, mentioned above, were most probably of this type.

It is certain that virtually no figures were made in England in the period 1700–40; but when the first salt-glazed stoneware models did appear, it can be shown that they derive from old Dehua prototypes (plate 81). Just as the decoration on early slip-cast teapots can be traced to engraved sources of the late seventeenth century, so the Staffordshire potters turned to whatever ceramic figures they could find and copy, using the only available material that roughly

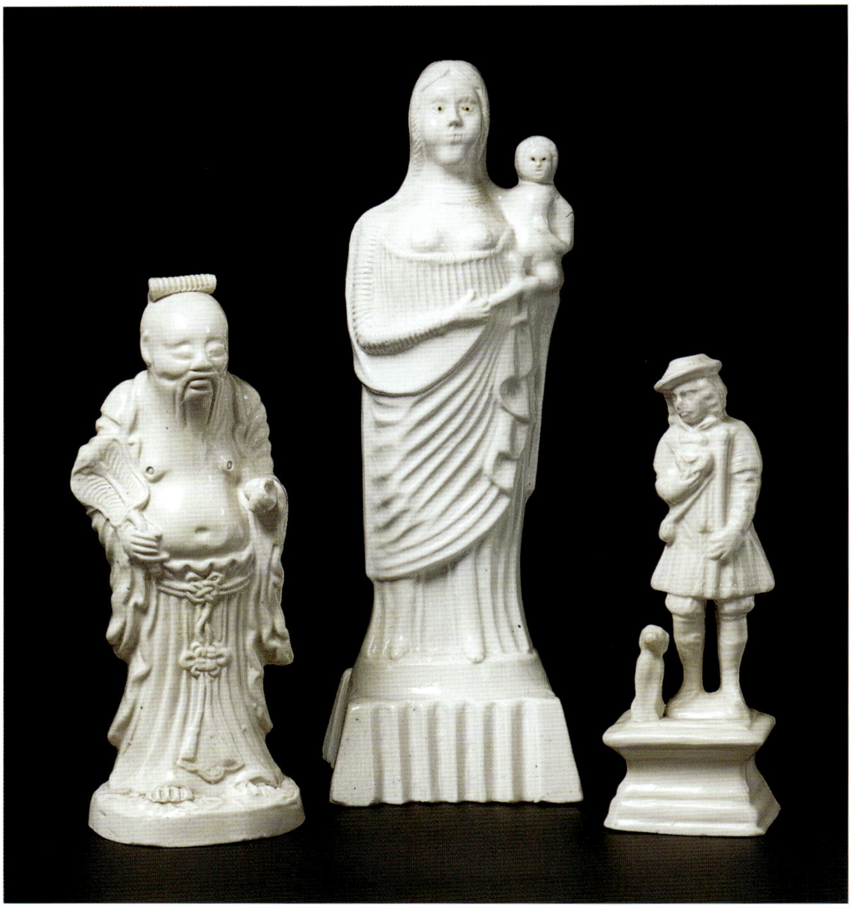

81
Slip-casting made possible the naïve attempts at figure-making in the 1740s. More exact copies, such as the Chinese deity which was also made in porcelain, were more successful. Max. height 18.4 cm (7¼ in.).
V&A: Sch.II 92, C.64–1940, Sch.II 88.

resembled white porcelain. Both salt-glazed figures and the Dehua figures themselves are now so rare that it is not easy to find exact matches between them. Some moulded models even appear to be unique survivors. There are, however, clearly related models that may be compared: crude figures of lion-like dogs on square bases clearly derive from versions of the Buddhist lion;[10] a Chinese boy lying on a lion is a sophisticated version of the Dehua 'men on beasts'; the crane backed by a hollow tree-trunk is a straight copy of the 'cranes with candlesticks',[11] datable by comparison with the similar Longton Hall examples to about 1749–53; the Virgin and Child with Chinese head-dress was copied from a Kuan Yin or 'Sancta Maria'; and the press-moulded two-piece cockerel figures must surely derive from the crude but more animated Dehua versions. The imported dogs, rabbits and horses mentioned above may well also have provided prototypes for Staffordshire figures, either salt-glazed or lead-glazed. Another figure that clearly takes its inspiration from China, but for which there seems to be no exact prototype, is the pair of so-called Shepherd and Shepherdess,[12] either mounted together on a rectangular base with a begging dog between them, or as single figures. These figures, which have been claimed by writers in the past to derive from a lost seventeenth-century bronze,[13] in fact most closely resemble the Dutch merchants of *circa* 1690 as found in a number of Dehua groups, with the man's long buttoned coats and breeches, and the woman's low-cut dress with curious flat-fronted skirt. They also provide vital clues in constructing a plausible pattern of evolution for these early figures, for the moulds were used to produce not only salt-glazed stoneware but also unglazed red stoneware and cream-coloured earthenware with coloured glazes. Thus the salt-glazed examples cannot pre-date the introduction of moulding techniques around 1740; red stoneware was not made before the late 1740s; and the earthenware fragments found on Thomas Whieldon's site at Fenton Vivian cannot be earlier than about 1747, when he moved there. We may therefore tentatively classify the period 1740–50 as one almost completely under the influence of Chinese Blanc de Chine.

Into this early group, ceramic historians have traditionally placed the extremely rare Pew Groups, as well as the elaborate, and clearly related, figures of mounted dragoons or hussars. In the complete absence of prototypes or other evidence, it seems much more likely that the inspiration for such military figures came from England's alliance with King Frederick of Prussia against the French in 1756, which was much celebrated on, for example, salt-glazed plates. If general similarities in technique are reliable indicators, then the partly moulded and partly hand-built Pew Groups are probably also of similar date, say 1755–60; and it is noteworthy that the Light Dragoon with helmet-cap was introduced into the British Army only in 1755. Much has been written about these groups, none of which has provenance further back than the early twentieth century, but whose authenticity has not been challenged, and which by 1913 were making huge prices of between £200 and £400. In the 1920s they were considered by Herbert Read as among the masterpieces of English primitive art in which 'the potter … himself a peasant with a simple mind and a simple sense of humour … blunders into beauty' – thus somewhat grudgingly elevating them to become essential keystones of any serious pottery collection.[14] But highly attractive and evocative though they undoubtedly are, combining the fresh sharpness of hand-modelled stoneware with the immediate appeal of a caricature, their influence on the future of figure-making in Staffordshire was slight: for the undoubted skills of these few makers, of whom three have been isolated through their notable idiosyncrasies of modelling, were not adaptable to commercial production.

82
At their best, mid-18th-century Staffordshire versions of Meissen figures skilfully enamelled in London came close to the spirit of the originals. Height 19.7 cm (7¾ in.).
V&A: Sch.II 173, 174.

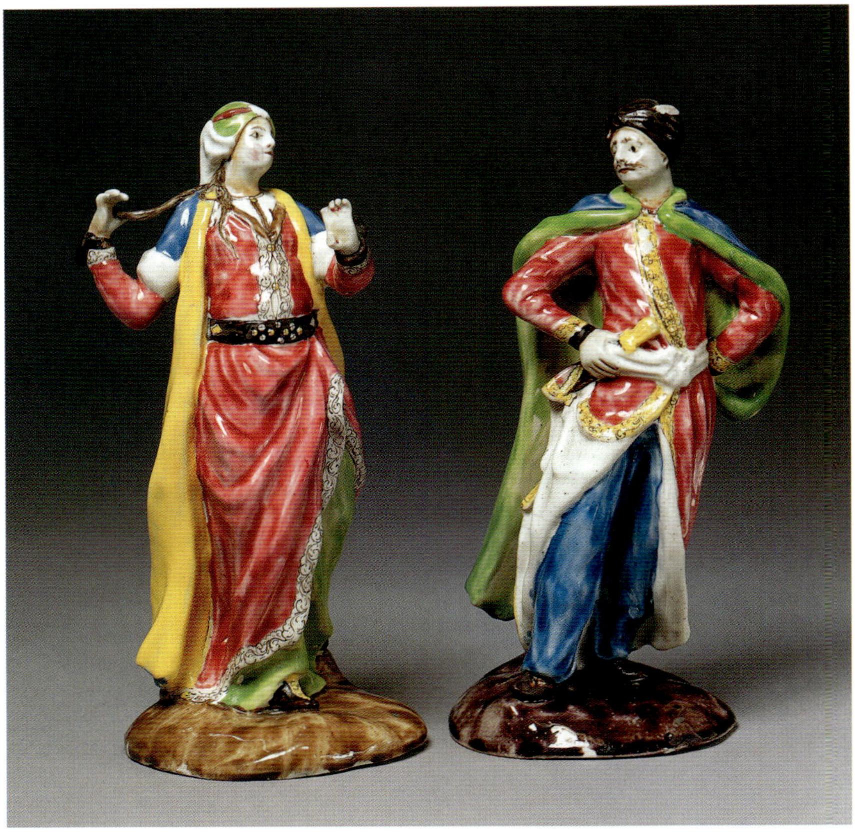

The simplest two-piece press-moulds were used for most of the early salt-glazed figures, which ranged from as big as 9 in. (23 cm) down to the smallest size into which a potter's finger might be inserted in order to smooth over and strengthen the seams. Since technical limitations restricted their decoration to the application of red-brown clay detailing and simple zigzag rouletting, when potters began to press-mould models of colourful animals and birds, it is not surprising that they experimented with the clay body itself, wedging differently stained clays together to form stripes or random patterns. Such toy figures, whether white or agate, plain or decorated with small stamps, are notoriously difficult to date, for it is likely that production carried on – like the comparable earthenware figures – well into the third quarter of the eighteenth century. Where there is a primitive bocage in imitation of porcelain, however, these must be dated after about 1760.

Much easier to place in the chronology of salt-glazed figures are the Staffordshire stoneware copies of sophisticated porcelain models. If the decade 1740–50 was one of dependency on China, then the one that followed it transferred allegiance from the East to the contemporary fashionable porcelains of Europe. As mentioned above, stoneware had been tough and white enough to copy Dehua porcelains with some success, but when the art of enamelling was applied to the material (as indeed 'cold' painted decoration and gilding had been applied by the Chinese to their Dehua figures), it could aspire to imitate the much more sophisticated German or English porcelain figures. It is known from the notebooks of William Duesbury that stoneware models were being decorated in London as early as 1751–3,[15] notably the 'Stone Birds', 'Stafordshire ladis' and 'Staffordshir lar[k] B[ir]ds', and perhaps also the 'swimming swans donn all over'.[16] Equally interesting are Duesbury's instructions for decorating a 'Turk Soldr': 'Cap the front Blue Back red of it the Wast Cote and Sleevs Blue the Sandals Yellow Breeches Red and Belt', which, if only we could match up the colours to surviving examples, would surely point to Duesbury's studio. Despite their excellent effect, however, the numbers of enamelled stoneware figures must always have been a tiny minority compared with painted teawares, and it is clear that the great bulk of Duesbury's business consisted of painting or repairing smarter porcelain figures – Chelsea, Dresden or Chinese – for the London china dealers, as well as adding metal 'branches' to convert figures into candlesticks. Although these rare and expertly painted stoneware figures (plate 82) may be attributed to Duesbury on grounds of probability, it is not known how many decorators he employed, or whether his studio was the only one involved in their decoration. Since some of the few white stoneware Italian Comedy figures modelled after Meissen originals were left undecorated (while the originals relied absolutely on bright colouring for their striking effect), it would seem that their anonymous makers may have missed the point and may never have intended that they should be enamelled. And if the enamellers hoped that they could compete with Chelsea, Bow and imported Meissen figures for the fashionable table decorations of the period,[17] then it was doomed to failure by the passing of the fashion during the 1750s, when figures began to acquire bocage and to move from the dining table to the mantelpiece.

Many plain white salt-glazed figures have survived, the most effective of which are perhaps the birds copied from white Meissen originals, sometimes via an intermediary source such as the copies made at Bow and Chelsea. The same moulds were used for making the much more common earthenware examples with underglaze sponged oxide decoration. By the early 1750s, expensive Meissen figures[18] were commonly used in fashionable English table-settings[19] and could easily be borrowed and copied by enterprising modellers in Staffordshire. Given the strong links with Staffordshire of the proprietors of the Bow factory, and also the high output of porcelain figures by William Littler's Longton Hall factory in Staffordshire, it is not surprising that overlapping models are found, such as pugs and the pairs of elegant recumbent horses and deer on flat bases decked with applied flowers. An earthenware version of the horse with tree-trunk supporting candle nozzle with underglaze sponged decoration confirms the date of this type as *circa* 1750–60;[20] and in view of the fact that William Littler had been operating a salt-glaze pottery with his brother-in-law Aaron Wedgwood at Brownhills since 1745 and did not join the Longton Hall partnership until 1751, it is not improbable that it was Littler who copied these models so skilfully from porcelain.[21]

Although the material of white salt-glazed stoneware could effectively copy porcelain, cream-coloured lead-glazed earthenware had other advantages. Its main drawback, the necessity for extra biscuit-firing, was not only at a temperature much lower – and therefore cheaper – than required for stoneware, but was more than offset by the wide possibilities for underglaze coloured decoration. The earliest and simplest of these little 'images' were surely those made in a two-piece mould, like the salt-glazed figures that preceded them, whose complete lack of pretension suggests that they were intended as children's playthings. The name of Thomas Whieldon has become associated with these, originally for no better reason than that he was the leading Staffordshire potter of the mid-eighteenth century; but excavations on the Fenton Vivian site have proved that he did indeed manufacture such 'toys', supported by the documentary evidence from his Notebook that in 1749 he supplied 'To Jack for Mr Thos Payne, 12 pr Glazd Images, 6 pr d[itt]o unglaz'd'.[22] The excavated Whieldon fragments consisted of a biscuit earthenware version of the Dehua shepherdess (more commonly found in stoneware, and sometimes in red stoneware, as described above), and a foot from a Boy on Water Buffalo group, of which many survive, mostly with the streaky underglaze oxide colours traditionally associated with his factory (plate 83). In addition, a '*Tortoise Shell* ware' cat given by Enoch Wood to the Dresden factory museum was captioned by him as 'made by Whieldon & Wedgwood at their commencement of Business', which would suggest a date of *circa* 1754. Other known figures of this class are rare, consisting of one of the eight Taoist Immortals (also found in salt-glazed stoneware, and not unlike the porcelain versions marked 'Bristoll . . . 1750' made by Lund & Miller at Bristol) and one or two others such as birds on tree stumps copied from Meissen. This would seem to be further confirmation of the changeover from Chinese to European influence that took place in the middle years of the eighteenth century.

As for the two-part press-moulded creamware figures, these were made by other Staffordshire potteries, such as the swans of *circa* 1765–70 excavated on the Greatbatch site. A figure of Admiral Rodney (plate 84), datable to his great naval victory of 1782, demonstrates that these little figures remained popular, unaffected by changes of fashion, until quite late in the eighteenth century, eventually acquiring hasty dabbed or sponged patches of high-temperature colour as their only decoration. Outside Staffordshire, as far apart as Devon and the North-East, such modest figures caught the popular imagination and continued to supply local needs. Fragments of press-moulded cats and grouped pairs of children made at the Indeo Pottery, Bovey Tracey, hark back to Staffordshire products of the mid-eighteenth century.

Into this uncomplicated sequence of development ceramic historians of the past introduced a class of crude creamware figures on red clay bases, modelled as seated or marching musicians (plate 84), which could be collected and assembled into bands somewhat like lead soldiers – from which, indeed, it is tempting to think that they may have drawn their inspiration. These have acquired the generic name 'Astbury', solely on account of their combination of red and white clays, and, if they have a mottled glaze, 'Astbury-Whieldon'.[23] And because of this unfounded assumption, inevitably they have been dated earlier than Astbury's death in 1743. Although Herbert Read could confidently state in 1929 that he was 'not acquainted with any forgeries of the Astbury-Whieldon type',

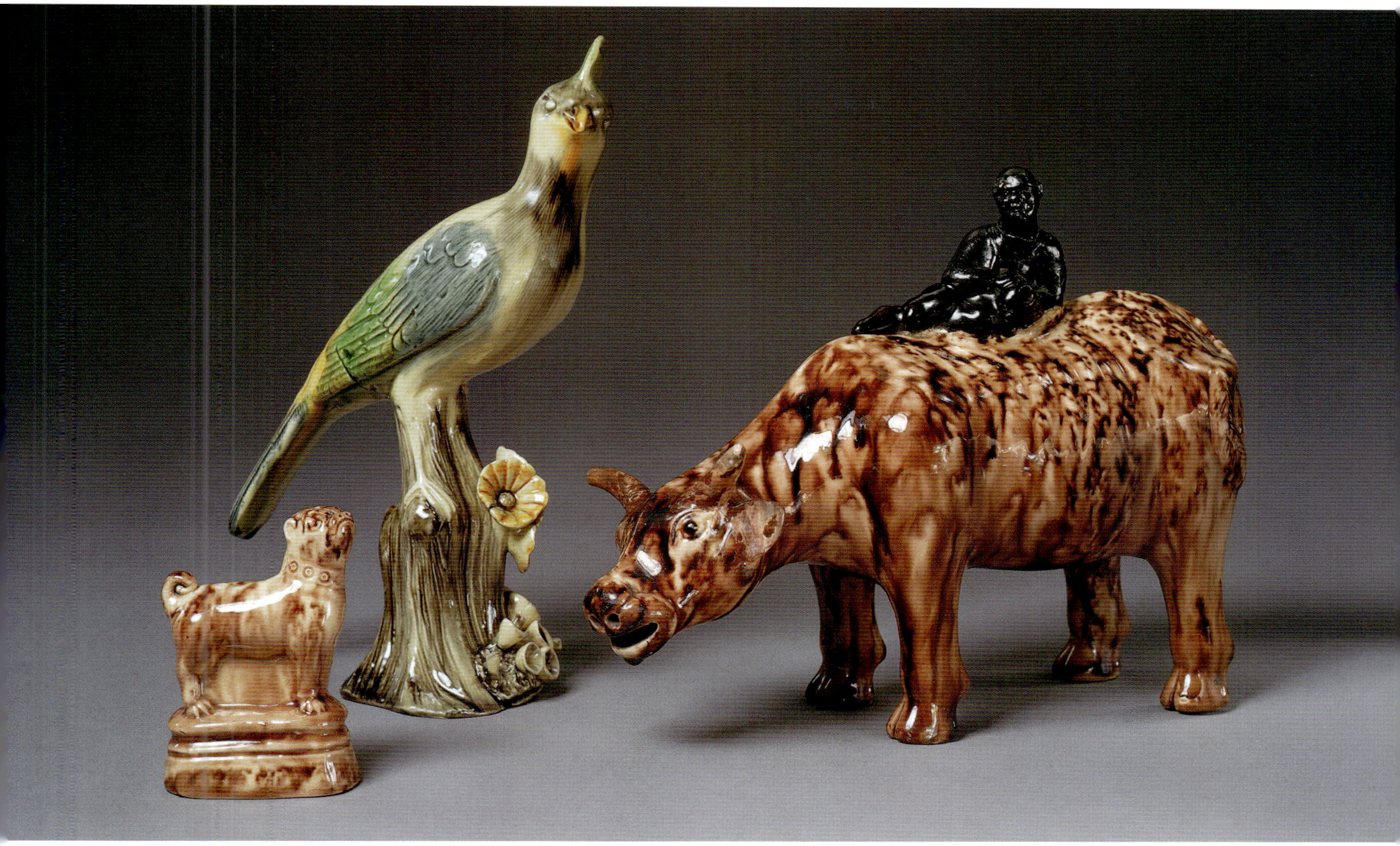

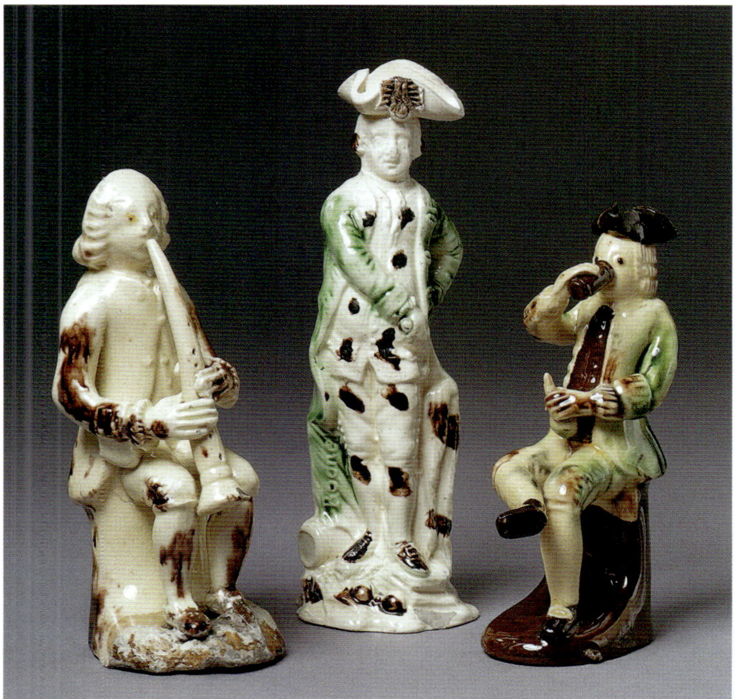

83
Colour-glaze and tortoiseshell, though far from naturalistic, proved effective for animal figures. Max. height 21.6 cm (8½ in.).

V&A: Sch.II 254, Sch.II 258, Sch.II 269.

84
A so-called Astbury figure with red base and of uncertain date is compared with a creamware figure of Admiral Rodney of *c*.1782 and a creamware musician of similar date. Max. height 14.9 cm (5⅞ in.).

V&A: C.194–1938, C.28–1940, Sch.II 253.

controversy has never been far away from these figures; yet because there are some examples (as in the controversial area of Jacobite Glass) that appear more genuine than others, no writer has gone as far as general outright condemnation. The matter of distinguishing between old fakes, older fakes and genuine must await a proper study backed by thermoluminescence testing. Meanwhile, the facts surrounding this class of creamware figure with red clay base are summarized as follows:

1. Not a single fragment of any of these figures has been excavated, either in Staffordshire or elsewhere.
2. Few of the large number of examples show any signs of wear or damage.
3. From both a technical and artistic point of view, they would be very easy to make in a small domestic workshop.
4. Those examples in the Willett Collection at Brighton, though having the oldest provenance, cannot be proved to be earlier than the 1890s.
5. The Schreiber Collection at the V&A has no examples. Given her demanding standards and predatory collecting policy, it may be significant that Lady Charlotte Schreiber managed only to acquire a single badly damaged creamware musician (without red clay base), added to her collection as late as 1884.
6. Captain R. K. Price states in his book *Astbury, Whieldon, and Ralph Wood Figures, Toby Jugs* (1922) that his extensive collection of figures was formed in the period 1907–17, that not a single figure was offered by Christie's during that period, but that in the year 1917 he purchased no less than 80 figures through the London trade. The Price Collection, still in the hands of the Price family, cannot be examined.
7. A faker of 'Astbury' figures working in the Vauxhall area was identified (but not then named) by the London antique trade in the 1930s.[24] Paradoxically, this wave of fakes in the 1930s, far from casting doubt on the existing figures, had the effect of making them appear more genuine.[25]

Moving on to the last quarter of the eighteenth century, this period witnessed the emergence of the Staffordshire earthenware figure from simple 'toy' to professionally modelled ornament, which, like the cream-coloured tablewares perfected by Wedgwood in the 1760s, could complement porcelain by exploiting those very qualities that made it both different and so much cheaper to produce. A number of other factors aided the promotion of these figures, including the extraordinary talents of the Wood family of modellers, the waning of the fashion for elaborate Rococo porcelain groups in favour of muted simple single figures in the Neo-classical taste, the growing infrastructure of 'Staffordshire Warehouses', which served the increasing market for fine earthenwares, and lastly the development of the raised cast-iron coal-burning hob-grate and its narrow chimney, framed by a neat wooden or painted slate mantelpiece that was soon to acquire a range of suitable over-mantle mirrors, pairs of candlesticks, spill vases and figures. As for the Wood family themselves, whose name is now synonymous with most earthenware figures of the period, it is essential to give a brief sketch of their tangled relationships.

The modellers and makers of block-moulds Ralph Wood I (1715–1772) and Aaron Wood (1717–1785) were brothers, Ralph being apprenticed to Dr Thomas Wedgwood of the Big House, Burslem, in 1731 and Ralph being employed by Josiah Wedgwood *circa* 1756–72. The next generation consisted of Ralph Wood's sons Josiah (1742–1789), John (1746–1797) and Ralph II (1745–1795), and Aaron Wood's son Enoch (1759–1840), who were all potters, and, with the possible exception of Josiah, all major producers of figures. John at first ran Wedgwood's London showroom from 1769 to 1772, after which he and Ralph II became partners in a pottery venture that failed, when John entered into a partnership with John Wedgwood, later building a factory at Brownhills, where he was a major producer not only of figures but also of white stoneware, creamware, Egyptian black, black-glazed wares, redwares glazed and unglazed, blue glaze, new china, and blue printed ware. After his early death in 1797 he was succeeded by his son John II, who married an heiress, Mary Baddeley, and diversified into banking, demolishing the factory in 1830. Unfortunately none of the products listed in his Sales Ledger of the 1780s at the Potteries Museum is distinctive enough to make any attributions possible. Ralph II began by running a Staffordshire Warehouse in Bristol in 1773, then started a pottery in 1784 with his cousin Enoch, the partnership dissolving around 1789, when Ralph II continued while Enoch left to set up his new Fountain Place pottery at Burslem. An order book from the partnership period, covering *circa* 1783–7, survives at the Potteries Museum. Ralph Wood II's pottery continued after his death in 1795, when he was succeeded by his son Ralph Wood III, who died in 1801. Enoch went from strength to strength by mass-producing utilitarian wares for export, eventually becoming the wealthiest man in Burslem, until his death in 1845.

It is highly likely that all these Woods made similar, and probably identical, figures from models that they shared among themselves: Enoch, undoubtedly the best modeller and the author of the ubiquitous bust of Wesley modelled in 1784, is a likely candidate for Chief Modeller, although he was considerably younger than his cousins, John and Ralph II. The only marked figures are a number impressed 'R.WOOD', 'R.Wood' or 'Ra.Wood Burslem', which are generally thought to date from the Ralph Wood II and Enoch Wood partnership of the years 1783–9 or the later factory of Ralph Wood II and III from 1789 to 1801,[26] and the later enamel-decorated examples impressed 'Wood & Caldwell' dating from Enoch Wood's partnership with James Caldwell, *circa* 1790–1818. The matter is further complicated by several series of mould numbers that are found impressed or painted on the bases of unmarked figures: some may be cross-referred to marked Ralph Wood and Enoch Wood figures, yet the many anomalies do not allow these numbers to be used for attribution purposes. But in the wider context, attribution to individuals is fairly unimportant: for the closely bonded factories of Staffordshire had good reason to produce anonymous and interchangeable products to encourage the smooth-running and furtherance of their trade.

The late eighteenth century was a period dominated by sentimentality and interest in the past, ranging from philosophers and heroes of the Ancient World to more recent influential British poets and writers such as Shakespeare, Milton and Prior. Inspired by the aristocratic Grand Tour, ever larger sections of society awakened to art, literature and the repertoire of classical mythology, for which Staffordshire potters soon provided well-modelled but cheap figures and busts. In this, the genius of native modellers was helped not only by a good range of porcelain prototypes to copy, but also by the ready availability of models produced by the leading London plaster shops of John Cheere, Hoskins & Grant, Peter Vanina, Charles Harris and Richard Parker. Wedgwood's Black Basalt proved an ideal material for translating these into a durable ceramic material, notably in those large downward-looking busts destined for the top of library bookcases; but other Staffordshire potteries made use of them, and sometimes a bust can be matched with a rare surviving plaster, such as the small *Isaac Newton* in the Victoria and Albert Museum. Ralph Wood II is recorded as asking for the loan of a foreign china figure to copy in 1785; but it was not until after about 1800 that the subjects of pottery and porcelain figures began to coincide closely, with professional modellers such as Pierre Stephan moving from the Derby factory to Shelton, followed in the 1830s by the Derby modellers Edward and Samuel Keys. By this date, Derby and Rockingham were the only factories outside Staffordshire making figures, while many new makers of 'china toys' had established themselves in Lane End and Shelton. It is fair to say that, in the Rococo Revival of the 1820s, it was not in porcelain but in pottery that the old bocage figures of the eighteenth century were to re-emerge.

The surviving sales ledgers of John Wood and Enoch & Ralph Wood give an excellent cross-section of the figures in vogue during the period 1783–7. These include 'Shepherds and Shepherdesses', 'Faith, Hope & Charity', 'Men with Lost Sheep', 'Clowns', 'Stags & Hinds', 'Sheep & Goats', 'Neptune & Venus', 'Spaniel & Pointer', 'Fox & Greyhound', 'Diana & Apollo', 'Mower & Haymaker', 'Lion & Panther', 'King David', 'Bacchus & Venus', 'Gardeners' and 'Sheep & Rams'. By 1810 a London retailer called Wyllie was supplied by Wood & Caldwell with some of the old favourites (for example, 'Faith, Hope & Charity', 'Lion & Panther', 'Stag & Hind', 'Diana & Apollo', 'Mower & Haymaker'), but also a new range of more elaborate models inspired by porcelain, often with bocage behind, including 'Justice & Peace', 'Sportsmen', 'Village Songster', 'Horn & Tambaurine [*sic*] players', 'Cupid & Dove', 'Seasons', 'Sir John Falstaff', 'Tailor & Mate', and a selection of birds and beasts such as leopards, swans, pheasants, cows and foxes.[27] Later entries for 1815 and 1823 in the Wyllie account-books show increasingly sentimental subjects, like 'Fruit Boys', 'Strawberry Gatherers', 'Boys & Girls with Dog & Lamb', being supplied by W. Moseley and T. B. Godwin. It is no surprise to find that some of the more appealing figures of the period around 1800, sometimes using children to illustrate adult life, have been identified as copies of Lunéville figures modelled by Paul-Louis Cyfflé after drawings by Boucher.[28] These, always with the addition of a square base, include the boy with bird's nest in his hand, a young falconer, a girl holding a box containing a marmot on a bed of straw, a huddled figure of Winter, a bagpipe player, 'tussling' boys, a cobbler and his wife, and the reclining Antony (taken from Cyfflé's group *Renaud et Armide*).

Oddly, not one of those neat enamelled miniature busts of, among others, Rousseau, Voltaire, Shakespeare, Milton, Prior, Thomson, Handel, Napoleon and Tsar Alexander II, mostly with circular marbled plinths, appear in any surviving ledgers or bills, nor are any of them marked. An obvious explanation would be that such pieces were conceived as desk furniture, for which purpose they were eminently suitable, and that they were supplied to stationers and booksellers rather than chinamen or Staffordshire Warehouses.

The introduction of toby jugs (plate 85), however, is well documented, since these were supplied by John Wood from 1783 to important London retailers

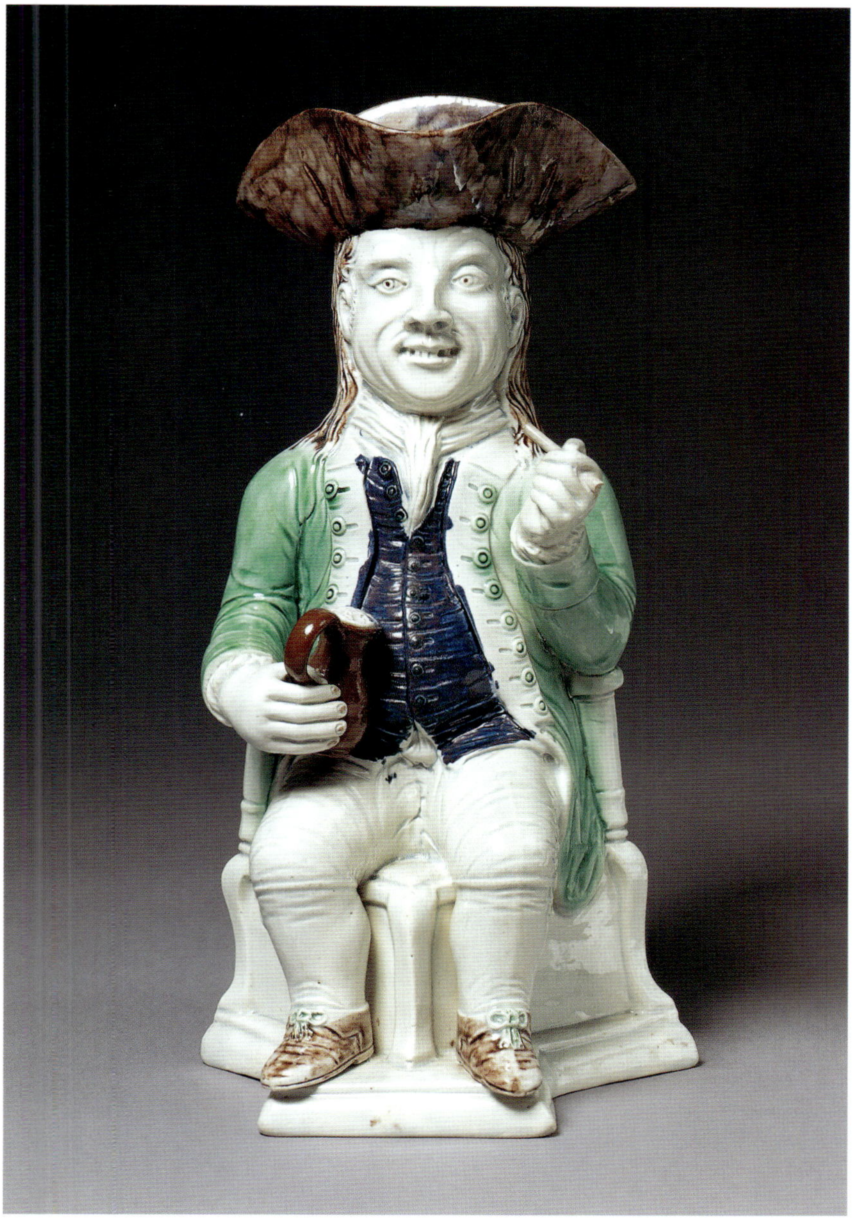

85
Toby jugs were supplied to the London retail trade from the 1780s and remained popular for decades. Early examples show the most vigorous modelling. Height 29.2 cm (11½ in.).
V&A: C.29–1930.

such as George Phillips and William Mortlock of Oxford Street, indicating that these self-consciously rustic objects were not, as one might think, intended for country pubs but for the more sophisticated population of the metropolis. In an age of nostalgia for a fast-vanishing Merrye Englande, such images of a self-indulgent country squire had an enduring appeal. The fat-bellied, beer-swilling pipe-smoking Sir Toby Philpott originally derived from an engraving by Robert Dighton of 1761, which accompanied verses from the song 'The Brown Jug' by the Revd Francis Fawkes, in which Sir Toby meets his end in the very act of drinking, concluding:

> His breath-doors of life on a sudden were shut,
> And he died full as big as a Dorchester butt

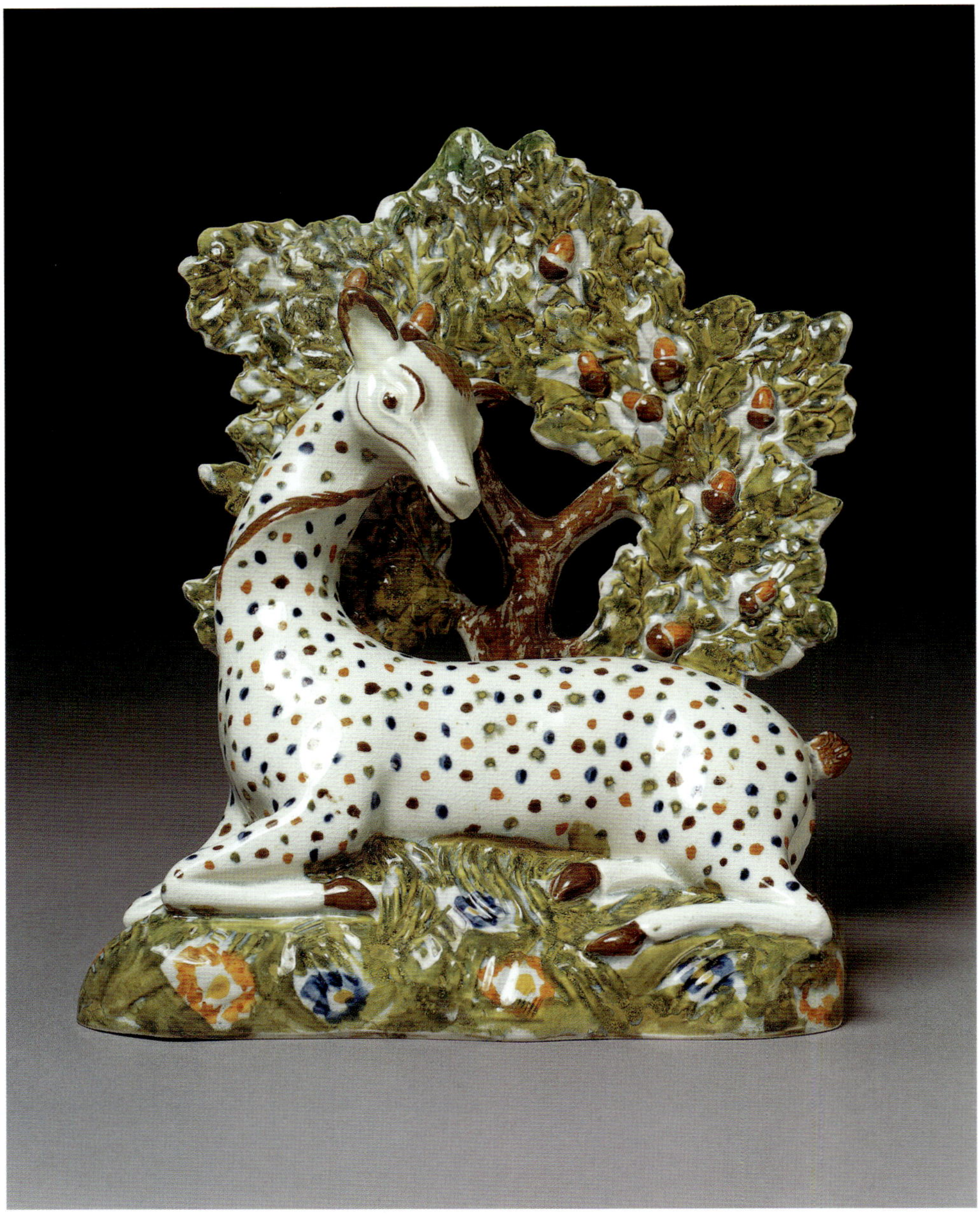

86
About 1800 high-temperature underglaze colours were successfully combined with a bocage background borrowed from porcelain figures of the 1760s. The muted colours suited both the bluish glaze and the spirit of the times. Height 20.3 cm (8 in.).
V&A: C.5–2002.

It is also perhaps no coincidence that Uncle Toby was the hero of Sterne's *Tristram Shandy*, published in 1768. But whatever the inspiration, the name not only stuck but must have added to its popularity. From about 1800 the same theme was taken up by Kishere's Mortlake pottery with the brown salt-glazed stoneware hunting jug, using sprigs and applied plaques of carousing 'tobies', until later in the nineteenth century a revival of interest in the simple life of Olde Englande brought reproductions of eighteenth-century toby jugs, and finally the deliberately grotesque 'character jugs' that are still made by Royal Doulton for a collectors' market.

Although the subjects of figures of the period 1770–1820 changed little, there were major developments in style and decoration that reflected changing fashions and markets, and which act as landmarks for dating purposes. For it is by these roughly chronological changes that figures of the period are now classified: *circa* 1780–1800, 'Colour Glazed' decoration where different coloured glazes are carefully painted onto adjacent areas of the biscuit earthenware; *circa* 1790–1840, high-temperature underglaze decoration in iron-brown, copper-green, cobalt-blue, antimony-yellow and manganese-purple (plate 86); *circa* 1790–1800, enamel-painted figures, of the type sometimes marked by Lakin & Poole, where the heavily cobalt-blue-stained lead-glaze gave a suitable background for sparse and delicate decoration in a limited range of rich enamel colours; *circa* 1810–20, enamel-painted Pearlware with large areas of brightly coloured enamel, and even sometimes gilding. Thus the character of these figures, and of course their price, varied widely: an average price for a simple figure would have been 10d, for coloured glaze 1s 3d, for plain and gilt 1s 9d, for coloured glaze and gilt 2s 3d, and for enamel-painted 2s 6d. Like engraved glass, any added decoration could double or treble the cost of the basic object. The more refined earthenware became, the more it could become a serious rival to porcelain, while maintaining a huge price advantage. Exact comparisons are difficult to find, but one might compare a large Derby figure of the actor Quinn playing Falstaff in 1779, which cost 16s, and a normal-sized Wood & Caldwell earthenware version (plates 87, 88) of the same model, which cost 5s in 1810. Although the Leeds Pottery produced a limited range of figures of excellent quality, in terms of sophistication the models of the Wood family put contemporary products of smaller Staffordshire potters, such as Theophilus Smith, and those of Yorkshire, Sunderland and elsewhere (plates 89), firmly into the shade. It is, however, these penny-or-two toys that modern taste has elevated to the status of folk art.

By about 1815 the sombre brown-lined square bases and bluish Pearlware of Neo-classical taste had begun to lose ground to a completely different class of figure (plate 90), gaudily painted all over and raised on a hollow mound base often with bocage, inspired directly by porcelain figures of 50 years before. But the old rectangular marbled bases coexisted with the new rustic types, as shown for example by the various different versions of the New Marriage Act of 1823. Square bases continued to be used for the better-quality portrait figures of the 1820s, such as the one-legged beggar Billy Waters and the clown Joseph Grimaldi, which can be attributed to Enoch Wood on the basis of matching

87

The more sophisticated enamelled Pearlware figures, such as the 'Falstaff' made by Wood & Caldwell, often derived from porcelain versions, modelled in this case by Pierre Stephan of Derby. Max. height 23.8 cm (9⅜ in.).

V&A: 2470–1901, 3018–1901.

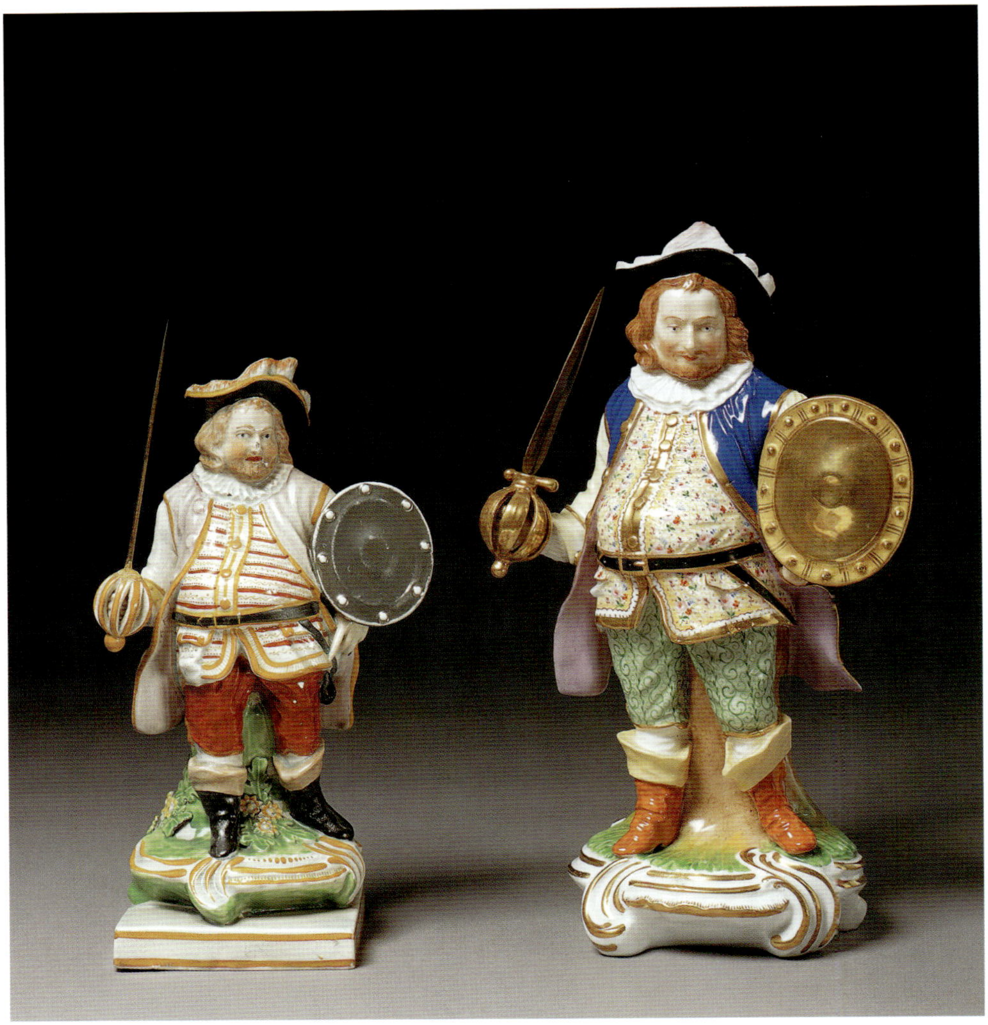

88

Falstaff was such a popular figure that Thomas Rowlandson depicted him on stage in an imaginary performance of Henry IV Part 1, illustrating 'Dr Syntax at Covent Garden' dating from 1809.

Private Collection.

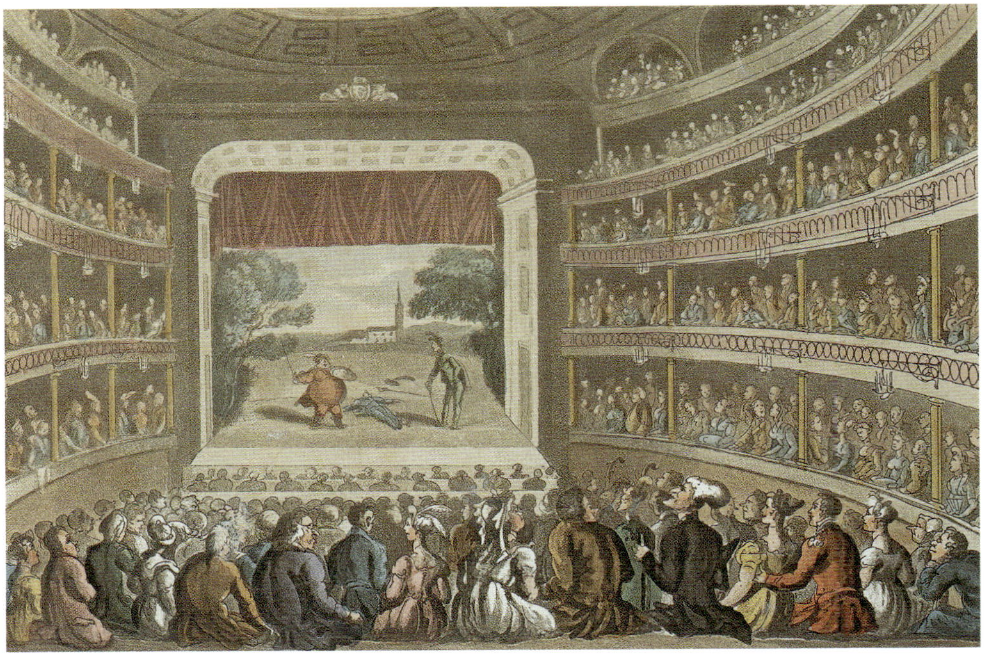

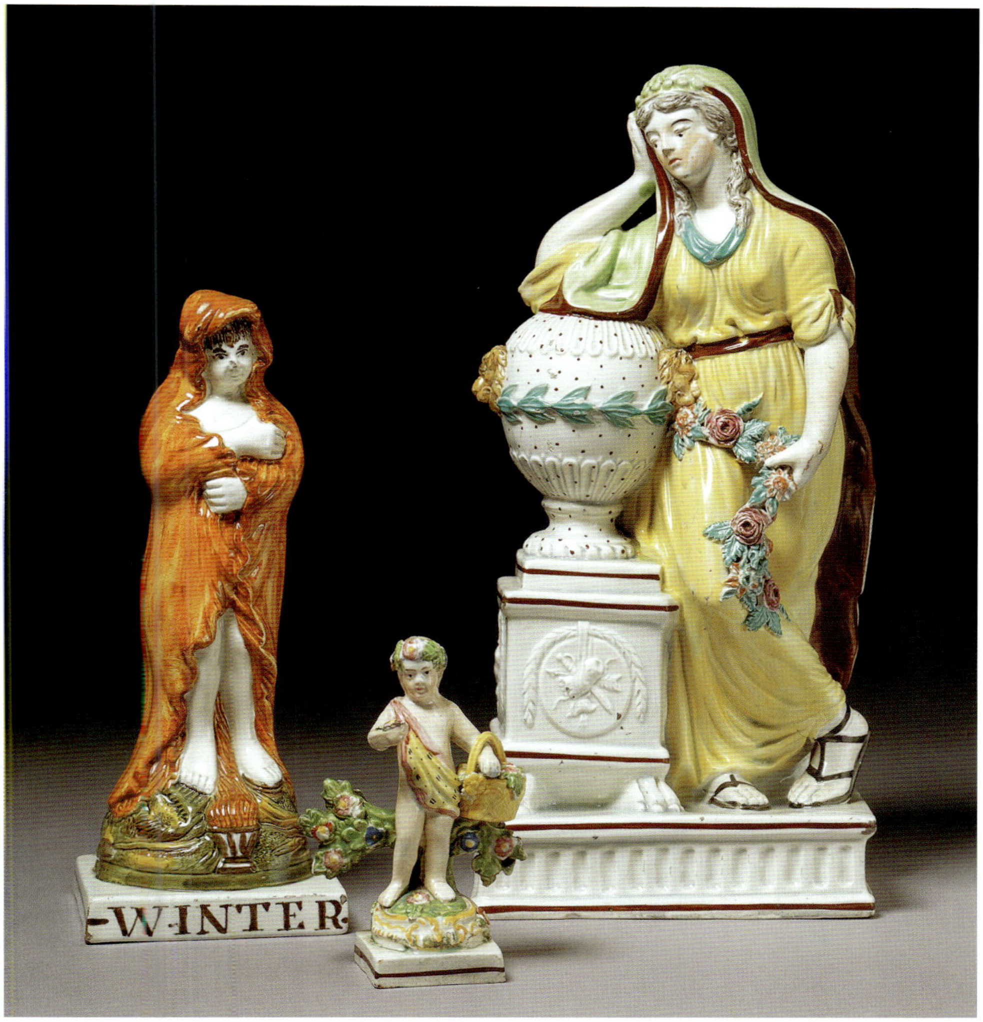

89

Figures made outside the Staffordshire Potteries were of variable quality. The 'Winter' with high-temperature colours made by Dixon & Co. of Sunderland and the boy marked 'Cambrian Pottery' copied from a Derby original do not compare well with the proficiently modelled figure of Andromache made at the Leeds pottery. Max. height 31.7 cm (12½ in.).

V&A: 3666–1901, 3470–1901, C.29–1955.

excavated fragments. The neat round pill-box base with gilded title preferred by contemporary porcelain factories such as Rockingham and Derby was but rarely attempted, perhaps because expensive gilding was out of the question while the alternative of *impressing* a title onto a tightly curved surface presented technical difficulties.

As with the Wood family in the 1780s, it was the most prolific self-advertiser who gave his name to the whole class of bocage figure with 'Rococo' base (plate 91), in this case John Walton of Burslem, who was listed in the local *Directory* from 1818 to 1835 – a period during which the number of figure makers doubled.[29] Unlike the dynastic Wood family, Walton's business passed to his son-in-law George Hood sometime in the 1830s, but did not outlast his death in 1848.[30] Other makers who marked their wares, such as Ralph Salt of Shelton, John Dale of Burslem and Charles Tittensor of Shelton, unwittingly laid the foundations of a rich collectors' field, which flourished a century later. Both the commemorative and the religious subjects of these little figures indicate that such pieces were increasingly aimed at a popular market with a distinct Nonconformist bias.

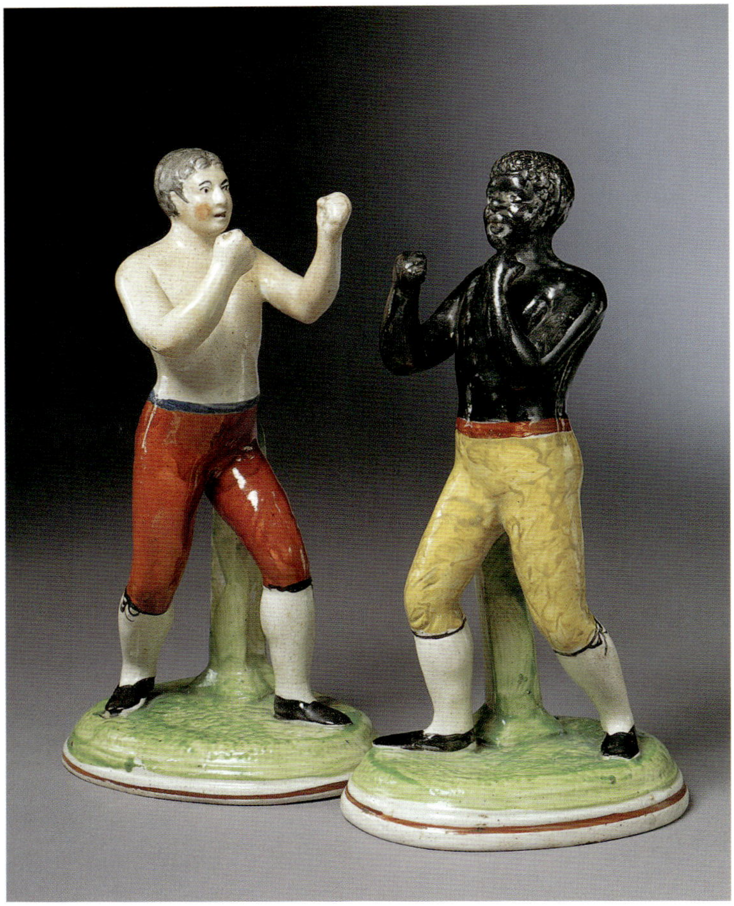

90

The bare-knuckle fighters Tom Cribb and the American Tom Molyneux fought their final decisive battle in 1812. Cribb was determined, Molyneux was out of condition after succumbing to the low life of London, leaving Cribb as a very popular British champion.
Height 22.3 cm (8¾ in.).

V&A: C.130:1, 2–2003.

91

Bocage figures of the 1820s–1830s are difficult to distinguish, although fortunately many are marked. Walton 'Earth' may be compared to the version by Dale, and the Walton 'Water' with its Dale counterpart.
Max. height 16.8 cm (6⅝ in.).

V&A: 2529–1901, 2657–1874, 2530–1901, 2658–1874.

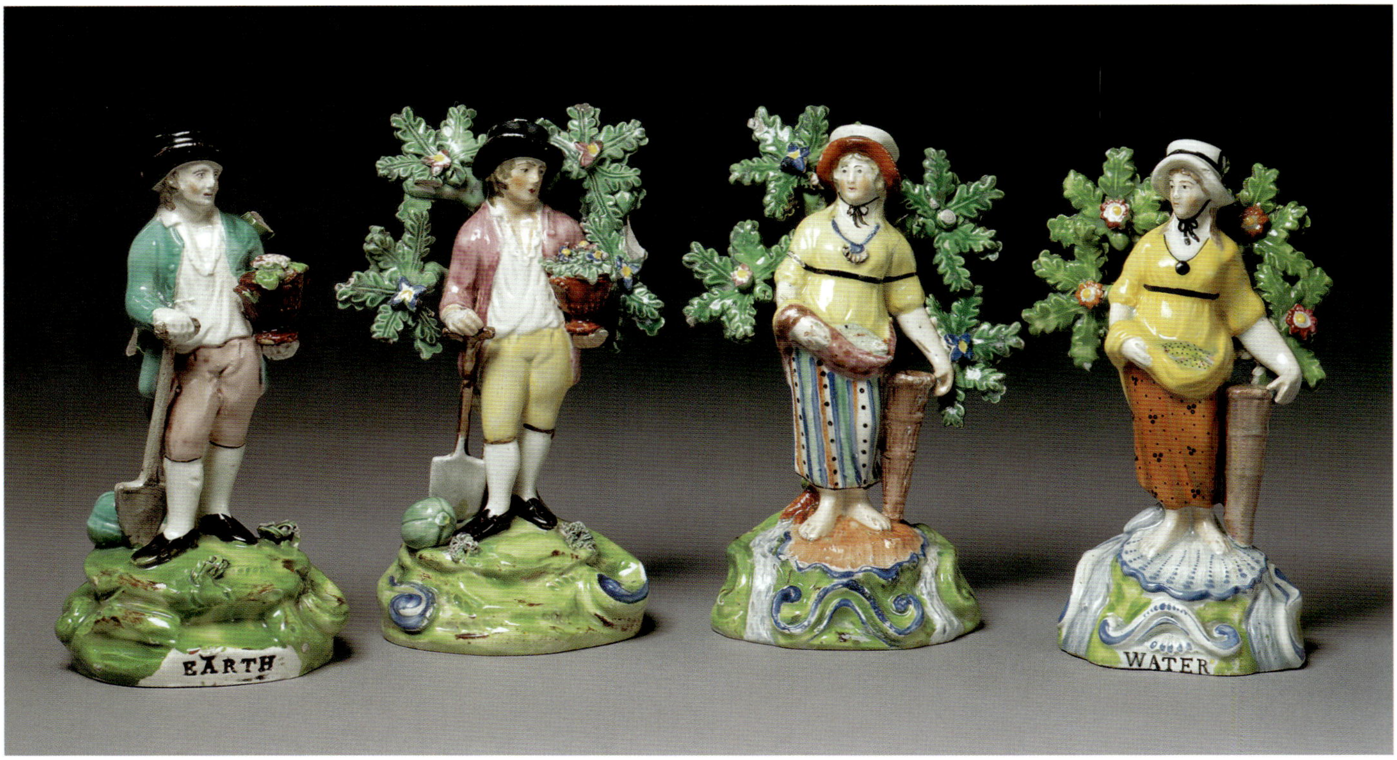

By about 1825 the great popularity of figures had led to ingenious new designs that began to reflect aspects of social history (plate 92), either contemporary events such as the New Marriage Act mentioned above, or the ever popular anti-clerical Tithe Pig group, which derived from a John Sadler print of the 1760s and which was also made in Derby porcelain. But the more ambitious the subject, the wider and stronger the base required to support it. Thus the so-called 'table base group' came into existence, a type that includes many of the models now regarded as masterpieces of the Staffordshire figure makers. In 1920 the writer George Wolliscroft Rhead, in his eagerness to find a single author for all these, picked upon the quaintly named but obscure Obadiah Sherratt of Burslem as the originator of the table base group. Despite the complete absence of any evidence,[31] and the fact that the only marked examples of Sherratt's work are two very undistinguished mugs, the myth has persisted. None is marked, and although it is clear that no single pottery could have made every table group, it is equally obvious from the many shared characteristics – the background towers of Gothic follies, moulded feet, sponged enamels, lustre – that a mere handful of ambitious makers was involved in their manufacture.

These groups were often made as pairs for larger mantelpieces. The simplest consisted of bold figures depicting popular subjects such as bull-baiting, or the tiger in 'The Death of Munrow' paired with the 'Roarin Lion', and of course the very elaborate Menageries, which, whether intentional or not, introduced a strong element of whimsy. 'Polito's Menagerie' (see plate 79) epitomizes the best of these groups. If these ambitious groups of Polito's and Wombwell's menageries could in theory be dated as early as 1814, when Polito died and his Royal Menagerie based at the Exeter Exchange in the Strand (plate 93) was taken over by Edward Cross, the treatment of the bases is so like that on the pair of 'Ale Bench' and 'Tee Total' that a date around 1830 is much more likely – the word 'Tee Total' entering the language only after 1834 when the temperance preacher Richard Turner at Preston added emphasis to the crucial word by repeating the first letter: 'T-total'. As so often, for example with the 'Death of Munrow', which referred back to the son of Sir Hector Munro being eaten by a Benghal tiger in 1792, Staffordshire potters borrowed not from the present and topical but from the well-remembered past, the harshness of the events softened by the passage of time.

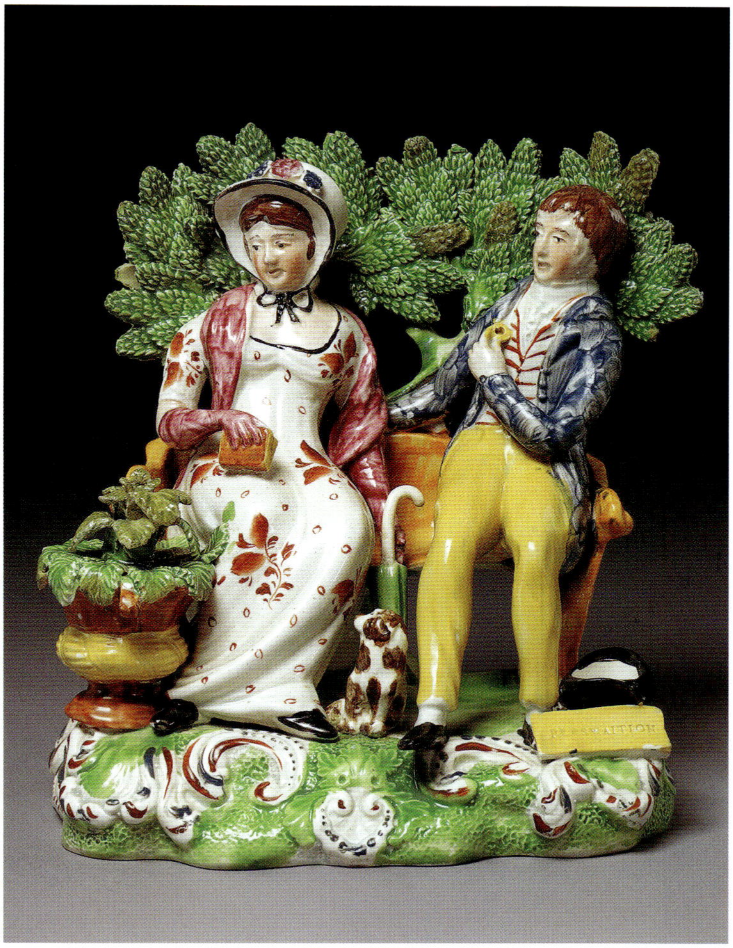

92
The larger sentimental figures made for a sophisticated middle-class market around 1830 seem to encapsulate the sort of emotional upheavals described by Jane Austen – even the title, 'Perswaition'. Height 19.4 cm (7⅝ in.).
V&A: C.137–2003.

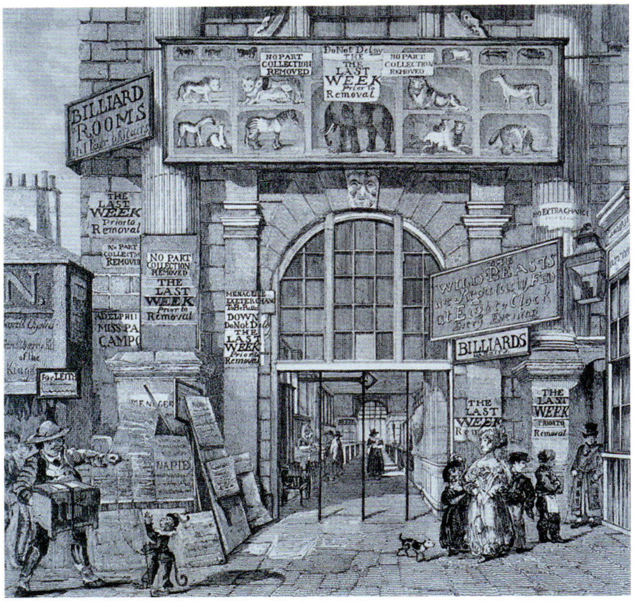

93
The Royal Menagerie was based at the Exeter Exchange in the Strand, where the public could watch the wild animals being fed every evening. Even though the business had changed hands when this print was made around 1820, the strong similarity between the painted sign above the door and the form of the Polito's figure group clearly points to its source.
Courtesy of Guildhall Library.

It is undeniable that the quality of Staffordshire figures deteriorated as rapidly as the demand grew, and as their increasingly topical subjects reduced them to the level of ephemera. Simple figures and groups press-moulded with a crude design and a plain back soon became the norm. Even with hand-modelled additions and bright enamel decoration in the newly available three colours derived from chrome oxide – bright pinks, greens and yellows – these represented a quite different class of figure aimed at a quite different market. Conceived solely in terms of cheapness of materials and speed of manufacture by the unskilled hands of women and children, inevitably they followed a basic functional form that may be compared with other contemporary mass-produced articles, such as the cruder types of moulded stoneware jug, or utilitarian 'flatback' cast-iron objects, such as door stops made in open moulds. So popular were these figures, and so appealing to the latter-day genteel inhabitants of English country cottages, that the firm William Kent of Burslem continued to manufacture a wide range from original moulds until their closure in 1962, when the moulds passed on to other hands.[32] From the second half of the nineteenth century onwards, we may imagine, with our condescendingly cosy mental picture of a romantic Victorian past, that no self-respecting cottage was without a pair of large shaggy dogs over or beside the fireplace – the natural successors, one might suggest, of those imported 'China lions' that started the whole craze two centuries before.

1. For example, note the depositing of 'white magic' witch bottles under hearth stones in the late seventeenth and early eighteenth centuries, described by David Allen (1991).
2. I am most grateful to Janet Spavold and Sue Brown for supplying nine references to figures from a total of 50,000 inventories covering the period 1692–1741, from many parts of England; also to Roger Massey for providing the reference to Northill Manor. The probates of 1754 are from Prob.3 in the Public Record Office.
3. See Weinstein (1984), pp.122–4. Similar examples from Port Royal published by Hume (1969). Others excavated at Anne Arundel County, Maryland, and in the British Museum.
4. Published by Allan (1984). For two similar delftware versions, see Grigsby (2000), pp.382–3.
5. Charleston (1968), pl.353.
6. Wills (1967).
7. Plot (1677), ch.9.
8. For example, Bimson (1961), Haselgrove & Murray (1979).
9. See Godden (1979) for details. A good range of Dehua models are illustrated in Marchant (1985, 1995), and Ken & Ayers (2002).
10. An example in the Greg Collection, illustrated in Burlington Fine Arts Club (1914) and Manchester City Art Gallery (1969), no.150.
11. A white example in the Fitzwilliam Museum, Cambridge, Glaisher no.812. Enamelled version in the Weldon Collection, a double version formerly in the Wallace Elliott Collection.
12. Pair on single plinth in Fitzwilliam Museum (Glaisher no.798); single 'shepherdess' with sitting dog, Sotheby's, 12 April 1964, lot 162; red stoneware shepherd, V&A: C.58-1921; Whieldon fragments illustrated by

Halfpenny (1991), pp.45–7.

13. Rackham (1930), p.24, gives the source as a seventeenth-century English bronze formerly in the collection of Mr Vauncey Salt. There seems, however, to be no known engraving of this work that potters might have copied.
14. Read (1929), p.22.
15. English Porcelain Circle (1931).
16. Compare the pair of enamelled swans in the Schreiber Collection, V&A: Sch.II 170 and 171.
17. As early as 1733 the Duke of Atholl was purchasing a pound of 'Guilded men & Creaturs etc.' from the dealer John Bodie in Edinburgh, following a fashion for marzipan or sugar figures as 'themed' table decoration, which spread to England from Germany, to be supplemented in the 1740s by Meissen figures and their later English porcelain copies. The quote of 1753 from Horace Walpole about 'Tables laid with harlequins, gondoliers, Turks, Chinese and shepherdesses of Saxon china' on the table is well known: but an interesting illustration of their use at a picnic, laid on a tablecloth, taken from the *Scribleriad* of 1751, was published by Wills (1961).
18. So expensive that they were often hired out at a charge of 10 per cent of their value: for example, in 1755 the china dealer Mrs Been of London hired '4 dresdon puggs' valued at 6s each and '2 dresden figurs of the Seasons' valued at £1 6s each. The local products, Chelsea and Bow figures, were slightly cheaper.
19. See note 17.
20. Weldon Collection, no.212. A pair to this, but in white salt-glazed stoneware, in the Glaisher Collection, Fitzwilliam Museum, Cambridge.
21. An attribution suggested by Read (1929) for the pairs of musicians and Turks in plates 12 and 13.
22. 'Unglaz'd' implies that they were left in the biscuit state to be painted with cold colours.
23. Earle (1915), p.xxi, comments: 'To Astbury, in a generic sense, are attributable those of the early little figures showing the adoption of two clays in their manipulation – a series of musicians are included in this class, as also are some actors and soldier figures'.
24. Stonor & Evans made a full-page announcement in the *Connoisseur* of April 1932. A short piece about the faker appeared in the *Evening News* of 3 January 1937, quoting a warning from the British Antique Dealers' Association (BADA) and comments by Frank Stoner, and claiming that the faker had been operating 'for nearly two years'. The identity of this faker (who seems unlikely to be the same man operating around 1917) is now known to be Brooker of Vauxhall Bridge Road, as divulged by A. J. B. Kiddell of Sotheby's to Anthony du Boulay and published by him in 2002.
25. Various authorities in the past, such as Arnold Mountford, Keeper of Ceramics at Stoke-on-Trent Museum, have claimed to be able to distinguish between the fake and the genuine figure. See also Elliott (1939), and the definitive study by Taggart (1967).
26. Fully discussed by Halfpenny (1991).
27. Fully discussed by Werner & Eatwell (1991).
28. Letters of 1926–7 from the great collector Stuart Davis to Herbert Read in the library of the V&A Department of Ceramics and Glass identify several of these Cyfflé models, with photographs.
29. Halfpenny (1991) states that the number of specialist makers rose from 12 in 1822 to 24 in 1834, and to 39 in 1841.
30. See the harrowing account of working at this run-down factory by Charles Shaw (1903, reprinted 1977).
31. Obadiah Sherratt, a master-potter, was listed as a toy and figure maker at Hot Lane in 1822 and in 1834 a person of the same distinctive name kept an ale-house at Longton.
32. An undated early twentieth-century typed price list of a selection of these figures stocked by S. L. Goodall 'Antiques & Curios' of Chiswick shows prices ranging from 1s for a pair of sitting hounds to 6s 3d for a large pair of Newfoundland Dogs, and 8s 6d for a 'very fine' Britannia. These were all artificially aged 'by our Special Process'.

CHAPTER EIGHT 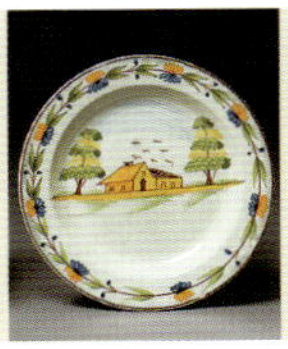

Cheap Pots, Big Profits

The story of how mass-produced salt-glaze opened the way for lead-glazed creamware, which in turn usurped the place of traditional delftware, pewter and ordinary Chinese porcelain and introduced modestly priced sophisticated tableware to millions of homes throughout Europe, has been told in previous chapters. These chapters, however, have necessarily concentrated on the mainstream developments, ignoring the many divergent routes taken by the makers of fine industrial creamware and stoneware after the lower ranks of society awoke to the possibility of affordable, useful, stylish and colourful pottery. The factor common to all these diverse types of pottery is that of cheapness. In most cases they represent inventions or reinventions specifically designed for the lowest markets, where undiscriminating customers would happily accept very basic products provided that they were functional and endowed with some superficial veneer of fashionable style. For manufacturers, the great advantage of producing simple repetitive wares was not only that they could be made in vast numbers by cheap, unskilled labour, but that the expanding population at home and overseas provided a constant and almost insatiable demand. Thus makers such as Enoch Wood, whose great modelling and business talents could easily have directed him towards the elitist market covered by Wedgwood, Turner, Neale, Mayer, Spode and others, instead chose to make easy money from rough-and-ready goods, at the same time ploughing back some of the profits into paternalistic good works for the inhabitants of his native Burslem: unconsciously providing, perhaps, a role model for the later Victorian industrialist (plate 95).

It was the appearance of 'shell edge' at the Wedgwood factory in the 1770s that brought creamware within reach of a larger number of manufacturers and a much wider public. Following the contemporary fashion for shell ornament, this constituted an inspired successor to the many previous types of moulded edge, from metalwork-derived gadrooning on salt-glaze to the 'cock's tails' on early creamwares. The great advantage of the shell edge, for maker and consumer alike, was that although the *intaglio* designs produced by the plate-mould were minimal, the cobalt-blue or copper-green painted onto the biscuit body tended to pool in the crevices and accentuate the design. Soon the basic shell was expanded to include relief-moulded borders with every manner of acanthus leaf, scroll and geometric edge moulding, and by the 1780s cobalt-blue- and copper-green-edged Pearlwares were stocked by every Staffordshire Warehouse in the country. They also continued to be exported in vast numbers by manufacturers such as Enoch Wood;[1] and their popularity continued until the second quarter

94
In the early years of the 19th century, many smaller factories found bluish Pearlware ideal for overglaze printing with bright enamel decoration in Oriental style. It could not, however, offer the heat resistance enjoyed by contemporary porcelain. The marked 'Stevenson' tea bowl and saucer and 'Harley' teapot date from *c.*1810. Max. height 15.2 cm (6 in.).
V&A: 2579–1901, C.46–1948.

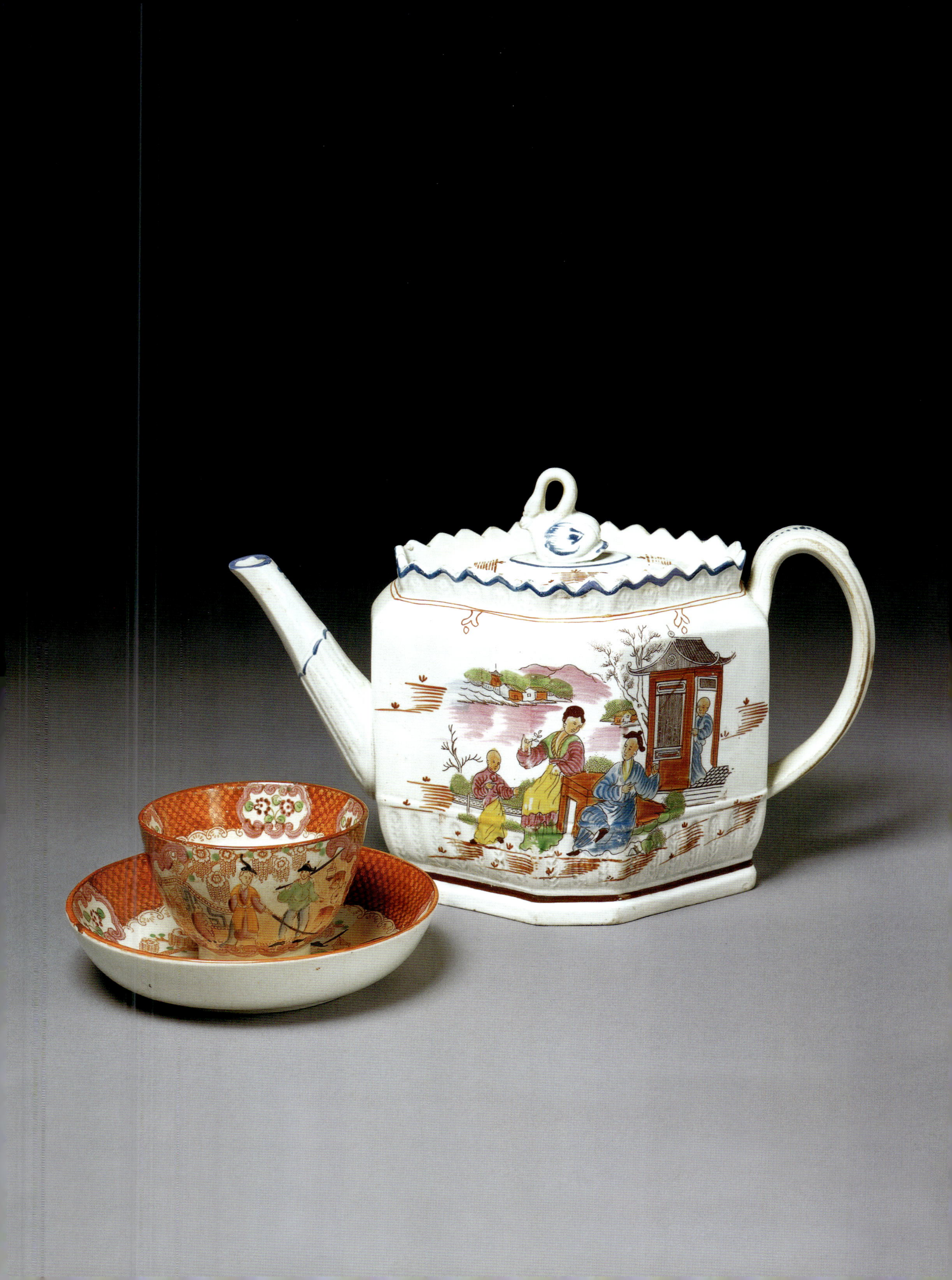

95
The extensive façade of Enoch Wood's factory at Burslem, viewed from Fountain Place.
Courtesy Potteries Museum, Stoke-on-Trent.

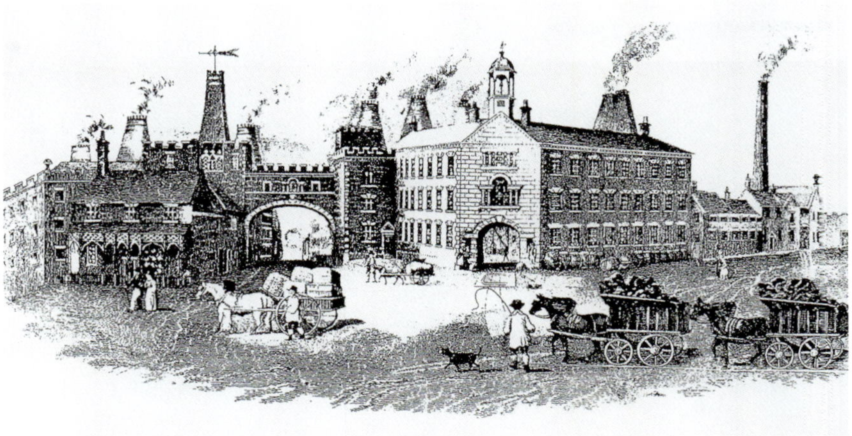

of the nineteenth century, particularly among the many smaller but prolific potteries from the North-East to Bovey Tracey in Devon.[2] Few were marked, but examples by the great exporter William Smith of Stockton-on-Tees (*circa* 1825–55) are known. The vast majority of such plates were plain, although simple patterns in muted underglaze oxide colours remained a popular export during the period 1790–1820. Mainly for the American market, simple but attractive painted and sponged patterns were developed, the most popular of which depicted a fantastic bird and foliage (plate 96).

Another major development allied to cream-coloured earthenware was so-called banded ware. The individual techniques of slip-dipping and lathe-turning were by no means new, but the combination of both succeeded in producing an entirely new class of ware that was to influence domestic pottery such as kitchen wares until well into the twentieth century (plate 97). From around 1782, when ale mugs commemorating Rodney's victories were made, the forms and colours of these 'industrial slipwares' grew quickly, from the first adopting the green or blue edge of contemporary tablewares, but having the intaglio edge decoration applied on the lathe with a metal roulette wheel. Orange, putty, buff or grey slips were used, often with applied sprigged decoration to give, with minimal effort, three layers of decoration: raised, surface and impressed. The range of effects obtainable with contrasting coloured slips, either inlaid into rouletted, chequered or Greek-fret bands with contrasting slip, or cut through a slip ground on an engine-turning lathe (known simply as an engine lathe), was almost limitless. Many such engine-turned designs are illustrated among surviving pattern books of the Leeds Pottery (plates 98, 130). And besides these mechanical processes, a more homely hand-made look was achieved from the early nineteenth century onwards through an earlier slipware makers' technique of using several liquid coloured slips, either separately applied to the leather-hard body and swirled or agitated to form surface marbling, or laid fan-like in a shallow receptacle into which the curved surface of

96
Pearlware plate of about 1800 with sponged decoration in high-temperature colours, one of the most popular patterns made for export. Diameter 24.2 cm (9½ in.).
V&A: C.808–1925.

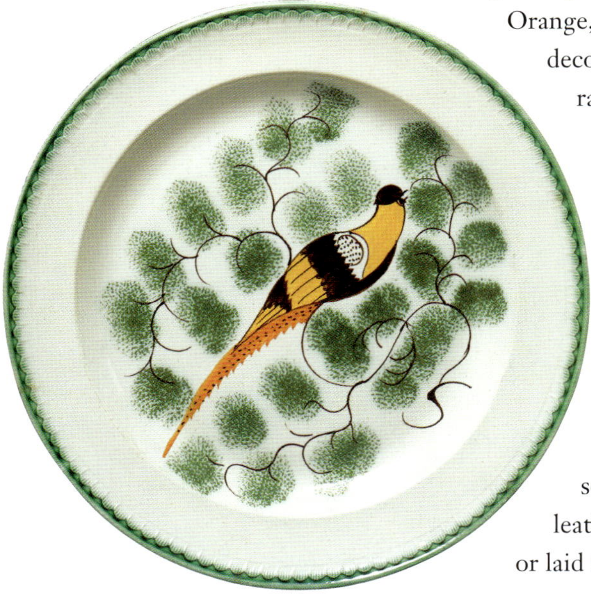

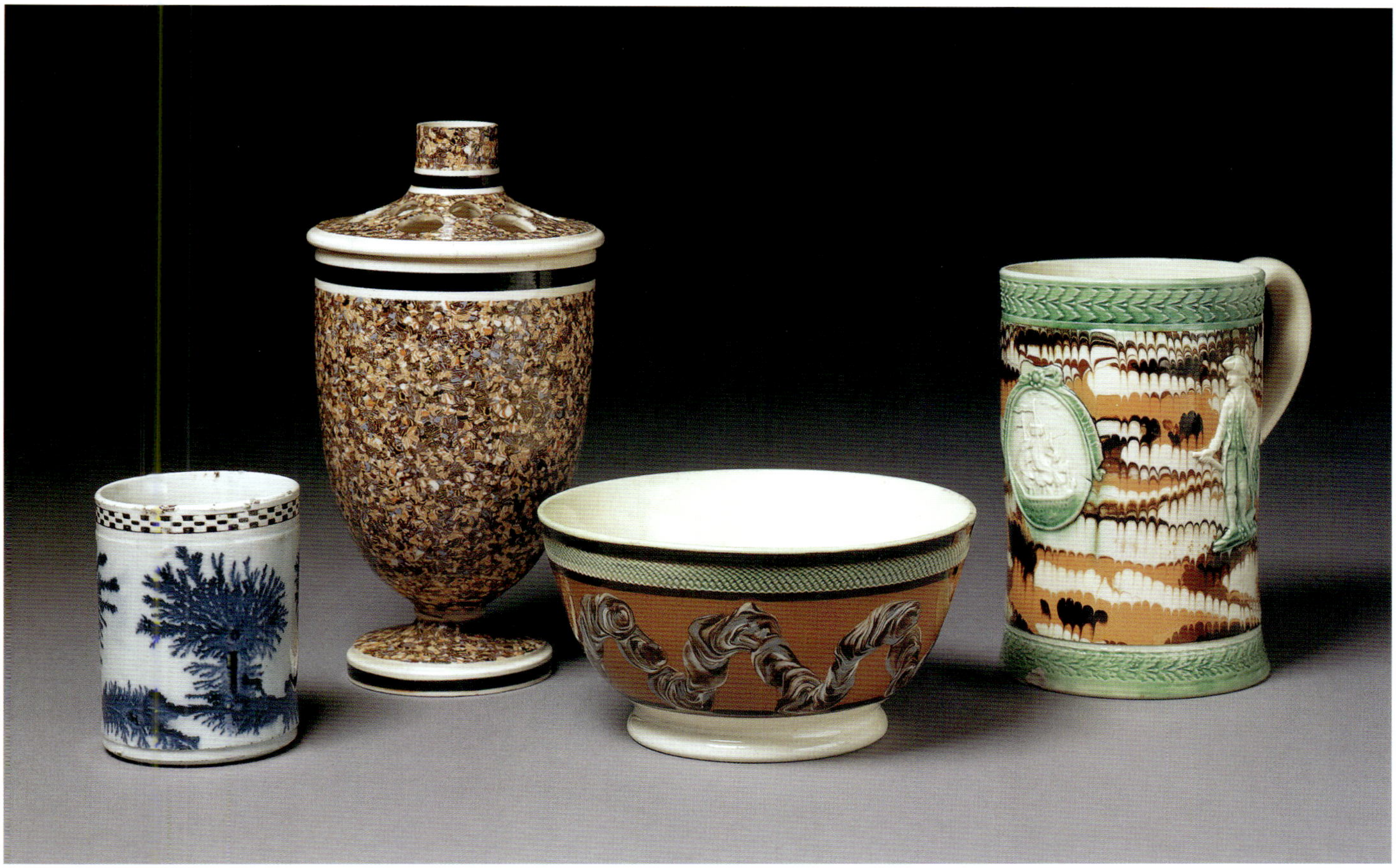

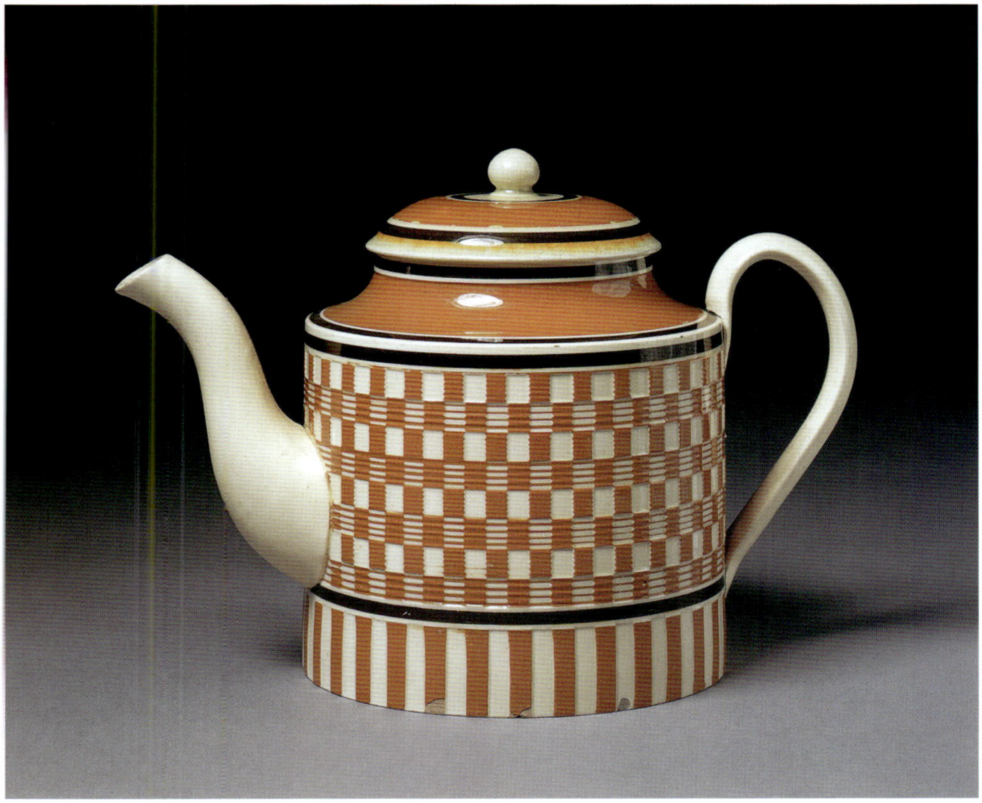

97
The variety of banded wares made around 1790–1810 was huge, including Mocha, Terra Tersia, snail trail and marbling (the mug here commemorating Admiral Rodney). Max. height 12.7 cm (5 in.).

V&A: C.15–1916, 3653–1901, C.9–1945, Sch.II 459.

98
Industrial chequer pattern slipware made at the Leeds Pottery. For the design, see plate 130. Height 16.5 cm (6½ in.).

V&A: 3558–1901.

a pot might be dipped to reproduce the pattern exactly. Other types of decoration involved a slip-trailer with several compartments, each with its own nozzle, which could either trail contrasting lines or drop globules of multi-coloured slip in individual blobs or in a series of loops to form a 'cable' or 'worm' pattern.[3] Production of these functional wares with their simple patterns enjoyed a long life: fragments have been excavated at many pottery sites, including that of Enoch Wood at Burslem, the Warburtons or the Clews at Cobridge, and even the Copeland factory as late as the 1840s. Outside their home territory of Staffordshire, they also became a staple product in the potteries of Yorkshire, the West Country and Wales.

In the 1790s a further experiment was attempted, using dry coloured clay particles rather than liquid slips. These crushed granules were applied to a wet slip ground, and could be either left whole as rough encrustation or rolled into the surface and eventually cleaned up on the lathe to give a smooth, finely dappled surface somewhat resembling solid agate. 'Bouquetiers' (bough pots) of this 'Terra Tersia' were included in the closing sale of Ralph Wedgwood's London showroom in 1794, though its rarity today suggests a short period of production. In fact, it may well have been ousted by a very much simpler form of decoration which appeared in the 1790s and soon became standard for well over 100 years: Mocha ware.[4]

Much has been written about Mocha, which emerged during the last decade of the eighteenth century.[5] Unlike many wares of the period, the name, alluding to the exotic fern-like markings of the type of chalcedony known as Mocha Stone from Arabia, is original and not a later collectors' term. The discovery of the technique, simply an acidic mixture of manganese, tobacco juice and (by tradition) stale urine reacting against a wet alkaline clay slip, was doubtless accidental, for one may easily imagine a potter dribbling tobacco juice onto a freshly slipped pot. But its commercial success was immediate and long-lasting. The basic colours of the spreading random patterns could be varied, but were usually black or dark brown, while a certain limited control over the distribution and direction could be exercised by a skilled potter: in effect, anything from a bush to a forest could be created, but invariably deciduous and seen in silhouette. Since all the decoration was on the surface, and all the coloured banding could be easily applied on a slow-turning lathe, it was soon being made everywhere: in Staffordshire, Yorkshire, Derbyshire, Bristol, Bovey Tracey, Wales and, in the early nineteenth century, in France by migrating potters. Most particularly was it later adopted by potteries around the great brewing centre of Burton upon Trent to make vast numbers of beer mugs: for not only had salt-glazed stoneware tavern mugs long gone out of fashion, but, with the introduction of the larger-capacity Imperial Standard in 1824,[6] existing mugs were all rendered illegal for use in public houses. Many of these new mugs and ale measures bore a decorative sprigged device above the band of mocha trees, peculiar to each factory and incorporating words such as 'VR . . . Imperial Pint', which, like the 'WR' ale measure marks stamped on eighteenth-century brown salt-glaze mugs, can sometimes be used to identify the manufacturer.[7]

The powerful legacy of Wedgwood's Jasper ware took some three decades to reach the great mass of the general public. But by about 1800, when smart fashion was turning away from the Antique and towards contemporary France, the essential elements of blue Jasper with white sprigged Neo-classical decoration were adopted by lesser manufacturers as simple, often misunderstood, decoration for their jugs and porter mugs (plate 99). The best of these, precision-turned porcellanous stoneware made by factories such as Chetham and Spode, have been covered in chapter Six, but at a lower level mass-producers like Enoch Wood and Shorthose & Heath concocted cheap lead-glazed versions with blue dip and crude sprigging derived from most of the well-known designs of Wedgwood's modellers. For example, excavated post-1818 pieces marked 'E. Wood & Sons' at the Potteries Museum include blue and fawn-coloured jugs

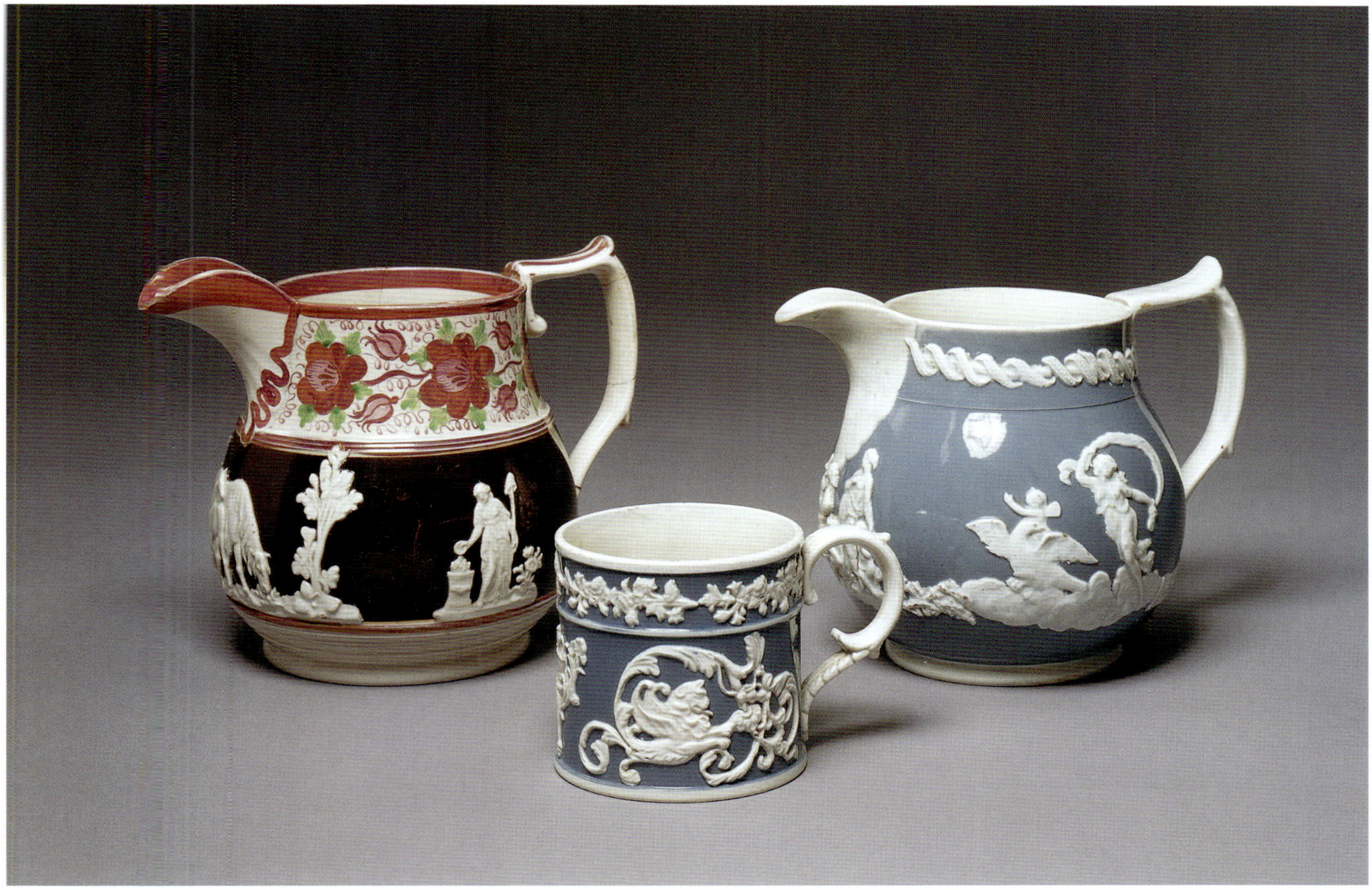

99
Enoch Wood was a major producer of export wares, particularly blue and white (the jug marked 'ENOCH WOOD & SONS'), but also lustre and coloured-ground wares. Shapes and decoration were distinctive. All *c.*1820. Max. height 14 cm (5½ in.).
Lustre jug V&A: C.42–1959, the others Private Collection.

with 'Dutch' and typical pear-shaped bodies, as well as a Campana-shaped spill vase, all with the ill-assorted sprigging characteristic of Wood's more humble products. Towards the middle of the nineteenth century, and after the demise of the Wood factory in 1845, the Wedgwood Jasper legacy reverted to true coloured stoneware in the capable hands of James Dudson of Hanley.

Allied to these late and meagre flowerings of the great eighteenth-century craze for Neo-classical ornament was something entirely new, 'lustreware',

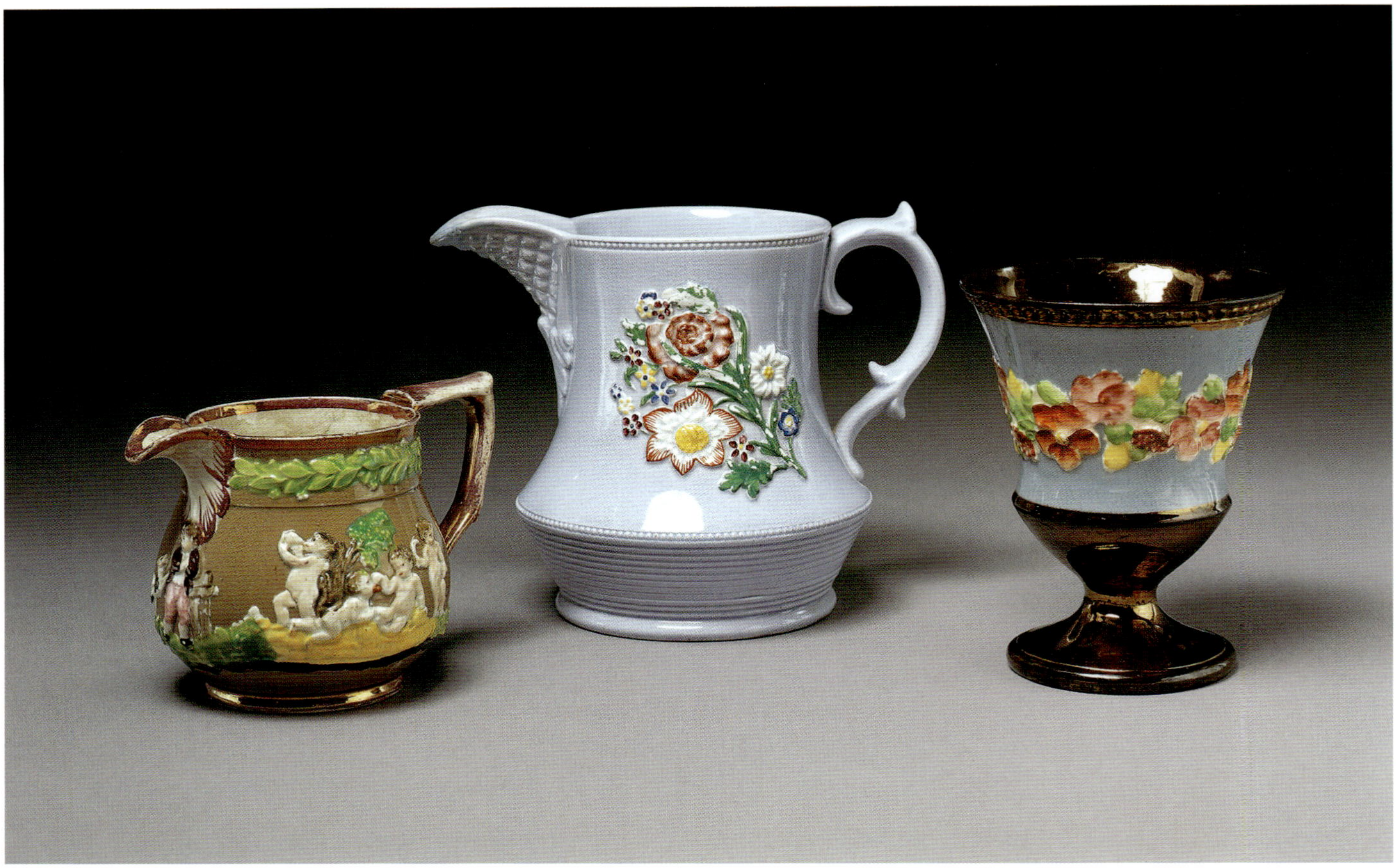

100

Coloured grounds with crude sprigs daubed with chrome colours provided cheap and effective decoration for many factories. Like the small 'Wood & Sons' lustre jug, these are datable to about 1835–40. Max. height 14 cm (5½ in.).

Lustre jug, V&A: C.52–1967, the others Private Collection.

which shared many of their characteristics and was made by the same factories. In this case, the reinvention of lustre was neither accident nor imitation, but the result of scientific research, and curiously it was originally intended to embellish not pottery but porcelain. Here again, much has been written,[8] and all the evidence now points to John Hancock as the inventor about 1805, while working at the decorating shop of Messrs Daniel & Brown within the Spode factory. This was, however, the silvery lustre produced with a microscopic layer of a newly discovered precious metal, platinum: but an entry in Daniel's notebook for late 1805 makes unequivocal reference to gold lustre: 'Mix well starch, and strong solution of gold equal parts – makes a pink lustre on china'.[9] This breakthrough, with all the possibilities it offered for making eye-catching cheap pottery with only the additional expense of a miniscule amount of gold and a final low-temperature firing, immediately spread throughout the potting fraternity of Britain. Even as early as 1807 the Fleet Street warehouse of the Cambrian Pottery at Swansea included on its trade card: 'Ware ornamented with an entire new Gold Lustre'. Apart from its ability to achieve maximum effect with minimum effort, the main appeal of lustre decoration lay in its versatility. With platinum, it would produce a non-tarnishing silver surface that, when applied to sturdy red earthenware pots, could achieve remarkably deceptive copies of contemporary silver or Sheffield plate teapots and cream jugs. The large collections of this ware in France and the Low Countries testifies to its wide popular-its, while at home it was also found that the two-handled silver-shaped chalice proved an ideal vessel for the Methodist communal 'Love Feast'. With gold, various delicate shades of pink and purple could be produced by painting it onto white earthenware, and on ordinary reddish-brown earthenware this same gold produced the famous 'copper' lustre. It could also be used either on its own, or to enhance enamel or printed decoration, or in conjunction with bands of coloured slip and enamelled applied sprigs (plate 100). These latter mixed techniques carried mass-produced 'copper' lustre well into the 1840s, with makers scattered throughout England, Scotland and Wales, and ready markets overseas, not just in North America but also in Europe.

The name of Sunderland is commonly linked to square slipware dishes, brown 'Portobello' wares with their curious printed Paisley patterns, and most

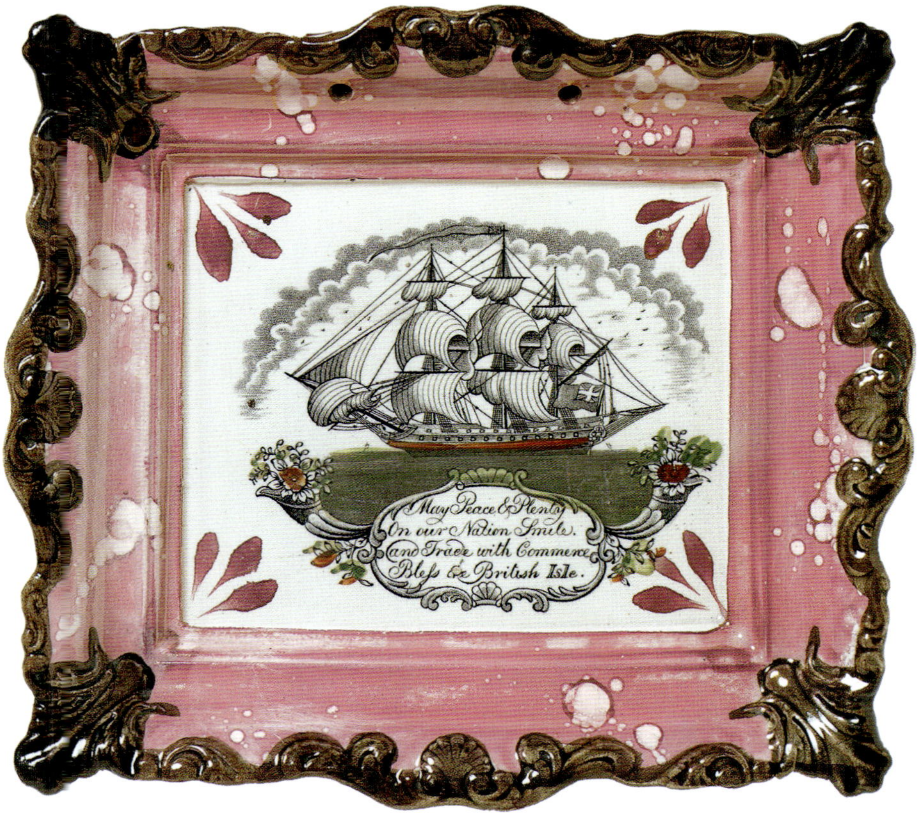

101

'Copper' lustre made with gold was a Sunderland speciality. Apart from jugs and mugs, it could also provide morally uplifting sentiments, such as 'Fear God' and 'Peace & Plenty'. Length 23.2 cm (9⅛ in.).

V&A: 3664–1901.

especially lustre (plate 101). Certainly the lustre technique may be said to have achieved its highest expression there, among a group of potteries noted as early as 1786 for being 'in an excellent situation for the Exportation of the manufacture to Norway, Russia or Holland & other foreign parts'.[10] Homely stout creamware jugs and mugs were traded via coal ships to ports around the east and south coasts of England, typical examples having printed verses or mottoes, evocative prints of sailors departing from their lovers, or the 70-gun *Northumberland*, which conveyed Napoleon into exile in St Helena. The archetypal product was, of course, the Dutch-shaped jug printed with the Sunderland Bridge, which had linked Sunderland to Monkwearmouth in 1796 (plate 102),[11] surrounded by freely painted lustre, which continued in production virtually unchanged until at least the 1850s: probably, in fact, until 1858, when the old printing plates were made obsolete by the reconstruction of the bridge.

Besides lustre, the discovery of chromium, and the diverse range of colours – apple green, bright pink, yellow and even orange – that could be produced from lead chromate, offered a simple palette suitable for equally simple decoration. It was already in use on hollow wares from about 1830, and rapidly became the dominating feature of cheap moulded Staffordshire figures. For bowls and dishes, for example, broadly brushed bright flowers and swags, painted in bold juxtaposed colours complemented by the addition of cobalt-blue, could fill the entire interior space. What American collectors have termed 'Gaudy Dutch' or 'Gaudy Welsh' rapidly became a favourite export, popular enough to

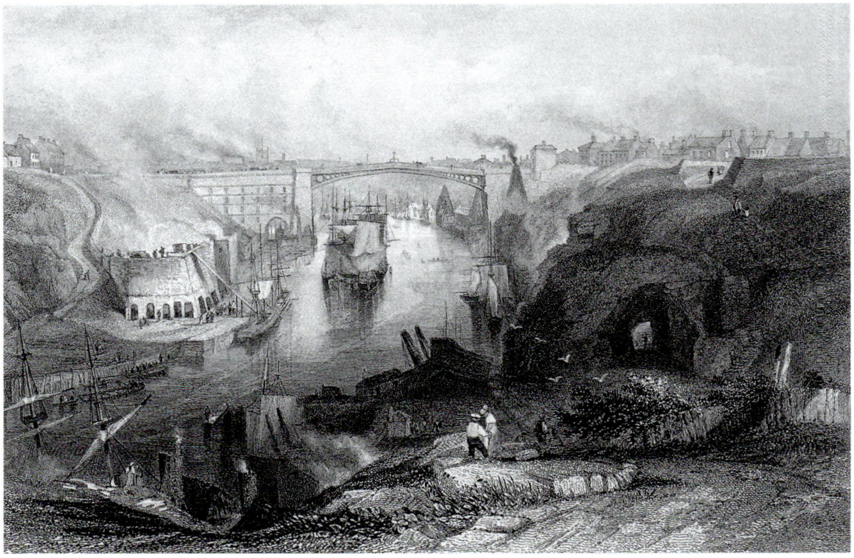

102
Print of Sunderland Bridge, showing kilns, glassworks and ship-building, after G. Balmer, engraved by W. Finden in 1839.
Private Collection.

be made widely in Britain and also copied in Holland by Petrus Regout at Maastricht from the mid-nineteenth century. Using exactly the same colours, but making geometric patterns with rows of small cut sponges, so-called Spatter Ware or Spongeware emerged at about the same time.[12] There is good reason to suppose that it was first made in Scotland, where it well suited potteries with a thriving export trade to North and South America, Africa and the Far East; but the technique is known to have been practised on a small scale in Staffordshire from the mid-1830s, becoming an important product in the following decade. In fact, so common was it in Canada that as late as the 1960s this 'Portneuf Ware' was still thought to have been a native product. The technique is said to have been introduced to Staffordshire via that great exporter William Adams after hiring Scottish potters in the period 1845–50.[13] So successful was spongeware as an export that today much of what is to be found in antique shops has been re-imported from India.

Printing on pottery had been developed in the 1750s not only to take advantage of the growing fashion for contemporary engravings, but also to facilitate mass production. With the perfection of creamware shortly afterwards and the new fashion for plain forms, overglaze black printing soon became firmly associated with those barrel-shaped creamware jugs with flaring necks and bases, as well as the popular cylindrical ale mugs – perfect vehicles for satirical prints and the spreading of political propaganda. By about 1800 the 'Dutch' jug was taking over, its globular belly decorated with a wide range of portraits or ephemeral political allusions aimed at both the British and the American markets.[14] Always aimed at a popular level, many of these were also of indifferent quality and clearly regarded as expendable: and so numerous and diverse were their subjects that at the end of the nineteenth century Henry Willett of Brighton was able to collect large numbers of them cheaply in order to illustrate English political and social life of the period.[15]

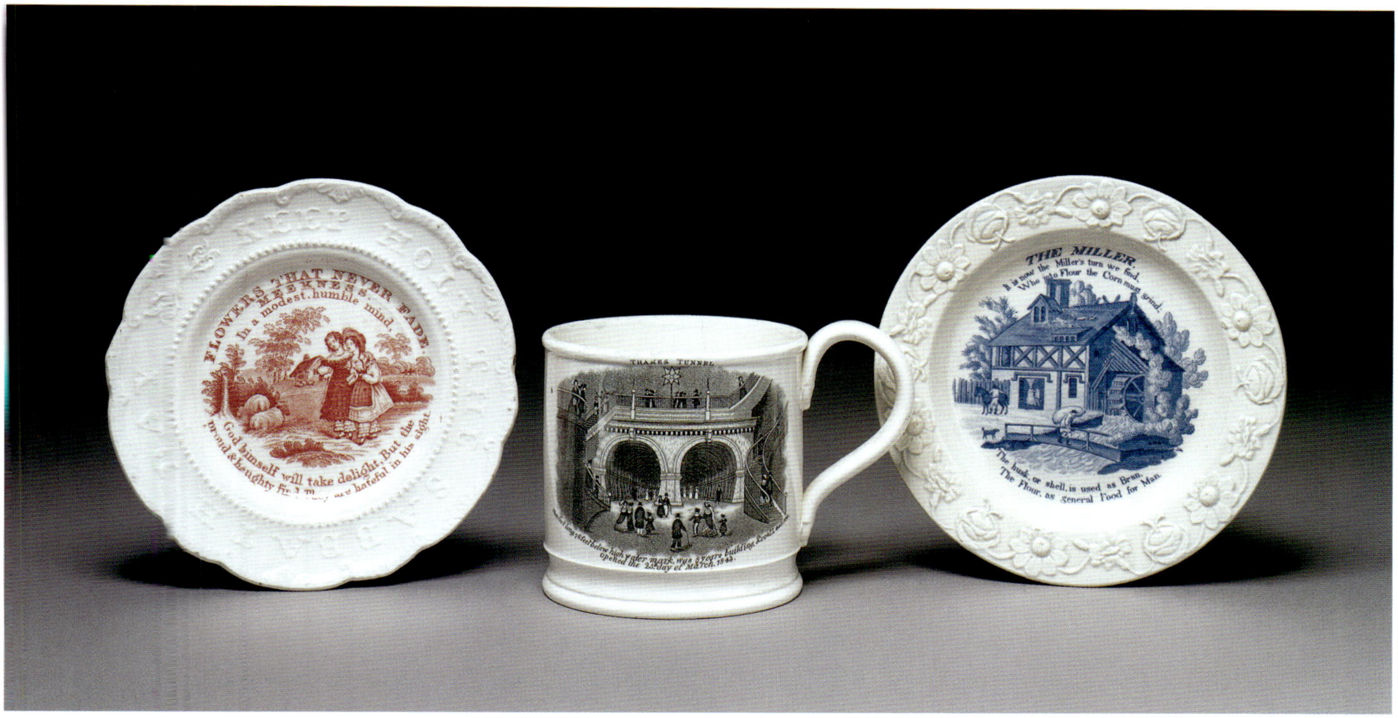

103
Popular printed wares included children's plates, often with a moral message and particularly made in the North-East, and ware commemorating great events such as the opening of Marc Brunel's Thames Tunnel in 1843. Max. height 15.2 cm (6 in.).
V&A: 738–1905, 1351–1924, 3641–1901.

By the 1820s an expanding population with a new-found lust for cheap 'folk' pottery began to demand wares for children: attractive, brightly coloured wares printed with an entertaining or moral message such as might be found in a contemporary rag-book or children's story (plate 103).[16] While named mugs offered a small surface for printing with the alphabet or wild beasts copied from woodcuts – those of Thomas Bewick in particular – the small plates moulded with an alphabet or daisy border, inspired by contemporary jugs moulded with allover flower heads, but coloured with chrome pink, green and yellow, became the standard form. Vast numbers of these were made during the second quarter of the nineteenth century, in endless variety with different prints and painted or lustre decoration, by many small potteries in Staffordshire, Bristol, Swansea, Stockton-on-Tees, Newcastle upon Tyne, Sunderland and in Scotland.[17]

It was, of course, underglaze blue printing that offered the most potential for mass production and, without the need for a third firing to fuse an overglaze print, bigger profits for the manufacturer. Some idea of the scale of manufacture of this staple commodity may be seen in the sale of William Turner's factory in 1829, which included 4,000 dozen (48,000, assuming that their size was rated at 12 to the dozen) blue-printed tablewares and teawares. As described in chapter Five, the style and colour of these printed wares progressed from about 1790 through coarse inky copies of Chinese designs of Willow Pattern type to the lighter blue of classical ruins, floral patterns and Indian Sports to the washed-out hazy blue of the 1830s and finally back to the dark blue in the 1840s. It was this dark smudgy blue, at first perhaps merely the result of hasty production, that was so welcomed by the American market that means were found to induce the effect chemically. To produce 'flow blue', where a cobalt-blue print bled into the surrounding glaze to form a halo or to stain the whole glaze, the insides of the saggars were washed with lime or chloride of ammonia.[18] This not only enabled potters to use cruder prints in the 1840s, including many American views, but also encouraged a range of thickly potted forms of almost monumental character, which set the style for the hugely popular plain 'Granite Ware' that followed. Major producers of 'flow blue' included Charles Meigh, Davenport and William Adams, and, of course, the factory of Enoch Wood in its final years.[19] Meanwhile, the home market had little use for such heavy pots, and instead of making 'flow blue', makers began to use the new chrome colours to produce pink and green prints, which finally came together to give the multi-colour printing pioneered by Davenport in the 1840s. And all the while, the Willow Pattern continued to pour out of factories such as William Smith of Stockton-on-Tees, whose 'Wedgewood' and 'Queen's Ware' backstamps may have fooled a few of the customers on the Continent.

Earthenware was quick to reproduce the Chinese and Japanese polychrome porcelains that came into fashion in the early years of the nineteenth century, using transfer-printed outlines and bold colouring by hand. These Pearlware copies of the teawares made by porcelain firms such as Minton and New Hall were cheap and attractive, but, to judge by their rarity, not very durable (plate 94). Significantly, many of these were produced by potteries outside Staffordshire, in areas where porcelain was not available. A much more durable product, of course, was Mason's Ironstone, already discussed in chapter Five, which relied entirely on printed and brightly painted patterns copied from Japanese export porcelain for its decoration. Although at first this was something of an elitist product aimed at the smart London market (see plate 114), rivalling Spode's new 'Stone China' of which Queen Charlotte bought a set in 1817, cheaper versions cleverly named 'Stone China', 'New Stone', 'Semi-Porcelain' and many others, and often marked deceptively with the royal arms, were immediately made by the mass of smaller Staffordshire potteries, in open defiance of the patent of 1813. Inevitably, the material descended into thick 'catering'-quality tableware, the coarseness of which was deliberately disguised by gaudy decoration. The Mason firm itself, compelled to follow the trend, became bankrupt in 1854, having shown a very indifferent range of wares specially made (and specially marked) for the Great Exhibition of 1851.

Besides printing, the various techniques of moulding were essential in the quest for quick production and easy profits. Although manufacture of both Staffordshire salt-glazed stoneware and delftware had ceased by about 1790, their basic techniques of simple press-moulding and a limited palette of *grand feu* oxide colours were combined and successfully reincarnated (plate 104).[20] This diverse class of pottery was so humble, and so universal, that it had no name until collectors discovered a handful of undistinguished pieces marked 'Pratt': one of the many potting Pratts, but nothing to do with William Pratt who made such fine stoneware around 1800 nor with the later pot-lid and red stoneware maker Felix Pratt of Fenton. Surprisingly, as well as the smaller potteries of

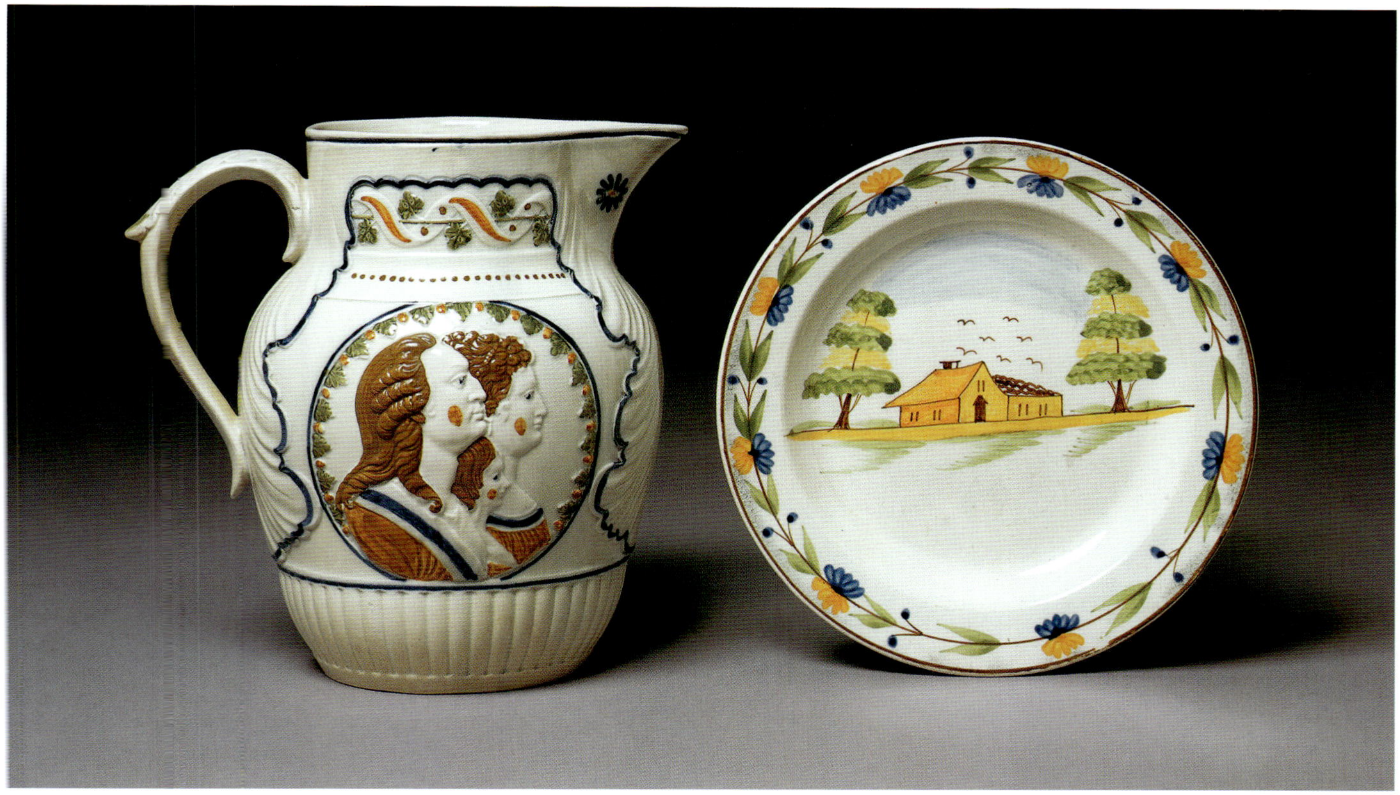

104
High-temperature underglaze colours, effective on cheaply moulded earthenwares as well as painted tablewares, became a speciality of potteries outside Staffordshire, particularly in Yorkshire and the North-East. The heads of Louis XVI and Marie Antoinette date the jug to about 1793; the plate is marked for the Ouseburn Pottery at Sunderland. Max. height 19 cm (7½ in.).
V&A: C.63–1952, C.570–1920.

Staffordshire, Yorkshire and elsewhere, some of the bigger creamware makers also stooped to make this popular product, as shown by surviving moulds from the Leeds Pottery. In some cases, it was made in the same moulds used by these same factories for basalt or felspathic stoneware of 'Castleford' type, but presumably at a much cheaper price. Tea canisters moulded with the 'Macaroni' figures that had been fashionable some twenty years before, endless jugs moulded with the heads of naval heroes or commemorating the brief Peace of Amiens of 1802, flasks, plaques, money boxes, figures, trick coiled pipes, toby jugs and many more cottage objects were made in profusion, the sole unifying factor being their technique of moulding combined with high-temperature colours of dull iron-red, sage copper-green, antimony-yellow and cobalt-blue – all oxides that would survive under the lead glaze and thereby, at the cost of having rather dull colours, save an extra enamel firing. Such cheap, largely anonymous wares remained popular until the mid-nineteenth century, remaining a staple product of many small potteries in Yorkshire, the North-East and Scotland.

At a lower social level, and partly in an urban rather than a rustic situation, brown salt-glazed stoneware offered an excellent opportunity for development from sanitary wares and containers into the domestic market (plate 105). During the late 1820s the potters of Lambeth conceived the idea of replacing their flat pocket spirit flasks (thrown on the wheel and flattened after removing an oval section from the base) with examples made in a two-piece decorated mould. Simultaneously, in Derbyshire the potters began to experiment with

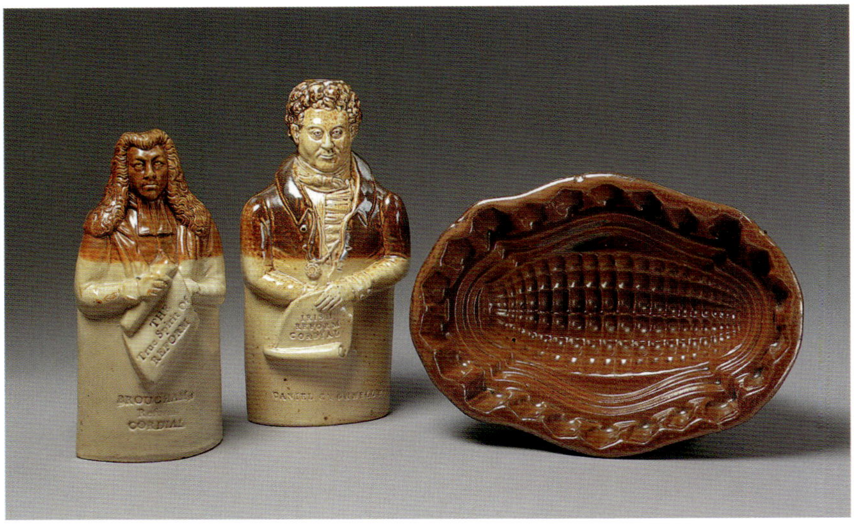

105
Stoneware gin flasks of the 1830s were among the first wares with moulded decoration to be made by potteries both in Lambeth and in Derbyshire. Later, kitchen wares such as jelly moulds became a staple product of the Brampton potteries. Max. height 18.1 cm (7⅛ in.).
Lord Brougham, V&A: 3783–1901, V&A: 3691–1901; Brampton blancmange mould, Private Collection

moulding the olive-brown wares of Denby and the honey-coloured wares of the Brampton/Chesterfield area, so that by 1832 'Reform' flasks moulded with the heroes' busts were being made both in London and Derbyshire.[21] The range of moulded stonewares increased rapidly, until by the 1840s almost every public house and kitchen in Britain would have been equipped with these indestructible objects, from bar casks to tobacco boxes to jelly moulds.[22]

In Derbyshire, and in many other places, a similar range of moulded vessels was offered in lead-glazed earthenware covered in 'Rockingham' glaze containing iron and manganese (plate 106). The glaze for these mottled treacle-coloured wares was not new, but rather a rediscovery of that made in Staffordshire in the 1690s, just before the secret of salt-glazing was unravelled. But, as the name suggests, the renewal of the fashion did indeed stem from the Swinton Pottery, which produced it as early as the 1770s; but it was fully exploited only by the Bramelds after 1806 as 'Rockingham' ware, well before the renaming of their Rockingham Works in 1826.[23] Their enamelled or finely gilt teapots produced at Swinton, several of which were ordered by the Prince Regent in 1807, set the fashion for a glaze that by the 1830s–1840s had ended up on

106
'Rockingham' glaze had many applications, from cheap Derbyshire flasks to fashionable 'Cadogan' and expensively gilt Rockingham wares. Max. height 22 cm (8¾ in.).
V&A: C.104–1994, 3172–1901, C.85–1950.

107
Moulded jugs made serious attempts to introduce artistic subjects with, for example, Minton's *Silenus* jug, Ridgway's *Tam O'Shanter* and Meigh's *Apostle* jug. Max. height 23.5 cm (9¼ in.).
V&A: C.4–1991, C.40–1969, Circ.133–1958.

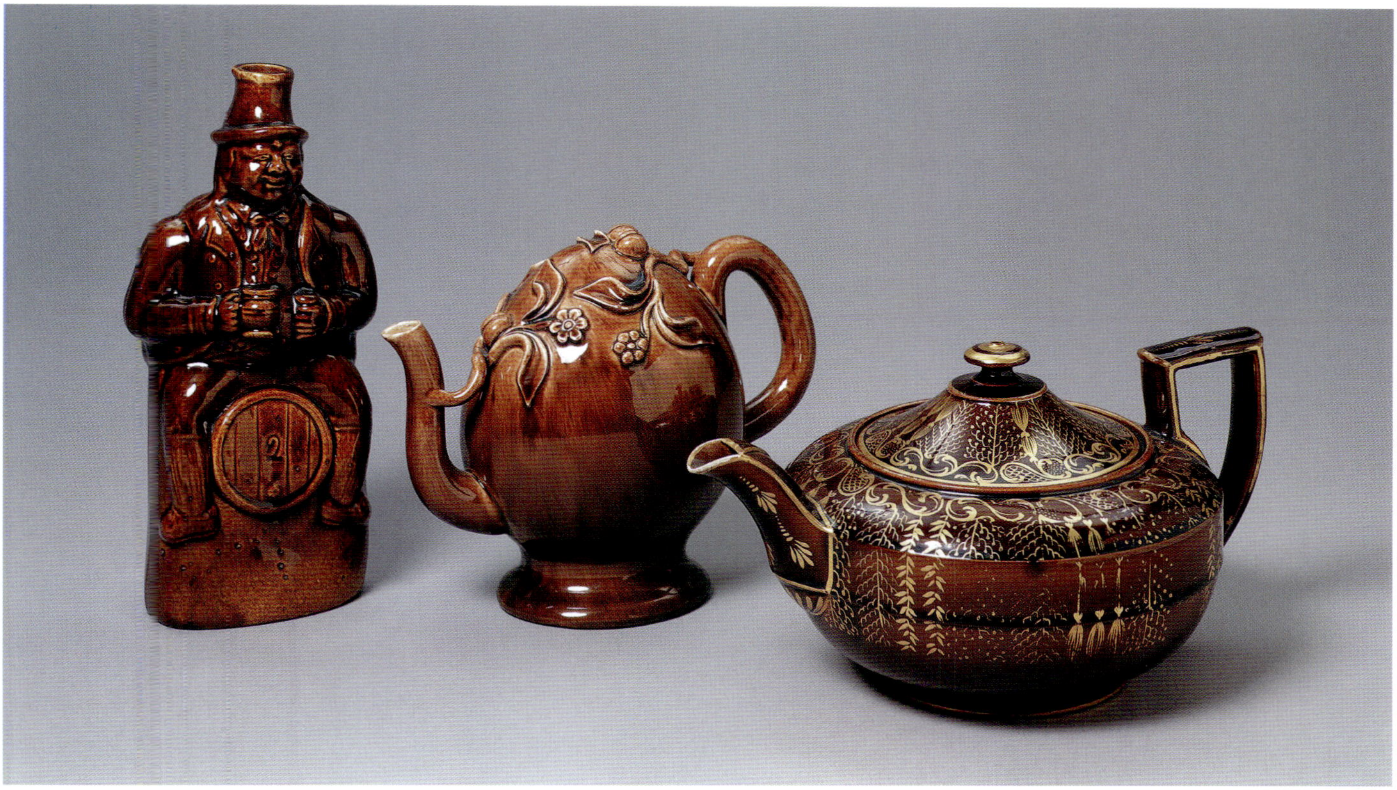

2

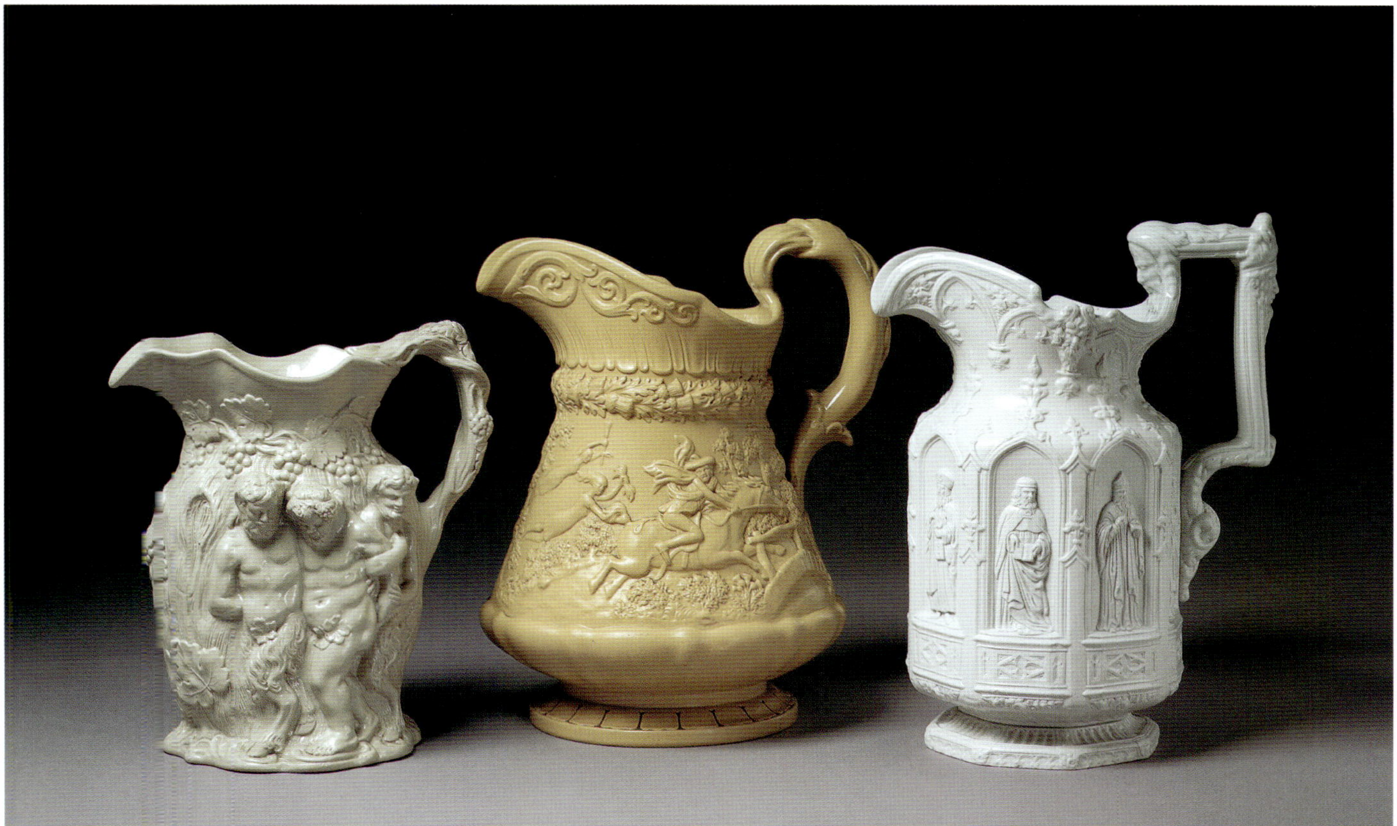

coarsely moulded furniture-leg supports, and copies of stoneware flasks made by fairly obscure potters, such as Joseph Thompson of the Wooden Box pottery, Ashby-de-la-Zouch, Derbyshire. Yet the glaze was greatly admired in the nineteenth century, for Llewellyn Jewitt declared it as 'one of the smoothest and most beautiful wares that has ever been produced at any place'.[24]

To finish the story of mass-produced pottery before the unrestrained explosion of eclecticism in the mid-nineteenth century, it is necessary just to lift the lid on moulded stoneware jugs.[25] The arrival of these in the 1830s was not entirely unexpected, for it was commercially sensible that the fine drab and putty-coloured smear-glazed stonewares of the previous decade should be reinvented in some form by ambitious potters keen to find ways of producing cheap, functional but artistic jugs for the tables of the middle classes. This was, after all, the period when the possibilities of other mouldable materials such as pressed glass, cast iron and papier-mâché were also being explored, and when manufacturers were obliged zealously to guard their designs by registering them according to the 'Act for encouraging the art of making new models and casts of busts, and other things therein mentioned' of 1798, or after the Copyright of Designs Act of 1842, to register and protect them with a 'diamond mark'. The first potters to offer an artistic fully moulded jug were probably the Ridgways, a progressive family of potters already responsible for fine drab and coloured stonewares: the *Pan* design, no.1 in the William Ridgway pattern book, was produced in blue around 1830. Thereafter the Minton factory quickly followed with their *Silenus* jugs around 1832, Ridgways with their *Tam O'Shanter* of 1835, the *Eglinton* jug of 1840, and a landslide of others by various makers, particularly Charles Meigh, who established his factory in Hanley in 1835 and made serious efforts to capture the market (plate 107). Highly successful examples of Meigh's output include his *Apostle* jugs of 1842, and the popular *Bacchanalian Dance* of 1844, which, with its borrowings from the works of Poussin and Rubens, was awarded in 1847 the Society of Arts Medal for the best model of a jug moulded in relief. All these jugs were of a single colour, limited to white and shades of buff, brown, blue and green; but an important breakthrough, particularly for makers of porcelain jugs, was the patent of 1843 by Richard Boote for a method of slip-casting using two separated colours. As the mass of designs expanded, so the quality suffered: new makers, such as William Brownfield, who began potting in Cobridge in 1850, vigorously exploited the fashion without achieving the striking originality of their predecessors.

Much has been written about moulded jugs, in which so many elements of Victorian taste may be traced: medieval Gothic (the *Eglinton* jug celebrating the attempted revival of jousting on a wet day in Perthshire in August 1839), Romanticism (Sir Walter Scott's *Tam O'Shanter*), Renaissance and Mannerist art (Poussin's *Bacchanalian Dance* and others), and imaginary scenes from the Bible and classical mythology. It is, however, difficult not to lament the decline of this excellent material during the second half of the nineteenth century, and the inherent suggestion that the worthy concept of art-for-all may be possible only when that art is diluted to the level of pastiche. But the vigorous reaction to this degeneration of manufacture and its inappropriate use of materials and decoration – from the Pre-Raphaelite Brotherhood, William Morris and the Arts and Crafts Movement – lie outside the scope of this book.

1. Of the many excavated Enoch Wood fragments in the Potteries Museum, Stoke-on-Trent, some have patterns so similar to those found at Bovey Tracey (see note 2 below) that the different types of rouletting may not be considered as diagnostic.
2. An extensive range of shell-edge borders illustrated by Adams & Thomas (1996), p.78.
3. The secrets of these processes have been unravelled and published by Carpentier & Rickard (2001).
4. The earliest known piece is a mug at Christchurch Mansion Museum, Ipswich, inscribed under the base 'M Clark 1799', illustrated by Godden (1974), pl.293. The earliest reference, 'Mocoa tumblers', appears in invoices of 1792–6 for Lakin & Poole of Burslem, mentioned by Jewitt (1878), p.252.
5. Lewis (1969), ch.19, Raybould (1984), Carpentier & Rickard (2001).
6. The original Elizabethan Ale Gallon measure remains in use in America.
7. A design of *c.*1835 by James Parr for a transfer-printed version is included in a volume of designs in the Victoria and Albert Museum (V&A: E.1288–1973). Capacity marks were sand-blasted after about 1887, and after the allocation of Official Stamp Numbers in 1890, it became possible to identify the exact area in which the mug or measure was used, if not manufactured. The key to these is given by Peal (1971).
8. Godden & Gibson (1991), Gibson (1999).
9. Gibson (1999), p.22.
10. *Leeds Mercury*, 30 May 1786.
11. The world's second cast-iron bridge after Ironbridge, thought to be the widest span in the world. For its history, see Phillimore (1941). Various versions of the prints are listed and analysed by Baker (1983).
12. Laidacker (1954).
13. Turner (1904), quoted by Cruickshank (1982). Of the 141 products listed in the price list of 1855 of Methven & Sons of Kirkcaldy, no less than 70 could be manufactured with the aid of sponges.
14. Drakard (1992), and Arman & Arman (1998).
15. The Willett Collection now at Brighton Museum and Art Gallery.
16. Riley (1991).
17. A group of such plates made at the Newbottle Pottery were given to the V&A by a descendant of the owners, W. H. Fairbairns, in 1905.
18. Snyder (1992). Acording to Reilly (1989), vol.II, p.347, the Wedgwood factory, which produced 'flow blue' patterns from 1841, used various mixtures of salt, lime and white lead.
19. Laidacker (1951) and Coysh & Stefano Jr (1981).
20. Lewis & Lewis (1984).
21. Hume (2001), ch.XIV.
22. Askey (1981) and Hildyard (1985).
23. Cox & Cox (1983).
24. Jewitt (1878), vol.I, p.498, quoted by Cox & Cox (1983), p.108.
25. Henrywood (1984) and Rumsey (1987).

CHAPTER NINE

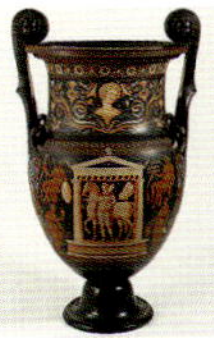

The Potting Trade and the Trade in Pottery

In many areas, and particularly in pottery production, England might be described as a late developer. Despite the glory and richness associated with the court of Queen Elizabeth I, by the end of her reign the British Isles were still lagging far behind the rest of Europe in adopting ceramic tablewares, nor had they begun to manufacture anything new, apart from partially green-glazed Border Ware copies of imported Rhineland mugs, and those early delftware tiles and pharmacy pots made by immigrants from the Low Countries in Norwich. Silver, pewter, turned wooden cups and trenchers, and basic earthenware bowls were sufficient for the needs of most social classes. Yet this general complacency was not instigated by Britain's isolation from the rest of continental Europe: but quite the reverse. Although lingering conservatism and coarse habits among the ruling classes cannot be denied, for those with wealth and the need to display it, foreign luxury goods could be imported by sea with the greatest of ease. Regular shipments of crystal and coloured fancy glass from Venice, painted maiolica from the Low Countries and Italy, and for the general population slipware from the Low Countries and Germany, colour-glazed moulded pottery from Beauvais, and the ubiquitous brown stoneware mugs and bottles from the Rhineland, all flowed into major ports, particularly London and Southampton. Importing proved a much softer option than risking capital in setting up new manufactures with the aid of foreign craftsmen, particularly when raw materials such as Norfolk clay and Cornish tin could be exported and reimported as finished pieces of maiolica.

The situation was altered, but by no means reversed, by the establishment of delftware manufacture in Southwark – the Netherlandish quarter across the river from the City – when the new Colonies in America could be supplied with quantities of these coarse imitations of outmoded Chinese porcelains.[1] But it was not until the mid-seventeenth century that industries outside London began to expand and export their pottery, first the delftwares of Brislington and Bristol, and then the slipwares of north Devon. Changes were also afoot in north Staffordshire, where, despite its land-locked position, the gradual refining of products made from local clays and early attempts at mass production using decorated press-moulds seemed to offer possibilities for future exports. In addition, with the Restoration of Charles II in 1660 came serious attempts to free Britain from its dependence on imports, at a time of social mobility when living standards were rising and the traditional image of the hunting squire with his draughty house, minimal furniture and sides of beef turning on a spit was becoming an object for lampoon rather than national pride. In order to protect the

108
The huge display jug, known to have been made by Bourne, Baker & Bourne for the showrooms of Messrs Neale & Bailey, which closed in 1834. The oval prints, designed for use on large meat dishes, are dwarfed by the jug, estimated to hold 30 gallons.
Height 70.5 cm (27¾ in.).
V&A: 53–1870.

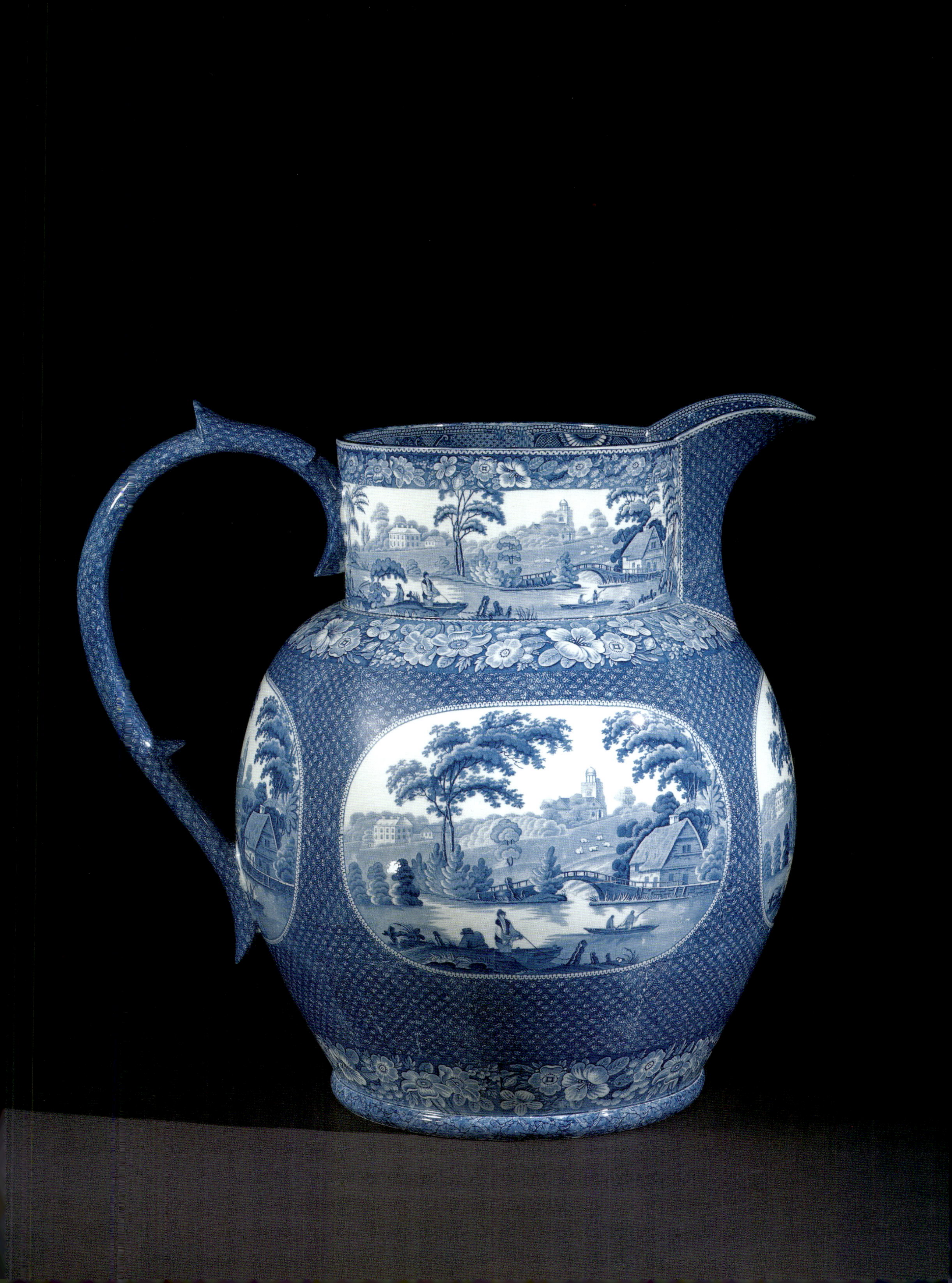

native delftware industry, in 1672 an Order in Council banned the importation of 'any kind or sort of Painted Earthen Wares whatsoever (except those of China, and Stone bottles and Juggs)'; but while encouraging delftware manufacture, this also effectively deprived the Colonies of a whole range of Continental goods, since the Navigation Acts required exports to the Colonies to be carried on British ships out of British ports. At the same time, the prevalent spirit of enquiry joined forces with a new entrepreneurial zeal to promote pioneering developments, such as the stonewares patented by John Dwight in 1672, the crystal glass that evolved from George Ravenscroft's patent of 1674, and the lathe-turned red stonewares of the Elers in the 1690s – all products that were greatly superior to the imports that initially they had tried to imitate. Such an expanding trade in pottery and glass required some central control, ably provided by the Glass-Sellers' Company which had received its Royal Charter in 1664, while all imports of Chinese porcelain were handled exclusively by the East India Company at its headquarters in Leadenhall Street.

Since the London potters were handicapped by having to import all their raw materials by sea – clays from Norfolk and Dorset, sand from the Isle of Wight, tin from Cornwall, cobalt from Saxony, salt and lead from the North-West, together with vast quantities of wood for firing – it was left to the energetic potters of Staffordshire to succeed in opening up new markets for pottery in the eighteenth century. In this, they were driven by a determination to use their natural advantages of having the heaviest raw materials at their doorstep, namely abundant local coal lying near the surface and the fireclay that was essential for kiln building and saggar making, to overcome the remoteness of Staffordshire from any seaport. There were also good local red-firing and yellow-firing clays with enough white pipeclay for making slipware, but the biggest single asset was coal: it has been estimated that the processing of every ton of clay required between five and twelve tons of coal,[2] and with the very heavy cost of transport, it is no coincidence that most of the potteries of the Five Towns – actually six, namely Burslem, Hanley, Tunstall, Shelton, Fenton and Stoke – were built directly on the coal measures with their associated seams of refractory clay. From this highly advantageous economic position, during the late seventeenth century Staffordshire slipwares began to be distributed on the backs of hawkers or 'crate-men' for markets within a 30-mile radius, and by mule, or later a string of mules led by a horse, as far afield as Northamptonshire, where they were still able to undercut the local slipware potters.[3]

In the years around 1720, when calcined flint and white-firing clays from the West Country were first introduced to the native salt-glazed stonewares, the need for improved transport became increasingly acute, resulting in the canalizing of the River Weaver, which, accessible from Winsford and linking the Potteries to Liverpool via the Mersey, was opened to traffic in 1733. There was already an established route eastwards involving an overland journey to Willington and thence via the River Trent to Hull. Although there was also an overland route to Chester, and another to Bristol via Bridgnorth and the River Severn, it was Hull in the east and Liverpool in the west that provided the source of the missing raw materials (white clays from Dorset and Devon and flint from Sussex, Kent, Lincolnshire and Yorkshire), and the outlets for the finished goods to London, continental Europe, Ireland, the West Indies and North America.

By the middle of the eighteenth century, major potters such as John Baddeley were exporting as many as 100 crates of white salt-glaze per month to Holland via Hull, and the port of Liverpool became more important towards the end of the century as it took over the lucrative slave trade from Bristol.[4] But land transport remained difficult until the roads could be properly maintained under the turnpiking system. Thomas Whieldon and Josiah Wedgwood were instrumental in supporting these improvements, for the Potteries were still at least 20 miles from the nearest river port. The solution was, of course, to join the Trent and the Mersey with 93 miles of canal, which, with its 75 locks and at the enormous cost of £300,000, was finally achieved in 1771. This reduced transport costs from 10d per ton per mile to 1½d, while enabling Wedgwood, who had already built his new Etruria pottery beside the proposed route of the canal, to offer free transport to anywhere in England.

The political turmoil of the last quarter of the eighteenth century, both at home and abroad, had a profound effect on the potting trade. In such a climate, the great boom that followed the popularization of Wedgwood's improved creamware proved impossible to sustain: in 1769 Wedgwood complained that there was 'Not a hand loose in the County to be hired, this Creamcolor has made the Trade in general so brisk', yet by the end of 1770 creamware was being stockpiled in warehouses and sales could not even cover the wages of his employees. It was apparent to his fellow master potters that the temporary slump could be overcome only by further cutting the prices already established by the first Price Agreement held at Newcastle under Lyme in that year. But firmly believing that the public would equate low price with low quality, Wedgwood adopted a bullish attitude and instead formed an opposition group later described as 'Our Little Society or Club of Potters at Hanley'. However, when matters came to a head in 1773 with the decision by the Potters' General Assembly to lower prices by 20 per cent, Wedgwood was compelled to comply.

The export market was always more important than the home market: by 1785 it was estimated that 'not less than five-sixths of the earthenware manufactured in Staffordshire is exported'.[5] Holland, already a major consumer of white salt-glazed stoneware, enthusiastically embraced the new creamware of the 1760s, which soon proved an ideal material for enamelling by Dutch decorating studios. During the 1770s Wedgwood, through his important political connections and helped initially by his dealings with the major exporting firm of Boulton & Fothergill of Birmingham, was soon able to break into new markets in Russia, the German States, Spain and Sweden, and by 1776 he even had a foothold in France through an agent in Paris. But this was also the decade of the American War of Independence, when this major export market was interrupted from 1775 until the establishment of the United States in 1783.

The French were determined to protect their indigenous faience potteries, which could offer little competition to the industrially produced creamwares of Staffordshire and Yorkshire. Persistent lobbying by Wedgwood and his fellow potters, however, was rewarded in 1786 by a Treaty concluded by the Minister, Vergennes, which fixed a reciprocal duty of 12 per cent on pottery and porcelain trade between Britain and France. From this time until the fall of the Bastille and the beginning of the Revolution in 1789, excellent and cheap English creamware flooded the French market. As expected, the faience industry suffered the same irreparable damage as English delftware a decade before, though some potteries continued to mass-produce unsophisticated wares for export to Canada and elsewhere. Despite the hiatus of the Revolution, by 1797 a French writer noted of Wedgwood pottery that

> its excellent workmanship, its durability, the advantage it possesses of withstanding the action of fire, its fire glaze impenetrable by acids, the beauty, convenience and variety of its forms, together with its moderate price, have created a commerce so active and so universal, that in travelling from Paris to St Petersburg, from Amsterdam to Sweden, from Dunkirk to France, one is served at every inn from English earthenware. The same fine article adorns the tables of Spain, Portugal and Italy, and it provides the cargoes of ships to the East Indies, the West Indies and America.[6]

By this time, Wedgwood alone had agents in Amsterdam, St Petersburg, Genoa, Hamburg, Brunswick, Antwerp and Frankfurt.

The hopes of the potters, already suffering from severe shortages of food and on the verge of civil insurrection, were raised by the Peace of Amiens in 1802 – significantly, the subject of many commemorative pots – only to be quickly dashed by the resumption of hostilities followed by Napoleon's Berlin Edict of 1806, which closed Europe to trade with Britain, and finally an embargo by America. As Josiah Wedgwood II noted in 1811, a year when no less than 30 potters were declared bankrupt, 'the business is not worth carrying on'.[7] At the same time shortages of food led to rioting in the Potteries, a lean patch made yet worse by the Anglo-American War of 1812 – which, however, did nothing to halt a black-market production of creamware jugs printed with anti-British sentiments. Surprisingly, although the end of the Napoleonic Wars in 1815 enabled both French and English manufacturers and consumers to resume 'business as usual', even by 1820 the important trade with America was still less than a quarter of its size in 1814.

An additional threat to trade was the willingness of potters to emigrate and take not only their skills but also the tools of their trade abroad, which Wedgwood took seriously enough to attempt to forestall it in 1783 with his address *To the Workmen in the Pottery on the subject of entering the service of Foreign Manufacturers*. Here he reminded his readers both of the miserable failure of previous attempts to settle in America in the 1760s and of the present dangers of being lured to France by false promises. Besides the loss of skilled potters, there was also the risk of losing secrets of manufacture through industrial spying, the value of which had been considerably raised by the huge success of creamware and Pearlware. As late as 1789 Wedgwood was called upon to examine a collection of pottery samples and books of technical notes that one 'Ljungberg' had gathered with the intention of setting up a pottery in Denmark.

The threat of migrant potters making English-style pottery abroad was a real one. An early attempt by Stacey & Co. of the Downshire Pottery near Belfast to make 'yellow-stone Ware' and 'Paris or Queen's Ware' in 1771 relied heavily for their success on the expertise of two emigrants from Staffordshire, Edward Ackers and Thomas Shelley. Further afield, various Staffordshire potters attempted to establish their own rival potteries in the New World, encouraged by a trade that, by the second quarter of the nineteenth century, had become so profitable that big suppliers of export ware such as Ridgway, Adams and Mayer maintained their own agencies in New York.[8] Initially, these potters were unable to produce fineware from local clays and posed little threat to the industrial might of England until, towards the end of the nineteenth century, they congregated at Trenton and East Liverpool to become major producers of whiteware.

As regards the Continent, it is well known that copies of English creamware were produced in France, Germany, Italy and Scandinavia as *faience fine*, *steingut*, *terra inglesia* and *flintgoeds* or *flintporslin*. It is less well known that this began as early as the 1740s with the intention of exploiting the popularity of Staffordshire salt-glaze: which incidentally gives further proof of the importance of the export trade even before the middle of the eighteenth century.[9] In Paris, a licence was obtained in 1743 to manufacture a type of white earthenware 'façon Angleterre' at Rue de Charenton, and later also at Pont-aux-Choux, a successful venture that, however, ended with the death of its director in 1788. At Montereau a 10-year patent was obtained for making salt-glaze, aided by an Englishman, John Hill, with such success that creamware manufacture was adopted, gold medals were won at industrial exhibitions of 1801 and 1802, and the factory taken over in 1819 by its rival at Creil, which had developed its finely printed creamwares. In common with others, during the 1830s 'opaque-porcelaine' or *faience feldspathique* was made as a response to the huge popularity of smear-glazed stonewares and Mason-type Ironstone. Even while Britain was at war with France, factories were being established by emigrants such as Robert Bray O'Reilly and John Hurford Stone, who founded the pottery at Creil in 1797, shortly to be managed by a Staffordshire man, James Bagnall, and eventually to take over Montereau. A factory at Sèvres was operating in the years 1798–1815 making 'terre à l'imitation de la terre Anglaise' under Charles Phillip Lambert. It produced some delicate brown-painted and printed creamwares of excellent quality. In provincial Bordeaux, highly creditable copies of Staffordshire-type stonewares, including even coloured moulded jugs, were made in large numbers by David Johnston during the period 1834–45. Many other French factories were involved in making either copies or local variants, ranging from the finest creamware to sponged ware and Mocha ware.

On the home front, there was also a growing threat from the natural reluctance of the workforce to accept new machinery to perform their manual work. Traditionally, water or wind power had been used for heavy work, such as grinding calcined flint, colours and the toxic lead-glaze, the well-understood hazards of which were reduced by various patents for wet-grinding with rotating pans containing iron or stone balls. These mills were dependent upon the weather, however, and by about 1780 John Turner had installed the first steam engine, a Newcomen 'fire-engine' of Cornish type, which raised water by vacuum in order to drive an overshot water wheel. Such an inefficient system had no appeal for Josiah Wedgwood, who in 1782 ordered from Boulton & Watt at Birmingham one of the new beam engines with flywheel and sun-and-planet crank, which found immediate full employment in several simultaneous operations of grinding and clay preparation. Another engine was ordered in the 1790s, to be delivered finally about 1802. Other manufacturers already had pumping engines to power water wheels, but the more ambitious soon opted for the Boulton & Watt directly driven system, despite the huge expense of more than £1,000: for example, engines were ordered by Josiah Spode in 1802 and again in 1810, and by Thomas Minton in 1819.

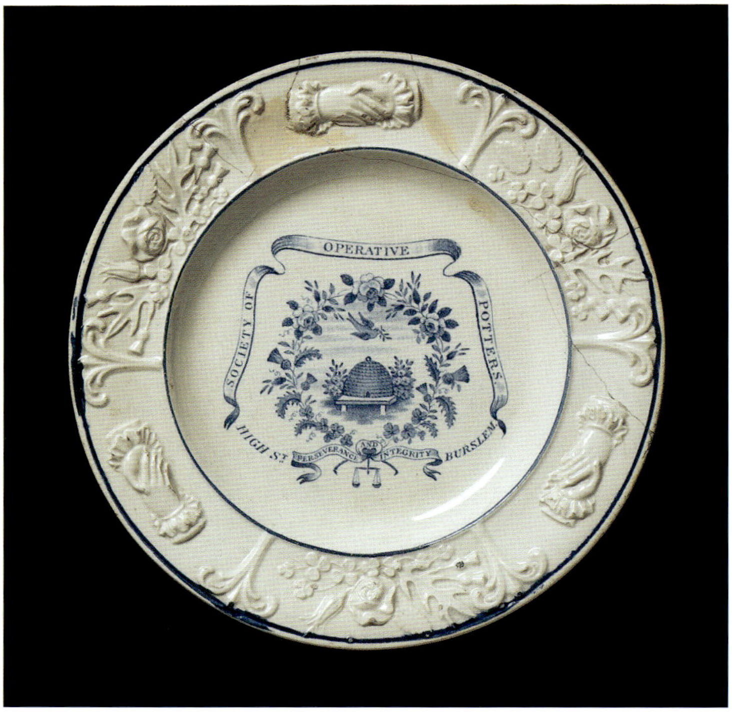

109
Moulded Pearlware plate marked 'Operative Union Pottery', with decoration alluding to productivity and industrial cooperation. This pottery at High Street, Burslem, is thought to have flourished briefly under the wing of the National Union of Operative Potters shortly after 1831. Diameter 17.8 cm (7 in.).
V&A: C.317–1931.

As for the comfortable rapport between a thrower or turner and his 'boy', however, old habits died hard and the application of steam to the potter's lathe and wheel is not known to have taken place much before its first mention in 1816,[10] despite its extensive use for deep cutting of lead-glass since at least 1800: an account in 1819 of the large and progressive Spode Works stated that, apart from grinding and blunging (mixing the clay mechanically), the 36 h.p. Boulton & Watt engine 'put in motion the throwing wheels and turning lathes, which, in other factories is effected by pedal and manual labour'.[11] This transition in the pottery trade seems to have been accepted without dispute, perhaps because the jobs lost had belonged to small boys rather than adults; but with the repeal in 1824 of the Anti-Combination Acts of 1799 and 1800, the way was open for pottery workers, already oppressed by the current Corn Laws and galloping inflation, to defend their rights vigorously through their own trade union. Without waiting to accumulate sufficient funding, this new body encouraged some sections of the workforce to stage strikes in 1824–5, which achieved very little at great cost. By 1831, however, most of the segments of the pottery trade had united themselves under the National Union of Operative Potters, a moderate organization that seemed set to flourish under the tolerant but watchful eye of the factory owners during the 1830s, and which appears to have founded its own modest and short-lived 'Operative Union Pottery' in the High Street,

Burslem (plate 109).[12] Further strikes in 1834 and 1836, however, were motivated by a need to link wages directly to prices, a fundamental issue to which some smaller potteries made gestures of appeasement, but which soon met concerted opposition from factory owners who were quite prepared to close down their works and wait for the union's strike funds to run out. It had undoubtedly been a mistake to polarize workers and management at a time when the pottery trade, and the factory owners in particular, were in a buoyant state. Striking potters were re-hired in 1836 only with reductions in their piece-work rates, while the union was left exhausted and heavily in debt.

In 1843 a new organization, the United Branches of the Potters' Society, was formed, with the intention of forcing factory owners to abandon their plans to apply steam power to the newly invented jigger and jolley, which directly threatened the livelihood of plate-makers and hollow-ware pressers. To make matters worse, this was also the decade when major manufacturers such as C. J. Mason of Fenton were attempting to introduce a new steam-operated printing press, derided as 'the rolling monster', to speed up production of printed wares. When it became apparent that the march of mechanization was too strong to resist, an alternative scheme was announced with the founding of the Potters' Joint Stock Emigration Society, proposing to raise £5,000 to purchase 12,000 acres of land in 'one of the Western States of the American Union' to accommodate any potters whose livelihoods were affected by new machinery. As with many utopian schemes, this well-meaning but ill-conceived plan to populate the Wild West with disgruntled Staffordshire potters was a disaster. For the founding and subsequent failure of Pottersville in Wisconsin in 1849 had repercussions that bankrupted not only the Emigration Society but also its parent, the United Branches of the Potters' Society, and caused irreparable harm to trade unionism in the Potteries. Ridgways and Masons, as well as potteries in other areas such as the North-East, were now free to lead the way by installing power-driven jiggers, jolleys and the Wall's Patent steam press, thereby reducing the workforce, enabling piece-work rates to be cut by tinkering with the accepted definition of a 'dozen' and increasing the profits for the factory owners.[13] Against such a background of strife were made so many of the pots that now seem to epitomize the perfect marriage of hand and machine.

Steam power did eventually prove a boon to the Potteries, with the passing in 1846 of three Acts that transferred ownership of the rapidly declining Trent & Mersey Canal (known as the Grand Trunk Canal) to a new consortium of railway promoters, under the title of the North Staffordshire Railway. Far from arousing opposition from potters, the cutting of the first sod of the new railway in September of that year was celebrated with a day's holiday, a public breakfast at Stoke Town Hall, and in the evening a ball and fireworks. A rail link with the outside world was of inestimable benefit, not only to the potters of the Stoke-on-Trent area, but also to its many iron foundries and engineering works.

As we have seen, the potting trade could generate for its masters considerable wealth, little of which reached the 'operative potters' themselves. But fortunes could also be made by Middle Men, the dealers whom potters were obliged to employ in order to sell the goods while they were busy at their potteries. And after the foundation of the Glass-Sellers' Company in 1664 centralized and channelled the trade in pottery and glass through the hands of its members, the more astute of these dealers later grew to become wealthy city tradesmen with considerable control over their suppliers. Then as now, important customers tended to favour one or two suppliers, such as Thomas Apthorp who provided the Earl of Bedford with all his ceramic requirements, including glass, Chinese porcelain, stoneware and delftware, from the 1670s to the 1690s. No doubt, on a domestic scale, delftware and glass could be bought direct from the factory, while the regular fairs, markets and hawkers could also cut out the middleman in order to keep the general public supplied with cheap household crockery. Even at this period there remained Dutch agents resident in London, since almost all Chinese porcelain from Holland, as well as the entire supply of Rhineland stoneware bottles and mugs from Germany, reached England via Dutch shippers. It is interesting to note that as late as the 1690s dealers with Dutch names continued to supply blue and white – either tin-glaze from Delft or porcelain from China – to great houses such as Petworth and Boughton. But the Glass-Sellers' Company took active steps to free themselves from this yoke by making an agreement to buy the entire output of John Dwight's Fulham Pottery in 1676, while also discouraging imports from the Rhineland. In 1699 thrusting British traders finally succeeded in obtaining direct access to Chinese merchants through their own trading station at Canton. Thus the Dutch lost their stranglehold, allowing both the East India Company and London 'chinaman' to flood the market with blue and white porcelain and tea, together with lacquer, fans and other exotic goods.

At this period London was still the heart of England, with a population that was to grow by the middle of the eighteenth century to at least 11 per cent of the total, and through it flowed most of the luxury goods imported from continental Europe and the Far East. Given the advantageous position in which London chinamen found themselves, therefore, it is surprising that their newspaper advertisements began to appear only after about 1720, and that it was not until the 1730s that they introduced those trade cards (with backs blank to be used as receipts) that are so useful to any modern study of the retailing trade. Although the Chinese porcelain purchased in huge lots from the sales of the East India Company was surely the most lucrative item stocked by chinamen, it was nevertheless impossible for them to ignore pottery of all kinds, which remained absolutely essential for even the humblest household. Thus the pottery retailing trade inevitably began by following that of porcelain and shared its fortunes.[14] At first, clustering for convenience around the premises of the East India Company at Leadenhall Street in the City, with ready access to wharfs on the River Thames to receive shipments of pottery from the Midlands via the River Trent and Hull, these dealers spread themselves on an east–west axis from the Tower along Leadenhall Street, Fenchurch Street, Cornhill, the Poultry, Fleet Street, Long Acre, the Strand and even as far as Pall Mall. With the expansion of London westwards, the trade followed where the money led, and from the mid-eighteenth century established dealers began to migrate, and new dealers began to congregate, in the area around St Paul's Churchyard, Ludgate Hill and Fleet Street, and further west in the Strand and Pall Mall. Some of the more adventurous moved north-west to the newly fashionable area around Soho, the Haymarket, St James's, Jermyn Street, Piccadilly and Bond Street, and even further towards Lincoln's Inn Fields and up to Oxford Street. After 1800, when many of the leading pottery and porcelain manufacturers had set up their own London showrooms in the most prestigious places, the trade began to centre itself around Bloomsbury, New Bond Street and the area around Oxford Street, including Hanover Square, Wigmore Street and South Audley Street. At the same time, a new breed of super-dealer came into existence, who at first acted as agents for far-flung factories such as Swansea or Coalport, and eventually began to take control of their output and, by claiming to be 'manufacturers' on their own backstamps, to force the actual makers into a subservient role. By the 1840s major dealers such as Phillips of Bond Street, Mortlocks of Oxford Street and Thomas Goode of South Audley Street wielded great power: Henry Cole was later to recall that in 1845 Herbert Minton was reluctant to mark his wares because 'he dreaded the retailers of London, who at that time ruled manufacturers with a rod of iron'.

To return to the beginnings of this trade, in the early eighteenth century the relationship between makers and dealers was one of cooperation in order to achieve the best sales, both responding to changing whims of fashions and the demands of the public. Staffordshire potters in particular needed outlets, for although later their factories maintained a smart frontage and catered for passing trade (see plates 95, 127), they were poorly situated for shopping expeditions by the public: for example, the Earl of Bedford buying pottery direct from Thomas Whieldon's factory in the mid-eighteenth century may be entirely explained through his wife's Staffordshire connections. It is, however, clear that the potters of Staffordshire were in touch with the London trade at least as early as 1719, when John Akerman of Cornhill advertised their latest 'white stoneware', a product that was evidently well respected by 1727, when the bankruptcy sale of William Watkinson of the Exeter Exchange included 'all sorts of fine white Stone Ware, all sorts of Earthen Ware fit for the Use of any Family of what Degree soever'. Direct links between Staffordshire and London came in the 1720s with the partnership of two members of North Staffordshire families, John Weatherby & John Crowther, who established a warehouse at St Catherine's near the Tower. Later, it was this partnership that brought the Bow porcelain factory into existence, facilitated by the expertise of many Staffordshire workmen, and their retailing business is known to have been supplied in 1748 by the prolific stoneware potters John & Thomas Wedgwood. A London pewterer, James Tidmarsh, established a pottery retailing business in Rosemary Lane about 1745, later becoming manufacturers at Cobridge and having some claim to be the inventor of the first 'Staffordshire Warehouse' in London.[15] There were many other exclusively earthenware dealers in London, for example, John White of Seven Dials, whose stock in 1744 consisted of 'all Sorts of Staffordshire,

110 (RIGHT)

Robert Fogg at the China Jar in New Bond Street, London, was one of the leading retailers of his day, father and son operating from *c.*1760 to *c.*1820. Although mainly a porcelain dealer, he also handled large amounts of creamware.

111 (FAR RIGHT)

The Portland Vase, made of sprigged blue-black Jasper dip but copying carved Roman cameo glass, was completed in 1790 and was regarded as one of Wedgwood's greatest triumphs. So popular was it that tickets for viewing were issued.

V&A: 22.12.71

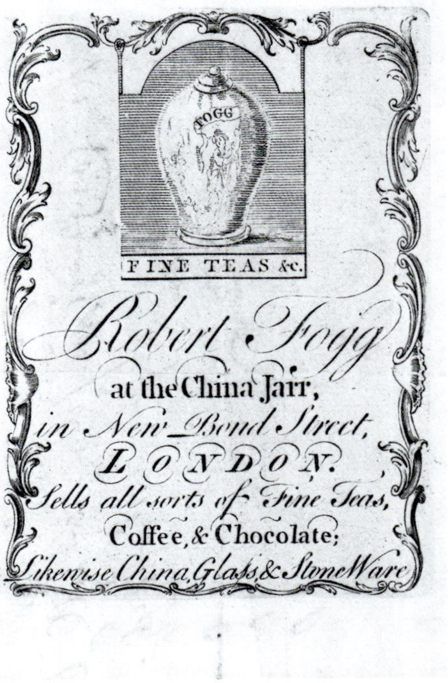

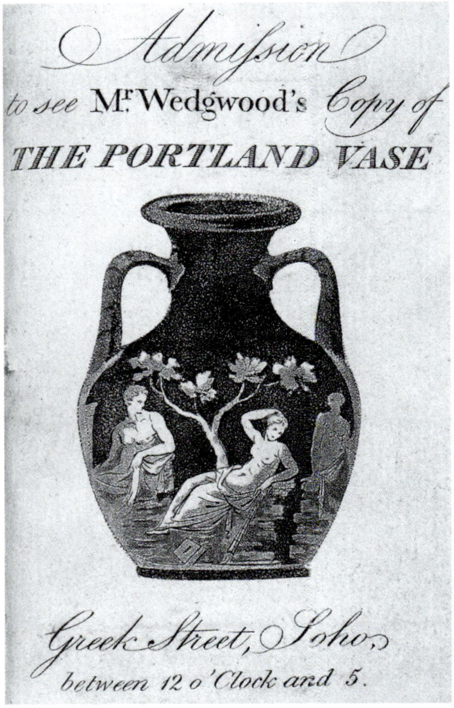

Nottingham, and Welch Ware, likewise all Sorts of Hampshire and Deptford Ware' – that is, every type of white and brown stoneware, slipware and lead-glazed earthenware. As production increased, so the prices seem to have fallen, if we take this advertisement from the *Daily Advertiser* of 30 August 1753 to be typical:

> To be sold under prime cost. The stock of a person leaving off business next door to the Blue Ball & Stag, in King Street, Bloomsbury, consisting of all sorts of Glass, Earthenware, Haberdashery & Grocery.
> Staffordshire White Ware at 1/6 per dozen
> Ditto Black Ware at 2/- per doz,
> Red China at 5/- per doz.
> Tortoiseshell at 6/- per doz.
> Blue at 12/- per doz.

A typical range of goods might include the following, as advertised in 1764 by the Staffordshire Stone Warehouse of Samuel Clarke in Fleet Street, whose Staffordshire connections are suggested by the fact that he had previously dealt in Longton Hall porcelain: 'red, black etc. Tea and Coffee pots, Sortable Wares, as Jugs, Mugs, Bowls, Basons, Baking Dishes, Boats, Tea Cups and Saucers, also Tureens, Bread Baskets, Candlesticks, pierced etc. figured Wares, and a large Assortment of fine Nottingham Ware'.

Apart from the prolific Wedgwood brothers at the Big House, Burslem, other major producers, such as John Baddeley, are recorded as supplying London dealers like James Abernethy of Leadenhall Street with many crates of earthenware during the 1760s. And once Wedgwood's improved creamware came into production at exactly that time, some dealers seem to have obtained exclusive agency rights with the larger Staffordshire makers, such as John Caravella of Oxford Street, whom Wedgwood accused in 1768 of acquiring his latest vases and immediately sending them to Humphrey Palmer to be copied for his shop, mentioning incidentally that the important chinaman Robert Fogg of New Bond Street (plate 110) had a similar arrangement with the potters Bagnall & Baker.

Elsewhere, factory outlets were established by emigrant Staffordshire potters far from either Staffordshire or London to supplement the trade handled by 'riders' (travelling salesmen) employed directly by the factory, by the numerous hawkers whom Parliament attempted unsuccessfully to ban in the 1780s, and by the growing number of provincial dealers. For example, Samuel Astbury 'Stafford-shire Earthen-ware maker and seller' advertised in 1771 that he had imported 'a great Variety of the most fashionable black, white and nankeen Ware' for his shop near the Custom House at Limerick. Ralph Wood, after an unsuccessful pottery venture at Burslem, set up in Tucker Street, Bristol, selling a large but typical variety of creamwares, and claiming 'by the most regular conveyance from the Manufactories in Staffordshire to get the earliest productions, finished in the best Manner and after the best antique and modern taste'. In Scotland, 'White Stone Ware for Exportation and inland Consumption, manufactured and sold by William Caddell and Sons and Company at Preston Pans' was advertised in 1767.

In London, the need to find markets for innovative delftwares led John Dunbibin to establish his 'Liverpool Warehouse' at Southwark, where he advertised

> all Sorts of Delft Ware, of their own making in Liverpool, wherein a large Assortment of Galley Tiles for Chimneys, of various patterns, in every respect equal to the Dutch, particularly Copper-plate printed tiles, of which they have got upwards of forty different patterns, which are the neatest Tiles ever made in England or Holland for Workmanship before; besides the above Sorts are also sold, all Sorts of White Stone Ware, Nottingham Ware, Welch Ware, Hampshire Ware, Deptford Ware, and Glass of all Sorts.

By this time also the new porcelain factories were establishing London showrooms, Bow at Cornhill in 1753, Chelsea moving to new premises in Piccadilly in 1755.

It was therefore logical that, in a climate where manufacturers' names were being attached to traditionally anonymous pottery and porcelain, Josiah Wedgwood should consider capitalizing on his appointment as Potter to the Queen in 1766 by opening the first single-factory *earthenware* showrooms in London. In this, he was helped greatly by his partner Thomas Bentley, who had already launched his export trade through his Liverpool mercantile connections, and who was now to play a vital role relaying back to Etruria every change in fickle London fashion. The location, Newport Street, was selected with great care in 1768 as being not the most fashionable, but in the heart of an area inhabited by men of culture and artists, notably Sir Joshua Reynolds; and, needless to say, the shop bore the sign of the Queen's Arms. By 1774, grander premises had been opened at Portland House, Greek Street (plate 111), with space adequate

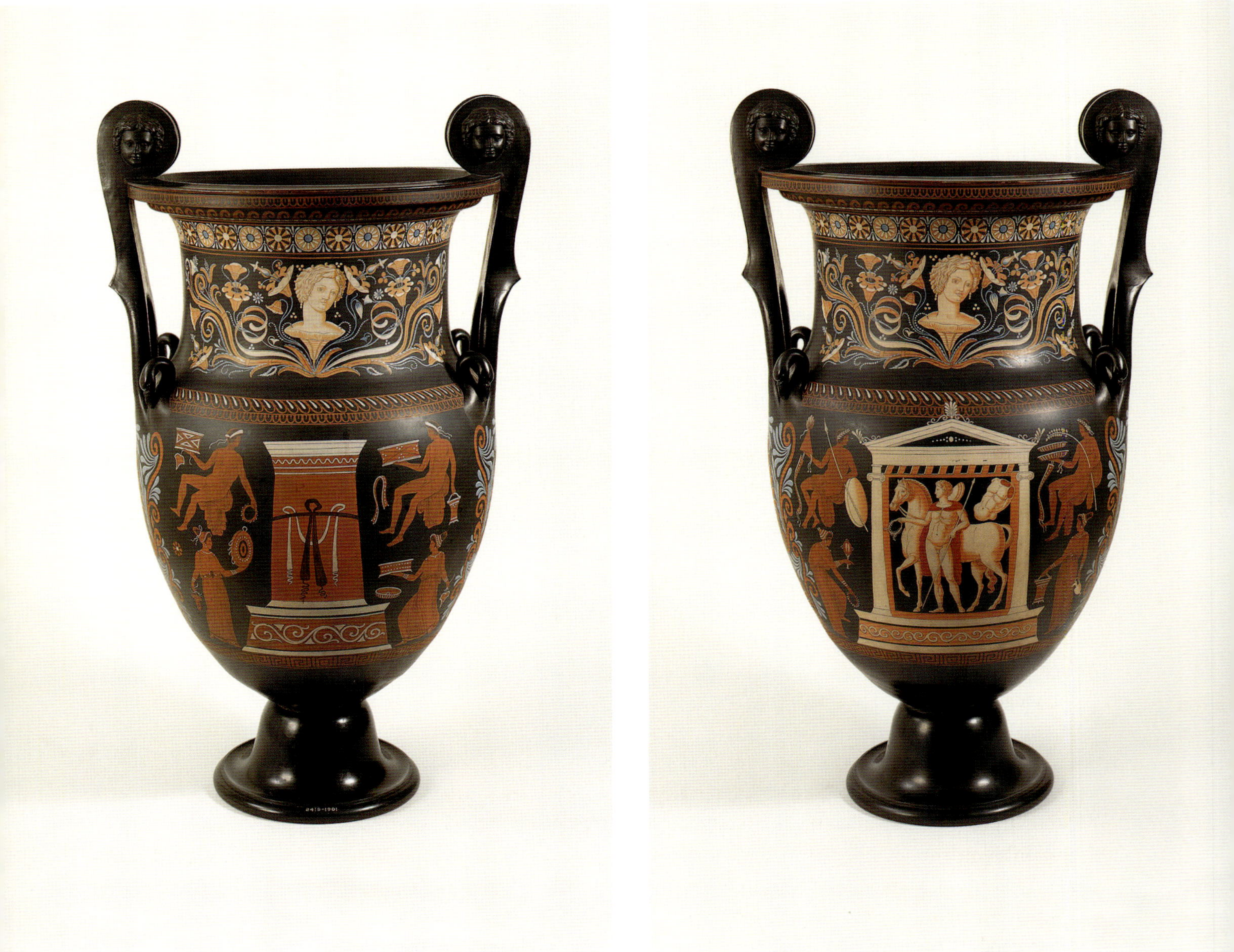

112
Huge Wedgwood Black Basalt krater with encaustic painting, after d'Hancarville, once a centrepiece at the showroom of the London glass manufacturer Apsley Pellatt, probably acquired after the closure of Wedgwood's own showrooms in 1829. Height 87 cm (34¼ in.).
V&A: 2419–1901.

to display Catherine the Great's famous Frog Service. Two years after Wedgwood's death, in 1797 the showroom moved further west to York Street, St James's Square, where in 1801 the sales of Messrs Wedgwood & Byerley amounted to as much as £18,813. But the glory days of smart carriages queuing up outside the Wedgwood showroom were past: the trade with America was seen as more important than that of London; Wedgwood products were stocked by all the smart dealers; and by 1829 the superfluous Wedgwood showrooms had closed.

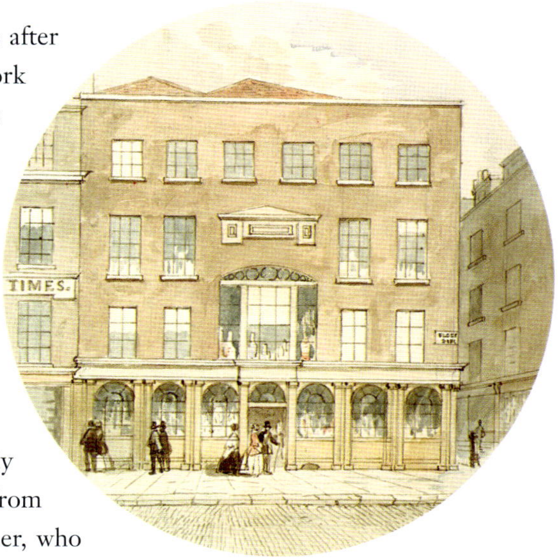

113
Frontage of Abbott & Mist, 82 Fleet Street, London. This old-established shop was taken over by Davenport in 1818.
Courtesy of Guildhall Library.

As regards the retailing of pottery for the fashionable market, Wedgwood was indeed the pioneer for others to follow (plate 112). But other Staffordshire contemporaries were already involved in supplying both the home trade and the export trade from warehouses within easy reach of the Thames, such as John Turner, who advertised in 1768/9 'Cream-coloured Staffordshire Ware for Merchants, Captains of Ships, and Shopkeepers', made at his thriving Lane End factory. An opportunity to move into more fashionable premises in Fleet Street came with his partnership with Andrew Abbott in about 1780.[16] Here the business flourished under various partnerships, notably with James Mist, until 1818 when the successful pottery and porcelain maker James Davenport obtained a 10-year lease (plate 113). Another important early retailer, James Neale, followed a similar path by moving from Wapping to St Paul's Churchyard in 1766, taking as partner his brother-in-law, the enterprising Humphrey Palmer, who was so quick to imitate the latest products of Wedgwood. By 1772 they could advertise:

> Greatest Variety of Articles in Earthen and Stone Ware, particularly complete Table and Desert Services in the Cream-coloured or Queen's Ware, Chamber Lamps [i.e., *veilleuses*] adapted to bear the sudden Approaches of Fire; Urns and Vases . . . Ornaments for the Cabinet or Closet . . . Arms, Devices etc. if ordered may be painted or impressed upon particular Setts . . . Great Variety of Glass.

The subsequent Neale & Bailey partnership (plates 108, 114), maintaining direct links with Staffordshire through the Neale and Wilson factories, lasted from 1789 to 1834.[17] Apart from trading in their own products, they stocked a full range of glass and were early promoters of Masons' Ironstone China.

From the early 1780s onwards the term 'Staffordshire Warehouse' became used increasingly to describe the flood of new retailers setting up business in busy provincial towns, taking advantage of the healthy creamware and pearlware market. Depending on their location, they might purchase direct from Staffordshire or through secondary trade with dealers in London as, for example, William Absolom of Great Yarmouth, or Elizabeth Studwell of Norwich, who advertised in the 1780s that they were 'just returned from London' with the latest goods.[18] In towns with local potteries and glasshouses, there were, of

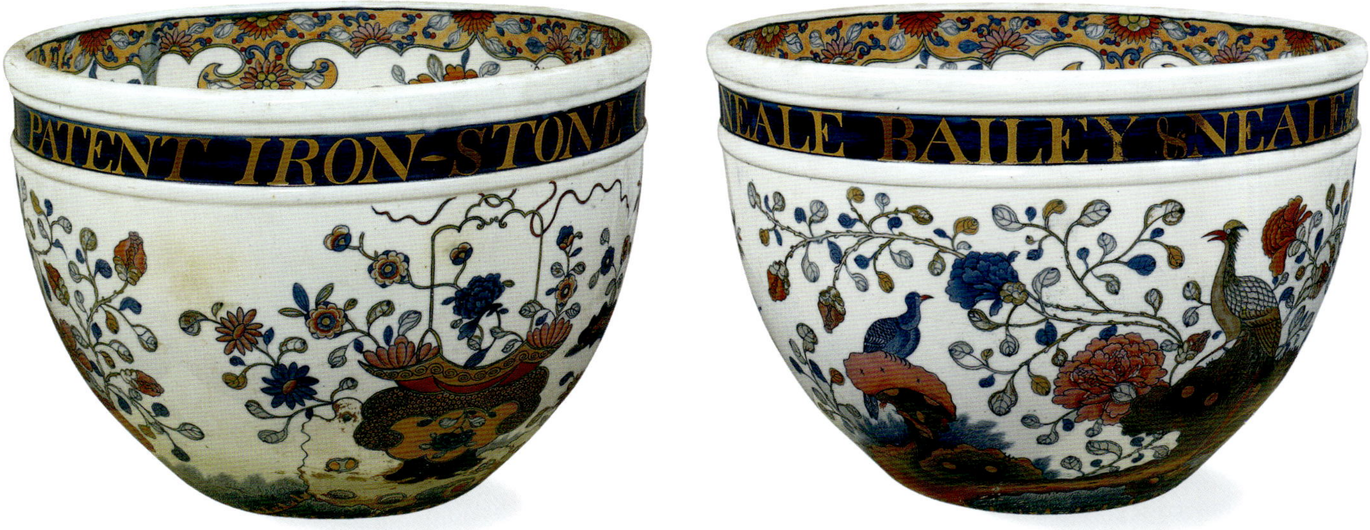

114
Documentary early Mason's punch-bowl inscribed 'Patent Ironstone', an advertising centrepiece from the showrooms of Neale Bailey & Neale at St Paul's Churchyard, datable to 1813–17. The turned wooden base has, alas, been lost since it was acquired in 1870. Diameter 48. 2 cm (19 in.).
V&A: 54–1870.

course, opportunities to sell direct to the public, these places including the major seaports of Liverpool and Bristol. The trade cards of glass works around 1800 sometimes show carriages and customers buying from a smart shop adjoining the factory, but smoking potteries generally maintained a separate shop in a more fashionable part of town (plate 115). From the 1780s also, pressure in the retailing trade began to be felt from a second generation of manufacturers after Josiah Wedgwood, makers who began with a basic creamware or Pearlware body for which the demand appeared to be unquenchable, and later expanded rapidly by exploiting to the full those two highly important technical advances of the 1790s: underglaze-blue transfer-printed pottery and bone china. For them, a showroom in London manned by a trusted family member could offer a direct outlet for their wares without paying commission, and a chance to keep their name in the public eye.

The earliest of this second generation was Josiah Spode, who started fairly modestly in 1778 with premises in Cripplegate under the shrewd management of his son, Josiah Spode II. By 1793 sales had risen to £9,485, and three years later they had taken over the premises of the well-known chinaman William Hussey at 5 Portugal Street (plate 116). With the double advantage of producing the finest dinner and tea services of both blue printed earthenware and bone china, the Spode factory flourished under subsequent partnerships and titles until in 1849 the showroom moved to prestigious New Bond Street.[19] Other makers whose achievements came after the early nineteenth century include Thomas Minton, whose brother Arthur established a showroom at Swallow Street in 1796, with a smallish turnover of £2,000 by 1800. With the huge export market later enjoyed by Mintons, this venture only lasted some 20 years, but while Mintons had been content at first to mass-produce unpretentious printed tablewares, more ambitious makers like Davenport, already having a large warehouse in Liverpool for the transatlantic trade, began to exhibit their wares in London from 1807, taking over Andrew Abbott's Fleet Street shop in 1818 and becoming 'Porcelain Manufacturers to their Majesties' in 1831. The basis for this huge expansion was surely not London, but rather their export trade with Russia, India and northern Europe, where Davenport warehouses were established in Hamburg in 1817 and Lübeck in 1826. One or two small but ambitious factories also briefly tried their hand at dealing, such as Yates & Co. of Hanley and Ralph Wedgwood & Co., who both took shops in St Paul's Churchyard in London around 1790. Some idea of the range stocked by an average dealer may be judged from Ralph Wedgwood's closing sale in 1794:

> plain and ornamented Wedgewood [*sic*] Table and Dessert Services, Water-plates, Broth Bowls, Oyster Barrels, Blancmange-Moulds, Ice Pails, Porcelain Tea Equipages, Jasper Vases, Tea and Sugar boxes, Terra Tersia Bouquetiers, Garden Pots and Jugs, large gilt, enamelled and black Figures, a large Assortment of blue printed Ware, black Egyptian Tea Pots, Mortars and pestles, Brass-mounted Vase-Lamps, and an extensive variety of useful and Ornamental Articles.

Josiah Wedgwood's decision to mark his wares consistently from about 1770 had been motivated partly by his insistence on charging more than others – this despite his supply to the public of 'Wedgwood' wares made by other factories. Only the most ambitious potters seem to have followed his example, in particular Spode, whose products were unequalled in the early nineteenth century. But the concept of retailers having wares marked with their own name by their suppliers was slow to appear (plate 117). As mentioned above, however, during the early nineteenth century the power of a few major London dealers grew to the point where, though acting as agents in selling 'named' products, they increasingly took control over the actual makers and began to insist on having their own elaborate backstamps, with or without that of the actual maker. In some ways, those makers who allowed their agents to assume such power became victims of their own success, for it was they who first promoted themselves as individual factories, superior to the great mass of others and capable of commanding greater prices. And if they lost direct access to their customers, at

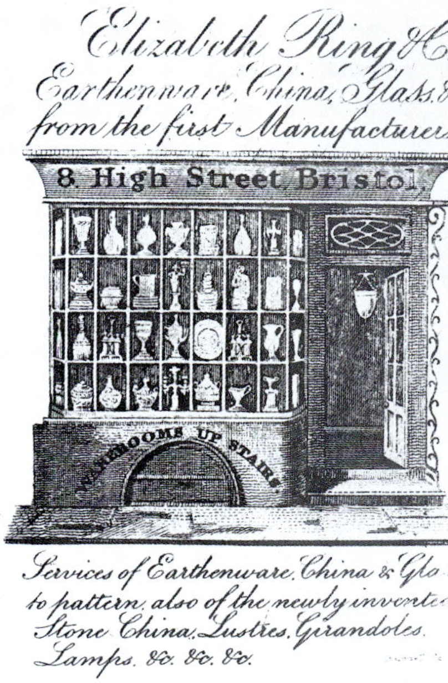

115
A typical provincial retailer, Elizabeth Ring's Bristol shop, from Matthew's Bristol Directory, 1835.

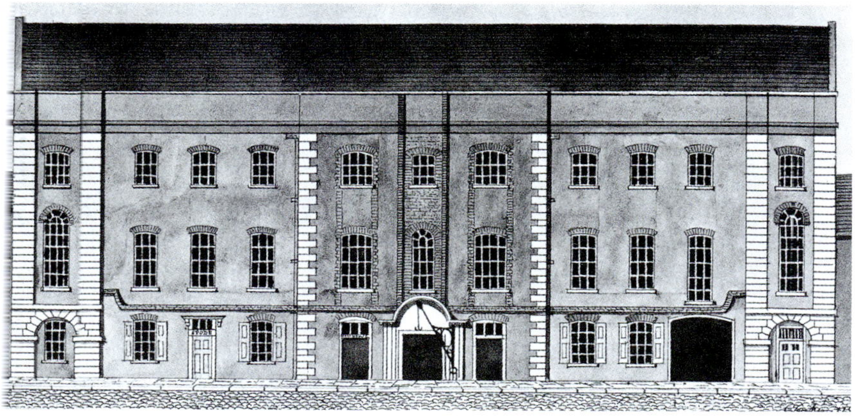

116
The grand frontage of Spode's showroom, 5 Portugal Street, London, in the early 19th century demonstrates the huge success enjoyed by this pioneering factory.

least they were spared the risks of a business that depended largely on credit and that could often end in bankruptcy.[20] But for the survivors like Mortlock, Phillips and Thomas Goode, there were big profits to be made.

This situation might have continued throughout the nineteenth century but for the great resurgence of pottery and porcelain manufacture in the 1840s, which, having thwarted the activities of the trade unions, was able to bring manufacturers' names back into prominence and break the stranglehold of the retail trade. In this they were greatly aided by the ever-widening railway network, which made it possible for the public to exclude the middleman and deal directly with factories in Staffordshire. Now the maker's mark began to form an integral part of the pot, often accompanied, after the Copyright of Designs Act of 1842, by a 'diamond mark' to discourage pirating. Great strides were made by

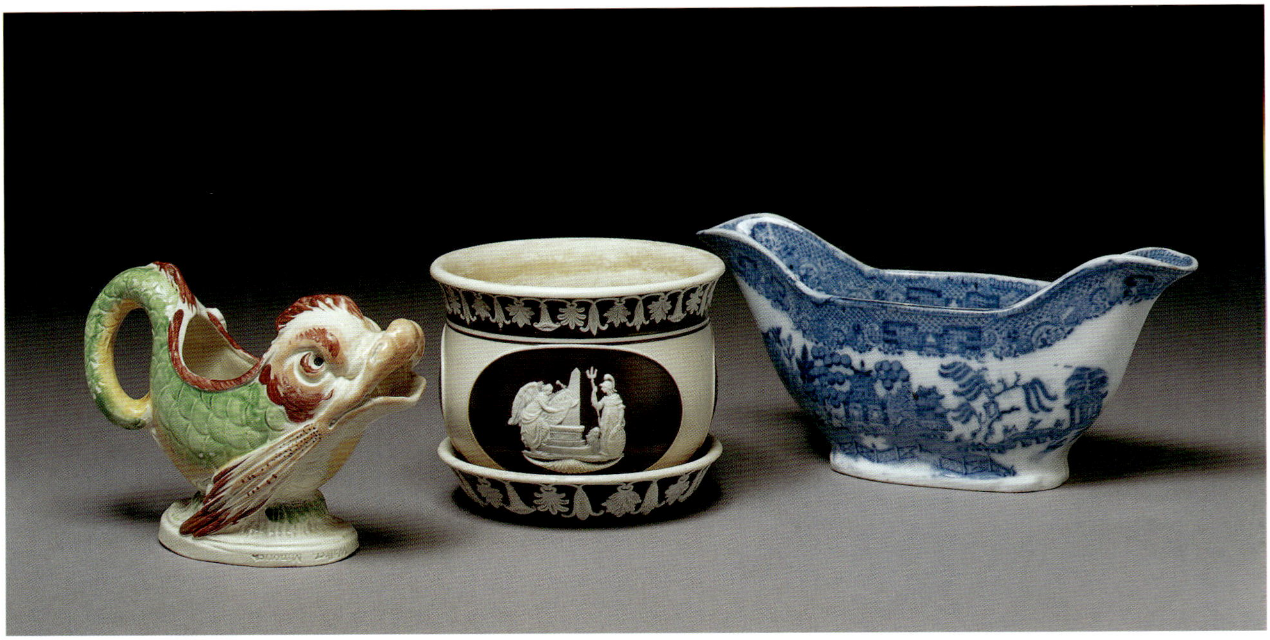

117
Retailers' marks are surprisingly rare, but they do exist. The creamware sauce boat marked 'Walker Minories' is datable to *c.*1784–*c.*1804, the stoneware pot commemorating Howe and Nelson marked 'Mist' for James Mist operating at 82 Fleet Street, London, 1809–15, the blue and white sauce boat impressed 'BURN' for John Burn, recorded at Clare Market in 1817. Max. height 9 cm (3½ in.).

V&A: Sch.II 425, Sch.II 564 &A, C.25–2002.

ambitious manufacturers in these years immediately preceding the Great Exhibition of 1851, particularly with regard to stoneware jugs moulded with subjects deemed to be artistic, and to the crowning achievements of majolica, Parian Ware and press-moulded encaustic stoneware tiles. Always at the forefront of such developments was Herbert Minton, in whose hands the Minton factory, after decades of mass-producing decent but unremarkable printed tablewares, was able to expand and dramatically raise its horizons. While the Wedgwood factory at Etruria had sunk so low as to be offered for sale in 1843, Herbert Minton's friendship with Henry Cole, later to become first director of the South Kensington Museum, ensured that the Renaissance art introduced into his manufactures came with the best pedigree and guarantee of success

It might appear that at this point history had repeated itself, that the Renaissance had done for Staffordshire potters in the mid-nineteenth century what the Antique had done for them in the 1770s. Yet there was an important difference: for now the guidance of public taste had passed from the private individuals, namely powerful aristocrats and collectors of the eighteenth century, through the hands of the London retail trade, and on to official Establishment bodies such as the Society of Arts, Manufactures and Commerce (later the Royal Society), which fostered improvements in design through exhibitions and prizes. At the same time, the seeds of Wedgwood's promotion of pottery as a tasteful fashion accessory were now to bear fruit on an unimagined scale, making Staffordshire the biggest producer of tableware in Europe throughout the nineteenth century.

1. Hume (1977).
2. Weatherill (1971), p.30.
3. An account of a potter John Wilden travelling with three asses and a hollow-eyed horse, Aris's *Birmingham Gazette*, 21 September 1747, quoted by Meteyard (1865–6), vol.I, p.267.
4. The slave trade was abolished in 1807, and slavery itself was ended in the British Empire in 1833.
5. From a resolution of the potters' minute book of 22 February 1785, quoted by Thomas (1971), p.116.
6. Saint-Fond (1797) quoted by, among others, Thomas (1971), p.116.
7. Correspondence between Josiah Wedgwood II and Thomas Sparks, Engraver, quoted by Whiter (1970), p.61.
8. Thistlethwaite (1958). The emigrants included members of dynastic potting families, such as William Ridgway, James Clews and Daniel Greatbatch.
9. Towner (1978), pp.181–7, and Guilemé-Brulon (1995).
10. Thomas (1971), pp.44–65.
11. Hassell (1819), quoted by Whiter (1970), p.60.
12. Two plates at least survive from the output of this pottery (V&A: C.317–1931, and another in the British Museum), which may either have been a cooperative venture, a means of raising funds for the Union, or both. This Union Bank Pottery was worked from about 1868 by Whittingham, Ford & Co.
13. The standard dozen was based on 12 mugs or jugs each with a capacity of one pint: two-pint vessels would therefore be 6 to the dozen, half-pints 24 to the dozen, and so on in proportion. With capacities of vessels often inexact and variable, this system was vulnerable to abuse by unscrupulous manufacturers.
14. Hildyard (2004).
15. A showroom jug inscribed 'Tidmarshe's Original Staffordshire Warehouse N 1775' in the Potteries Museum, published by Adams (1975–6). A delftware plate in the British Museum, inscribed 'James Tidmarsh 1736' with their shop sign of a hand and pewter tankard, illustrated by Lipski (1984), no.406. It is probable that, when changing from pewterers to pottery retailers, they simply altered their shop sign to the 'Hand, Buttercup [i.e., a butter boat] and Blue and White Dish', which was given in their advertisements from at least 1748.
16. Howarth (1996).
17. Edwards (1987).
18. Howell (1980).
19. Profits from mass production were nonetheless obtained only by calculating and keeping costs to the absolute minimum. As quoted by Whiter (1970), p.22, the Spode factory in 1833 estimated that 722 blue-printed dinner plates could be fired with one ton of coal.
20. Wedgwood's declared policy of accepting cash only was never put into practice. Aristocrats were often bad payers, shamelessly using their name as a guarantee of eventual payment. The situation with foreign trade, to Russia for example, was very much less certain.

CHAPTER TEN

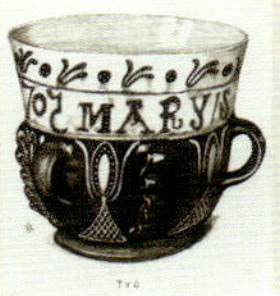

From Warehouse to Antique Shop: The Fashion for Collecting

The statement that 'Rapid advance in wealth, luxury, and leisure, in any country, is for the most part followed by an increased thirst for the investigation of its early history . . . into progress made from the most ancient times in its industrial and decorative arts' (Hodgkin and Hodgkin, *Examples of Early English Pottery, Named, Dated and Inscribed*, 1891) remains a valid assessment of the forces that first impelled eminent and cultured men to collect humble English earthenware. If literature on the subject is a reliable indicator, the origins may be traced back as far as the late eighteenth century, with antiquarian studies such as John Henniker's *Two Letters on the Origin, Antiquity, and History of Norman Tiles, Stained with Armorial Bearings* of 1794; and although such papers were concerned mainly with heraldry rather than the history of ceramics, the contemporary obsession with heraldry itself grew out of the need for a new class of wealthy tradesmen to establish a place in society, just as much as the simultaneous efforts by old established families to reassert their position in a shifting world. In an age when the upper sections of society considered the picturesque and the elegant as ideals of beauty, and when Joseph Wright of Derby saw only romance in the nocturnal blazing iron furnaces of Coalbrookdale, there was as yet no place for a serious study of manufacture in England. Despite the phenomenal commercial and social success of Josiah Wedgwood, the trade of potter remained, in the eyes of the prosperous and educated public, a comparatively lowly one.

Thus it was that the impetus to celebrate the potter's craft came from the industry itself. While Wedgwood himself is now known to have written the self-eulogizing entry for the Staffordshire potteries in *The County History of Stafford*, an entirely objective approach to the subject was taken by Enoch Wood, whose production of unpretentious earthenware for export and the mass market at his Fountain Place works at Burslem brought him enormous wealth and the opportunity to indulge a passion for the old and unconsidered products of his fellow potters. As early as 1816 Wood's factory museum opened its doors to show the fruit of years of avid collecting in the Potteries area: starting with a nucleus of salt-glazed block-moulds made by Aaron and Ralph Wood, he soon amassed good examples of local pottery from the late seventeenth century onwards, including the earliest recorded slipware chargers. Shortly afterwards, the historical and technical aspects were taken up by Simeon Shaw (plate 119), whose *History of the Staffordshire Potteries* (1829) recorded from local people a wealth of truth, half-truth and pure myth that has continued to perplex authors ever since. Ward's *The Borough of Stoke-upon-Trent* (1843) further promoted the Potteries'

118
This fine inscribed Parian portrait bust of Llewellyn Jewitt was produced by W. H. Goss for presentation to his son in 1879. Height 39.3 cm (15½ in.).
V&A: C.1–1982

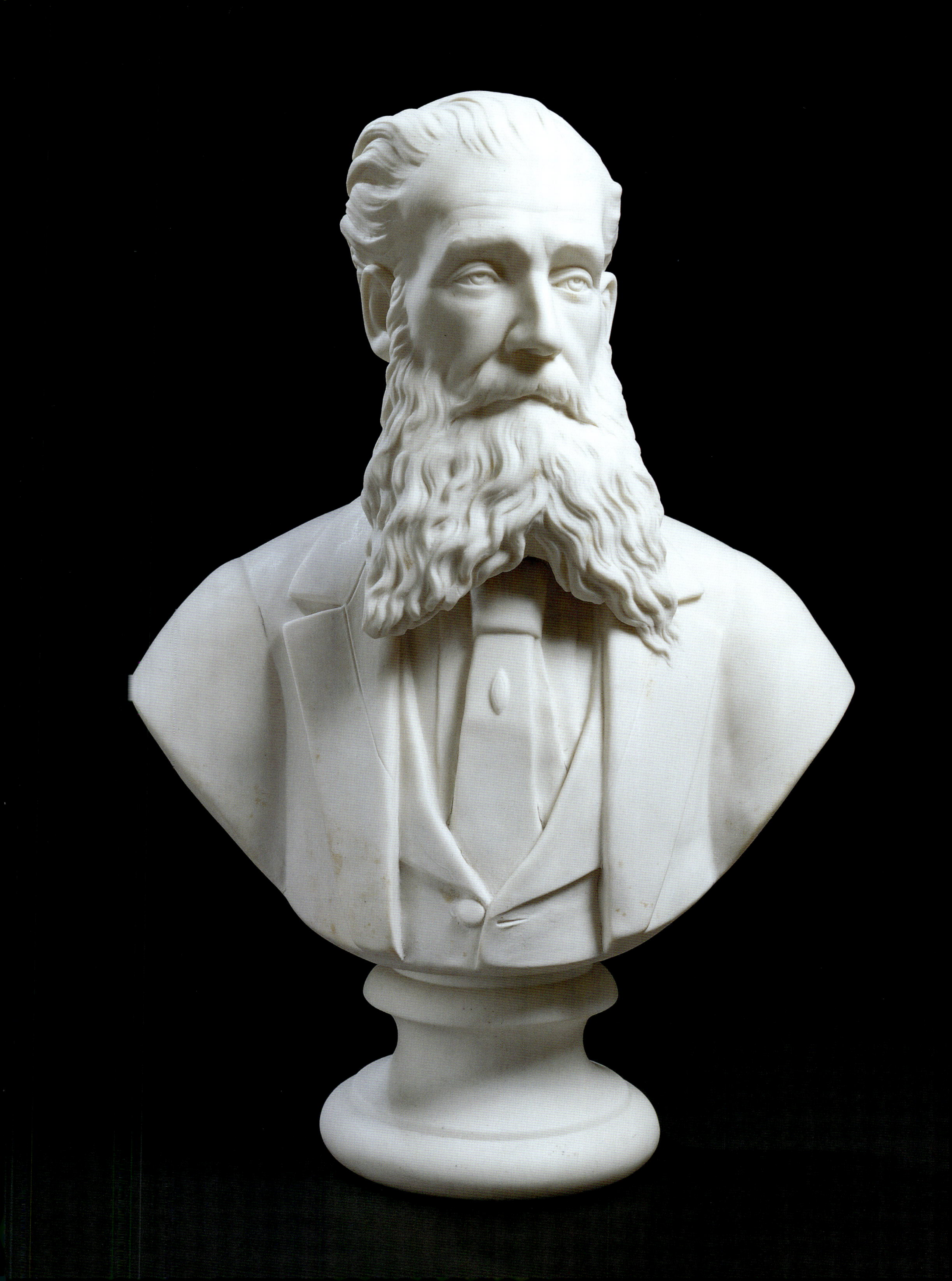

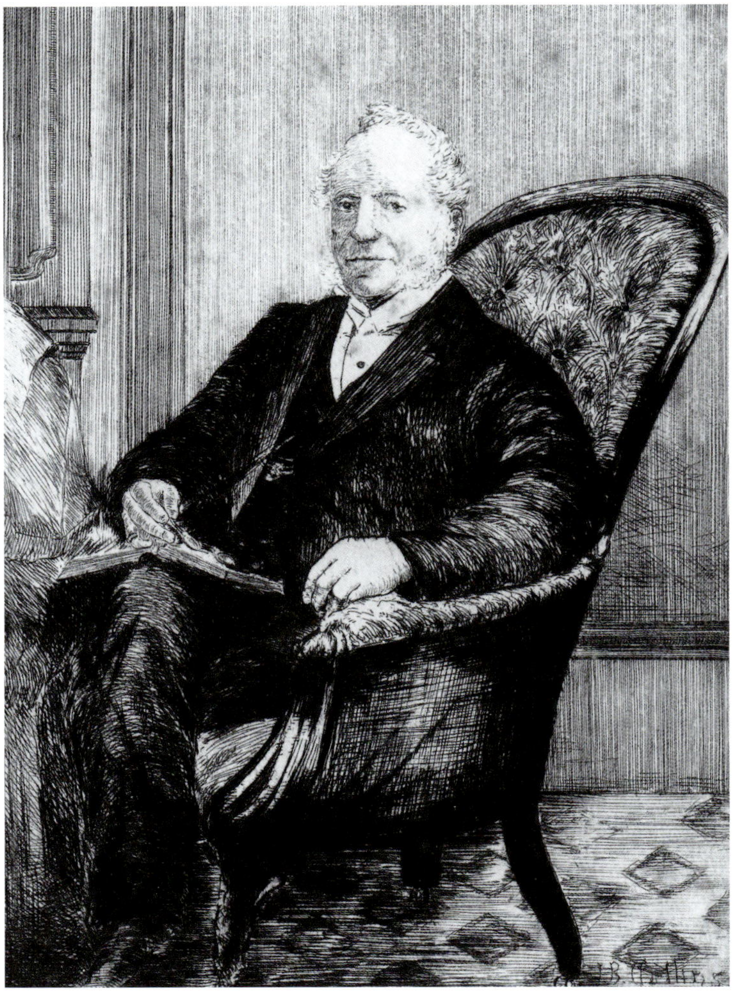

119
Simeon Shaw in old age, a hitherto unpublished engraving.
V&A, library of Ceramics and Glass Collection.

pre-eminence, at a time when the Geological Survey of Britain had decided to demonstrate the transformation of earth to art in the establishment of the Museum of Practical Geology in Jermyn Street, London.

Unhappily, Enoch Wood's pioneering museum – some five years in advance of Alexandre Brogniart's Musée Céramique at Sèvres – died with him. One hundred and twenty pieces had already been presented to the Royal Collections at Dresden, where most still survive, while after some years of abortive negotiation with the Government, the remaining collections were divided between the Museum of Practical Geology, the Mechanics' Institute at Hanley, Herbert Minton (who presented his share to the Museum and Art Gallery at Stoke), and the new South Kensington Museum.

It was, in fact, the relationship between these institutions and their common goals in uniting museum with manufacture, Art with Industry, that was to shape the future of ceramics, and pottery in particular, as a separate field of study. The critical point of fusion came as a by-product of the Great Exhibition of the Art and Industry of All Nations in 1851, the first world trade fair, which, as far as Britain was concerned, was a deliberate attempt to shame native manufacturers into improving the artistic quality of their goods, and to convince them that mere cheapness of manufacture should not be used to justify their poor design. The effects were manifold. On the one hand Renaissance ornament was added to a design repertoire already overloaded with eclecticism, and on the other came a new awareness by the public of Britain's artistic place in Europe, and a desire to trace the artistic antecedents of great new British inventions such as Parian Ware and Minton's majolica: the application of genealogy to manufacture, so to speak. In anticipation of the Great Exhibition, the first general work on ceramics had appeared in 1850, Joseph Marryat's *A History of Pottery & Porcelain, Mediaeval and Modern*, a major work whose later editions included some colour-printed plates. Others soon followed. After nearly 50 years as director of the Sèvres porcelain factory and as the driving force behind the establishment of the factory museum that opened in 1824, Alexandre Brogniart's great work, *Traité des arts céramiques ou des poteries*, was published in 1854. The following year the first catalogue of the Museum of Practical Geology by Sir Henry de la Beche and Trenham Reeks appeared, while at South Kensington in 1856 J. C. Robinson catalogued the Soulages Collection of mainly

French pottery, whose direct influence on the artists of the Minton factory is well documented.

There was a flurry of activity during the 1860s, with the first of many editions of William Chaffers's *Marks & Monograms on Pottery & Porcelain* appearing in 1863. This year also witnessed Gladstone laying the foundation stone of the Wedgwood Memorial Institute at Burslem, which provided a focus for the first non-autobiographical accounts of the man and his achievements. Both Llewellyn Jewitt's *Life of Josiah Wedgwood* and Elizabeth Meteyard's two-volume *The Life of Josiah Wedgwood from his Private Correspondence and Family Papers* came out in 1865, stimulating an existing interest in collecting the factory's best ornamental products, which had been continually copied but never surpassed since Wedgwood's death in 1795. Meteyard followed this up in 1873 with a lavishly illustrated book on Wedgwood's decorative wares in the Neo-classical taste, *Wedgwood & His Works*, which no doubt played its part in fuelling the Neo-classical Revival of the late nineteenth century.

No sooner was the fashion for making ceramic collections established as a pastime for the enquiring and prosperous amateur, than it adopted faces to fit all types of collectors. At an aristocratic level, serious collecting of pottery was by no means new. Grand late seventeenth-century Dutch Delft tulip pyramids still remained from an earlier collecting phase in country houses such as Chatsworth and Blaise Castle, while *istoriato* Italian maiolica was sometimes collected on the Grand Tour, like the Fountaine Collection in Norfolk. The many aristocratic customers of Wedgwood still retained their creamwares, Jasper wares, Basalt and marbled vases. But initially it was the passion for old porcelain that fuelled a collecting mania that eventually spread to encompass many types of Continental pottery, and eventually also English pottery. In order to trace its roots, a brief digression is required.

Fine enamelled Chinese vases in the English taste (and even, in the case of *famille rose*, decorated with English-made enamels) were imported on East India Company ships throughout the eighteenth century, usually as private rather than Company trade. Despite their size and technical excellence, the *cachet* of these luxury objects, as well as of the huge armorial services ordered from China through agents in London, eventually declined through the ready availability of cheap Chinese blue and white tablewares. The invention of porcelain at Meissen in 1709 and its spread throughout Europe would eventually seal the fate of the trade in finely enamelled Chinese imports, for not only were these new European products decorated by highly skilled artists, but the factories themselves, often established by aristocrats in order to enhance their prestige, enjoyed wealthy and royal patronage for their exclusive products. The King of Saxony's factory at Meissen provided porcelain figures from the 1730s; the Chelsea factory – independent but patronized by royalty – was active from the 1740s; Louis XV's factory, first at Vincennes and later at Sèvres, produced services to order from the mid-eighteenth century and seldom managed even to cover its costs. Though purchased for domestic use, when not in use these objects served a secondary function as decoration, either laid on the dining table or in china cabinets. In England, it was possible to enhance these core collections through expensive purchases from the London trade: in the late eighteenth century china dealers advertised not only second-hand Continental porcelains but also Chelsea to supply an aristocratic market for flamboyant forms, rich ground-colours and lush gilding. In fact, the craze for Sèvres porcelain was augmented rather than diminished by the Revolution of 1789 and the Napoleonic Wars. Wealthy collectors such as William Beckford took advantage of the chaos in France to acquire more porcelain; and when in 1801 the supply dried up with Alexandre Brogniart's decision to abandon the labour-intensive manufacture of elitist soft-paste, replacements were quickly found. At first, large quantities of redundant soft-paste blanks were sold by Sèvres in 1802 to coincide with the brief Peace of Amiens, and later these blanks, elaborately decorated in England, were joined by a mass of copies, fakes and 'improved' originals. In an age of increasing national wealth, the taste for luxury products of the *ancien régime* spread rapidly, so that those who could not collect the real thing were soon to be supplied by London china dealers with convincing substitutes. Unaware that the special characteristics of snowy-white Sèvres soft-paste derived from the ingredient alum, Billingsley's potteries at Swansea and Nantgarw produced a glassy porcelain that was equally beautiful but highly unstable, while from about 1815 large Staffordshire manufacturers such as Spode and Minton, and particularly the Coalport factory in Shropshire, offered a reliable solution to the problem by adding feldspar to their bone chinas.

After Waterloo, aristocrats such as the future Duke of Atholl not only continued to buy from dealers in England (for example, the purchase of 32 Sèvres plates at the enormous price of 30s each from Louis Fleschelle in Bond Street in 1817), but also satisfied their lust for large quantities of soft-paste by purchasing directly from Paris dealers. It was the exclusiveness of these porcelains and their aristocratic and royal association that made them attractive not only to the old aristocracy, but also to the newly wealthy, among whom bankers were to become the most active collectors. To a lesser extent, the same pattern is discernible in the field of Chelsea porcelains and ornamental Wedgwood: for the exclusiveness that they all shared was guaranteed by the decisive watershed of the French Revolution, the closure of the Chelsea factory in 1769 and by the death of Wedgwood in 1795. Above all, it was Francophilia that remained supreme and unshakeable among the wealthy throughout the nineteenth century, culminating after the mid-nineteenth century in huge imitation châteaux such as Waddesdon, Mentmore and what is now the Bowes Museum at Barnard Castle, all built as decorated showcases for their owners' collections of *objets d'art*.

As for pottery, although it might appear that original buyers of Wedgwood were demonstrating patriotism in preferring native products, in reality they were merely following the well-established taste for the Antique. While the porcelains of Meissen and Sèvres were unable to break out of their Baroque and Rococo mould and take on the mantle of pure Neo-classicism, Wedgwood's modellers could use his new adaptable earthenware and stoneware bodies to produce modern, and technically much superior, versions of classical artefacts supposedly in the styles of Rome, Greece and Egypt, as interpreted by the leading contemporary architects and designers. When wealthy collectors did begin to turn their attention to early pottery towards the middle of the nineteenth century, at first they were beguiled by the glamour of Continental lead-glazed earthenware with its obvious and reassuring artistic qualities – a reassurance that was difficult to find in quaint, idiosyncratic pre-Industrial English pottery. Not surprisingly, they first gravitated towards highly decorated French 'Palissy' wares or the grander German stonewares of the Renaissance period, which not only clearly declared their origin but which also survived in large numbers. These numbers began steadily to increase as fakers found a new lucrative market.

As mentioned above, it was the Great Exhibition of 1851 that proved to be a milestone for pottery collecting in Britain. After a phenomenal attendance of more than six million visitors, the public was left with not only a new awareness of Britain's ceramic achievements, but also with a greater interest in world ceramics. As well as extolling the virtues of the modern efficient factory, the Exhibition paradoxically also generated interest in English life before the Industrial Revolution, accompanied by a growing sense of nationalism that was fuelled by a certain puritan revulsion felt by an enlightened middle class to the uncritical aristocratic worship of foreign luxury goods.

At the same time, English museums were beginning to recognize the importance of native manufacture and to build up representative collections. In 1857 the collections of the Museum of Ornamental Art at Marlborough House were re-housed at South Kensington with generous funding from the profits of the Great Exhibition, under the directorship of Henry Cole, whose close friendship with Herbert Minton forged vital links with the both the modern ceramic industry and its past. Starting with a nucleus of early pottery and block-moulds purchased from the Enoch Wood collection in 1854, the South Kensington Museum began to build up its collections, acquiring the first (and arguably the best) Thomas Toft slipware mermaid charger in 1869 for the comparatively modest sum of £15. Meanwhile, at the British Museum from 1851 the first Keeper of the Department of British and Mediaeval Antiquities, Sir Augustus Wollaston Franks, was building up a superb personal collection in order to illustrate different branches of British archaeology. Having donated this to the British Museum in 1887, the following year he purchased for the museum the important and complementary collection of early pottery formed by Henry Willett of Brighton. Pottery specialists also appeared in the major provincial cities. At Liverpool Free Library & Museum, Joseph Mayer, a descendant of that great Staffordshire potting family, championed the cause of pottery, while at Bristol a local antiquarian, Hugh Owen, firmly established the importance of local pottery (and in particular the neglected delftware) with his *Two Centuries of Ceramic Art in Bristol* (1873), a work surpassed only much later by W. J. Pountney's *Old Bristol Potteries* (1920).

By the 1870s, when museums in London were still attempting to define aspects of pottery as either geology, archaeology or art, a new breed of private collector and ceramic author emerged with completely different aims and criteria, perhaps inspired by the early edition of Chaffers's *Marks & Monograms* (1863). When these private collections reached a critical point, opportunities to publish naturally presented themselves, as was most certainly the case with the huge collections amassed by Lady Charlotte Schreiber (plate 120). After the death of her husband Sir John Guest in 1852, she had married her children's tutor Charles Schreiber, and from about 1865 embarked on a collecting spree that lasted until his death in 1884, when she donated most of her collection to the South Kensington Museum. Although her first husband had been the richest industrialist in the world, employing some 20,000 steelworkers in Wales, as a widow with ten children her funds were not unlimited: but her enthusiasm for the pursuit of a bargain knew no bounds. Apart from the interest for ceramic historians of a major nineteenth-century collection surviving completely intact, the copious documentation that accompanied the gift to the Museum has offered other useful insights into the world of Victorian collecting. For the pottery section not only closely reflected her taste, and no doubt the tastes of the period with its predilection for enamelled and elaborately moulded salt-glazed stonewares, but it was formed at a time when many of the pieces were less than 100 years old, and when the unfired oil-gilding on sprigged stonewares, on Littler's Blue and iron-manganese-glazed 'Jackfield' wares still remained. Because her Journals show that many of these pieces were acquired during her 23 trips to the Continent, particularly Holland, it is also possible to reconstruct at least some areas of the huge export trade between north Staffordshire and the Low Countries. Given the size and national importance of the collection, it is not so surprising that when Lady Charlotte Schreiber began to write the catalogue of her collection, to be published in 1885, Sir Augustus Wollaston Franks of the British Museum offered his assistance. As the first museum catalogue of eighteenth-century English ceramics, this serious publication gave the official seal of approval to the subject as an independent field of study. It was to be revised and divided into three volumes by Bernard Rackham, the first volume appearing in 1915 with a second complete series published after the First World War in 1928, 1930 and 1924 respectively.

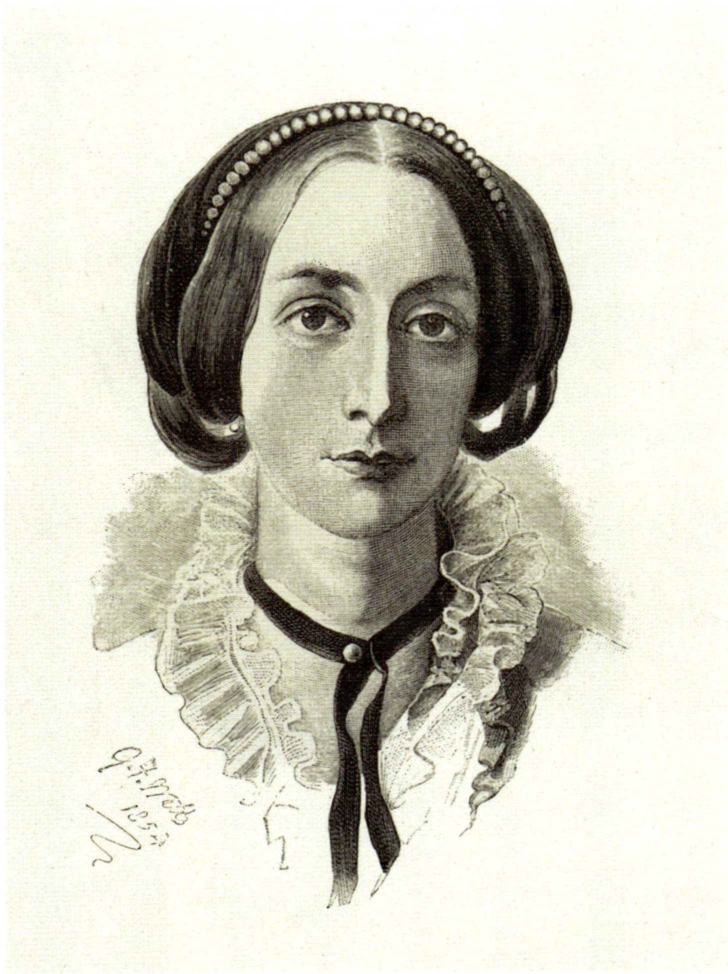

120
Lady Charlotte Schreiber, engraving after a drawing by G. F. Watts, from the Schreiber Catalogue

Ceramic authors were not always collectors. History could be written either from surviving objects, or from surviving documents, or both. Llewellyn Jewitt (see plate 118) defined his approach in his introduction to *The Ceramic Art of Great Britain* (1878) as a belief in '*work*, in hard unceasing labour, in patient and painstaking research, in untiring searchings, and in diligent collection and arrangement of facts'. The wealth of interesting facts and figures included in his two volumes goes a long way towards justifying such a philosophy, although the reader would look in vain for informed aesthetic judgement. Collectors continued to publish, however, and often contrived to combine history with aesthetics. Five years after Jewitt's great work, Marc Louis Solon, the French Art Director of Mintons, produced his superb limited edition, *The Art of the Old English Potter*, consisting of a romantic romp through the history of English pottery up to the mid-eighteenth century based on 50 pieces from his own collection. In keeping with the sumptuous binding and handmade paper, it was illustrated throughout by Solon's sensitive etchings – themselves reproduced by photogravure, a photographic process ably demonstrating a perfect marriage between art and science (plate 121). The narrative, based closely on Simeon Shaw, was rambling and whimsical, and infused by a mission to awaken the British to the unrecognized treasures of their past. Fortunately, the trained ceramist in Solon jibbed at repeating the preposterous myth about Palmer of Bagnall discovering salt-glazing by observing the effects of an over-boiling pan of salt water. Surprisingly for the chief exponent of pâte-sur-pâte decoration, Solon declared that he was 'attracted towards primitive works, always sound, fresh and rational' in a world 'saturated with sophisticated embellishments'. But by the 1880s the Arts and Crafts Movement and the cult of Japanese minimalism had deeply penetrated the British aesthetic sensibility; and if the primitive stonewares of Seto and Bizen could be admired for their spontaneity, then why not English peasant pottery? Certainly, from this point onwards English pottery, and slipware in particular, was to be treated increasingly as art in its own right. Solon went so far as to mount his slipware dishes in ebonized frames to hang on the wall, in much the same way that sets of colour-printed Pratt pot lids had been framed in order to create a miniature picture gallery.

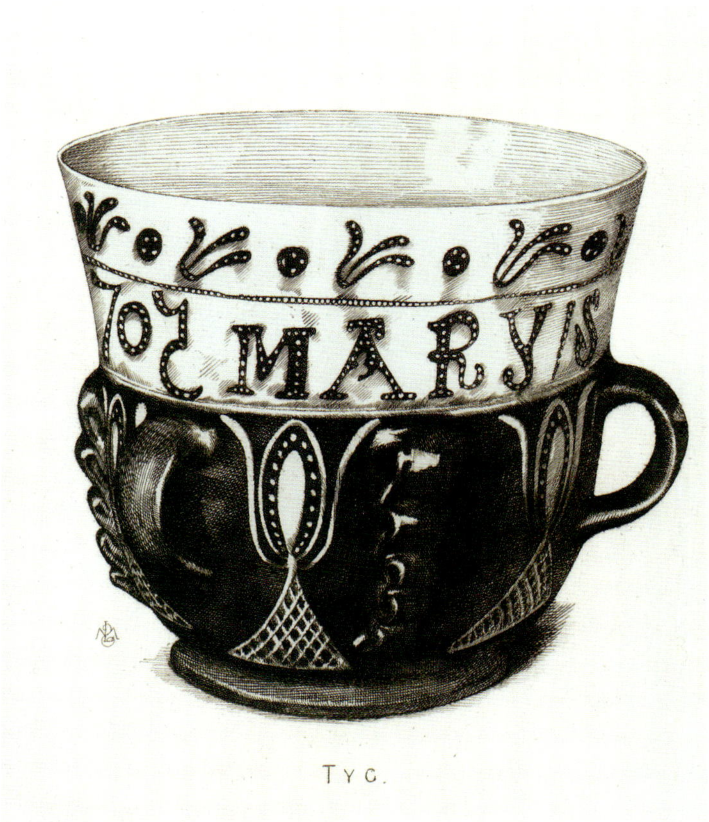

121
Illustration from *The Art of the Old English Potter* (1897) showing the sensuous subtlety of the photogravure technique as practised by Marc Louis Solon, Minton's Art Director and master of the *pâte-sur-pâte* technique.

By the 1880s a number of other specialized English pottery collections were reaching that state of eminence that seemed to require a permanent record of their existence. Since the framework of ceramic history had already been established by works such as Arthur Church's *A Collection of English Pottery* (1870) and William Chaffers's *Keramik Gallery* (1872) – a pictorial supplement to *Marks & Monograms* which was illustrated by lantern slides used in his lectures to the

Society of Arts in 1867 and no doubt inspired by the opening of the Ceramik Gallery (now the Silver Gallery) at South Kensington Museum in the late 1860s – the whole subject began to separate into smaller, more focused, fields of collecting and study. In particular, English pottery, perceived as a product of a golden pre-industrial age that accurately mirrored the social history of its period, was taken up by collectors in wealthy provincial cities, notably Manchester, where a friendly rivalry developed between Dr Sidebotham, Edward Sheldon, Frank Falkner (all supporters of the Manchester Museum Committee) and Charles Lomax. The romantic vision of peasant life that lay at the root of many collections formed by the wealthy professional classes may have been a myth, but it suited such people – then as now – to decorate their comfortable homes with what they considered as primitive artefacts. Perhaps also there was a perceived need to counterbalance the worship of expensive old Chelsea, Worcester, Sèvres and Meissen by wealthy London-based collectors. A much more serious interest in social history was taken by Henry Willett of Brighton, whose primary collection of early pottery had already been acquired by the British Museum in 1888. His extraordinarily comprehensive secondary collection, built up with the idea that 'the history of the country may to a large extent be traced on its homely pottery', was lent in 1899 to the Bethnal Green Museum (a branch of South Kensington Museum, originally intended as the first of four, which, in a consciously paternalistic way, would serve the poorer parts of London, the East End in particular), and eventually bequeathed to Brighton Museum, where it continues admirably to fulfil its owner's intentions. The original official catalogue of 1899, priced at 6d, has yet to be superseded.

Further private collections were published, mainly in lavish format. John Eliot and Edith Hodgkin chose to focus on a single aspect of pottery collecting by compiling, from both public and private sources,

> a list as nearly complete as may be of all the pieces of selected kinds of Early English Pottery which tell us anything about themselves, which say *when they were made or where, or by whom or for whom, or for what purpose*, thus standing out distinctly from the mass of specimens which on all these points are *dumb*.

If we excuse the authors for not only deliberately omitting, but incidentally attributing to Staffordshire, the entire class of late seventeenth-century delftware charger with 'very rude representations of Adam and Eve . . . and of portraits of contemporary celebrities', this is still a most useful reference work. It was not until 1919 that the credibility of these attractive tin-glazed earthenwares was established by the Revd E. A. Downman with his pioneering work *Blue Dash Chargers*. After Hodgkin and Hodgkin, the equally handsome book by Mr and Mrs Frank Freeth, *Old English Pottery* (1896), limited to 100 copies, formed a catalogue fully illustrated by excellent group photographs facing each page. The extent and seriousness of the collection – eighteenth-century Staffordshire salt-glaze and creamwares, pottery from Yorkshire, Liverpool, Bristol and

Sunderland, with miscellaneous Pratt and lustrewares, toby jugs, delft and a single slipware charger – owed much to the writings of Arthur Church, and may be seen as a model for many future collections of English pottery, notably Burnap in the 1920s–1930s. Freeth continued to contribute interesting articles on the subject, mainly in the *Connoisseur*, until 1921. At exactly the same period Thomas Greg, a descendant of the owners of Styal Mill and a sometime barrister, solicitor and country gentleman, joined the race to accumulate the best collection of early English pottery. Even with considerable wealth, this proved a challenge. But long after his outstanding collection was offered to Manchester in 1904, Greg continued to track down rarities such as slipware of Toft type, until his death in 1920 when the gift was made final. The 1,000 objects were catalogued and published by Dr E. J. Sidebotham three years later with a preface by Herbert Read. In 1969 a popular booklet with a selection of 222 pieces was published under the title *The Incomparable Art*.

By this time, yet another Manchester collector, Charles Lomax (plate 122), had built up by far the best collection of English slipwares, eventually to be published in 1909 as *Quaint Old English Pottery* with a glowing preface by Solon. This book set out in a somewhat rambling way the known history of Tudor, Wrotham, Metropolitan, Staffordshire, Derbyshire and West Country slipware. Taking his cue from the earlier writings of Solon, Lomax attempted to excuse the obvious lack of sophistication shown by these pots: referring to potters of the seventeenth century, he said that

> men who produced this pottery, reared as they were in a hard school, and without the aid of chemical science, accomplished much, and considering they were catering for the peasant classes, from which they themselves were drawn, and considering the poverty and other hardships that oppressed them, a generous view should be taken in passing judgement upon their contributions to fictile art.

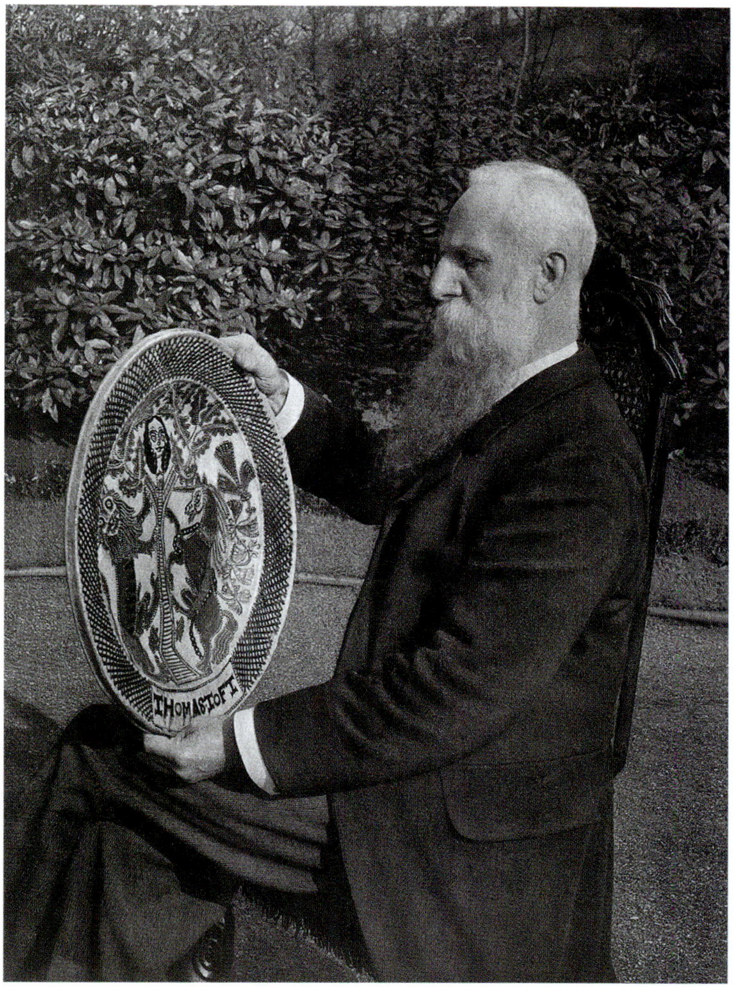

122
Charles Lomax holding one of his Toft dishes, from his *Quaint Old English Pottery* (1909).

It may be argued that the book carried less influence in the long term than the Lomax collection itself, which, further supplemented by delft and Staffordshire fine earthenwares and stonewares, was sold in 1937 and eagerly snapped up by a new breed of collector in America.

After 1900, with the new century, ceramic literature took a more serious turn, becoming both more specialized and more diverse. Museum catalogues, books dealing with the technicalities of pottery production and social conditions, and magazine articles, catered for collectors with widely differing interests and income. Significantly, also, the Staffordshire figure (of which the later 'flatbacks' were still in production) emerged as a separate field of study. That great champion of pottery Bernard Rackham joined the South Kensington Museum (shortly to become the V&A) in 1898, just in time to deal with the massive influx of pottery transferred after the closure of the Museum of Practical Geology at Jermyn Street. At the British Museum in 1903 R. L. Hobson produced his great *Catalogue of the Collection of English Pottery*, listing the entire museum holdings from medieval tiles to the beginning of the nineteenth century, the period that he described as 'one of stagnation and decadence, imitation taking the place of progress'. Excellent though the catalogue is, his dismissal of the first half of the nineteenth century as 'a period of mediocrity' is now difficult to condone, but it appears to have been a view shared with Arthur Church, who could write of Ironstone China in 1904 that 'Mason's potting was good, but the artistic value of his productions slender'. Such sentiments explain how Henry Willett had been able to acquire, with apparent ease, such huge numbers of commemorative jugs and figures of that despised period.

The year 1904 saw Church's answer to Hobson, with his Victoria and Albert Museum Art Handbook *English Earthenware*, and a serious introduction to the subject by the potter William Burton, *A History and Description of English Earthenware and Stoneware (to the beginning of the nineteenth century)*. Into this world of spiralling pottery collecting now came a new authoritative voice from the very centre of manufacture, that of Josiah C. Wedgwood, whose *History of the Wedgwood Family* of 1908 and *Staffordshire Pottery and its History* of about 1910 were works of admirable thoroughness and considerable scholarship. Concentrating on local history rather than art history, matters of the social, religious and trading conditions under which pottery making flourished in Staffordshire were fully discussed and analysed. A more intimate account of the whole family was given by Wedgwood's great-granddaughter Julia Wedgwood in *The Personal Life of Josiah Wedgwood the Potter* of 1915, published after her death. At this point also the Staffordshire figure rose to prominence, in particular those that had been made in moulds for series production and, unwittingly, for future collectors whose ambitions were to own 'one of everything'. Frank Falkner's *List of Staffordshire Figures* in 1903 was to be supplemented by a large number of figures in Major Cyril Earle's *The Earle Collection of Early Staffordshire Pottery* of 1915 (a collection that was sold by Messrs Charles Butters & Son at Stoke-on-Trent for high prices in 1919), and later Captain R. K. Price's *Astbury, Whieldon, and Ralph Wood Figures, and Toby Jugs* of 1922. The craze for figures became so heated that the introduction of fakes onto the market, though quite sudden, was largely ignored: Captain Price expressed no surprise at being offered 80 so-called Astbury-Whieldon figures in 1917, and even Glaisher was deceived into paying £500 for a spurious pew group in 1925. Effectively closing the

Edwardian period of pottery collecting, the Burlington Fine Arts Club's *Illustrated Catalogue of Early English Earthenware* of 1914 comprised a magnificent assemblage of pieces of all the main types, borrowed from all the great collections in private hands or in regional museums, with introductory essays by Hobson and Glaisher. A romantic and wistfully nostalgic view still prevailed, of a 'purely native product, a rustic craft, home grown and racy of the soil . . . quaint, homely and unsophisticated'. Not surprisingly, a considerable number of these examples of English folk art are now to be found in American collections.

At the end of the nineteenth century and the beginning of the twentieth, it was still possible to assemble an outstanding collection of British pottery on a limited budget. J. W. L. Glaisher, a noted Cambridge mathematician, began methodically to collect interesting and documentary delftware in the early 1880s, at a time when inscribed delftwares were plentiful and fairly inexpensive, branching out into slipware and industrial Staffordshire wares some years later, when his interest also turned to modern Art Pottery and Continental pottery and porcelain. His pioneering lecture on 'Delft-Ware' to the Society of Arts in 1897 was followed by three lectures to the Cambridge Antiquarian Society between 1899 and 1901 on Staffordshire pottery and Nottingham stoneware. At this point the earliest collections, formed during the latter part of the nineteenth century, began to appear on the market. In 1913 he selected and bought 19 pieces ('quite the pick of the collection') from the Hodgkin collection, then in the hands of a London dealer, Wilfred Harding. Already very well known, most of Dr Glaisher's collection came to the Fitzwilliam Museum in 1928, to be catalogued and published in two great volumes by Bernard Rackham in 1935.

The artistic and cultural advances that accompanied the upheavals of the First World War, such as the establishment of the Omega Workshops by the exponent of abstract art Roger Fry, and a new appreciation of simple or undecorated 'artist' pottery, had their effect on the attitude to the collecting of old English pottery in the 1920s. That great art critic and champion of modernism, Herbert Read, who joined the Victoria and Albert Museum under Bernard Rackham in the early 1920s, saw early Staffordshire pottery as untutored native art worthy of exposure to serious art criticism. Their collaboration soon resulted in *English Pottery: Its Development from Early Times to the End of the Eighteenth Century* of 1924, which made a point of isolating the unwelcome strands of foreign influence and which set out to 'treat the subject from a critical point of view, and to introduce standards which may be helpful, not only to collectors who turn to the past for aesthetic enjoyment, but also to designers and craftsmen whose aim it is to develop the English tradition in the future'. Read went further in *Staffordshire Pottery Figures* of 1929, claiming that the peasant potter unconsciously 'blunders into beauty', and finding parallels between Staffordshire figures and the work of the French primitive painter Henri 'Douanier' Rousseau. Truly, early English pottery had arrived in the art market. By firmly linking it in the public mind with both modern art and the burgeoning studio pottery movement, and by holding them all up on equal terms for comparison and serious criticism, these two seminal books established a view of pottery appreciation that still holds sway. By 1948 W. B. Honey could state in his foreword to Rackham's *Mediaeval Pottery* of 1948 that these simple pots 'may be claimed, quite simply, as the most beautiful pottery ever made in England'.

Simultaneously the fashion for more general pottery collecting reached a wider public through books such as G. Wooliscroft Rhead's *The Earthenware Collector* of 1920 and the versatile J. F. Blacker's *ABC* series. Specialist areas were more extensively but amateurishly covered by Charles F. C. Luxmoore's *English Saltglazed Earthenware* of 1924 and Major R. G. Mundy's *English Delft Pottery* of 1928. The latter work, while illustrating a very fine collection, was laced with spurious attributions to individual painters.

Towards the end of the 1920s both the collecting drive and the spate of ceramic books ran out of energy, happily coinciding with the founding in 1928

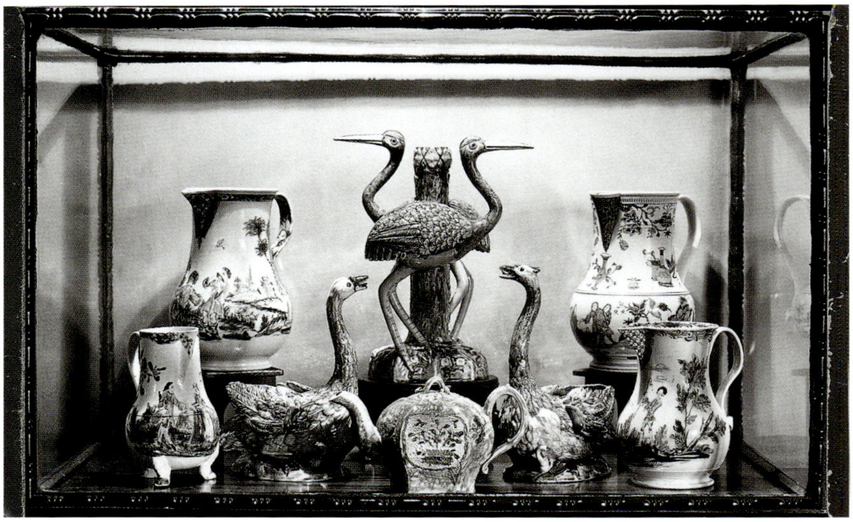

123
Wallace Elliott's massed display of salt-glaze, photographed sometime in the early 20th century.
From the Wallace Elliott scrapbooks, V&A, library of Ceramics and Glass Collection.

of the English Porcelain Circle, which in 1932 admitted English pottery and restyled itself the English Ceramic Circle. From this point, it was possible for museum curators, amateur collectors and researchers to publish original research in the Circle's *Transactions*, the list of early authors including W. B. Honey on stoneware and on the Elers in 1934, Bernard Rackham on slipware in 1935, Robert Hall Warren on delftware, F. H. Garner on delftware and on the seventeenth-century potters John Dwight and Rous & Cullen in 1937, Rackham on early Tudor pottery, John Drinkwater on brown salt-glaze, Mrs Esdaile on John Dwight, and Rackham on the 'Virtues of English Pottery' in 1939. Such illustrious authors helped to raise the prestige of pottery to a level where pottery and porcelain became linked in the public mind as equals. Bernard Rackham at the V&A made a few acquisitions, mainly from bequests such as that of Wallace Elliott in 1938 (plate 123), which included slipware chargers and a Dwight 'mouse-coloured' bottle with white sprigs; but his interests in the 1930s seem to have been turning more towards stained glass and maiolica, while the cataloguing of the Glaisher Collection in the years 1928–35 must have left him little time. In any case, the 1920s and '30s were a period when the energies of the Ceramics

Department were being channelled into building up an unparalleled collection of English glass, notably from the Rees-Price Collection of 1925 and the Buckley and Harding collections of 1936.

For museum curators and the collecting public alike, widening scholarship seemed not to increase pottery collecting so much as to provide a substitute for it. And if a discernible hesitancy among this second generation of collectors was caused partly by the uncertain financial climate of the 1930s, there was also an unprecedented rise in prices, the root causes of which lay in the scholarly ceramic literature of the time. In terms of collecting, greater scholarship meant greater discrimination. For the writings of Bernard Rackham and Herbert Read had successfully argued that early English pottery was Art, and more especially Folk Art, with the consequence that, from the late 1920s, the whole genre was taken up with unstoppable energy and unlimited funds by the New World.

When, after the First World War, the booming oil, steel and munitions industries of America had produced some of the wealthiest individuals the world has seen, it was almost inevitable that some of this industrial money should be turned towards examining the country's idyllic and rustic past, attempting to recreate – and in many cases reinvent – the lost innocence of a vanished, uncommercialized America. At Williamsburg, William Rockefeller used surviving fragments and excavated remains of the old town to fulfil his personal vision of an authentic eighteenth-century American town. Excavations showed what artefacts had been in use, and money did the rest. England was combed for slipware, delftware and Staffordshire tablewares. Absurdly, a reference to the Governor's palace having Chelsea figures led to the purchase of a massive collection of these luxury objects, since published as a book. Just as the South Kensington Museum had acquired in the nineteenth century huge numbers of foreign luxury goods of types that would never originally have been imported, so America began to fill with the finest English wares designed specifically for the more discriminating home market.

Almost on a whim, Frank and Harriet Burnap of Kansas began to acquire pottery on their antique-hunting trips to England in the late 1920s. A whim became an obsession, and the obsession resulted in a superb collection, spanning pottery of the medieval period to about 1820, the date that Frank Burnap considered the end of manufacture by hand. The massive collection was presented to the Nelson-Atkins Gallery of Art in Kansas City in 1941, and constantly increased by Frank Burnap until his death in 1957. The catalogue of 1953 was revised and updated by Ross E. Taggart in 1967 to include a number of major pieces, particularly delftware, added in the 1950s. It also included an appendix of collection labels that reveal numerous purchases from the Lord Revelstoke (Cecil Baring) sale of 1934, the Lomax sale of 1937 and many others. His decision to give it to Kansas – well away from New England and the areas of early settlement – was influenced both by loyalty to his home town and by his friendship with the then director, Paul Gardner.

Although Burnap started collecting late, about the time of Glaisher's death in 1927 he nonetheless managed to assemble a collection that remains one of the most comprehensive in America. Nor was he alone in siphoning off early pottery from England, for apart from Rockefeller at Williamsburg, other wealthy American industrialists were frenetically engaged in recreating a kind of utopian vision of Olde England. At about the time that Burnap became enthused by English pottery, the Du Pont family at Delaware also began to convert their huge mansion Winterthur into a showcase for displaying early American room-settings. Wealth generated by manufacturing explosives for the two world wars of the twentieth century was lavishly applied to the furnishing of some 75 rooms with seventeenth- and eighteenth-century artefacts, together with large reserve collections.

A pivotal role in supplying America with the English pottery they lacked was played by the Tilley family, whose rather shabby shop just off Sloane Square

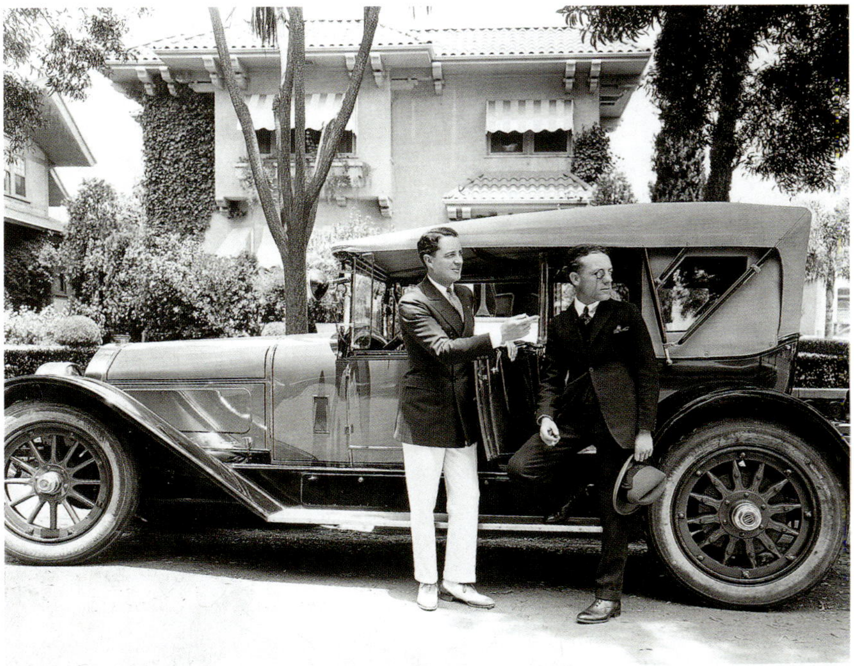

124
The London dealer Frank Tilley poses with his wealthy client, probably Rockefeller, and his elegant and expensive Locomobile Sportif 48 of 1927. Like many of its clients, the Locomobile company failed to survive the financial crash of 1929.
From Tilley family photographs in the library of the V&A Ceramics and Glass Collection.

in London masked a major trade in English pottery and porcelain. As a collector with an enquiring mind and a dealer with a sharp eye for boosting his trade, from the 1930s Frank Tilley contributed a steady stream of worthwhile articles to *Connoisseur* and *Apollo* in Britain, and to *Antique Collector* in America, spanning nearly 40 years. He was also chosen to appraise the unknown Kidd Collection at Sherbourne, Warwickshire, when it was acquired by Williamsburg in 1964. The collection, which had been formed from the early years of the century, won approval from Tilley as excluding wares made after the beginning of the nineteenth century, when, as he said, 'commercialism and decadence joined hands'. Some idea of his own high-flying commercialism and (to modern eyes) decadence may be gleaned from family photographs (plate 124), and a trunk full of decaying paperwork, deposited in the library of the Ceramics Department and now part of the V&A Archives.

After the Second World War, the threads of pottery research were picked up and new collections begun, mostly on a tight budget and very narrow in scope. These were supported by the equally specialized publications in the 1940s and '50s that owed much to research encouraged by the English Ceramic Circle. Garner's paper of 1946 on 'London Pottery Sites', which came at a time when much of London south of the river was about to be rebuilt after the ravages of the Blitz, was followed in 1948 by the first informed monograph on the subject, his *English Delftware*. By this time the Faber & Faber Monograph Series, to be edited successively by W. B. Honey, Arthur Lane, Sir Harry Garner and Robert Charleston, also included Rackham's *Mediaeval Pottery* and Honey's *Wedgwood Ware*, followed in 1951 by Rackham's *Early Staffordshire Pottery*, Donald Towner's *English Cream-Coloured Earthenware* in 1957, Reginald Haggar and Elizabeth Haggar's *Adams's Mason Porcelain and Ironstone, 1796–1853* of 1977 and Towner's revised and retitled *Creamware* of 1978. The last of these pottery monographs, which covered hitherto neglected subjects, of necessity contained much new research and were expensive: Williams-Wood's *English Transfer-Printed Pottery & Porcelain* of 1981, Oswald, Hughes and Hildyard's *English Brown Stoneware* of 1982, and Cox and Cox's *Rockingham Pottery & Porcelain, 1745–1842* of 1983. By the time the last monograph appeared, Adams and Redstone's revised *Bow Porcelain* of 1991, the price for the series had risen from the original one guinea (£1.05) in the 1940s to £85. Informative, elegant, compact and well-illustrated though these monographs were, continuance of the series was deemed not to be a commercial proposition.

Following exactly the same format as the Faber series, but under the editorship of Geoffrey Godden, Barrie & Jenkins launched an excellent series of *Illustrated Guides*. Alan Smith's *Liverpool Herculaneum Pottery* of 1970 was joined the following year by D. G. Rice's *Rockingham Pottery & Porcelain*, Godden's *Mason's Patent Ironstone China* and Arnold Mountford's *Staffordshire Salt-Glazed Stoneware*. Geoffrey Godden's energetic publishing machine was soon producing standard reference works at regular intervals, covering a wide range of ceramic areas. Attempts to put the whole of British pottery into context, however, were limited to a few works such as Bevis Hillier's contribution to Weidenfeld & Nicolson's Social History of the Decorative Arts series, *English Pottery and Porcelain* of 1968, followed by Griselda Lewis's *A Collector's History of English Pottery* and Geoffrey Wills's *English Pottery and Porcelain* of 1969, and Geoffrey Godden's *British Pottery* of 1974. Such books were, of course, backed up by regular articles by a variety of authors in *Apollo*, *Antique Dealer & Collectors' Guide*, and the five issues of the short-lived magazine *Ceramics* of 1985–6.

Inevitably, as research proliferated, so ceramic literature became yet more focused. Branches of the subject developed their own champions and their own literature – Garner, Ray, Lipski, Britton and Archer on delftware, Cooper and Grigsby on slipware, Price and Barker on red stoneware, Haggar, Balston, Pugh, Oliver and Halfpenny on Staffordshire figures, Little, Coysh, Henrywood, Drakard and Copeland on blue-printed earthenware, Bimson, Horne, Oswald, Hughes and Hildyard on brown stoneware, and many others. As before, prominent dealers such as Jonathan Horne, to whose entrepreneurial skills we owe the astonishing escalation of the delftware and slipware market over the last 30 years, now publish specialist books, while the Antique Collectors Club publishes original manuscripts, as well as offering reprints of rare books at a modest price. The collector is also well served by the English Ceramic Circle, the Northern Ceramic Society founded in 1972, and specialist groups such as the Wedgwood Society and the Wedgwood International Seminar, both begun in 1956. After the founding of the Society for Post-Medieval Archaeology in 1967, the study of English pottery from the Tudor period onwards has made great strides, tempering those assumptions about pottery that has survived above ground with hard facts about ceramic production, distribution and consumption.

To the old-established collections in London, Cambridge, Manchester and Brighton, and at Williamsburg, Winterthur and Kansas, may now be added more recent collections in America. The Mellanay Delhom wing at the Mint Museum, Charlotte, Carolina, was opened in 1968; the Chipstone Foundation at Milwaukee is not only available to the public, but has entered the field of publishing on a grand scale with Ivor Noël Hume's *If These Pots Could Talk*, and the introduction of an annual volume of essays, *Ceramics in America*, while a catalogue by Leslie B. Grigsby of the Syd Levethan collection of early and rare delftware and slipware entitled *The Longridge Collection* was published in two superbly illustrated volumes in 2000. A second edition of the catalogue of Henry Weldon's great collection, by Peter Williams and Pat Halfpenny, includes a useful appendix on the group of fakes that had been identified and isolated from the earlier volume, *English Pottery, 1650–1800: The Henry H. Weldon Collection* by Leslie Grigsby. Often collections are too valuable to remain intact for longer than the lifespan of the owner, or the sated appetite of the owner decrees a move to another field of collecting; and when these famous collections come onto the market, sale price records are always broken. Unfortunately these sales – such as Lipski in the years 1981–3, Rous Lench in 1986 and Kassebaum in 1991 – while recirculating huge numbers of objects, have so focused the objects onto a small band of wealthy rival collectors that now museums are virtually excluded from the bidding. But well away from the pressures of the marketplace, archaeology constantly widens the field by bringing to light forgotten types of everyday pottery and by putting expensive types of surviving pottery in their contexts – not necessarily to their advantage. The humble makers of seventeenth-century slipware or delftware chargers would have been astonished to know that their products would eventually command prices of several hundred thousand pounds.

When considering the history of selling and collecting English pottery, much can be learned from a study of those tiny sticky labels so often found on the bottom of pots, comprehensive illustrated lists of which are to be found in Ross E. Taggart's revised catalogue of the Burnap Collection (1967) and Michael Archer's *Delftware* (1997). Like botanists gathering specimens, collectors lost no time in classifying and numbering their acquisitions, using a wide variety of labels – mostly printed but others originally blank, to be filled in by meticulous antiquaries with name and number using a fine mapping-pen. Where collectors were entitled to coats of arms, their crest might be used as a motif, thus perpetuating the old custom of marking ('putting their stamp on') possessions such as deed-boxes with red sealing wax and signet ring: some collectors were even able to chart their rise through the social ranks, such as the banker Cecil Baring, whose later labels show him ennobled as Lord Revelstoke. The more adventurous collectors had highly personal motifs designed to reflect their interests, such as the slipware charger with the signature 'Thomas Toft' around the rim altered to 'Lomax Collection'. Dealers often felt obliged to add 'Guaranteed Genuine' to their labels, an addition that in later years they might come to regret. Although a minor facet of the collecting world, it is clear that such labels appealed to those with antiquarian tastes: they also fuelled interest, bestowed individuality to inanimate objects, created provenance and reinforced claims to authenticity.

After America entered the race to collect English pottery around 1930, museums too often found themselves outbid. Since the V&A can no longer attempt major purchases without sponsorship, inevitably some areas of the collections continue to lack crucial pieces; for it is often the rarest objects that are the last to be found. Most rare, however, does not necessarily equate to most valuable, so that significant gaps may sometimes be filled at comparatively small expense or through unexpected gifts, such as the salt-glazed hawk from Mrs B. Simpson in 1976 and the wonderful Rococo salt-glazed sauce boat from Mrs Darlington in 1993. More recently, the great generosity of Julie and Robert Breckman has enabled the Museum to acquire Staffordshire figures of the first quality and greatest rarity. But a systematic approach to gap-filling must be adopted in order to keep pace with advances in ceramic knowledge, and to ensure that rare moments of solvency can be matched with sudden availability of rare objects. Thus the Staffordshire Pew Group was acquired in 1975, the Enoch Booth proto-creamware teapot in 1989, and in recent years, with the help of the V&A Friends, the equally rare experimental seventeenth-century Woolwich and Killigrew stoneware bottles, and the Grand Tartar teapot. There is some prospect of finding a combed slipware owl, but, with the notable exception of the magnificent charger depicting King Charles and his children acquired in 1998 from the Chequers Trust with generous help from the National Art-Collections Fund and Sir Harry Djanogly, the prospects for major purchases in the pottery field are not bright. Nevertheless, a glance through the Acquisition Registers of the Ceramics & Glass Department, which go back as far as 1844, demonstrates that the Collections, of which at least 50,000 objects are on permanent display, may claim to be the most comprehensive in the world. To these Collections and to their creators, this book is dedicated.

Materials and Techniques: An Illustrated Glossary

Agate The eighteenth-century name for a material introduced by Staffordshire potters in the 1740s, composed of coloured clays wedged together, cut and worked until the desired scale and complexity of the 'agate' pattern was achieved. Vessels were sometimes made by the press-moulding process so as not to distort the patterning: even globular lathe-turned teapots could be made from two moulded hemispheres of agate clay joined around the girth – on finely variegated wares, the seam is barely visible. Bands of agate clay, mainly white with simple markings, were sometimes inlaid into the red earthenwares produced during the second quarter of the eighteenth century. Coarser country pottery made with red and white clays could be thrown on the wheel, but always with a spiral effect.

Ball clay So-called because it was transported from the West Country, notably Dorset, in cubes roughly rolled into balls, weighing about half a hundredweight (that is, 56 lbs or about 25 kg) and designed to be handled easily by one man. Otherwise known as 'blue clay', its natural raw colour before firing white. This clay had been used by John Dwight of Fulham for his 'ffine white' stonewares, and later formed the basic ingredient, along with calcined flint, of the white stoneware made in vast quantities by Staffordshire potters after about 1715.

Basalt Developed by Josiah Wedgwood in 1768 as *Black Basaltes* or *black porcelaine*, in order to imitate Greek vases – then thought be Etruscan – to which he could add his patented polychrome 'encaustic' painting. Since the idea of black stoneware was not new, Wedgwood made no attempt to patent it; but he correctly identified the best moment to develop it, using as a colouring agent a slurry rich in iron oxide, known as Carr, which was extracted from local mines. Having good turning and casting properties, this adaptable material, generally known in the trade as Black Egyptian, was soon being mass-produced in Staffordshire and Yorkshire, effectively replacing the ubiquitous red teapot with a black one.

Bat A disc or lump of clay to be worked, for example, by being pressed over a plate-mould or into a hollow-ware mould. Traditionally, thin pieces were produced by being cut, like cheese, with a string or wire from a larger piece, but rolling and beating methods were also used.

Bianco sopra bianco Literally white-on-white, the term and technique borrowed from Italian maiolica, whereby a pure white tin-glaze was used to paint lace-like patterns onto a blue-tinted ground. In England, it is found mainly on the delftware of Bristol and London. The use of subtle painting in white porcelain slip was well known to Chinese potters.

Biscuit The first firing of raw clay vessels, before the application of glaze and decoration. The two-firing cycle was essential for making delftware, for which also absorbent calcareous clay was chosen in order to absorb and bond with the opaque tin-lead glaze. In Staffordshire, biscuit-firing was in use for red earthenwares by the early 1720s, and perhaps earlier. It was fundamental to the production of underglaze sponged oxide decoration, such as the popular tortoiseshell made from the 1740s.

Block-moulds (plates 125, 126) The positive master-mould from which subsequent plaster moulds were taken, almost always solid and made of salt-glazed stoneware, the thin glaze of which sealed the surface without obscuring the fine detail of the moulded design. Practically indestructible, a large number of these have survived, particularly those rescued by Enoch Wood in the early nineteenth century from the residue of blocks modelled by Aaron and Ralph Wood. The high value of these, as shown by surviving accounts, indicates that the acquisition of a working set of blocks represented a major investment for a pottery, but thereafter the various bodies and spouts could be mixed and matched in many different formats and used for any type of stoneware or earthenware, either press-moulded or slip-cast.

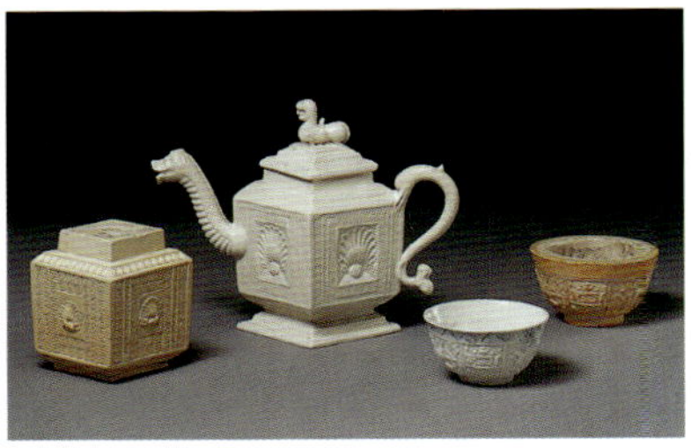

125. Square teapot block-mould with matching teapot, V&A: 2160–1901, Sch.II 113, and cup with matching block-mould, V&A: 2215–1901, 3098–1852.

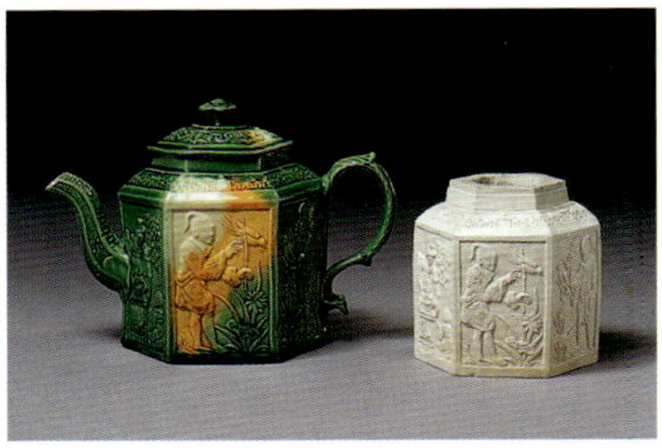

126. Moulded chinaman teapot and matching block, V&A: C.26–1946, Sch.II 123.

Bristol glaze A vaseline-coloured liquid stoneware glaze invented by Anthony Amatt at Bristol about 1835 and supplied by the mills of J. & J. White of Bristol to the stoneware potters of Lambeth before they developed their own, almost clear, glaze, which began to replace the traditional brown salt-glaze after about 1870. The formula consisted of zinc oxide, potash of lime, silica and alumina.

Caneware A buff-coloured stoneware body, made from local marl clay and flint, first produced by Josiah Wedgwood in 1770 but significantly improved over the next two decades by the addition of Cornish china stone. Its heyday coincided with the fashion for bamboo during the Regency period, *circa* 1800–20. A coarse version was used for so-called pastry ware about 1800. Other notable makers were Spode, Davenport, Elijah Mayer, Turner and the Herculaneum factory.

China clay With china stone, the other essential ingredient of true porcelain. Discovered by William Cookworthy sometime before 1768 and much used thereafter in clay bodies, especially after the expiry of Champion's patent in 1796. See **China stone** below.

China stone, or Growan Stone China clay and china stone were the two ingredients essential for making translucent hard-paste porcelain of Chinese type. Both ingredients, as granite in different stages of decomposition, were discovered together in Cornwall by William Cookworthy, who obtained a patent and established his porcelain factory at Plymouth in 1768. After moving the factory to Bristol, the patent passed to Richard Champion, who first renewed it and then sold it in 1781 to the partnership that comprised the New Hall factory at Shelton. Under the terms of the patent, fiercely contested by several Staffordshire potters led by Wedgwood, porcelain could not be made, but both ingredients could be added to pottery. Mining licences in Cornwall were obtained by several Staffordshire potters in the late eighteenth century, and after the patent expired in 1796, more use was made of Cornish ingredients, particularly for the new bone china, which was half true porcelain and half bone-ash, and for hybrid stoneware bodies, such as the felspathic 'Castleford' wares.

Chrome colours The properties of chromium sulphate were discovered and developed in order to produce a range of bright new colours from a single metallic oxide: sugar pink, apple green and bright yellow. It was in use on Staffordshire wares by about 1830, and later formed the basis of sponged decoration on 'rainbow spatter ware' and 'gaudy Dutch' made for export, and for the decoration of Staffordshire flatback figures.

Clays Although it was the discovery of beds of suitable throwing clay that first led to potteries being established – for example, the beds of white-firing clay on the Surrey-Hampshire borders – later on it was the fuel supply that became the deciding factor. For example, the Staffordshire Potteries owed their initial predominance entirely to the combination of cheap, easily accessible coal and refractory clays for kiln-building, which constituted the heaviest materials in pottery-making, while after about 1720 the potters became entirely dependent on imported clay and flint for making their finewares.

For delftware, a calcareous open-bodied clay was required, for which Norfolk clays were found so ideal that they were regularly exported to Holland. The high-firing clays needed for stoneware were obtained by John Dwight from Poole in Dorset, also the main source used for Staffordshire white stoneware from around 1720. Since stoneware clays were often found together with seams of coal, this led to the huge expansion of the brown stoneware industries of Nottingham and especially Derbyshire. When china clay and china stone were discovered in Devon, and leases on quarries obtained by Staffordshire potters in the late eighteenth century, these ingredients were increasingly added to pottery and stoneware bodies to produce various highly refined wares, often porcellanous and semi-translucent.

The preparation of clay was a long process. First it was reduced to slip by adding water and mixing, then it was sieved to remove impurities and poured into tanks for the water to be evaporated – either by the sun or, with industrialized factories, by being boiled for 12 hours. The clay was cut into lumps and beaten, then stored for as long as possible before being wedged on the bench to remove any trapped air, when it was finally ready to be passed to the potter for throwing or moulding.

Cobalt The essential blue used by the Chinese for their porcelain, and imported into England from Saxony, first for dyeing and then for delftware. By the late eighteenth century, when it was required in large quantities for blue and white porcelain as well as transfer-printed Pearlware, it was discovered both in Scotland and in Cornwall. A furnace for refining cobalt was established in the Staffordshire Potteries by Roger Kinnaston around 1772. An impure form, zaffre, was used for scratch-blue, and for the dip that produced Littler's Blue.

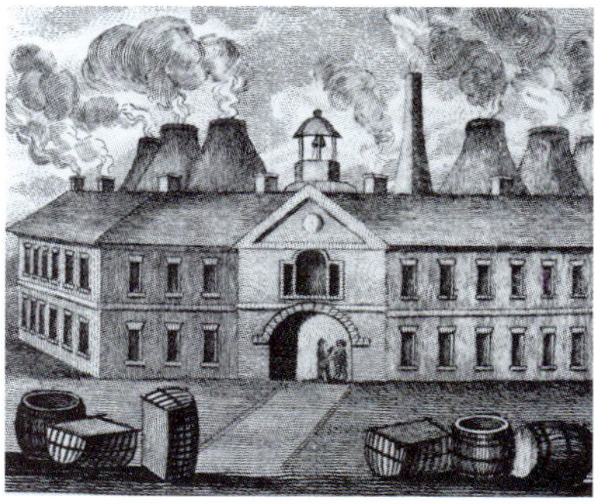

127. Yard of Enoch Wood's factory about 1830, showing pottery being packed into crates, observed by well-dressed customers.

Crate (plate 127) The crate was the basic container for transporting pottery and porcelain from the factory to anywhere in the world. Made of broad interwoven strips of willow, and packed with straw, these were considerably bigger than a tea chest, but carefully designed to be handled by one man, carried on a horse, and ultimately stacked on canal boat or sailing ship. They always bore numbers and letters for identification by sender and recipient, but many failed to arrive and breakage was common. The larger factories would have employed crate-makers on the premises; and by the mid-nineteenth century the stoneware factories of Derbyshire are recorded as growing their own pollarded willow for the purpose.

Enamels and enamelling Simeon Shaw stated that the technique of enamelling was introduced by Dutchmen to the factory of the Warburtons in Hot Lane, Cobridge, around 1740, a theory that it has never been possible to prove or disprove. It is nevertheless clear that the technique was available in England at this period, notably in the first porcelain factories at Chelsea and Bow, and certain that it was being practised in Holland. But it must have been known to English goldsmiths and silversmiths, not to mention clockmakers. Although certain factories such as Warburtons had their own decorating shops, which catered for the needs of neighbouring potteries, in general it was very much a specialist trade, with freelance enamellers migrating between factories and working on glass, porcelain or stoneware. It may be supposed that the standard enamelled patterns found on salt-glaze were executed at the factory, while the rarer and wilder Chinoiseries were added by talented artists, some of whom appear to be linked to Liverpool.

With the perfection of creamware, a new market opened up. At first Josiah Wedgwood sent his plain wares to Robinson & Rhodes of Leeds, where they were enamelled and sold – a cumbersome but successful arrangement that lasted from 1760 to 1766. But the need to enamel crests and arms onto dinner services for the London market, and especially the major task of painting the Frog Service for the Empress Catherine of Russia, led him to recruit David Rhodes to run his new decorating shop at Chelsea in 1768. Many freelance decorators in London, Bristol and elsewhere continued to advertise their services during this period, operating a muffle kiln with which they could also effect repairs to broken china by fusing the broken edges. By the early nineteenth century, some of these decorators were embellishing both pottery and porcelain with elaborate flower-painting and signing their work.

Enamels were prepared and stocked by specialist dealers. 'Cakes' of coloured glass could be bought and ground up as required, but a wide range of loose enamel powder was available, sold by the ounce. For example, in 1766 Mr Juniper, an apothecary in Macclesfield Street, Soho, advertised 'Fine dark yellow, fine pale yellow, Scarlet Purple, fine dark ditto, dark red, light Rose,, dark Rose, dark blue, light ditto, black, brown, light Rose Purple, black for Dial Plates', and in 1769 'The fine Indian Rose Colour prepared for Use, adapted to suit almost any Glaze' was available from Mr Spicer of Fish Street Hill at 30 shillings an ounce – reflecting its derivation from gold. Since these enamels did not necessarily fuse at the same temperature, several firings were generally required: no doubt this was responsible for the style of early decoration on salt-glaze, with its separate blobs of colour. The gilding used in England had the lowest firing temperature and was therefore applied last.

Engobe Used to describe the thin layer of slip, containing calcined flint, into which the first Staffordshire white salt-glazed stonewares were dipped before firing. When the stoneware body itself was strengthened and whitened during the 1720s, the practice of dipping continued to be used for the cheaper and coarser wares.

Fettle, fettling The essential process of removing mould-marks and tidying up the leather-hard pot before glazing and firing, using a knife, scraper or burnishing tool or even the traditional 'cow's lip'. Prominent mould seams on a finished pot, however, should not be taken to indicate a small factory or lax quality-control.

Firing The firing of clay vessels could vary between about 900 and 1,350 °C, that is, between soft delftware and stoneware or porcelain. Depending on the firing conditions – notably *oxidizing*, when the flues were open to draw in fresh air, or *reducing*, when the flues were closed and the kiln starved of oxygen – different effects could be achieved. Until the late eighteenth century, the control of the firing was a highly specialized job that entailed removing a bung and inspecting the kiln through a spy-hole. The spoiling of a whole kiln, though not uncommon, represented a great financial loss to the pottery. Science was eventually applied to the problem: by 1786 Josiah Wedgwood was selling his newly invented Pyrometer as a boxed set with pellets of different composition, which, during the firing, could be extracted and their shrinkage accurately measured to indicate the temperature of the kiln. At a later date, a similar principle was used for Buller's Rings. But a different system was devised by Hermann Seger (1839–1893), technical director at the Berlin porcelain factory, whose Seger Cones would melt and collapse at given temperatures.

Flatware Plates were made by placing and pressing a bat of clay over a convex, dampened plaster plate-mould mounted on a swivelling stand or wheel-head, trimming the edges with a knife and forming the foot with a profiling tool usually made of earthenware. After drying for 24 hours, the plate was removed from its mould and the edges smoothed by fettling.

The process was semi-mechanized by the development of the jigger, a simple hinged arm carrying the profiling tool, which could be swung over and lowered onto the rotating plate: by the 1840s steam power was applied to both the jigger and its hollow-ware equivalent, the jolley, with disastrous effects on labour relations.

Flint Flint had been used by glassmakers such as George Ravenscroft in the late seventeenth century for his 'fflint glass', and its use as an ingredient in stoneware was known to John Dwight of the Fulham Pottery. However, it was only used on a major scale when Staffordshire potters rediscovered it for their white stoneware in the period 1715–20. Thereafter it was in great demand, being shipped around the coast from the South-East to Liverpool and thence to Staffordshire. Processing consisted of calcining by building an enclosed 'clamp' of alternate layers of coal and flint that was allowed to burn for two days, the resultant softened nodules being wet-ground in rotating tubs containing loose angular crushing stones. The pulverized flint was then added to the clay slip, which was dried in heated tubs for about 12 hours, blunged (mixed mechanically) to remove the air, and then wedged before being worked by the potter.

Flow blue In order to satisfy the demand from the American market for dark blue transfer-printed wares, in the 1830s–1840s coarser prints were developed and the cobalt-blue was encouraged to run and stain the glaze during the firing by washing the saggars with lime or chloride of ammonia. The American taste for 'flow blue' remained strong throughout the nineteenth century, but was never popular in Britain.

Fuel Wood fuel, which burned cleanly for the updraft delftware kilns and which could give a superb gloss to lead-glaze with a last-minute 'flash firing' of green brushwood or furze, was universal until the early eighteenth century, when Staffordshire salt-glaze potters developed their typical bottle-kiln with up to eight fire-mouths – presumably inspired by glass-furnaces, which had been prohibited from using wood since 1615. The availability of cheap fuel was one of the main factors governing both the siting of potteries and the likelihood of their commercial success: it had a major effect on both the rise of the Staffordshire Potteries and the decline of the delftware industries of London, Bristol, Liverpool and elsewhere, which was hastened not just by the threat from Wedgwood's creamware but by the disadvantage of importing all their raw materials. Experimental use at Dublin and Glasgow of Henry Delamain's method for firing delftware with coal in the mid-eighteenth century came too late. Even the Fulham Pottery continued to use wood until at least 1780, and perhaps also the Nottingham stoneware industry, which used square up-draught kilns. But by the end of the eighteenth century coal was

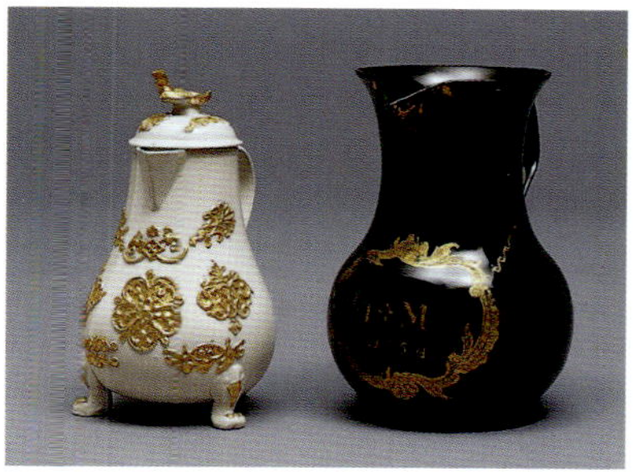

128 Gilding: white salt-glaze milk jug with 'cold' gilded sprigs and blackware jug with 'burnt in' gilding dated 1754. V&A Sch.II 73, Circ.357–1923.

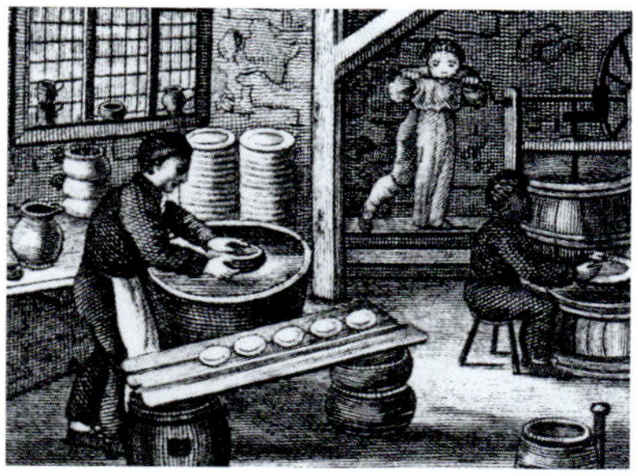

129. Glazing, from an illustration of a visit to the Enoch Wood factory around 1830.

universally used. An interesting comparison of the cost of raw materials is given by an account of the Cambrian Pottery, Swansea, in 1802: local coal cost 5s a ton, ball clay 12s, and flint 20s.

Gilding (Plate 128) Two kinds of gilding were used on pottery: first *cold* gilding where gold leaf was stuck to the pot with gum and heated lightly to harden the glue, and secondly fired or *burnt in* gilding, where the gold is permanently fused to the glaze. The earliest use in England was probably by the Elers Brothers, who were silversmiths by trade and who sometimes used cold gilding as a background for the slip-cast panels of Chinoiserie on their hexagonal teapots. With the development of vine-leaf sprigs in the 1740s, gold leaf was often affixed to the raised ornament of black wares, tortoiseshell wares, green-glazed wares and white salt-glaze. On the shiny surface of Littler's Blue and plain blackwares, some delicate painted Chinoiseries were attempted in the 1750s–1760s, inspired by Oriental lacquer. The technique was rarely applied to delftware, except occasionally on Scottish armorial wares.

Fired gilding was used on English porcelain from the 1740s but its preparation and application became a specialist trade. When Wedgwood needed to gild the green-and-gold tea service ordered by Queen Charlotte, he was forced to track down the only man who supplied the 'gold powder', a Mr Shenton, whose address was known to the London decorator James Giles. His own experiments solved the problems in a few months, however, and from 1768 his Chelsea decorating studios, under the management of the experienced David Rhodes from Leeds, could offer gilding as well as enamelling.

The technical difficulties of 'burning in' gold onto ceramics were twofold: first the conversion of solid gold into powder form, and secondly the identification of the chemical additives that would make it adhere to the glaze. J. G. Höroldt was the first to invent a satisfactory method at Meissen around 1723, dissolving gold in acid, drying it and adding ferrous sulphate and lead silicate. This method had the disadvantage of requiring a higher firing temperature than the enamel decoration. In France, a different system was developed, wasteful of gold but highly effective, whereby gold leaf was pulverized in a mortar, mixed with gum and applied to the glaze. Later honey was used during the grinding process ('honey gilding') and garlic used to provide the sulphur needed for adhesion. When hard-paste was introduced at Sèvres in the 1780s, the use of mercury was borrowed from makers of ormolu, to produce a hazardous amalgam that was cheaper but less durable. English porcelain makers combined the two French methods, dissolving the gold in acid but adding both ferrous sulphate and mercury. This would have produced the 'gold powder' that Wedgwood was seeking in 1765, and since it fired at a temperature below that required for enamels, it could be applied last, with the ability to hide any ragged enamel edges. It was not until 1827 that 'liquid gold' was developed by H. G. Kühn at the Meissen factory, a convenient, economical method that was widely adopted but which could produce rather anaemic results.

Glaze and glazing Lead-glaze in various forms was the dominant glaze for earthenware, either applied in dry form as powdered lead ore sprinkled onto the upper surface of combed slipware baking dishes, or mixed as a liquid into which delftwares and most Staffordshire-type wares were dipped by hand (plate 129). Glazers, assisted by boys, suffered early deaths from lead poisoning – often as young as 30. Although lead-glazed tablewares were not considered hazardous to the users, pickle jars were usually made of salt-glazed stoneware to eliminate the absorption of lead from the acidic contents. Experiments, such as the prize-winning leadless glaze recipe of Job Meigh in 1822, which was designed to resist the acids of jams and pickles, eventually overcame the problem. Salt-glazing, in which the rock salt, vaporized at the peak of the firing at around 1,200–1,400 °C, combined with the alumina and silica of the clay body to form a thin coating of glaze. This vitrified stoneware was thus doubly impervious to liquids.

Glost The trade name for glazing, as in the 'glost firing' that followed the 'biscuit firing'.

Handles, handling Always solid, but usually made as light and elegant as possible, handles required considerable skill to make and apply. Fully moulded handles on Staffordshire salt-glaze and red earthenwares were usually made in two-piece plaster moulds, although some brass versions survive at the Wedgwood factory. For mass production, ribbed handles could be made in a wooden 'dod box' by extruding the clay through a metal plate cut with the desired section, the resulting strip being cut up into suitable lengths ready for the handler. Alternatively, clay could simply be rolled by hand into tapering worms, or for fancy shapes the plain round-section clay extruded from a dod box could be cut into lengths and pressed into two-piece plaster moulds – up to 24 at a time according to an account in 1802.

Jasper ware A semi-porcelain, unglazed but with a sealed surface, perfected by Josiah Wedgwood at the end of 1774 after several years of trials, and generally acknowledged as his one original invention. The body was analysed by William Burton, who found that it contained 10 per cent flint, 59 per cent barium sulphate (the flux), 2 per cent barium carbonate, and 29 per cent silica and alumina (refractory clay). This basic material, with an impervious surface sheen, was initially white but could be coloured as required, either as a solid colour or, as later, by the more economical method of dipping in coloured slip. Versions were produced almost immediately by many other factories, notably John Turner, whose Jasper was a semi-porcelain that lacked the barytes and thereby infringed Richard Champion's hard-paste porcelain patent.

Kilns The design of kilns varied widely, from the simple square up-draught type illustrated by Piccolpasso to the archetypal 'bottle kiln' of the Staffordshire Potteries. Delftware needed only the square wood-fired kiln, with or without some chimney arrangement on top, around which workshops and drying rooms could be built to use the surplus heat. John Dwight's salt-glazed stoneware was also fired in square wood-fired kilns, but at a much higher temperature and necessitating special holes in the roof for throwing in the salt at the peak of the firing. But during the eighteenth century coal-firing became almost universal, and for this the bottle kiln was developed, no doubt inspired by the 'glass cone', which consisted of a conical brick 'hovel' acting as a chimney for the coal-fired furnace with its crucibles of glass serving the glass workers surrounding it, and built over large underground flues to provide the draft. But for pottery kilns, the hovel was smaller, protecting the oven or kiln and covering the fire-mouths, which were constantly stoked for many hours to achieve maximum temperature before being closed and allowed to cool. The method of salt-glazing is described fully in chapter Four.

Muffle kilns were used for low-temperature work, such as enamelling and gilding. The essential features were that the oven should be completely isolated from the smoke and flames of the fire, and that it should be controllable to accommodate the different firing temperatures of the various enamel colours. Some of these kilns were small enough to be set up in a domestic situation, and could be dismantled and moved.

Lathe, engine-turning lathe The use of lathes in pottery-making came with the development of finewares: that is, close-grained tough stoneware bodies that could be thinly turned in the leather-hard state and yet keep their shape in the firing and remain strong enough for practical use. Thus it was that the Elers Brothers, immigrant Dutch silversmiths, were the first to use them at Bradwell Wood for finishing their slip-cast red stonewares. By the early eighteenth century they were certainly in general use, the earliest mention being the will of the Staffordshire potter Aaron Shaw in 1714.

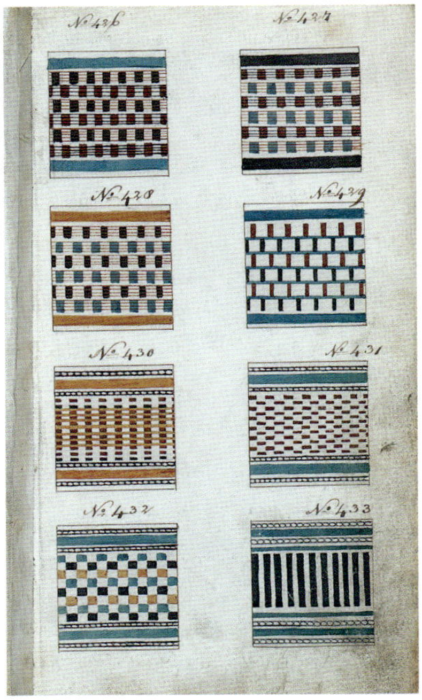

130. Page from Leeds Pottery Pattern Books 1–3, showing engine-turned decoration. Compare with plate 98. V&A: E.578–1941.

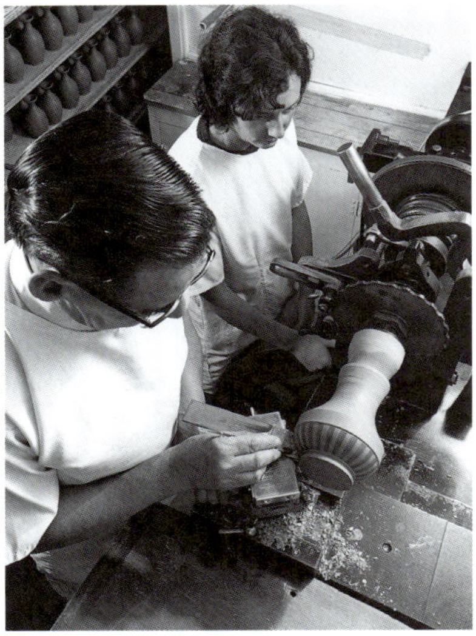

131. Wedgwood's engine lathe, as rebuilt and used today. Courtesy Trustees of the Wedgwood Museum.

The engine-turning lathe (plate 130), originally invented for use in decorating metal, ivory and hardwood, represented a highly sophisticated development, whereby the slowly revolving headstock was made to oscillate back and forth guided by the lobes of a 'rosette'. According to which type of rosette was fitted, a variety of diced, fluted or basketweave patterns could be produced, the decorative qualities of which could be greatly enhanced by cutting through a layer of coloured slip (plate 131). As with many technical advances, it was Josiah Wedgwood who pioneered their use by acquiring the first example from Matthew Boulton's Soho Works at Birmingham in 1763, after which their use spread throughout the potteries of Staffordshire and Yorkshire. Parts of Wedgwood's original machine appear to have been incorporated into a lathe still in use at Barlaston.

Lustre The process of depositing a microscopic layer of metal, painted onto a lead-glazed pot in liquid form, and fused in a low-temperature firing with a reducing atmosphere. Invented in the Middle East, it spread along with the tin-glazed earthenware technique to Moorish Spain and thence to Italy, where it was applied to maiolica by specialist workshops at Gubbio and Deruta. In England, it was rediscovered by John Hancock working at the Spode factory in 1805, first using platinum to give silver lustre and then using gold to produce pink on a white body or copper on red earthenware. See also under *Platinum*.

Lute, luting The process of attaching sprigged decoration, handles, spouts, etc., to a leather-hard pot, using clay slip to help adhesion. A sharp knife-blade (literally, a penknife) could pick up the delicate sprigs without leaving an ugly scar.

Mocha ware Invented in the 1790s, probably by accident, and much exploited for more than a century for utilitarian beer mugs and jugs. The technique consisted of dripping a special 'tea' composed of acidic tobacco juice, manganese and, by tradition, stale urine onto a surface freshly dipped in coloured alkaline clay slip. The reaction between the acid and alkali would spread the brown mixture into frond-like forms resembling the Mocha Stone from Arabia, which to a certain extent could be controlled by a skilled potter. The lathe-turned rims and feet were usually finished with simple trailed bands of slip.

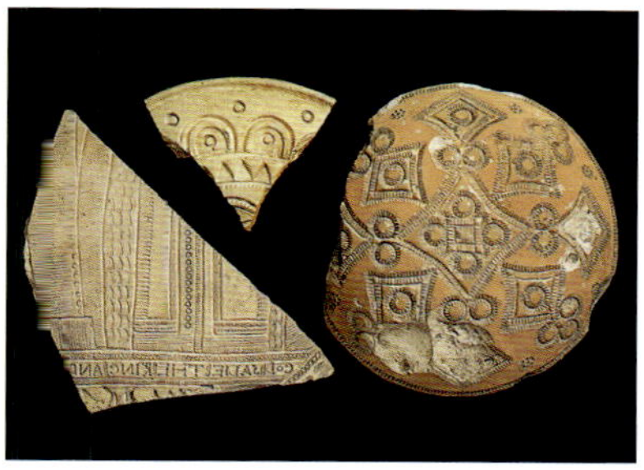

132. Slipware dish moulds, late 17th to early 18th century, the largest, V&A: 2298–1901, incised 'Thomas Wedgwood', V&A: 2298–1901, 5648–1901, 4774B–1901.

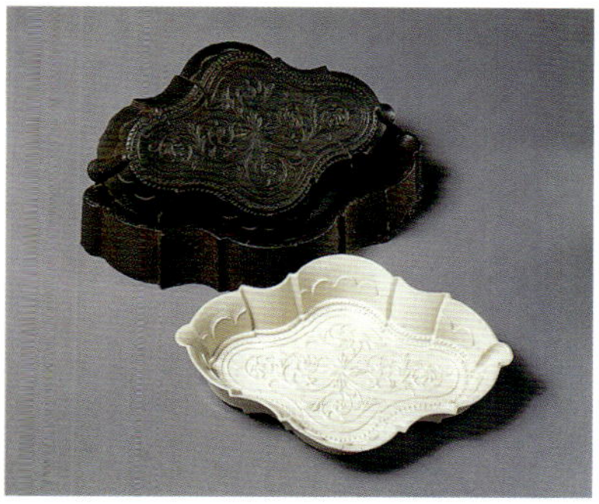

133. Brass and iron spoon tray mould and matching salt-glaze spoon tray. Length of mould 20.3 cm (8 in.). V&A: 2225–1901, 2224–1901.

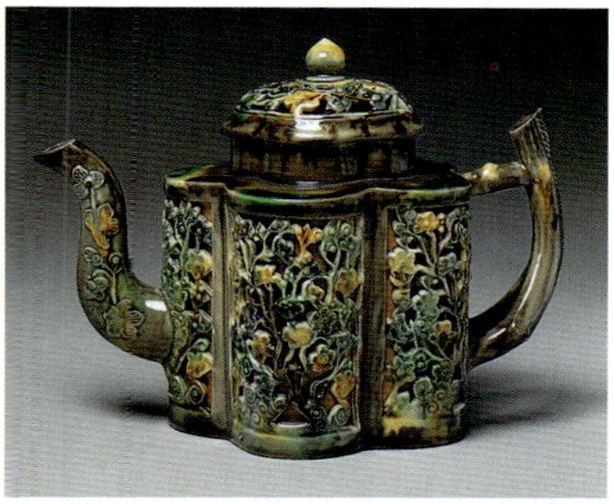

134. Reticulated Whieldon-type teapot of c.1750–6c. Height 14 cm (5½ in.). V&A: C.75–1948.

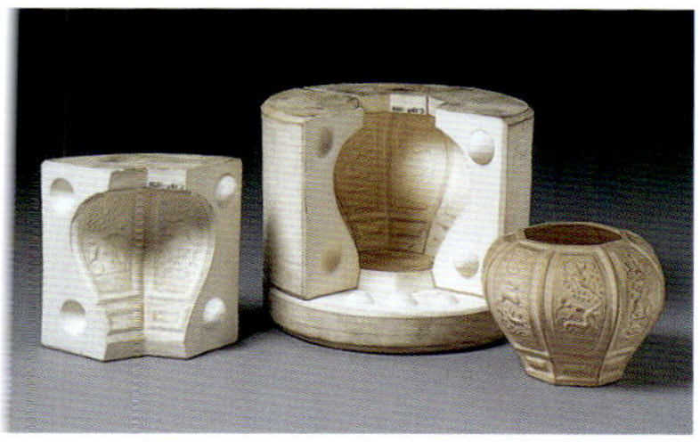

135. Recreated set of plaster moulds and slip-cast teapot. V&A: C.19–1928.

Moulding The two basic techniques, *press moulding* (plates 132, 133) and *slip-casting* (plate 135), were adopted by the Staffordshire potteries around 1740. Later, some degree of mechanization was introduced by using a jigger to profile the spinning backs of plates already on the mould, and a jolley for hollow ware, this consisting of a profile or rib that could be lowered and forced into a negative mould already lined with clay. The application of steam power to these basic machines was to cause great unrest towards the middle of the nineteenth century. See also *Block-mould, Plaster of Paris.*

Pearlware The successor to creamware, having a whitened body with a glaze stained with cobalt-blue. Initially known in Staffordshire as 'china glaze', this was a conscious attempt to compete with grey imported Chinese porcelain; but when Josiah Wedgwood was finally compelled to make his version of a material he actively disliked, his name 'Pearl White' was the one that prevailed. Pearlware formed the basis for shell-edge, for blue-painted wares and, above all, for underglaze-blue transfer-printed earthenwarers from the late 1780s onwards. The 'pearl ware' said by Simeon Shaw to have been made by Chetham & Woolley around 1800 is almost certainly their porcellanous stoneware body with blue dip and white sprigs.

Pierced decoration (plate 134) Designs could be cut freehand through a double-walled vessel ('reticulation'), as on Nottingham stonewares and some mid-eighteenth-century Staffordshire wares that closely imitated Chinese examples, or made with tiny punches (like pastry cutters), which removed lozenges, trefoils and other simple shapes to form larger patterns. On double-walled vessels, the waste pieces would simply fall through the open bottom. For flatwares, and open moulded vessels like chestnut baskets, the piercing became increasingly intricate during the last quarter of the eighteenth century, particularly at the potteries around Leeds.

Plaster of Paris Made from calcined gypsum, which is found in Cheshire and elsewhere, and used to take casts from a solid master-mould ('block-mould'), which then became the moulds for producing hollow-wares (plate 135). The plaster would rapidly absorb water from either the solid clay or the liquid clay slip, allowing the clay to shrink and detach itself from the mould; after drying out it could be used repeatedly until the plaster began to deteriorate. The discovery in Staffordshire around 1740 of the slip-casting technique enabled fancy hollow forms to be made, but until the invention of chemical deflocculents in the early twentieth century, the method was cumbersome and not widely used. Press-moulding, on the other hand, immediately revolutionized the mass production of hollow-wares.

Platinum Discovered in the late eighteenth century and thought to have been used first for 'silver' decoration by the Berlin porcelain factory. In England, its capability for producing 'silver' lustre was discovered by John Hancock working at the decorating shop of Messrs Daniel & Brown within the Spode factory in 1805. After a brief period as 'silver' decoration on Spode porcelain, it was almost immediately taken up by earthenware makers. Whole silver-shaped vessels of red earthenware, notably teawares, could be completely covered, or reserves could be introduced by masking with wax ('wax resist').

'Pratt Ware' A type of coarse moulded lead-glazed white earthenware introduced in the 1790s, decorated with a range of high-temperature underglaze colours, including cobalt-blue, copper-green, iron-orange and antimony-yellow – these having been used previously as the basis for polychrome delftware. The misleading collectors' term 'Pratt' arose solely because of a handful of marked pieces, but it was mass-produced also in Yorkshire at, for example, the Leeds Pottery and by Wedgwood & Co. of Ferrybridge.

Printing The application of printing to ceramics took place during the 1750s, combining the unconnected experimental work of three men: John Brooks in Birmingham with his patent applications of 1751, 1754 and 1755 for printing enamel boxes and china; John Sadler of Liverpool with his patent application for printing tin-glazed tiles in 1756; and Robert Hancock, who had perfected both overglaze and underglaze printing at the Worcester porcelain factory by 1757. Its use on creamware was quickly recognized by Josiah Wedgwood, who engaged the services of the partners John Sadler and Guy Green from 1761 to decorate glazed creamwares, which were sent to Liverpool in ever increasing numbers. About half

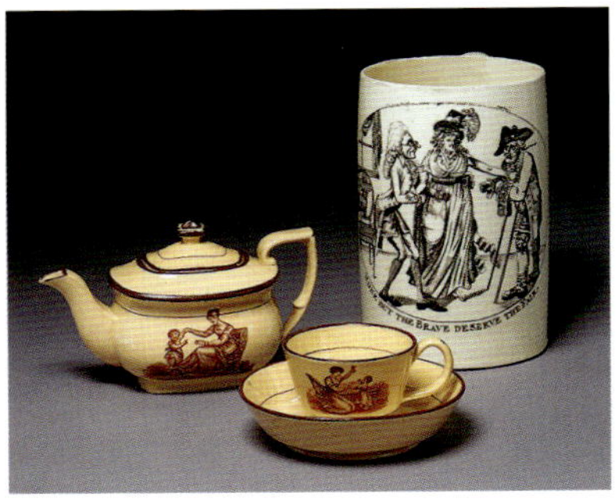

136. Overglaze printing: bat-printed drabware, and creamware mug, the print 'None but the Brave' signed *John Aynsley Lane End Staffordshire*. Max. height 15.5 cm (6⅛ in.). V&A, from a child's miniature tea service, C.85 to 92–1911 and C.88–1973.

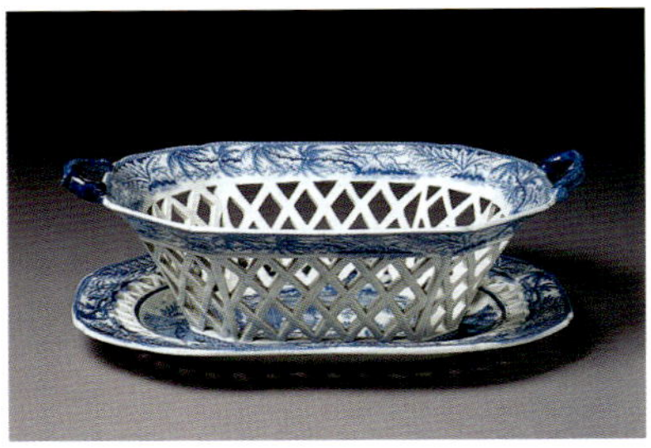

137. The designs of underglaze printing were effective even when interrupted by pierced surfaces, as on this finely potted Davenport basket and stand. Max. height with stand 9.6 cm (3¾ in.), length of stand 26.1 cm (10½ in.), length of basket 27.5 cm (11 in.). V&A: 3944–1853.

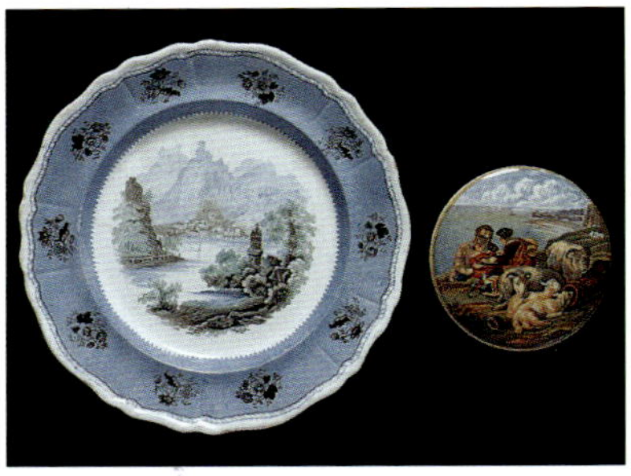

138. Colour printing: Davenport plate *c.*1845, F. & R. Pratt pot lid printed with 'Peace'. Diameter of plate 21.6 cm (8½ in.). V&A: C.415–1920, C.24–1977.

of these were returned, while half were retained by Sadler & Green for sale on their own account. Surprisingly, this mutually beneficial but cumbersome arrangement lasted until 1793, by which time many smaller factories had set up their own printing shops.

The various techniques for printing on pottery were adapted and modified to meet changing fashion and demand. For overglaze printing (plate 136), the basic method consisted of rubbing an engraved copper plate with oil and wiping off the surplus, taking an impression onto thin paper and transferring the oily print to the glazed earthenware surface, which was then dusted with finely ground pigment of the desired colour – usually black – and blown or shaken to remove an unwanted powder. A short time in the muffle kiln would soften the glaze, burn off the oil and leave the print firmly bonded to the surface. This 'pluck and dust' method could be varied by transferring the oily print onto a 'glue bat', a slab of flexible gelatine that could be laid on the bench while a globular pot was carefully rolled over it.

Neither of these methods could be used for underglaze printing (plate 137), for the powdered pigment would irreversibly contaminate the porous surface of the biscuit earthenware. Therefore, a simple improvement was made whereby the heated copper plate was charged with a mixture containing the cobalt-blue, which was transferred to thin paper and pressed onto the biscuit body before being softened with water and gently peeled away. The print was then hardened on in a muffle kiln to make it resistant to the glaze-dipping, and fired in the 'glost' kiln in the usual way. It was found that a simple subject, deeply engraved, gave the best results under glaze. This method, perfected at Worcester by 1757, was adopted in Staffordshire as late as the 1780s: according to Simeon Shaw, by Josiah Spode in 1784, on principles developed by Ralph Baddeley of Shelton.

A further method, *bat printing*, was used to reproduce the soft grey stippling made popular by engravers such as Bartolozzi at the end of the eighteenth century. It was found that the hand-held glue bat was effective in picking up and transferring the tiny punched dots on the oiled copper plate, so that it was taken up in the period 1800–20 by major porcelain manufacturers such as Spode, Minton and Mason, and occasionally used on earthenware for vignettes depicting children and motherhood after the popular engraver Adam Buck (plate 136).

By about 1800 engraving shops and specialist makers of transfer-paper had set up business in the Potteries: the shop of John Cutts, sometime proprietor of the Pinxton porcelain factory, was said later to have employed 40 persons, and many of his designs are included in a volume at the Victoria and Albert Museum containing more than 900 pen-and-ink designs typical of the period around 1830. According to the sale catalogue of William Turner's factory in 1829, a table service required ten copper plates to print all the various parts, while tea services needed between six and ten plates.

Printing in colours apart from blue was slow to appear (plate 138). The breakthrough was made by Jesse Austin, who had worked for Davenport in the 1820s–1830s, and was later to make famous the pot-lids of F. & R. Pratt of Fenton, in partnership with Alphonso Toft some time in the early 1840s. At this time Davenport was making tentative experiments by using a single plate inked with several colours, which produced an effect somewhat like a Japanese woodcut, but Austin's superior method involved the use of several plates, each engraved with separate parts of the whole design, and each inked with different colours. Crucially, each individual transfer print was carefully registered with the others by aligning dots concealed in the design.

Resist The technique of masking areas of a pot with wax, associated particularly with lustre. The protecting wax would burn away in the firing.

Saggar The drum-shaped protective casing in which pottery was fired, made of fireclay reinforced with ground sherds ('grog'). Making these was an important specialist job: a wide band of clay about an inch thick was wrapped around a wooden drum, the edges joined, and the resulting cylinder of clay affixed to a matching base beaten flat by the 'saggar-maker's bottom knocker' – the butt of many a joke. Designed to be reused as many times as possible, in practice the rough handling, accidents in the kiln and glaze encrustation called for constant replacement, and the stocks held by biggish potteries were considerable: the sale of William Turner's factory in 1829 included 800 Biscuit Saggars and 800 Glazed Saggars.

Designed to be stacked in the kiln in columns, the size and type of saggars

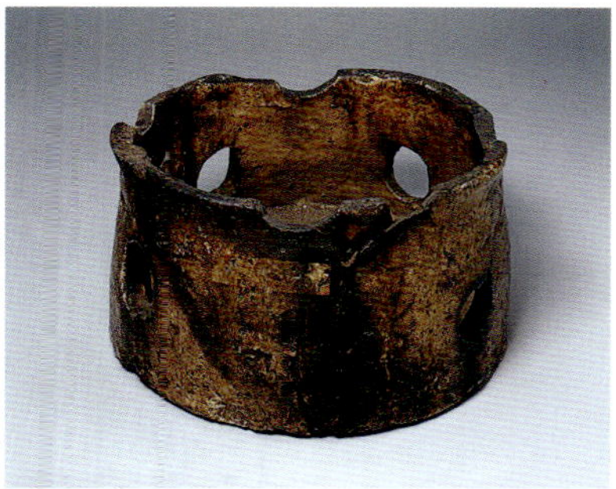

139. Salt-glaze saggar with slot ventilation holes, of a type used throughout the 18th century. Diameter 40 cm (15¾ in.). V&A: 2157–1901.

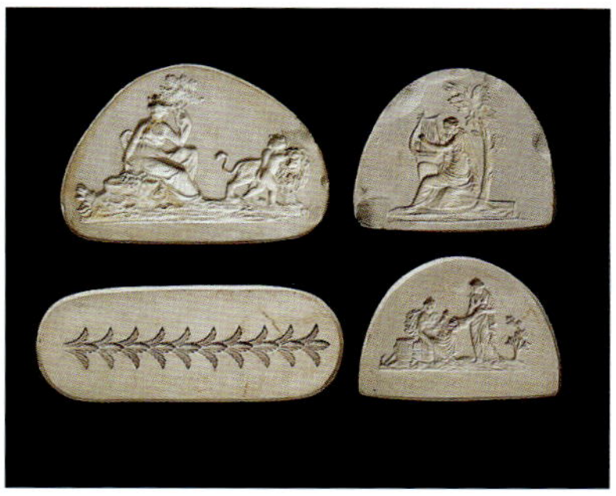

140. Wood & Caldwell sprig moulds of *c.*1815, one marked, one with mark erased, probably by subsequent owners. V&A: C.158–1937, C.79, 80, 81–1932.

varied widely: for delftware, triangular holes were punched radially around the saggar to hold the three triangular pegs on which each plate rested in both biscuit and glaze ('glost') firing. For salt-glaze stoneware, oval ventilation slots were cut to allow the vapour glaze to penetrate (plate 139), and plates were piled up and separated with small clay 'bobs'. For individual finewares, such as John Dwight's experimental mugs, small saggars were made with a slot to accommodate the projecting handle. Various kiln supports were used, from 'bobs' to several types of triangular 'stilts', while sherds or grit were used to prevent pots sticking to the bottom.

Salt Could be extracted by evaporation from sea water, but was also mined from earliest times at Droitwich, Middlewich and Northwich. Large amounts were required for the salt-glazing process: Angerstein records that in the years 1753–5 an average salt-glaze firing required 6 bushels, or 336 lb – that is, 3 cwt sacks or about 155 kilograms.

Scratch blue Inspired by Westerwald salt-glazed stoneware, where an incised outline was used to prevent cobalt-blue painting from running, the English version used the incised line itself to hold the cobalt and create a design or inscription. Zaffre (impure cobalt) as dry powder or liquid slip was rubbed into the scratched or combed lines and scraped clean. Iron-brown was occasionally used.

Sgraffito An Italianate (but not strictly Italian) term applied by art historians to the technique of drawing a design with a sharp point through a layer of dried (usually white) slip over a red clay body. The technique was especially developed by slipware makers in the West Country and Wales, where pots were customarily dipped in white slip to disguise the coarse local red clay. On a much smaller scale, delftware decorators sometimes scratched fine details through solid areas of cobalt-blue painting.

Slip, slipware Clay reduced to liquid form, either during its preparation and purification, for casting in plaster of Paris moulds, or for decoration by dipping or trailing. Trailed slipwares imported from North Holland provided the inspiration for a type of ware that was to flourish for three centuries, first perhaps at the beginning of the seventeenth century in an isolated pocket at Wrotham, but shortly after on a commercial basis at Harlow in Essex. By the mid-seventeenth century press-moulded slipware dishes were being produced in Staffordshire, where later the slip-trailed technique was developed into an art form. Combed slipware baking dishes were produced by country potteries until at least the mid-nineteenth century.

Smear glaze A very light surface sheen that became popular at the end of the eighteenth century, and which would help to keep the clay body clean. From the 1830s onwards it was used on moulded jugs. The method involved washing the interior of the saggars with either salt solution or creamware lead-glaze, which would deposit a thin vapour glaze on the clay body.

Sponge and spongeware As part of the potters' repertoire of tools made from natural materials such as a cow's lip or pieces of carved wood, the sponge played an essential part in producing 'tortoise-shell ware', where the iron and manganese oxides were sponged and dabbed onto the biscuit earthenware before glazing. Sponged cobalt-blue decoration is also often found on delftware, especially for rendering trees and bushes. From the 1840s, tiny sponges were cut into simple printing-stamps used to make polychrome patterns on 'spongeware', which formed an important export market for many potteries in Staffordshire, the North East and Scotland.

Spouts Spouts, like handles, were always applied separately, and necessarily after the process of lathe-turning. Many salt-glazed block-moulds of the mid-eighteenth century survive, these having been used to make the two-piece plaster moulds for press-moulding. Typically, each side of the mould would be lined with thinly rolled clay, a string with small wet sponge attached would be laid along it, and the two halves closed up. Then the 'pull-through' would be pulled through to seal the interior seams, and the ends trimmed with a knife.

Sprigging (plate 140) Moulded relief decoration applied to a pot before firing when it was 'leather hard'. The sprigs were either pressed into moulds of plaster or fired clay ('pitcher') and teased out of the mould by rubbing with a spatula to be picked up on the point of a small knife and accurately placed on the pot, or small sprigs could be pressed into curved brass moulds, wetted with slip and pressed onto the pot, in the manner of sealing wax and leaving behind a visible mould-mark. A set of John Dwight's brass sprig-moulds of about 1690 with Chinoiserie subjects, of a type remarkably similar to those used by the Elers brothers, was found at the Fulham Pottery and is now at the British Museum. A large number of 'pitcher moulds', mainly of Neo-classical subjects, were acquired from the bankruptcy sale of the Turners in 1805–6 and are now at the Spode Museum, Stoke-on-Trent.

Stencilling Copied from the Chinese technique of blowing fine powdered pigment on porcelain to produce 'powder blue', and requiring a paper stencil to mask off the areas intended to remain white (the 'reserves'), the earliest use of stencilling on British pottery seems to be the Enoch Booth creamware teapot of the early 1740s in the V&A: on this there remain the outlines of string used to tie the stencils in place. Shortly after this, it

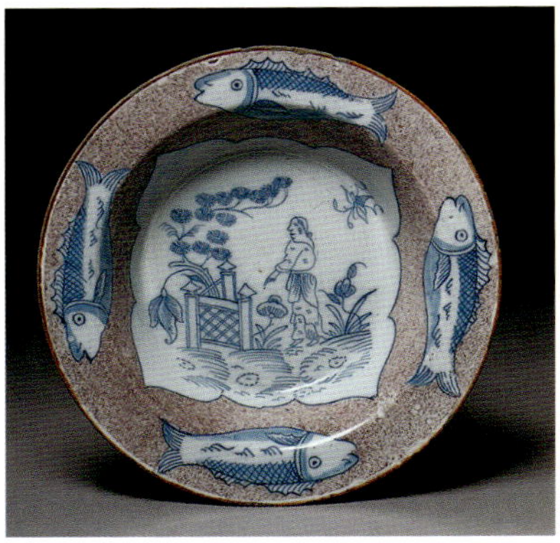

141. Stencilling, as copied from Chinese 'powder blue' porcelain: London delftware soup plate of *c.*1745–50. Diameter 22 cm (8⅝ in.). V&A: C.75–1965

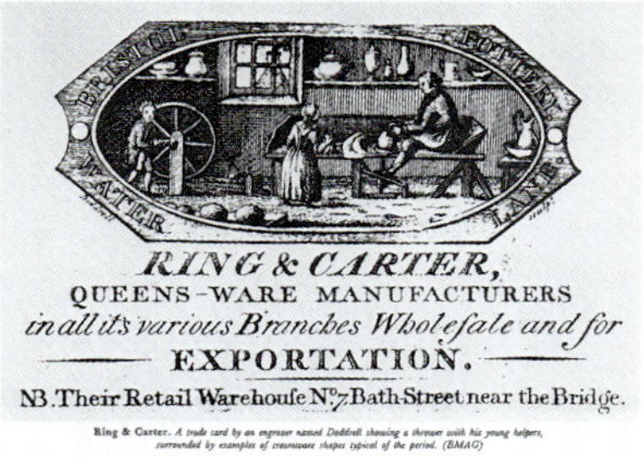

142. Trade card of Ring & Carter of Bristol, showing children turning the wheel.

was adopted by delftware makers (plate 141), especially for tiles, and was much used to decorate Bow porcelain in the years around 1760, with fan-shaped reserve panels. A much simpler method was developed using painted wax as a masking medium ('wax resist'), extensively employed with silver (platinum) lustre in the early nineteenth century.

Tin, Tin-glaze Tin was supplied to both England and much of Europe by the Cornish tin mines, which never recovered from the introduction of creamware in the 1760s: for the new material rapidly began to replace not only delftware but pewter as well. Tin-glaze – in reality, a lead-glaze rendered opaque by the addition of tin oxide – was invented in Mesopotamia and was spread by migrating potters successively to Moorish Spain, Italy, France, Holland and England. The absorbent biscuit-fired body was dipped in the (highly poisonous) glaze, and when dry this powdery surface could be painted deftly in cobalt-blue to produce the typical 'in-glaze' blue and white decoration widely used in Europe from about 1600 to copy imported Chinese porcelain. Overglaze *petit feu* polychrome decoration, developed to a high standard in France and Germany, was practised to a small extent at Liverpool. The great popularity of Wedgwood's perfected creamware led to the demise of the British delftware industry in the late eighteenth century, and had severe repercussions in France and elsewhere in Europe. Known as *maiolica* in Italy, *faience* in France, *fayence* in Germany, and in England, from the early eighteenth century, as *delftware*.

Tortoiseshell Decoration imitating tortoiseshell, applied as iron and manganese oxides sponged onto the biscuit earthenware body before glazing and re-firing. Associated particularly with the factory of Thomas Whieldon from the late 1740s, but made by all the major potteries of the period until at least the end of the century, by which time it may have been chiefly aimed at export to continental Europe: in 1796 the Swinton Pottery still listed *Tortoise Shell* as one of their products. Complete tea and dinner services were made, the sprigs on teawares often embellished with unfired gilding. They were affordable by many. For example, in 1753 tortoiseshell plates were advertised at 6s per dozen (6d each), four times as much as plain white salt-glaze, but half the price of Littler's Blue.

Wheel The basic tool of the potter, a heavy rotating head rotating on a spindle and powered either by a flywheel kept in motion by the potter ('kick wheel'), a foot-operated crank arrangement, or cord-driven by a small boy turning the handle of a large wheel, which transmitted power to a much smaller pulley below the head of the potter's wheel, on the same principal as a spinning wheel (plate 142). For repetitive work, carefully measured or weighed balls of clay were passed to the thrower, who centred each one on the rotating wheel and raised the pot using both hands. By about 1810, a few progressive manufacturers were beginning to adapt steam power to power wheels and lathes, although most continued throughout the rest of the century to use man rather than machine.

Useful Sources

Angerstein, R. R. *R. R. Angerstein's Illustrated Travel Diary, 1753–5* (London, Science Museum, 2001)

Barker, David. 'Bits and Bobs: The Development of Kiln Furniture in the Eighteenth Century', *ECC Transactions* (1998), vol.16, pt 3, pp.318–41

Britton, Frank. 'Some Sources of Delftware Clay', *ECC Transactions* (1987), vol.13, pt 1, pp.24–32

Copeland, Robert. 'Pottery Manufacturing Processes of the 18th and 19th Centuries', *Welsh Ceramics in Context*, part 1, ed. Jonathan Gray (Swansea, 2003), pp.39–52

Elliott, Gordon. *The Design Process in British Ceramic Manufacture, 1750–1850* (Stafford, 2001)

Goodby, Miranda. 'Moulds and Modellers in the Early Eighteenth-Century Staffordshire Potteries', *ECC Transactions* (2000), vol.17, pt.2, pp.216–28

Hunt, L. B. 'Gold in the Pottery Industry', *Gold Bulletin* (1979), no.12 (3), pp 116–27

Searle, Alfred B. *An Encyclopedia of the Ceramic Industries*, 3 vols (London, 1929)

Smith, Alan. '*The Illustrated Guide to Liverpool Herculaneum Pottery* (London, 1970), Appendix III: 'The Tomkinson Papers', pp.121–9 [contains recipes for many glazes and bodies]

Sussman, Lynne. *Mocha, Banded, Cat's Eye and Other Factory-Made Slipware*, Studies in Northeast Historical Archaeology, no. 1 (Boston, 1997)

Young, Hilary. 'Evidence for Wood and Coal Firing and the Design of Kilns in the Eighteenth-century English Porcelain Industry', *ECC Transactions* (1999), vol.17, pt 1, pp.1–14.

Chronology

1600	East India Company founded
1602	Earliest dated piece of English delftware, plate inscribed 'The Rose is Red'
1612	Earliest dated Wrotham slipware pot, by John Livermore
1613	Patent for delftware obtained by Hugh Cressey and Edmund Bradshawe
1614	Stoneware monopoly obtained by Thomas Browne, Tobie Steward and Nicholas Burghley
1626	Stoneware patent obtained by Rous & Cullen
1628	Delftware patent obtained by Christian Wilhelm of the Pickleherring Pottery
1636	High-temperature kiln patented by David Ramsay
1647	Trade in Chinese porcelain ceased due to civil wars in China
1649	Execution of Charles I, start of Commonwealth Period
1651	First coffee house opened, the Angel Inn at Oxford
1658	Earliest advertisement for tea sold in London
1660	Restoration of Charles II
1672	John Dwight's first patent for salt-glazed stoneware
1683	Vauxhall Pottery established
1683	Trade in porcelain resumed after establishment of Emperor Kangxi
1684	John Dwight's second patent for salt-glazed stoneware, red stoneware, etc.
1685	Accession of James II
1688	Flight of James II, accession of William and Mary
1690	David Elers running a pothouse in Vauxhall
1693	Elers brothers and others sued by John Dwight
1695–8	Earthenware Tax in force
1698	Expiry of John Dwight's second patent for stoneware and redware
1700	Elers brothers bankrupt
1700	Act compelling potters to mark standard tavern mugs with 'WR' and crown
1701	Accession of Queen Anne
1703	Death of John Dwight
1714	Death of Queen Anne, accession of the Hanoverian George I
1719	Earliest mention of 'white stone ware', sold by John Akerman of London
1720	Traditional date for the first use of ground flint and West Country clays
1724	Samuel Bell's redware pottery established at Newcastle under Lyme
1726	Accession of George II
1729	Samuel Bell's patent for 'red marbled stoneware'
1733	River Weaver opened to navigation
1740	Traditional date for adoption of press-moulding and slip-casting techniques
1744	Death of redware makers John Astbury and Samuel Bell
1745	Invasion by Prince Charles Edward Stuart, crushed the following year
1747	Thomas Whieldon established his pottery at Fenton Vivian, closed 1780
1749	Earliest mention of 'Cream Colour', made by Thomas Whieldon
1754–9	Partnership of Thomas Whieldon and Josiah Wedgwood
1756	John Sadler's patent for printing delftware tiles
1756	Transfer-printing began at Worcester porcelain factory

1761	Accession of George III
1761	Wedgwood's transfer-printing contract with Sadler & Green of Liverpool
1762	William Greatbatch established his own factory by this year
1763	Engine-turning lathe installed by Wedgwood
1763	Wedgwood's creamware to be decorated solely by Robinson & Rhodes at Leeds
1766	Wedgwood appointed Potter to the Queen
1768	William Cookworthy patented the use of china clay from Cornwall
1768	Wedgwood's Chelsea decorating studio established, managed by David Rhodes
1768	Wedgwood's showroom opened at Newport Street, moving to Greek Street in 1774
1769	Ornamental branch of Josiah Wedgwood's factory at Etruria opened
1770	Potters' first Price Agreement
1770	Leeds Pottery established
1773	Black Basalt perfected by Wedgwood
1774	'Frog Service' displayed in Wedgwood's London showrooms
1775	Jasper ware perfected by Wedgwood
1776	American War of Independence
1778	Spode's showroom opened in London
1779	'Pearl White' perfected by Wedgwood
1780	Thomas Whieldon's factory closed and turned into a garden
1782	Rodney's naval victories over the French fleet
1782	Wedgwood ordered the first steam engine to be used in the Potteries
1784	Josiah Spode said to have introduced blue-printed earthenware
1786	Boxed sets of Wedgwood's Pyrometer made available to the pottery trade by this year
1786	Treaty of Vergennes, whereby France agreed to accept imports at 12 per cent duty
1787	Cane or Bamboo ware perfected by Wedgwood
1791	East India Company ceased to import Chinese porcelain
1795	Potters' second Price Agreement
1795	Death of Josiah Wedgwood
1796	Expiry of Richard Champion/William Cookworthy hard-paste patent
1796	Minton showroom opened in London
1799	Earliest dated piece of 'Prattware'
1800	Regency Period began
1805	Silver (platinum) lustre invented by John Hancock at Spode's factory
1810	'White porcelain' or 'White Bisque' introduced by Wedgwood factory
1812	Anglo-American War, Washington burnt
1813	C. J. Mason Ironstone China patent
1820	Accession of Prince Regent as George IV
1822	Job Meigh's successful leadless glaze
1824	Imperial Measure introduced to replace the Elizabethan ale gallon
1824–5	Strikes in the Potteries
1830	Accession of George IV's brother as William IV
1831	National Union of Operative Potters founded
1832	Reform Bill became law
1834, 1836	Further strikes in the Potteries
1835	Bristol Glaze invented by Anthony Amatt
1837	Accession of Queen Victoria
1840	Marriage of Queen Victoria and Prince Albert
1841	Wedgwood factory began production of 'flow blue' tablewares
1842	Copyright of Designs Act, protecting against pirating of designs
1843	United Branches of the Potters' Society founded
1846	North Staffordshire Railway brought to Stoke-on-Trent

Bibliography

Adams, Elizabeth. 'James Tidmarsh at Cobridge', *Northern Ceramic Society Journal* (1975–6), no.2, pp.31–7

Adams and Thomas. *A Potworks in Devonshire* (Bovey Tracey, 1996)

Aikin, Dr J. *A Description of the Country from Thirty to Forty Miles Round Manchester* (1795)

Algar, Light and Copland-Griffiths. *The Verwood & District Potteries* (Trowbridge, 1987)

Allan, J. P. 'Post-Medieval Finds from Exeter, 1971–80', *Exeter Archaeological Reports No.3* (Exeter, 1984)

Allen, David. 'Four Bellarmine "Witch Bottles" from Abbotts Ann, Hampshire', *Custom & Ceramics: Essays Presented to Kenneth Barton*, ed. E. Lewis (Wickham, 1991)

Allen, Phillip N. 'Yixing Export Tea Wares of the 17th and 18th Centuries', *Transactions of the Oriental Ceramics Society* (1988–9), 53, pp.87–92

Angerstein, R. R. *R. R. Angerstein's Illustrated Travel Diary, 1753–5* (London, Science Museum, 2001)

Archer, Michael. *Irish Delftware* (Castletown House, Co. Kildare, exhib. cat. 1971)

—. *Delftware: The Tin-glazed Earthenware of the British Isles* (London, 1997)

Arman and Arman. *Anglo-American Ceramics*, part 1 (Portsmouth, New Hampshire, 1998)

Arthur Herbert Church, 1834–1915, privately printed memorial including his obituaries and portrait photographs (London, 1917)

Askey, Derek, *Stoneware Bottles from Bellarmines to Ginger Beers, 1500–1949* (Brighton, 1981)

Austin, John C. *British Delft at Williamsburg* (Williamsburg, 1994)

Baines, John Mainwaring, *Sussex Pottery* (Brighton, 1980)

Baker, John, *Sunderland Pottery* (Tyne & Wear County Council Museums, 1983)

Barker, David. 'A Group of Red Stonewares of the 18th Century', *ECC Transactions* (1991), vol.14, pt 2, pp.177–98

—, *William Greatbatch, a Staffordshire Potter* (London: Jonathan Horne, 1991)

—, 'Stoke-on-Trent Discovery', *Antique Collector* (June 1992)

—, *Slipware*, Shire Publication no.297 (1993)

—, 'To Put You in Mind of a Red Pot Teapot: English Red Stoneware of the Eighteenth Century', *Ars Ceramica* (1996), no.13, pp.39–52

Bemrose, Paul. 'The Pomona Potworks, Newcastle, Staffs, Parts I and II', *ECC Transactions* (1973), vol.9, pt 1, pp.1–18; (1975), vol.9, pt 3, pp.292–303

Bimson, M. 'John Dwight', *ECC Transactions* (1961), vol.5, pt 2

Blacker, J. F. *The ABC of English Salt-Glaze Stone-Ware from Dwight to Doulton* (London, 1922)

Blake Roberts, Gaye. 'Josiah Wedgwood and Queen's Ware', *The Green Frog Service*, ed. M. Raeburn, L. Veronikhina and A. Nurnberg (London, 1995)

—, ed. *True Blue: Transfer Printed Earthenware* (Wedgwood Museum exhib. cat. March–July1998)

Blakey, Harold. 'Newcastle Potters and the Export of Earthenware from Newcastle-upon-Tyne', *Northern Ceramic Society Journal* (2001), vol.18, pp.113–52

Bossert, H.T. *Peasant Art in Europe* (London, 1927)

Brears, Peter C.D. *The English Country Pottery: Its History and Techniques* (Newton Abbot, 1971)

—, *The Collector's Book of English Country Pottery* (Newton Abbot, 1974)

Brereton, *Sir William: Travels in Holland etc., 1634–5 by Sir William Brereton Bart*, ed. E. Hawkins (Folio Society, 1844)

Britton, Frank. *English Delftware in the Bristol Collection* (London, 1982)

—. *London Delftware* (London, 1987)

—. 'French Influence on the Decoration of English Delftware', *ECC Transactions* (1989), vol.13, pt.2

—. 'The Pickleherring Potteries: An Inventory', *Post-Medieval Archaeology* (1990), vol.24, pp.61–92

—. 'Bernard Palissy and London, Delftware', *EEC Transactions* (1991), vol.14, pt 2

—. 'Delftware Inventories', *ECC Transactions* (1993), vol.15, pt 1

Brown, Peter B. *In Praise of Hot Liquors: The Study of Chocolate, Coffee and Tea-Drinking, 1600–1850* (Fairfax House, York, 1995)

Burlington Fine Arts Club, *Illustrated Catalogue of Early English Earthenware* (London, exhib. cat. 1914)

Carpentier, Donald, and Jonathan Rickard. 'Slip Decoration in the Age of Industrialisation', *Ceramics in America* (Chipstone Foundation, Milwaukee, 2001), pp.115–34

Charleston R.J., ed., *World Ceramics* (1968)

Coleman-Smith and Pearson. *Excavations in the Donyatt Potteries* (Chichester, 1988)

Cooper, Ronald G. *English Slipware Dishes* (London, 1968)

Copeland, Robert. *Spode's Willow Pattern & Other Designs after the Chinese* (London, 1980)

—. 'Copeland and the Hudson's Bay Company, 1836–1872', *ECC Transactions* (1993), vol.15, pt 1

—. 'Pottery Manufacturing Processes of the 18th and 19th Centuries', *Welsh Ceramics in Context*, part 1, ed. Jonathan Gray (Swansea, 2003), pp.39–52

Coysh, A.W. *Blue-Printed Earthenware, 1800–1850* (London, 1972)

Coysh and Henrywood. *Blue & White Printed pottery, 1780–1880*, 2 vols (Woodbridge, 1982–9)

Coysh and Stefano Jr. *Collecting Ceramic Landscapes: British and American Landscapes on Printed Pottery* (London, 1981)

Cox and Cox. *Rockingham Pottery & Porcelain, 1745–1842* (London, 1983)

Cruickshank, Graeme. 'Scottish Spongeware', *Scottish Pottery Studies* (1982), no.1

des Fontaines, Una. 'Wedgwood Blue-Printed Wares, 1805–43', *ECC Transactions* (1983), vol.11, pt 3

Davis, Cottreau and Niven. *Artifacts from Eighteenth Century Halifax* (Saint Mary's University Archaeology Laboratory, Halifax, 1987)

Drakard, David. *Printed English Pottery: History and Humour in the reign of George III, 1760–1820* (London, 1992)

Drakard and Holdaway. *Spode Printed Ware* (London, 1983)

du Boulay, Anthony. 'English Ceramics in National Trust Houses', *ECC Transactions* (2002), vol.18, pt 1, p.179

Dudson, Audrey. *Dudson: A Family of Potters since 1800* (Stoke-on-Trent, 1985)

Duysters, Kristin. *Theepotten Steengoed: Roodstenen Theepotten uit Yixing en Europa*

(Historish Museum het Burgerweeshuis Arnhem, 1998)
Earle, Cyril. *The Earle Collection of Staffordshire Pottery* (London, 1915)
Eatwell and Werner. 'A London, Staffordshire Warehouse, 1794–1825', *Northern Ceramic Society Journal* (1991), vol.8
Edwards, Diana. *Neale Pottery and Porcelain: Its Predecessors and Successors, 1763–1820* (London, 1987)
—. *Black Basalt: Wedgwood and Contemporary Manufacturers* (Woodbridge, 1994)
Edwards, Diana and Rodney Hampson. *English Dry-Bodied Stoneware* (Woodbridge, 1998)
—. *White Salt-Glazed Stoneware of the British Isles* (Woodbridge, 2005)
Edwards, Rhoda. 'London, Potters *circa* 1570–1710', *Journal of Ceramic History* (1974), no.6
Elliott, Gordon. *John and David Elers and their Contemporaries* (London, 1998)
—. *The Design Process in British Ceramic Manufacture, 1750–1850* (Stafford, 2001)
—. 'Staffordshire Red and Black Stonewares', *ECC Transactions* (1977), vol.10, no.2, pp.84–94
Elliott, Wallace. 'Reproductions and Fakes of English Eighteenth Century Ceramics', *ECC Transactions* (1939), vol.2, no.7.
Emmerson, Robin. *British Teapots and Tea Drinking* (London, 1992)
English Porcelain Circle. *William Duesbury's London: Account Book, 1751–1753* (London, 1931)
Ewins, Neil. '"Supplying the Present Wants of Our Yankee Cousins…": Staffordshire Ceramics and the Amercian Market, 1775–1880', *Journal of Ceramcs History* (1997), vol.15
Exeter, Royal Albert Memorial Museum. *By Potters Art and Skill: Pottery by the Fishleys of Fremington* (Royal Albert Memorial Museum, exhib. cat. 1984)
Fishley Holland. *Fifty Years a Potter*, Pottery Quarterly (Tring, 1958)
Francis, Peter. 'Irish Creamware: The Downshire Pottery in Belfast', *ECC Transactions* (1995), vol.15, pt 3, pp.400–25
—. *Irish Delftware* (London, 2000)
Freestone and Gaimster, eds. *Pottery in the Making* (London, British Museum, 1997)
Gaimster, David. 'The Archaeology of Post-Medieval Society, *c.*1450–1750: Material Culture Studies in Britain since the War', *Building on the Past* (Royal Archaeological Institute, 1994)
—. *German Stoneware, 1200–1900* (London, 1997)
—. 'Regional Decorative Traditions in English Post-Medieval Slipware', *Pottery in the Making* (London, British Museum, 1997)
Garner and Archer. *English Delftware* (London, 1972)
Gibson, Michael. *19th Century Lustreware* (Woodbridge, 1999)
Godden, Geoffrey A. *Minton Pottery and Porcelain of the First Period, 1793–1850* (London, 1968)
—. 'A London Chinaman', *Antique Collector* (April 1972), pp.68–72
—. *British Pottery* (London, 1974)
—. *Oriental Export Market Porcelain* (St Albans, 1979)
—. *Godden's Guide to Mason's China and the Ironstone Wares* (Woodbridge, 1980)
—. *Godden's Guide to Ironstone & Granite Wares* (Woodbridge, 1999)
Godden and Gibson. *Collecting Lustreware* (London, 1991)
Grant, Alison. *North Devon Pottery: The Seventeenth Century* (Exeter, 1983)
Grant, Captain M. H. *The Makers of Black Basaltes* (Edinburgh and London, 1910)
Graves, Alun. *Tiles and Tilework* (London, Victoria and Albert Museum, 2003)
Green, Christopher. 'John Dwight's Fulham Pottery: Excavations 1971–9', *Archaeological Report 6* (English Heritage, 1999)
Griffin, John. *The Don Pottery, 1801–1893* (Doncaster, 2001)
Grigsby, Leslie B. *English Pottery, 1650–1800: The Henry H. Weldon Collection* (London, 1990)
—. *English Slip-Decorated Earthenware at Williamsburg* (Williamsburg, 1993)
—. 'Johann Nieuhoff's *Embassy*', *Antiques Magazine* (January 1993), pp.172–83
—. 'John Stalker and George Parker's *Treatise*', *Antiques* (June 1993), pp.886–93
—. 'George Edwards and Matthew Darly's *Chinese Designs*', *Antiques* (February 1994), pp.296–305
Grigsby, Leslie B. and M. Archer. *The Longridge Collection of English Slipware and Delftware*, vols.I & II (London and Milwaukee, 2000)
Guilemé-Brulon, Dorothée. *Le faïence fine française, 1750–1867* (Paris, 1995)
Halfpenny, Pat. *English Earthenware Figures, 1740–1840* (Woodbridge, 1991)
—. 'Creamware: Its Origins and Development', *Catalogue of the International Ceramics Fair and Seminar* (1993), pp.19–27.
—. 'Thomas Whieldon: His Life And Work', *ECC Transactions* (1997), vol.16, pt 2, pp.237–54
—, ed. *Penny Plain, Twopence Coloured, Transfer Printing on English Ceramics, 1750–1850* (City Museum & Art Gallery, Stoke-on-Trent, exhib. cat. 1994)
Hallesy, Helen L. *The Glamorgan Pottery, Swansea, 1814–38* (Llanysul, 1995)
Hamilton Foyn, W. 'Dated Brown Saltglazed Hunting Mugs, 1713–1775', *ECC Transactions* (2000), vol.17, pt 2, pp.253–74
Hassell, John. *A Tour of the Grand Junction Canal in 1819* (1819)
Haselgrove, Dennis. 'Steps towards English Stoneware Manufacture in the 17th Century, Part 1: 1600–1650' and 'Part 2: 1650–1700', *London Archaeologist* (1989), vol.6, no.5, pp.132–8, and (1990), vol.6, no.6, pp.152–8
Haselgrove and Murray. 'John Dwight's Fulham Pottery, 1672–1978: A Collection of Documentary Sources', *Journal of Ceramic History* (1979), no.11
Henrywood, R. K. *Relief-Moulded Jugs, 1820–1900* (Woodbridge, 1984)
—. *An Illustrated Guide to British Jugs* (Shrewsbury, 1997)
Herman, Michael. *Wedgwood Jasper Ware* (Atglen, Pennsylvania, 2003)
Hildyard, Robin. *Browne Muggs* (Victoria and Albert Museum, London, 1985)
—. 'A Group of Dated Southwark Delftwares', *Connoisseur* (May 1990), pp.354–5
—. 'Country Classical', *Antique Collecting* (September 1997)
—. *European Ceramics* (London, 1999)
—. 'London Chinamen', *ECC Transactions* (2004), vol.18, pt.3
Hillier, Bevis. *Master Potters of the Industrial Revolution: The Turners of Lane End* (London, 1965)
Hodgkin and Hodgkin. *Examples of Early English Pottery, Named, Dated and Inscribed*, (London, 1891)
Honey, W. B. *The Art of the Potter* (London 1946)
—. *English Pottery & Porcelain* (London, 1947)
Horn, Barbara. 'Ceramic Bills paid by Alexander, 4th Duke of Gordon', *ECC Transactions* (1995), vol.15, pt.3, pp.435–9
Horne, Jonathan. *John Dwight* (Jonathan Horne Antiques, London, exhib. cat. 1987)
Howarth, Jack. 'Andrew Abbott and the Fleet Street Partnerships', *NCS Journal* (1996), vol.13, pp.75–117
Howarth and Hildyard. *Joseph Kishere and the Mortlake Potteries* (Woodbridge, 2004)
Howell, John. 'William Absolon of Great Yarmouth', *ECC Transactions* (1980), vol.10, pt 5, pp.314–33
Hume, Ivor Noël. *Pottery and Porcelain in Colonial Williamsburg's Archaeological Collections* (Williamsburg, 1969), p.22
—. 'Stoneware Gin Flasks: Legacy of the Damned', *Antiques* (February 1975)
—. *Early English Delftware from London, and Virginia*, Colonial Williamsburg Occasional Papers in Archaeology (1977), vol.II
—. *If These Pots Could Talk* (Milwaukee, 2001)
Hurst, Neal and van Beuningen. *Pottery*

Produced and Traded in North-West Europe, 1350–1650, Rotterdam Papers VI (The Hague, 1986)
Jennings, S. 'Eighteen Centuries of Pottery from Norwich', *The Norwich Survey, East Anglian Archaeology 13* (1981)
Jewitt, Llewellyn. *The Ceramic Art of Great Britain* (1878)
Kansas City. *The Frank P. and Harriet C. Burnap Collection of English Pottery in the William Rockhill Nelson Gallery of Art* (1953)
Kerr and Ayers. *Blanc de Chine: Porcelain from Dehua* (Singapore, 2002)
Kiddell, A. J. B. 'Wrotham Slipware and the Wrotham Brickyard', *ECC Transactions* (1954), vol.3, pt 2, pp.105–18
Kinder, Philip. *Collections towards a History of Derbyshire* (*c.*1650; manuscript in Bodleian Library, Oxford)
Laidacker, Sam. *Anglo-American China*, parts I and II (Bloomburg, Pennsylvania, 1951–4)
Lawton, H. C. 'Silver Lustre', *Connoisseur* (May 1904, July 1904)
Lawrence, H. *Yorkshire Pots and Potteries* (Newton Abbot, 1974)
Leech, John E. 'Staffordshire Pew Groups', *Antiques* (September 1936)
Leese, M. E. 'The Turner Moulds', *Northern Ceramic Circle Journal* (1987), vol.5
Lewis, Griselda. *A Collector's History of English Pottery* (1969 and later expanded editions)
Lewis, J. M. *The Ewenny Potteries* (Cardiff, 1982)
Lewis and Lewis. *Pratt Ware* (Woodbridge, 1984)
Lipski, Louis L. and Archer, D. M. *Dated English Delftware* (London, 1984)
Little, W. L. *Staffordshire Blue* (London, 1969)
Lockett, Terence. 'Pearlware: Origins and Types', parts I and II, *Antique Collecting* (April 1996, June 1996)
Lockett and Godden. *Davenport: China, Earthenware, Glass* (London, 1989)
McKendrick, N., J. Brewer and J. H. Plumb, *The Birth of a Consumer Society: The Commercialization of Eighteenth-century England* (London, 1982)
McVeigh, Patrick. *Scottish East Coast Potteries, 1750–1840* (Edinburgh 1979)
Mackerness, E. D., ed. *The Journals of George Sturt, 1890–1927* (Cambridge, 1967)
Mallet, John. 'John Baddeley of Shelton: An Early Staffordshire Maker of Pottery and Porcelain' parts 1 and 2, *ECC Transactions* (1966), vol.6, pt 2, pp.124–66, and (1967), vol.6, pt 3, pp.181–247
— 'Rotherham Saltglaze: John Platt's Jug', *ECC Transactions* (1973), vol.9, pt 1, pp.111–14
Manchester City Art Gallery. *The Incomparable Art* (1969)
S. Marchant & Son. *Exhibition of Blanc de Chine* (London, 1985 and 1995)
Massey, Pearce and Howard. *Isleworth Pottery and Porcelain: Recent Discoveries*, English Ceramic Circle (Museum of London, exhib. cat. 2003)
Meteyard, Eliza. *The Life of Josiah Wedgwood*, 2 vols (London, 1865–6)
Miller and Berthoud. *An Anthology of British Teapots* (Wingham 1985)
Miller and Hunter. 'How Creamware Got the Blues: The Origins of China Glaze and Pearlware', *Ceramics in America* (Milwaukee, 2001)
Morley-Hewitt, A. T. 'Early Whieldon of the Fenton Low Works', *ECC Transactions* (1954), vol.3, pt 3, pp.142–54
Morris, Christopher, ed. *The Journeys of Celia Fiennes* (London, 1947)
Mountford, Arnold. *The Illustrated Guide to Staffordshire Salt-Glazed Stoneware* (London, 1971)
—. 'Thomas Whieldon's Manufactory at Fenton Vivian', *ECC Transactions* (1972), vol.8, pt 2, pp.164–82
—. *Thomas Wedgwood, John Wedgwood and Jonah Malkin, Potters of Burslem* (unpublished thesis, University of Keele, 1972)
—. 'Documents relating to English ceramics of the 18th & 19th Centuries', *Journal of Ceramic History* (1975), no.8
Mountford and Celoria. 'Some Examples of Sources in the History of 17th-century Ceramics', *Journal of Ceramic History* (1968), no.1
Museum of London. *Pewter: A Celebration of the Craft, 1200–1700* (1989)
Newton and Bibbings. 'Seventeenth-century Pottery Sites at Harlow, Essex', *Transactions of the Essex Archaeological Society* (1960), vol.25, pt.3, pp.358–77
North, Anthony, and Andrew Spira. *Pewter at the Victoria and Albert Museum* (London, 1999)
Northern Ceramic Society. *Stoneware & Stone Chinas of Northern England to 1851* (Stoke-on-Trent, exhib. cat. 1982)
—. *Creamware & Pearlware* (Stoke-on-Trent, exhib. cat. 1986)
Oswald and Hughes. 'Nottingham and Derbyshire Stoneware', *ECC Transactions* (1974), vol.9, pt 2, pp.140–89
Oswald, Hughes and Hildyard. *English Brown Stoneware* (London, 1982)
Outlaw, Merry Abbitt. 'Scratched in Clay: Seventeenth-century North Devon Slipware at Jamestown, Virginia', *Ceramics in America 2002* (Chipstone Foundation, Milwaukee, 2002), pp.17–38
Peal, C. A. *British Pewter* (London, 1971), pp.70–73
Phillimore, John. 'A Famous Bridge in Pottery and Glass', parts 1 and 2, *Apollo* (January 1941, February 1941)
Player, Cyril. 'Old Foxhead and Houndhead Cups', *Antique Collector* (September 1933), vol.4, no.9
Plot, Robert. *The Natural History of Oxfordshire* (1677)
—. *History of Staffordshire* (1686)
Pococke, Dr. *Dr Pococke's Journey into England from Dublin by Way of the Isle of Man* (1751).
Price, R. M. 'English Redware', *Apollo* (April 1963)
—. 'Some Groups of English Redware of the Mid-Eighteenth Century', parts I and II, *ECC Transactions* (1957), vol.4, pt 5, pp.1–9, and (1962), vol.5, pt 3, pp.153–68
Pryor and Blockley. 'A 17th-century Kiln at Woolwich', *Post-Medieval Archaeology* (1978), vol.12
Pulver, Rosalind. 'An Early Eighteenth Century China Shop', *ECC Transactions* (1985), vol.12, pt 2
Rackham, Bernard. *Catalogue of the Schreiber Collection: Earthenware, vol.2* (1930)
—. *Catalogue of the Glaisher Collection of Pottery & Porcelain in the Fitzwilliam Museum Cambridge*, 2 vols (Cambridge, 1935)
—. 'A Dated Staffordshire Mug in the National Museum of Wales, Cardiff', *ECC Transactions* (1942), vol.2, no.8, pp.145–8
—. *Early Staffordshire Pottery* (London, 1951)
Rackham and Read. *English Pottery: Its Development from Early Times to the End of the Eighteenth Century* (London, 1924)
Ray, Anthony. *English Delftware Pottery in the Robert Hall Warren Collection, Ashmolean Museum, Oxford* (London, 1968)
—. *English Delftware Tiles* (London, 1973)
Raybould, K. A. G. 'Some Aspects of Mocha Ware', *ECC Transactions* (1984), vol.12, pt 1, pp.41–4.
Read, Herbert. *Staffordshire Pottery Figures* (London, 1929)
Reilly, Robin. *Wedgwood*, 2 vols (London, 1989)
—. *Josiah Wedgwood, 1730–1795* (London, 1992)
Reilly and Savage. *Wedgwood: The Portrait Medallions* (London, 1973)
—. *The Dictionary of Wedgwood* (Woodbridge, 1980)
Riley, Noël. *Gifts for Good Children: The History of Children's China, 1790–1890* (Shepton Beauchamp, 1991)
Roussel, Diana Edwards. *The Castleford Pottery, 1790–1821* (Wakefield, 1982)
Rumsey, Jill. *Victorian Relief-Moulded Jugs* (Richard Dennis, London, exhib. cat. 1987)
Saint-Fond, F. de. *Travels in England* (1797)
Sharp, Rosalie Wise. *Ceramics: Ethics & Scandal* (New York, 2002)
Shaw, Charles. *When I Was a Child* (1903, reprinted 1977)
Shaw, Simeon. *History of the Staffordshire Potteries* (1829)

Sheenah, Smith. 'Norwich China Dealers of the Mid-Eighteenth Century', *Transactions ECC* (1974), vol.9, pt 2
Smith, Alan. *The Illustrated Guide to Liverpool Herculaneum Pottery* (London, 1970)
Snyder, Jeffrey B. *Flow Blue* (West Chester, Pennsylvania, 1992)
Solon, M. L. *The Art of the Old English Potter* (London, 1883)
—. 'The Slip Decorated Dishes of Chirk Castle', *Burlington Magazine* (April 1907), vol.XI
Stockspring Antiques, London, *Isleworth Pottery & Porcelain* (exhib cat. 2003)
Strong, H. W. *Industries of North Devon* (Barnstaple, 1889, reprinted 1971)
Sussman, Lynne. *Mocha, Banded, Cat's Eye and Other Factory-Made Slipware*, Studies in Northeast Historical Archaeology, no. 1 (Boston, 1997)
Taggart, Ross E. 'John Astbury – 1730 or 1930?', *Art Quarterly* (1967), vol.XXX, no.1
Tait, Hugh. '"Blocks" for Spouts', *British Museum Quarterly* (1963), vol.XXVI, no.3–4
—. 'Samuel Malkin and the "SM" Slipware Dishes', parts 1 and 2, *Apollo* (January 1957, February 1957)
—. 'Southwark (alias Lambeth) Delftware and the Potter, Christian Wilhelm', parts 1 and 2, *Connoisseur* (August 1960, February 1961).
—. 'The First English Ceramic Coffee Pot', *Ars Ceramica* (1987), no.4, pp.50–52
Thistlethwaite, F. 'The Atlantic Migration of the Pottery Industry', *Economic History Review* (1958), vol.XI, no.2, pp.264–78
Thomas, John. *The Rise of the Staffordshire Potteries* (New York, 1971)
Thorpe, W. A. in *Society of Glass Technology* (1938), vol.22, pp.166–205
Towner, Donald. *The Leeds Pottery* (London, 1963)
—. 'The Melbourne Pottery', *ECC Transactions* (1971), vol.8, pt 1, pp.18–30
—. 'Robinson & Rhodes, Enamellers at Leeds', *ECC Transactions* (1974), vol.9, pt 2
—. *Creamware* (London, 1978)
Turner, William. *William Adams, an Old English Potter* (London, 1904)
Valfré, Patrice. *Yixing Teapots for Europe* (Poligny, France, 2000)
Walton, Peter. *Creamware and other English Pottery at Temple Newsam House, Leeds* (London, 1976)
Ward, John. *The Borough of Stoke-on-Trent* (1843; facsimile, 1984)
Weatherill, Lorna. *The Pottery Trade and North Staffordshire, 1660–1760* (Manchester, 1971)
—. 'The Business of the Middleman in the English Pottery Trade before 1780', *Business History* (1984), vol.28
—. *The Growth of the Pottery Industry in England, 1600–1815* (New York, 1986)
Weatherill and Edwards, 'Pottery Manufacture in London, and Whitehaven in the late 17th Century', *Post-Medieval Archaeology* (1971), vol.5. pp.160–81
The Selected Letters of Josiah Wedgwood, ed. Ann Finer and George Savage (London, 1965)
Letters of Josiah Wedgwood, 1762–1795, 3 vols (Manchester, 1973)
Weinstein, Rosemary, 'Pipeclay Figurines' in 'Excavations at Aldgate', *Post-Medieval Archaeology* (1984), vol.18
James and Charles Whitehead, Manufacturers, Hanley, Staffordshire (Birmingham 1798; reprinted Milton Keynes, 1974)
Whiter, Leonard. *Spode* (London, 1970)
Williams-Wood, C. *English Transfer-Printed Pottery & Porcelain* (London, 1981)
Williams, Peter, and Pat Halfpenny. *A Passion for Pottery: Further Selections from the Henry H. Weldon Collection* (London, 2000)
Wills, Geoffrey. 'Ceramic Causerie', *Apollo* (May 1961), pp.145–6
—. 'English Pottery in 1696: An Unpublished Document', *Apollo* (June 1967)
The Sales Ledger of John Wood of Brownhills (1746–1797) (un-numbered manuscripts in Stoke-on-Trent Museum)
Wood, Pamela. *'Made at Nottm': A History of Saltglazed Stoneware* (Nottingham, 1980)
Young, Hilary. *English Porcelain, 1745–94* (London, 1999)
—, ed. *The Genius of Wedgwood* (Victoria and Albert Museum, exhib. cat. 1995)

Index

Index notes: italicised page numbers refer to illustrations and their captions. Chapter notes are not indexed.